Explorer Italy

Tim Jepson

AA Publishing

Written by Tim Jepson
Revision verified by Tim Jepson
Original photography by Clive Sawyer
Cover design by Carroll Associates
Reprinted with new cover 1999
Revised third edition 1998
Reprinted 1996
First published 1994
Edited, designed, produced and distributed by AA Publishing, Norfolk House, Priestley Road, Basingstoke, Hampshire, RG24 9NY.
Maps © The Automobile Association 1994, 1996, 1998.

The contents of this publication are believed correct at the time of printing. Nevertheless, the publishers cannot be held responsible for any errors or omissions or for changes in the details given in this guide or for the consequences of any reliance on the information provided by the same. Assessments of attractions, hotels, restaurants and so forth are based upon the author's own personal experience and, therefore, descriptions given in this guide necessarily contain an element of subjective opinion which may not reflect the publishers' opinion or dictate a reader's own experiences on another occasion. We have tried to ensure accuracy in this guide, but things do change and we would be grateful if readers would advise us of any inaccuracies they may encounter.

A CIP catalogue record for this book is available from the British Library.

ISBN 0 7495 1877 4

Published by AA Publishing (a trading name of Automobile Association Developments Limited, whose registered office is Norfolk House, Priestley Road, Basingstoke, Hampshire, RG24 9NY. Registered number 1878835).

Colour separation by Fotographics Ltd
Printed and bound in Italy by Printer Trento srl.

Titles in the Explorer series:
Australia • Boston & New England • Britain • Brittany • California Caribbean • China • Costa Rica • Crete • Cyprus • Egypt • Florence & Tuscany • Florida • France • Germany • Greek Islands • Hawaii Indonesia • Ireland • Israel • Japan • London • Mallorca • Mexico Moscow & St Petersburg • New York • New Zealand • Paris Portugal • Prague • Provence • Rome • San Francisco • Scotland Singapore & Malaysia • South Africa • Spain Thailand • Tunisia Turkey • Turkish Coast • Venice • Vietnam

AA World Travel Guides publish nearly 300 guidebooks to a full range of cities, countries and regions across the world. Find out more about AA Publishing and the wide range of services the AA provides by visiting our Web site at www.theaa.co.uk.

Front cover (a): Campania, Ravello (b): Tuscan landscape near Sienna (c): Raphael's painting *St Catherine of Alexandria* (d): a Ferrari in Florence **Back cover:** the columns of San Paolo Fuori de Mura **Page 3:** Positano, Amalfi Coast, Campania **Page 4:** Sacro Monte, Varallo, Piedmont **Page 5 (top):** the Forum, Rome **Page 5 (right):** market stalls, Palermo **Pages 6 and 7 (top):** inventive Italian pasta **Page 8:** Portovenere, Riviera di Levante

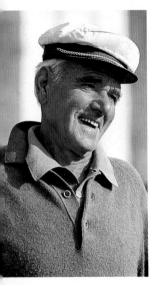

How to use this book

This book is divided into five main sections:

❏ Section 1: *Italy Is*

discusses aspects of life and living today, from politics to the family

❏ Section 2: *Italy Was*

places the country in its historical context and explores those past events whose influences are felt to this day. This section also discusses important periods in Italian art

❏ Section 3: *A to Z Section*

is broken down into regional chapters, and covers places to visit, including walks and drives. Within this section fall the Focus-on articles, which consider a variety of subjects in greater detail

❏ Section 4: *Travel Facts*

contains the strictly practical information vital for a successful trip

❏ Section 5: *Hotels and Restaurants*

lists recommended establishments throughout Italy, giving a brief résumé of their attractions

How to use the star rating

Most of the places described in this book have been given a separate rating:

▶▶▶ **Do not miss**

▶▶ **Highly recommended**

▶ **Worth seeing**

Not essential viewing

Map references

To make the location of a particular place easier to find every main entry in this book has a map reference to the right of its name. This comprises a number, followed by a letter, followed by another number, such as 176B3. The first number (176) refers to the page on which the map can be found, the letter (B) and the second number (3) pinpoint the square in which the main entry is located. The maps on the inside front cover and inside back cover are referred to as IFC and IBC respectively.

Contents

Quick reference   6–7

My Italy   8
by Tim Jepson

Italy Is   9–18

Italy Was   19–38

A to Z
Rome   39–61
The Northwest   62–77
Lombardy & Emilia-Romagna 78–93
Venice   94–113
The Northeast   114–31
Florence   132–47
Tuscany   148–63
Umbria and Le Marche   164–79
Lazio and Abruzzo   180–95
Campania   196–211
The Deep South   212–25
Sicily   226–43
Sardinia   244–56

Travel Facts   257–70

Hotels and Restaurants   271–83

Index   284–8

Picture credits and
  contributors   288

This quick-reference guide highlights the features of the book you will use most often: the maps; the introductory features; the Focus On articles; the walks and the drives.

Maps

3-star sights and regions	IFC and IBC
Rome	40–1
Vatican museums	49
The Northwest	62–3
Lombardy & Emilia-Romagna	78–9
Venice	94–5
The Northeast	114–15
Dolomites drive	121
Florence	132–3
Tuscany	148–9
South of Siena drive	155
Siena	160
Umbria and Le Marche	164
Assisi	168
Heart of Umbria drive	172
Valnerina and Monti Sibillini drive	178
Lazio and Abruzzo	180–1
Southern Lazio drive	191
Campania	196
Pompeii	202–3
Amalfi Coast drive	211
The Deep South	212–13
Sicily	226–7
Sardinia	244
The Logudoro	251

Italy Is

Italians	10
The family	11
The Church	12
Food and wine	13
Politics	14–15
North and south	16
Language	17
Cinema	18

Italy Was

Early history	20
The rise of Rome	21
The Roman Empire	22
The Dark Ages	23
Popes and emperors	24
The city states	25
Foreign domination	26
Unified	27
The world wars	28
Modern times	29
Classical art	30
Byzantine art	31
Romanesque and Gothic	32
Pre-Renaissance	33
The Renaissance	34–5
Baroque	36–7
Art in decline	38

Focus On

Il Vaticano	48–9
The Colosseum	50
St Peter's	55
Walking in Northwest Italy	70–1
The Hanbury Gardens	73
The Turin Shroud	75
Walking in Lombardy	86
The Last Supper	90
The Mosaics of Ravenna	93
Venetian art	98–9
Basilica di San Marco	100

The Lagoon 104
Venice in peril 105
Walking in Venice 110
Dolomites activities 122–3
Opera 127
Andrea Palladio 131
The Grand Tour 136
Walking in Florence 144
The Palio 162
Saints 169
Truffles 174
Walking in Umbria 179
The Etruscan towns 186–7
Tivoli 189
Parco Nazionale d'Abruzzo 194–5

Vesuvius 200
Pompeii 201–3
Herculaneum 205
Museo Archeologico Nazionale 207
Romanesque Apulia 218
Matera 221
Trulli 223
Magna Graecia 231
The Mafia 236–7
Piazza Armerina mosaics 241
Prehistory 249
Bandits 256

Walks

Through Rome's piazzas to
the Spanish Steps 56
Northwest Italy 70–1
Lombardy 86
Venice 110
Florence 144
Umbria 179

Drives

The Valle d'Aosta 76
La Grande Strada delle Dolomiti 121
Through Tuscany's heart 155
The heart of Umbria 172
From Spoleto 178
The Roman countryside 191
The Amalfi Coast 211
The Logudoro 251

Piazza Navona, Rome

My Italy by Tim Jepson

Tim Jepson's love of travel began with a busking trip through Europe, and has since taken him from the drowsy calm of the Umbrian hills to the windswept tundra of the Yukon and far north. Hopelessly in love with Italy – like many a romantic Englishman before him – he has lived in Rome, Venice and Tuscany, but has plans to leave the warmth of the Mediterranean for the Arctic and the hidden mountains of South America. He has written several guides for the AA, including AA *Explorer* guides to *Italy, Florence & Tuscany* and *Canada*

It's not difficult to fall in love with Italy, but it is hard to escape its fatal charm once the love affair has matured. No country, in my opinion, is as rich, no people as passionate, no landscapes as beautiful. And if you don't warm to the Italians, or you find countryside elsewhere more beguiling, what about the food and wine – some of the world's best – or the art and architecture? The world would be a poorer place without pasta and pizza, not to mention the artistic legacy of the Renaissance, or the cultural patrimony of the Greeks, Etruscans, Romans, Arabs and other civilisations that have left their imprint on the Italian peninsula.

I first visited Italy 20 years ago, and have been going back there every year since. Even now there are corners of the country I have yet to explore, churches to discover, paintings to see, seas to swim, mountains to climb, operas to hear and food to eat. I'm lucky – I've made a start. For those on their first or second trip, the discovery is just beginning. There are many countries that could warrant a lifetime's study, but in how many would you really want to spend a lifetime? For me, Italy is one, although equally, I have no desire to 'go native', and have few illusions about Italy's faults, for no country is perfect.

Yet Italy is more perfect than most. Just 50 years ago it was little more than a peasant-based agricultural country, ravaged by war and years of dictatorship. Today it's one of the world's leading industrial nations, a byword for style, fashion and flair, and in many ways a long way from the spaghetti, mandolins and Sophia Loren-type clichés of popular imagination. Yet vivid slices of the old Italy still survive, its perfection being a blend of the old and the new: black-clad peasants and the glories of Rome, Florence and Venice combined with family, passion, opera, olive oil, Latin lovers and all things which will be forever Italian. Revel in these and other delights, but be warned: once Italy ensnares you, it has you for life.

■ 'We have made Italy,' said Cavour, founding father of the Italian state, 'now we must make Italians.' Some 130 years on, how many Italians, from the German-speaking burghers of Alto Adige to the blue-eyed Sicilians of Norman descent (unless united behind their football team), still feel bound by the idea of a single nation? ■

Stereotypes Everybody has a picture of the typical Italian: philandering Latin lover; son-smothering *mamma*; pasta-bloated patriarch; louche Mafia Godfather; black-clad widow; deranged driver; sensuous sex-siren (*à la* Sophia Loren). Picking national stereotypes is always a dangerous game, but in Italy it is more than usually fraught with pitfalls. The country was unified only 135 years ago, having been divided for centuries, a historical legacy that has produced countless regional variations of character. For every Italian who conforms to type, there is another who proves the exception to the rule.

❑ 'And don't, let me beg you, go with that awful idea that Italy's only a museum of antiquities and art. Love and understand the Italians, for the people are more marvellous than the land.' E M Forster. ❑

Region by region The cool arrogance of the Florentines, for example, is at odds with the fierce honour of the Sicilians; the mild-mannered Venetians are a world away from the more abrasive Romans; and the dignified reserve of the Piedmontese provides a foil for the mannered efficiency of the Milanese. Italians also stand by their regions, proclaiming themselves Tuscans first and foremost, or Sicilians, Sardinians, Umbrians, Calabrians ... Others are divided from compatriots by language and cultural tradition (German in the Alto Adige, Slovene in Friuli, French in Piedmont, Greek and Albanian in Sicily and Calabria).

Characteristics Despite these contrasts we instinctively recognise Italians, not only from the way they look (fashion is a fierce leveller in Italy) but also from their outlook on life, whether a pragmatic aptitude for survival – born of constant political upheavals and foreign invasions – or a natural instinct for spontaneity and sensual self-indulgence in anything from food and friends to family and football. We admire their apparent free spirit – while lamenting their occasional inefficiency – and wonder why, when most nations have something to teach, Italians seem to have much more.

■ **For all the Italians' intrinsic differences, there is no doubt that the family – though diminishing in size and losing its hierarchical rigidity – is still a major force in the mainstream of Italian life. Mother and son are its pivotal members, children its sentimental axis, and marriage and death its dynastic climaxes.** ■

History The family, with its ties of loyalty and obligation, is as much a metaphorical as a literal force, binding Italians to nearest and dearest rather than neighbour and nation. Its roots lie in Italy's agricultural past (when survival demanded co-operation), firmly grounded in Catholicism's familial teachings, and reinforced by times when it became essential to preserve family (or family-like) groups – either in the wake of emigration or in the face of outside interference.

Economic necessity Demography and social change are weakening family ties – witness Italy's drug problem and the numbers of old people living alone – with divorce and abortion now readily available, and attitudes modified by the student and feminist movements of the last 20 years (less so in the more traditional south). Yet children often continue to live at home into their thirties – unable to move away to study (there are few grants) and unable (or unwilling) to buy their first home alone. At least 65 per cent of working Italians, moreover, are dependent on a family economy, a structure that still strongly binds extended families.

Mother and child *Mammismo* – the attachment of Italian men to their mothers – is as strong as ever. Christ, runs the old joke, was an Italian, brought up at home for 30 years in the belief that his mother was a virgin and he was the son of God. Psychologists say the search for a woman that replicates the mother's selfless devotion is the key to the Italian family, resulting in the south's elevation of virginity as the *sine qua non* of feminine virtue, the male's constant philandering (and eventual return to the nest) and the matriarchal structure that, for all men's sexual *braggadocio*, leaves women the rulers of the Italian roost.

The Church

■ **The Catholic Church has been bound up with Italian life for almost 2,000 years. Although now in apparent decline and no longer obsessed with political power, it still plays a part in national affairs and impinges – however subtly – on many aspects of day-to-day life.** ■

Decline In many respects Italy is no longer a Catholic country. Although 97 per cent of Italians are baptised, only around 10 per cent regularly attend Mass. Divorce, abortion and birth control are freely available, and the Church's political influence is now almost negligible.

Christian focus At the same time, Italy qualifies as one of the holiest spots on earth, not only for its saints, shrines and churches (and myriad religious festivals) but also because it contains the Vatican. Attitudes towards the latter are ambivalent, for on the one hand it was Italy's only real unifying force after the fall of the Roman Empire, yet on the other it opposed political unification, only

Religious mementos on sale

reluctantly relinquishing the Papal States in 1870. It is remembered as a poor ruler, bleeding regions dry and giving little in return – still a source of anti-clericalism in much of Italy.

Structure It is important to differentiate between the Vatican and the Catholic Church. The Vatican (with the pope at its head) rules 850 million Catholics worldwide (including those

in Italy), while the Italian Church is ruled by a cardinal and the Italian Episcopal Council (composed of 29 bishops). Overseeing all is the pope – *Il Papa* in Italian, from the Greek *pappas*, 'father' (Pope John Paul II, elected in 1978, is the 263rd such spiritual successor to St Peter). Pontiffs enjoyed political power until 1870, when they retired to the Vatican, only emerging in 1929 after Mussolini's Lateran Treaty (which formalised Church and State relations and created the independent Vatican territory). Once all 10 major posts in the Curia, or church government, were held by Italians: now only one or two are likely to be native incumbents, a measure of the degree to which Catholicism's power base has shifted away from Italy.

Pagan inheritance Italy's holy heritage goes back to ancient Rome's taste for myth, superstition and pagan observance. Wandering Rome's Forum you might have sampled dozens of recipes for salvation – Mithraism, Judaism, Christianity, Manichaeism, the worship of Isis, Osiris and Atargatis, even oddities like the cult of the goddess Cybele, whose priests were expected to indulge in ritual self-castration.

The burial of apostles Peter and Paul in Rome put Christianity firmly on the Italian map. Unable to shake off the pagan trappings of its antecedents, it merely incorporated them. Festivals were given new names – December's *Saturnalia* became Christmas, Isis' day of the dead became November's All Souls' – and churches were raised all over Italy from temple ruins. Incense, holy water, even marriage rites were all taken from Roman ceremonies.

Food and wine

■ **Eating is one of Italy's greatest pleasures. Its cuisine – fed by the natural bounty of land and sea – ranks among the world's greatest, and if the plaudits for its wines are less resounding, there are still good wines that perfectly match the simple genius of the cooking.** ■

A culinary voyage around Italy is a pleasant surprise. There are many specialities unique to each region – and even if you stick to the classics, pizza or *spaghetti bolognese* taste better in their places of origin.

Restaurants The outside appearance of a restaurant has little bearing on the quality of food on offer. *Ristorante, osteria* and *trattoria* are now fairly interchangeable terms; a *tavola calda* or *pizzeria* is more humble (though the food can still be excellent). Nowhere do you have to wade through the entire menu (*la lista*) – Italians themselves often stick to a plate of pasta and salad; nor should you overlook bars and markets as sources of cheap snacks. Avoid fixed-price tourist menus – usually a false economy.

Meals Smarter hotels may offer you the breakfast (*prima colazione*) you eat at home, but Italians tend to start the day with sweet croissants (*una brioche* or *un cornetto*) and coffee (*espresso* or the longer *cappuccino* and *caffè latte*).
In Sicily or German-speaking Alto Adige, breakfast might include wine, salami and grilled cheeses.
Lunch (*pranzo*) is no longer the extended and overblown occasion of days gone by. Save the blow-out until evening and stick to something light – a picnic or bar snack with rolls (*panini*) and sandwiches

(*tramezzini*). In bars pay first for what you want at the cash-desk (*cassa*) and take your chit (*lo scontrino*) to the counter, where a L200 tip slapped on the bar works wonders with staff.

Full-scale meals start with *antipasto* (an *hors d'oeuvre*), followed by the *primo piatto* (first course), which may be soup, pasta or rice, and then by the main meat or fish dish (the *secondo*). Vegetables (*contorni*) or salad (*insalata*) follow separately and the meal is rounded off with cheese (*formaggio*), fruit (*frutta*) and/or a pudding (*dolce*).

Washing it down Italy produces more wine than any country in the world. The DOC classification system is no real indicator of quality; ask instead for local wines (*vini locali*) or house wines (*vini della casa*), and treat yourself to more famous tipples in the appropriate regions – notably Piedmont (*Barolo* and *Barbaresco*) and Tuscany (*Chianti, Brunello* or *Vino Nobile*). Happily, standards are rising among small, independent producers (notably in Umbria, Trentino–Alto Adige and the Veneto).
Try firewaters like *grappa* at least once, as well as aperitifs (Cinzano, Campari and Cynar) and liqueurs like *amaro* (a bitter digestif), *amaretto* (a sweet almond-based drink) and the aniseed-flavoured *sambuca*.

13

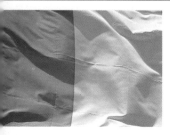

■ **Turnout at Italian elections is higher than anywhere else in Europe, yet for all this apparent enthusiasm most Italians treat politics with the resignation or weary disdain it largely deserves. Only recently have corruption scandals and a crumbling of the old order challenged indifference to the system and made political progress a real possibility.** ■

The system Italy has been a republic since a referendum in 1946, overseen by a largely symbolic president (who occupies Rome's Palazzo Chigi), and underpinned by a decision-making lower house, the Chamber of Deputies. Housed in Rome's Palazzo Montecitorio, this has around 630 deputies, of whom about 30 are ministers. Near by lies the upper house (Palazzo Madama), comprised of 315 senators, made up of six representatives from each Italian region plus various senators-for-life, appointed for their service to the state (such as ex-presidents of the Republic).

Local government Italy's 21 regions (*regione*) also enjoy a large measure of self-government, some – usually those in 'problem' or multi-ethnic areas – being semi-autonomous (notably Sicily, Sardinia, Trentino–Alto Adige and the Valle d'Aosta). Each region is divided into provinces (*provincia*), and each province is then further divided into a series of local councils (*comune*).

Publicity material for the Leghe

Democracy The Italian post-war political system rose from the ruins of Fascist dictatorship – with all the democratic frailties and insecurities that implies. Despite its many faults it has been behind (if not always directly responsible for) the transformation of Italy from an agricultural backwater to one of the world's leading industrial nations. Its institutions, if now looking increasingly moribund, were framed to prevent a throwback to Mussolini and seemed initially to match the country's particular needs.

Voting Voting is written into the Italian constitution as a 'civic duty', being seen after the war as an act in support of the very idea of democracy. Failure to vote can in theory be marked on a citizen's criminal record. A complicated system of proportional representation led to the series of coalition governments whose corruption finally brought about their own downfall (see opposite page). In August 1993, parliament voted in an electoral reform bill, whereby 75 per cent of both upper and lower houses are elected by a first-past-the-post system, the remaining 25 per cent by proportional representation.

Italians also occasionally vote in referenda, held when 500,000 or more signatures are collected on an issue, a democratic device that decided such crucial issues as divorce and abortion in the 1970s and electoral reform in 1993.

A crooked waltz For all the 50 or so post-war governments in Italy elected under the old voting system, ultimate control remained all but unchanged, power and position

14

being shared out around the coalitions in a gentle waltz of slowly changing partners.

The largest party, the broadly centre-right *Democrazia Cristiana* (Christian Democrats), commandeered the four- or five-party coalitions, sharing the spoils of government with the Socialists (PSI), Republicans (PRI), Liberals (PLI) and Social Democrats (PSD) – and keeping out the popular Communists (now renamed *Partito Democratico*

❏ 'And what is the prize eventually to be won? The rebirth of democracy. The glorious prospect of being able one day to choose their rulers from a list of powerful men, most of whose corruptions are already known and accepted with weary resignation.' – Norman Lewis with the Allies in Italy in 1944. ❏

---

della Sinistra, Democratic Party of the Left). None of these parties has survived untainted by corruption, which has crept in largely under the cover of *clientelismo* – the hidden links, votes for favours, kickbacks and the like that have characterised Italian political life since Machiavelli, but which recently seem to have become too much even for the long-suffering Italians.

In 1993 politicians agonised over the formation of a new electoral system

Present and future Italian politics are currently undergoing a sea change. Scandal after scandal has revealed the breadth and depth of corruption, with the highest in the land, in politics and industry, under investigation for bribery, misappropriation of billions of lire – even murder. Such was the disgust with politicians that in April 1993 the president asked the respected governor of the Bank of Italy to form a government. Carlo Azeglio Ciampi was Italy's first non-parliamentarian prime minister this century. New parties are springing up, notably the *Leghe* (Leagues), northern coalitions in favour of a federal Italy (see page 16) and *La Rete* (The Network), a southern-based party directed against political collusion with the Mafia. Further signs of public disenchantment with the old parties were seen with the creation of 'Forza Italia', a centre-right party formed by media mogul Silvio Berlusconi, and the centre-left party under Romano Prodi which currently enjoys power. However, new parties have sprung up before, such as the Radicals and Greens in the 1970s, and there is some doubt – especially given Italian bureaucracy's Byzantine obduracy – whether the present upheavals really mark the death throes of old-style Italian politics.

■ **Geography and history have always marginalised southern Italy – which starts somewhere between Rome and Naples – leaving it not only considerably poorer than the north, but also the victim of an unholy trinity comprising prejudice, corruption and organised crime.** ■

Problems Some of the south's problems will never go away. Little can be done to alter Italy's shape, which leaves the region far from markets, thus crippling industrial initiative; nor to alter its climate, whose harshness leaves agriculture hamstrung; nor to change its geology, which offers nothing by way of energy sources or raw materials. Nor, it appears, can much be done to tackle the Mafia, whose tentacles strangle legitimate enterprise and discourage long-term investment.

Calabrian women

Potential for change Others of the south's problems can perhaps be resolved, principally those rooted in the autocratic Spanish regimes (from 1559) that stifled the south for centuries – corruption, poor education, crumbling infrastructure and latent feudal hierarchies. Money has been thrown at the region for decades, every so often hitting its targets – notably in the eradication of malaria and in the building of new roads – but more often than not falling into the pockets of Mafia barons.

Emigration The south has known two great periods of emigration: the first to the United States at the turn of the century, the second to the industrial heartlands of the north (Milan, Turin and Venice), where cheap southern labour fuelled the economic boom of the 1950s and '60s. While boom has hardly turned to bust – they say Italy without the south would be Europe's richest country – southerners are now resented by some with a virulence which amounts to racism.

New bigotry Northerners have always looked with mock horror on the south. In the wake of recent political disillusionment, looks and attitudes have taken a more ugly turn, manifest in graffiti telling *terroni* (peasants) to go home (or worse) and the rise of the *Leghe* (Leagues), increasingly popular political parties who – angered at what they see as the north subsidising the south – argue for a more federal, even partitioned, Italy. This is unlikely to happen, but the longing – some 135 years after unification – is a symptom of some greater malaise in the Italian soul.

Symbol of the prosperous north

■ **Italy has long hummed with a babel of dialects descended from Greek, Latin and the languages introduced by foreign invaders over the centuries. Regional differences still define Italian character, but the advent of mass media is gradually eroding the country's linguistic diversity.** ■

History Italian draws the bulk of its vocabulary from Latin, and is still the closest of the Romance languages to its Roman roots. It has evolved in its present form from the educated language of Tuscany, primarily because this was the regional dialect used by medieval writers such as Dante, Petrarch and Boccaccio. Even today an Italian saying describes how 'Tuscans polish the air around them', while the best Italian is said to be *la lingua toscana in bocca romana* (a Tuscan tongue in a Roman mouth).

Usage For all its occasional verbosity, Italian is one of the most beautiful languages, its musical cadences more seductive to the heart than the mind. Its particular spell was well captured by Charles Vs, the Holy Roman Emperor, in his famous observation that he spoke Spanish with God, French to his courtiers, German with his horse and Italian to women. He might have added that Italian is one of the best languages for displays of anger and passion.

Dialects Italy's particular shape, its remote mountain enclaves and a chequered past have all fostered an estimated 1,500 different dialects, a diversity so rich that it is estimated

only two per cent of Italians are unable to speak some form of dialect. Some even speak a different language, notably in the Valle d'Aosta (French), Friuli (Slovene) and Alto Adige (German). Venetian has words of Spanish and Portuguese origin (a legacy of its seafaring tradition). Lombardy has German imports (having been ruled by Austria), while Piedmont is heavily laced with French. Spanish and French crop up in Neapolitan, while a bastardised Greek and

Albanian is spoken in parts of Calabria. Sicily boasts a sprinkling of Arabic, French and Spanish, similarly Sardinia, which has its own language, Sardo (as well as a Catalan enclave in Alghero). And small pockets of *Ladino* (Ladin) still exist in certain remote Alpine valleys. In as little as a generation, however, with the levelling influence of television, Italy may find itself speaking a standard Italian, its dialects no more than quaint memories.

■ **Cinema is among Italy's major contributions to the mainstream of 20th-century culture, having not only influenced a generation of post-war film-makers, but also defined a particular image of Italy with films like *La Dolce Vita* and stars such as Sophia Loren, Marcello Mastroianni and Isabella Rossellini.** ■

Epics and escapism Italian cinema launched itself in Turin with blockbusting silent films like Enrico Guazzoni's *Quo Vadis?* (1913), before moving to Rome – to take advantage of its climate and ready-made locations – where lack of funds and its head-on encounter with Fascism saw it crash to near oblivion in the 1930s. Films made under Fascist auspices were usually ideologically approved propaganda or the so-called *telefoni bianchi*. These were sentimental and escapist palliatives named after the white telephone that always appeared in the heroine's bedroom – symbol of the exotic Hollywood fairy-tale for Italians who had never owned a telephone, and much less a white one.

Neo-realism Rome's great studios, Cinecittà, opened by Mussolini in 1938 with the words 'cinema is our greatest weapon', became Italian cinema's spiritual home, inhabited after the war by a generation of young film-makers whose new-found freedom produced the revolutionary genre known as Neo-realism (which greatly influenced

American *films noirs* and the French New Wave of the 1960s). Its earliest exponents were Luchino Visconti (*Ossessione*, 1942) and Roberto Rossellini, whose *Roma, Città Aperta* (1945), with its real locations, visceral style, jerky camerawork and almost documentary footage, prepared the ground for classics in the same genre such as Vittorio de Sica's *Ladri di Biciclette* (*Bicycle Thieves*, 1949).

To the present day Tastes changed during the boom years of the 1950s and 1960s, when the Neo-realists' mantle was taken up by Federico Fellini, Francesco Rosi and Michelangelo Antonioni (though Pier Paolo Pasolini continued to chronicle the new underbelly of Italian urban life in films like *Accatone* and *Una Vita Violenta*). Fellini's distinctive view is seen in *La Strada* (1954), *La Dolce Vita* (1960) and *Otto e Mezzo* (*8½*, 1963). Antonioni is perhaps best known for *Blow-Up* (1966), whose English-language lead was taken up by Bertolucci (*The Last Emperor, Last Tango in Paris*) and the Taviani brothers (*Good Morning Babylon*). Cinecittà's reputation, meanwhile, saw it grow fat on American epics like *Ben Hur* and *Cleopatra*, before television and rising costs reduced it to peddling so-called 'spaghetti westerns', soft porn and money-spinning potboilers. Of recent hits, perhaps the most familiar to foreign audiences is Giuseppe Tornatore's *Cinema Paradiso*, set in Sicily, though monuments to longevity like Bertolucci are still making films.

Top: Roma, Città Aperta
Left: Ossessione

OSSESSIONE a film by LUCHINO VISCONTI   a BFI release

■ **Italy's archaeological record goes back over half a million years to early Stone Age hunters. Generations came and went, leaving few traces of their passing, until the advent of the Greeks and Etruscans, who brought Italy into the light of history. Soon a great civilisation was born.** ■

Prehistory The first modern human remains found in Italy date from palaeolithic times around 20,000 BC. More advanced cultures made their appearance between 3000 and 1800 BC, notably the Ligurians (who settled modern-day Liguria), the Siculi (Lazio and southern Italy) and the Sards (who developed a pastoral culture in Sardinia). They were followed by migratory peoples, principally the Picini and Messapians, who crossed the Adriatic from the Balkans, as well as the Veneti, Latins and Umbrii, who moved down the peninsula from the north.

Phoenicians and Carthaginians By 800 BC the Phoenicians had drifted along the African coast and established colonies in Sicily and Sardinia (introducing an alphabet into Italy for the first time). One of their leading African cities, Carthage, eventually became a power in its own right, establishing footholds in southern Italy, Sicily and Sardinia at about the same time as Greek and Etruscan influence emerged elsewhere.

Greeks The first Greek colonies on Italian soil were established around 735 BC in Sicily, eventually developing into a network of independent cities all over southern Italy known as Magna Graecia (Greater Greece). Despite internecine wars and conflicts with the Carthaginians (in Sicily) and the Etruscans (in Campania), the colonies immeasurably enriched Italy's indigenous cultures in the realms of art and architecture, while in agriculture they introduced two great staples – the vine and the olive.

Etruscans The Etruscans occupied much of present-day Lazio and Tuscany, in an area roughly bounded by the Arno and Tiber rivers (though they occasionally expanded beyond these borders). Where they came from is one of history's great mysteries, but they were probably a mixture of indigenous and foreign peoples, who became linked by a common language and assimilated neighbouring tribes (like the Ligurians and Umbrians) to forge a loose political (and religious) affiliation based on a 12-city confederation. Like the Greeks, they were culturally, technologically and agriculturally advanced, though militarily they were to prove no match for the Romans, who by about 350 BC had all but defeated their leading cities.

Engraving depicting a Phoenician merchant fleet

The rise of Rome

■ **After obscure beginnings, Rome conquered its Greek and Etruscan neighbours. Its sophisticated republican structure evolved through periods of social disorder into an empire that endured almost a thousand years and whose limits touched almost every corner of the known world.** ■

Beginnings According to legend, Romulus founded Rome in 753 BC. However, the city's earliest archaeological remains date from around 1200 BC (though it may be 2,000 years older). By 900 BC Rome formed the border between the Etruscan and Latin spheres of influence, possibly ruled until around 600 BC by the Tarquins, an Etruscan royal dynasty.

The Republic The Etruscan kings were ousted by the Romans in 509 BC and replaced by a Republic (*res publica*), where in theory the 'people were kings'. In practice the city was riven by disputes between the plebeians (the lower classes) and the patricians (the military and political élite). The plebeians were partly placated by the tribune (494 BC), a magistracy which looked after their interests, and an uneasy consensus allowed Rome to expand, first into Etruscan and Samnite territory, and then into Greek-dominated southern Italy.

*Right: Julius Caesar
Below: The Roman
Forum*

The Punic Wars Rome's expansion brought it into conflict with Carthage. The struggle for supremacy took the shape of three protracted campaigns – the Punic Wars – the first of which (264–241 BC) saw Rome seize control of Sicily, Corsica and Sardinia. In the second (218–202 BC), Carthage dispatched Hannibal and his army – elephants and all – across the Alps to inflict defeats on Rome at Cannae and Trasimeno. Scipio Africanus at last defeated Hannibal at Zama in 202 BC. The Third Punic War (149–146 BC) left Rome master of the Mediterranean and territories as far flung as Jerusalem and Asia Minor.

Julius Caesar In Rome the city's internal divisions simmered on. Popular revolt exploded in the Social Wars (90–88 BC), bringing about an increasingly authoritarian response from the Senate. The general Sulla was installed to restore order, followed by Pompey, who with two other leading figures – Crassus and Julius Caesar – formed the First Triumvirate (60 BC).

The Roman Empire

■ **Julius Caesar became dictator of Rome, but it was his grand nephew and adopted son and heir, Octavius, who first assumed the title of emperor (as Augustus). He ushered in a period of reforms, public works and military consolidation that saw Rome emerge as the cultural, religious and political centre of the known world.** ■

22

The Ides of March Caesar's military prowess eventually made him pre-eminent, a dictatorial position he used to heal the scars of a century's civil strife. Institutions were reformed, and new temples and civic buildings blossomed. Jealousy mounted, however, and in 44 BC, on 15 March (the Ides), he was assassinated.

Assassination of Julius Caesar

The age of Augustus The Second Triumvirate – Lepidus, Mark Antony and Octavius – was then formed. Designed to wage war on Caesar's assassins, it soon became a battleground for control of the empire. Antony compromised his chances by dallying with Cleopatra, leaving the field clear for Octavius, who sealed his position with victory at the Battle of Actium in 31 BC. He took the title of *princeps* in 27 BC, changing his name to Augustus Caesar. The Augustan Age was to mark the high point of the Roman civilisation.

The Emperors Few subsequent emperors were able to emulate Augustus (27 BC–AD 14), but the immense spoils accruing from the empire masked their more grotesque

deficiencies. Three of the more decadent incumbents followed – Tiberius (14–37), Claudius (41–54) and Nero (54–68) – followed in turn by the Flavians (Vespasian, and his sons Titus and Domitian), under whom the empire enjoyed a period of relative peace and prosperity. This golden age continued under the Antonines, the great military emperors Trajan (98–117), Hadrian (117–138) and Marcus Aurelius (161–180).

Decline and fall After Aurelius' death, revolts broke out against the Roman yoke across the empire; emperors came and went with increasing rapidity; cultural life stagnated; and political, military and economic institutions teetered on the brink of collapse. Diocletian divided the empire in two (East and West), bringing a partial recovery sustained under Constantine, whose Edict of Milan (313) allowed Christians freedom of worship. In time the capital of the Western Empire was moved to Ravenna (with Constantinople the capital in the East).

The Mausoleum of Augustus, Rome

■ **Neither the Dark Ages nor the succession of barbarians who swarmed into Italy after the fall of the Roman Empire were as black as they are usually painted. Today, however, little evidence remains of the Goths, Franks and Lombards who dominated the peninsula for more than three centuries.** ■

Barbarians Raids by 'barbarians' (outsiders, or foreigners) had preoccupied Rome for centuries, but as the empire floundered they became more coherent, and the means to withstand them less forthcoming. When Rome itself was sacked in 410 by Alaric the Goth it sent a tremor around the civilised world. Subsequent incursions came to a head in 476, when Odoacer the Goth displaced the last Western Emperor, Romulus Augustulus. In 493 Theodoric, another Goth, seized Ravenna, and with it control of the old empire's western territories.

Byzantines Constantinople – modern Istanbul – prospered as the capital of the Eastern Empire (Byzantium), and to a large extent escaped the turmoil that marked the demise of its western counterpart. Between 536 and 552 its emperor, Justinian, retook large areas of Italy (through his famous general Belisarius), the so-called Gothic Wars producing a Byzantine hegemony over parts of the country that was to survive for centuries. At the same time the Church emerged as a temporal power, taking advantage of uncertain political times to assert an increasing influence on Italian affairs.

Lombards and Franks Territorial gaps left by the Byzantines were partly filled by the Lombards (568–774), a race from the north, who established three duchies in Italy centred on Pavia, Cividale and Spoleto. They were later joined by the Franks, a Christian race from Gaul, whose loyalties were divided between two rival factions – the Carolingian and Merovingian dynasties. Pepin the Short, a Carolingian, resolved the division in 754 by appealing to Pope Stephen III, who – in anointing him with holy oil – sanctioned his rule (a symbolic gesture of immeasurable consequence). In return, Pepin and his son, Charlemagne, defeated the Lombards (774), handing over large areas of conquered territory to the papacy – lands which were to form the papal states and source of the papacy's temporal power. On Christmas Day in 800 Charlemagne was crowned 'Emperor of the Romans' by Pope Leo III, an act which forged enduring links – and guaranteed centuries of conflict – between the popes and northern-based emperors.

Charlemagne, Holy Roman Emperor

Popes and emperors

■ **The centuries following Charlemagne's death saw a struggle for ascendancy between the papacy and the Holy Roman Empire. With the popes claiming the right to crown emperors, and the emperors the right to sanction popes, opposed camps began to emerge across Italy – the Guelphs (papal supporters) and Ghibellines (imperial supporters).** ■

24

Rival powers The Frankish empire disintegrated, but the office of emperor stayed intact – though emperors increasingly remained in their northern power bases, entering Italy only intermittently in attempts to assert imperial authority. While the fortunes of empire and papacy waxed and waned, there were rarely periods when they were not at one another's throats.

Tit for tat The most famous encounter came in 1076, when Emperor Henry IV rejected Pope Gregory VII and his proposals for radical political reforms. Gregory in turn excommunicated Henry, thus – in theory – freeing his subjects from imperial allegiance. Although this squabble was resolved diplomatically, others were to be more violent, notably the rampaging campaigns of Frederick I (Barbarossa) against northern Italian cities from his base in Germany in 1155. Papal

fortunes hit rock bottom in the 14th century with the move from Rome to Avignon, followed by the Great Schism, when three rival popes vied for recognition.

Arabs and Normans While northern Italy swayed between pope and emperor, events in southern Italy followed a more orderly path. The Saracens (Arabs) invaded Sicily in 827 and assumed control for two centuries. Elsewhere the Byzantines held sway until supplanted by the Normans (11th century), who after arriving in the region as mercenaries carved out a kingdom (including Sicily) under Robert Guiscard and his successors Roger I and Roger II.

Anjou and Aragon The marriage of a Norman princess and Emperor Henry VI brought the south within the imperial orbit. Unfortunately the Norman kingdom had been legitimised by the papacy, thus creating the same dilemma that dogged papal and imperial relations in the north. Italian-born emperor Frederick II briefly dominated the south in defiance of the papacy, but his heirs were defeated by Charles of Anjou (1265), brother of the French king, who received Naples and Sicily as a 'gift' from a grateful papacy. The Anjous (Angevins) ruled most of the south for two centuries, except for Sicily, which they forfeited to Spain (Peter III of Aragon) after the uprising known as the 'Sicilian Vespers' in 1282. In 1442 Alfonso V of Aragon was named heir to the last of the Angevins and the south was united under Spanish control until the 18th century.

GREGORIVS·VII·PAPA·SAONENSIS

The city states

■ **City states have been a constant feature in Italian history, but they reached their zenith during the 14th century – when 400 of them stretched across the north of the country – riding high on increased trade and the relative decline of papal and imperial authority.** ■

Climate for change Rivalry between pope and emperor left a power vacuum in which cities could evolve independently. This was especially true by 1300, after which few emperors could combine control of Italy with their dynastic obligations in northern Europe. For the papacy's part, after a dispute with Philip of France, it fell under French domination, and in 1307, hopelessly compromised and subordinate, moved to Avignon under the protection of the French kings (The Great Schism).

Meanwhile, the maritime republics (Amalfi, Pisa, Genoa and Venice) and cities which stood on trade routes (Bologna, Milan, Verona and Florence) grew rich on commerce.

The Comune Many cities initially developed a quasi-democratic structure known as the *comune*, a ruling council consisting of merchants,

guildsmen and minor nobility. As cities prospered, so they acquired magnificent *palazzi* and cathedrals. This was the period of Dante (1265–1321), Petrarch (1304–74) and Boccaccio (1313–75), all pillars of Italy's literary tradition, and of the first stirrings of artistic change heralding the Renaissance.

The Signoria As cities fought one another, or were fractured by internal power struggles, so they increasingly abandoned the *comune* and looked to one man (*signore*) to cut through the muddle. Despotic rule followed, usually under a powerful noble, merchant or *condottiere* (a mercenary employed by the cities to fight on their behalf). Thus rose the Visconti (Milan), Gonzaga (Mantua), Este (Ferrara), Montefeltro (Urbino), Medici (Florence) and many other powerful families.

■ **An agreement in 1455 between Italy's major powers – Milan, Florence, Venice, Naples and the papal states – cemented a period of calm which endured until the death of Lorenzo de' Medici in 1492. Thereafter Italy became a pawn in the hands of foreign players – first France and Spain, then Austria.** ■

France France entered the equation in 1494 when the Duke of Milan, after a quarrel with the Neapolitan king, invited Charles VIII of France to conquer the Kingdom of Naples. Charles for his part claimed the throne on the basis that his Anjou ancestor formerly ruled Naples and southern Italy (see page 24). He captured the kingdom easily, but stayed only three months, after which it was regained for Spain by Ferdinand II of Aragon. A later French king, François I, took Milan in 1515, basing his claim on a marriage between a Visconti (former rulers of Milan) and the French royal family.

Napoleon in all his glory

Spain Spain joined France in the scramble for territory in Italy in the person of Charles V (1500–58), Holy Roman Emperor and Habsburg heir to the Austrian and Spanish thrones. His troops ransacked Rome in 1527, and defeated the French at Pavia (1526) and Naples (1529). The Treaty of Cateau-Cambrésis (1559) ratified Spanish rule over Sicily, Sardinia, southern Italy, Milan and parts of Tuscany for 150 years. France held other pockets, leaving only Venice and the papal states independent of foreign powers. It was against this background that the great religious movements of the Reformation and Counter-Reformation were played out.

Austria and Napoleon Spain's stranglehold slackened following the War of the Spanish Succession, which saw Lombardy, Mantua, Naples and Sardinia pass by treaty to the Austrians (1713). Machinations later in the 18th century saw further realignments (Lorraine took Tuscany, Piedmont was ruled by the Savoys, and in 1734 the Spanish Bourbons took southern Italy). Austria meanwhile remained in control of the north under Maria Theresa (1740–80) and her son Joseph II (1780–92).

All changed with Napoleon's Italian campaigns in 1796 and 1800. He succeeded in conquering the Italian peninsula, establishing a republic which, for all that it was short-lived, reduced papal power, reformed feudal hierarchies, and – perhaps most importantly – suggested the potential for a single Italian state. The Vienna Settlement (1815) restored Austrian control, but over the next 50 years did little to halt the momentum of the unification movement.

■ **Three obstacles lay in the path of a unified Italy – Austria (who ruled northern Italy), the papacy (rulers of central Italy) and the Spanish (rulers of Sicily and the south). Although unification was ultimately engineered by Italian patriots, it was only made possible by conflict and collusion between foreign powers.** ■

Leading players Unification's Italian protagonists were Giuseppe Mazzini (1805–72), a political agitator, and Giuseppe Garibaldi (1807–82), an inspired military leader. Both favoured linking royal and republican efforts towards unification, the former spearheaded by Count Camillo Cavour (1810–61), prime minister of Piedmont, an independent kingdom ruled by the Savoys, Italy's future kings. Externally, Napoleon III of France was motivated by concerns for French Catholics and the survival of the papacy. Britain favoured the end of Spanish (Bourbon) domination in southern Italy, and Austria was opposed to unification at the expense of its position in northern Italy.

Garibaldi, military genius of unification

The 1848 Republics Revolutionary unrest swept Europe in 1848. In Italy, it sparked off a war against Austria in Lombardy (under Carlo Alberto, the Savoy king), and the restoration of Venice's Republic of San Marco (again in defiance of the Austrians). In Rome, the pope fled from rioting and Mazzini established the Roman Republic (Garibaldi organised the city's defences). The republics were short-lived. Austria crushed the northern uprisings and French troops relieved Rome, restoring the *status quo* of a year earlier.

The 1859 campaigns In 1859 Cavour engineered an alliance with Napoleon III against the Austrians, joining the French armies to those of Piedmont (under the Savoy king, Vittore Emanuele II). The Austrians were defeated at Magenta and Solferino, after which Napoleon III – to Cavour's frustration – signed an armistice with them. Meanwhile, revolts elsewhere had gathered a momentum of their own, with uprisings in Tuscany and Emilia, both of which were annexed by Piedmont (along with Lombardy, won at Solferino).

Unification In 1860 the job of unification was only half complete. To finish it, Garibaldi left Genoa with 1,000 volunteers (the *Mille*) to overthrow the Bourbons in the name of Vittore Emanuele II. Sicily and Naples fell within four months, the papal states surrendered to Cavour, and the Kingdom of Italy was proclaimed in February 1861. The Austrians were removed from Venice and the Veneto in 1866 (defeated following an alliance with Prussia), and Rome and the papacy were taken in 1870 after the withdrawal of the French garrison (precipitated by the fall of Napoleon III, defeated by Prussia that year in Sedan).

■ **Italy entered both world wars in the hope of territorial gain – after piecemeal colonial expansion in Eritrea, Libya and Abyssinia. Success in 1918 bred only debt and disappointment, and gave rise to Fascism, while failure in 1943 – ironically – laid the foundations of progress and the country's present prosperity.** ■

World War I At the start of the Great War, Italy was neutral, but by 1915 had joined the Allied cause, lured by promises of colonial rewards and the chance of gaining the partly Italian-speaking regions around Trento and Trieste. Its ill-prepared army lost several bitterly fought battles, notably at Caporetto in 1917, before a last-ditch victory at Vittorio Veneto. Although denied certain territories, Italy's gains at the peace conference included (present-day) Trentino–Alto Adige and Friuli–Venezia-Giulia, though at a high cost: national assets fell by 26 per cent, and 40 per cent of the 5.5 million Italians mobilised were killed or wounded.

Fascism Italy's government was unable to deal with the social and economic chaos unleashed by the war, creating a power vacuum quickly filled by Mussolini, whose high-sounding promises pandered to the panic-stricken middle and upper classes. A threatened general strike in 1922 provided the excuse for his 'March on Rome', after which – fearful of civil war – the king refused to sanction the incumbent government and handed power to Mussolini (then with an intimidating mob presence on the streets, but still only a tiny showing in parliament itself). By 1925 Italy was ruled by a dictatorship, held together with bluster and brute force, and bolstered by imperial adventures in north Africa.

World War II After a hesitant start, Mussolini took Italy to war in June 1940, emboldened by Hitler's success and eager to share in the spoils of victory. After successes in the Adriatic, he suffered defeats in Greece, heavy casualties in Russia and the loss of Sicily (August 1943), all of which led to his downfall and an armistice with the Allies. The Nazis assumed control, installed Mussolini as the head of a puppet republic, and confronted the Allies – and a force of 450,000 partisans – as they inched up the Italian peninsula to liberate Rome on 4 June 1944. Mussolini's end came in April 1945, shot and strung up in Milan's Piazzale Loreto.

Fêting the triumphant Mussolini

■ **Italy's progress since World War II has been remarkable, developing in less than a generation from an agricultural backwater to one of the world's leading industrial nations. In its wake, however, the transformation has brought social tensions, terrorism and the inexorable rise of organised crime.** ■

The Fifties A referendum in June 1946 voted narrowly (54–46) to replace Italy's monarchy with a republic. With the help of Marshall Aid, the hardships of the immediate post-war years gave way to an economic boom bolstered by cheap, compliant labour and most Italians' thirst for the world of cars, televisions and material well-being. This was the era of the *dolce vita*, Sophia Loren, baby Fiats, and mass migrations from the south to the industrialised cities of the north. In 1957 the Treaty of Rome was signed, and Italy became a founder member of the European Community.

The Sixties The boom tailed off somewhat in the 1960s, and the orthodoxy of past governments (dominated by the centre-right Christian Democrats) gave way to coalitions in which the left demanded a voice. Inflation soared, and social tensions surfaced, the bitter fruit of Italy's sudden wrench from traditional ways of life. Unrest culminated in the *autunno caldo* (hot autumn) of 1969, when strikes and student demonstrations crippled the country.

The Seventies Matters became worse in the next decade, when at times it appeared Italy was on the brink of disintegration. Right- and left-wing terrorism was rife, culminating in 1978 with the kidnap and murder of Aldo Moro, a former prime minister, by the *Brigate Rosse* (Red Brigades). These were the so-called *anni di piombo* (years of lead), named after the period's weight of bullets, but also evocative of the gloomy and apocalyptic mood of the times.

The Eighties and Nineties By about 1985 the economy steadied and terrorism was all but defeated. Italy continued to prosper (at least in the north) despite its upheavals and political scandals, progress occurring despite rather than because of its institutions. Today, however, after 40 years of corrupt government, the country seems to be approaching the millennium with a heartfelt desire for institutional reforms. If they succeed – and the problems of the Mafia and the south are addressed – Italy may finally pull itself into this century in time for the next.

Rome, April 1968: student protests were brutally put down by riot police

■ **Italy's artistic heyday was perhaps not the Renaissance, but the centuries from which it borrowed, when Greek, Etruscan and Roman artists and sculptors produced the classical masterpieces which still lie scattered across the country's museums and archaeological sites.** ■

Greek influences Greek art came to Italy with the colonies of Magna Graecia around 800 BC (see page 231), making its mark on much of southern Italy and influencing the Etruscan and Roman cultures that followed for more than a millennium. Particularly influential were the temple architecture of Sicily and southern Italy (Paestum provides supreme examples), and the semi-circular Greek theatres, fine examples of which survive in Taormina and Siracusa. Hellenistic painting, by contrast, has almost vanished, though its influence permeates the tomb paintings and decorated vases of Etruscan culture. Sculpture was of incalculable significance, and Greek bronzes and ceramics also served as models for Italian craftsmen.

Etruscan art While borrowing from Greek models, Etruscan art retained a distinct character, its often earthy naturalism in marked contrast to the idealised strivings of Greek artists. Tomb paintings survive in Tarquinia and Chiusi, mixtures of visionary, realistic and superstitious tableaux, testimony to the Etruscans' vivacious and outward-looking culture. Bronze and terracotta, rather than marble, were favoured for sculpture (perhaps because the materials were at hand), producing beautiful and sophisticated pieces, many of which are now on show in Rome's Vatican and Villa Giulia museums. Little is known of Etruscan architecture, though it probably made use of the arch and vault, forms later adopted by the Romans.

The Romans Roman art's debt to Greece and Etruria was immeasurable, from the use of mosaics and Etruscan sarcophaghus reliefs to the masterpieces of Roman sculpture copied from Greek originals. The derivative nature of Roman sculpture in no way detracts from the often sublime execution, but for originality one must look to architecture (and engineering) with innovations such as the basilica, triumphal arch, and commemorative column. There are Greek borrowings in the Colosseum and Pantheon, and in villas, palaces and baths, but all are unmistakably Roman. Wall paintings, widespread in their day, but now limited mainly to fragments uncovered at Pompeii and Herculaneum, also showed a Hellenistic bent.

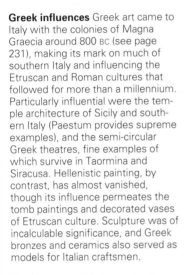

Etruscan vessels of exquisite workmanship

■ The stylised Madonnas and mosaic tradition of Byzantium look stilted today, but they were to influence Italian art until at least the 13th century. Together with aspects of Roman art and architecture, they formed the backbone of Christianity's earliest artistic tradition. ■

Old forms, new themes Christianity presented art with new themes and iconography, and was to be its chief inspiration until the Renaissance. In its earliest incarnations Christian art remained wedded to the prevailing tastes of the day: sculptures graced a few sarcophagi; paintings, except in a handful of catacombs, were rare – though it may be that early Christian artefacts have been lost. Church architecture aped the forms of Roman aisled basilicas, often relying for decoration on mosaics, the most prominent medium of early Christian art. Early mosaics – those of Rome's 4th-century Santa Costanza, for example – followed classical Roman models, but most quickly adopted the more highly coloured attributes of Byzantine models.

Byzantium Byzantine art was a hybrid of classical and oriental influences, introduced by Justinian, emperor of the eastern half of the Roman Empire, when he invaded parts of Italy in the 6th century (see page 23). It was distinguished by abstraction, gold backgrounds and a profusion of ornamental motifs, usually put to work in the service of mosaics. Notable examples are found in Ravenna (Byzantium's Italian capital), Rome (Santa Maria Maggiore and elsewhere), Milan (Sant'Ambrogio) and Aquileia (the Basilica). Not only did Byzantium's artistic hegemony spread over a wide area, it also proved remarkably durable, and Byzantine-influenced craftsmen were still producing mosaics in the 12th century (principally in Palermo's Cappella Palatina, the cathedrals of Cefalù and Monreale, and – most famously – in Venice's Basilica di San Marco, the apotheosis of Byzantine art, architecture and decoration).

Byzantine painting Byzantium's influence pervades three images that dominated Italian painting until the 14th century: portraits of saints; the iconic Madonna and Child; and

Santa Maria in Trastevere, Rome

Christus Triumphans, a large painted crucifix of Christ. All were distinguished by a mystical or reverential tone and stiff, formalised figures, with little attempt at verisimilitude. Byzantium is also ever-present in an oft-overlooked but vital artefact of the Dark Ages – the illustrated monastic manuscripts that carried art's banner for centuries.

Romanesque and Gothic

■ **Apart from mosaics and illustrated manuscripts, Italy's most conspicuous artistic flowering, as it emerged from the Dark Ages, appeared primarily in the Romanesque churches and then in the Gothic palaces and cathedrals that accompanied the growth of independent city states.** ■

Romanesque Romanesque architecture emerged during the 11th century, fostered by the upsurge of church-building in the emerging city states. Northern European (Lombard) and Italianate influences combined to produce a style distinguished by simplicity, round arches, and thick-walled buildings with cross vaults or exposed beam ceilings. Churches often had a basilical plan, with a raised choir and correspondingly sunken crypt.

Decoration was simple, usually confined to the apse or main portal, but often extended to separate campaniles and baptisteries.

The style emerges all over Italy, particularly in Lombardy (Modena, Parma and Cremona),

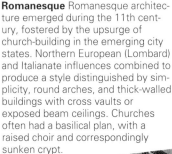

Milan cathedral, northern Italian Gothic at its finest

around Pisa (Lucca and Pistoia), in Sicily (Cefalù, Palermo and Monreale) and in Apulia, where Arab, Byzantine and Norman elements combined to create the hybrid known as Apulian-Romanesque (Bari, Ruvo, Trani, Troia and elsewhere). Masterpieces of Romanesque sculpture include the reliefs of Wiligelmus in Modena, Antelami's work in Parma, the doors of San Zeno (Verona) and the works of the Pisanos across central Italy.

Gothic Where Romanesque architecture was robust and earthbound, the Gothic, which originated in 13th-century France, was light and airy. Its emphasis was on verticality, its staples were the pointed arch, rose windows, stained glass, rib vaulting and flying buttresses. In Italy, Milan's Duomo, with its pinnacles and soaring lines, best shows the genre in all its characteristic glory.

Elsewhere, a lesser version of the Gothic appeared, its grandeur suited to the desire of cities to make conspicuous displays of their new prosperity. It distinguished the civic palaces (*palazzi pubblici)* of Siena (the Palazzo Pubblico), Florence (Palazzo Vecchio) and Venice, whose Palazzo Ducale captures Italian Gothic at its most dazzling. The style also emerged in the great cathedrals of central Italy, notably Pisa, Siena, Florence, and in the Basilica di San Francesco in Assisi (1228), an early Gothic masterpiece.

■ **During the Gothic period the Renaissance was prefigured by a handful of artists and sculptors who cast off the conventions of Byzantine art to sow the seeds of artistic renewal. It was at this time that regional schools began to develop a style which, while working on familiar lines, breathed new life into old traditions.** ■

Sculptors Nicola Pisano (*c* 1220–84) was the first of a trio of 13th-century artists whose marriage of Gothic and classical ideas was a harbinger of things to come. His graceful, sinuous style can be seen in four outstanding works – Fontana Maggiore (Perugia), Arca di San Domenico (Bologna) and pulpits in Pisa (the Baptistery) and Siena (the Duomo). Pisano's pupil and assistant, Arnolfo di Cambio (*c* 1245–1310), disseminated his influence in works scattered all over central Italy, though the influence of Pisano's son, Giovanni Pisano (*c* 1248–1314), whose figurative skill was revolutionary, was of still more resounding significance.

Painters Glimmerings of a new artistic dawn began with men like Pietro Cavallini (active 1273–1308), who began to explore the possibilities of fresco. After working in Rome (Santa Maria in Trastevere), he moved to the Basilica di San Francesco in Assisi, where he was joined first by Cimabue (*c* 1240–1302), whom

Vasari dubbed the 'father of Italian painting', and then by Giotto di Bondone (1266–1337), a seminal figure in the development of Italian art. Giotto introduced emotion, natural settings and narrative detail into his paintings (fresco cycles in Assisi and Padua in particular) that broke decisively with the stilted and stylised strictures of Byzantine art.

33

Above: Nicola Pisano's Fontana Maggiore in Perugia
Left: detail from Siena cathedral

Siena While Giotto preached innovation in Assisi's Basilica, the artists of Siena were reinterpreting the Byzantine tradition, forging the most dynamic of the schools of painting that sprang up across central Italy during the 13th and 14th centuries. Glorious swathes of colour and gold backgrounds dominated its early masterpieces, exemplified by the works of Duccio di Buoninsegna (*c* 1255–1318), features which were later wedded to the courtly and beautifully detailed style enshrined in the paintings of Simone Martini (*c* 1284–1344) and Pietro Lorenzetti (active 1306–45).

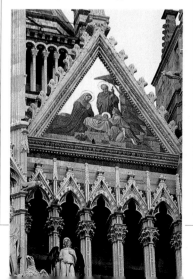

■ **A serendipitous mixture of social, artistic and intellectual ferment gave rise to the *Rinascimento* (Renaissance), which spread from Florence over the course of 125 years to become one of the greatest periods in the history of western art.** ■

34

What and why Several closely related factors helped bring about the Renaissance – the 'rebirth' of art and science. Humanist scholarship freed art of its devotional obligations and rediscovered Greek and Roman texts, from which it was a short step to a revival of the classical ideal in art. Where conservative Church patronage had previously stifled innovation, lay patrons like the Medici provided the financial wherewithal for voyages of artistic discovery. Free-thinking Florence, a prosperous and cosmopolitan city, provided an atmosphere in which creativity could flourish, attracting ever more artists as its reputation snowballed. And as more artists arrived, so the exchange of ideas and atmosphere of innovation intensified (particularly in crucial areas such as the study of anatomy and perspective).

Florence Three artists in three key disciplines ushered in the Florentine Renaissance. Filippo Brunelleschi (1377–1446) triumphed as an architect, not only creating a

dome for the city's cathedral, but also clarifying ideals of design and advancing the new science of perspective. The sculptor Donatello (1386–1466) produced staggeringly innovative work, returning the nude to the mainstream of artistic expression. And in painting Masaccio (1401–28) – together with Masolino da Panicale – pioneered techniques of perspective that dazzled contemporaries. An army of hallowed names followed – Paolo Uccello, Fra Angelico, Filippo Lippi, Benozzo Gozzoli, Luca della Robbia, Verrocchio, Ghirlandaio and Sandro Botticelli (not to mention architects like Michelozzo, Sangallo and Leon Battisti Alberti).

Outside Florence Florence did not have a monopoly on Renaissance talent. Piero della Francesca, from the Tuscan town of Sansepolcro, produced singular works that combined ethereal beauty with compositional precision. In Cortona, his pupil Luca Signorelli painted influential work distinguished by striking nudes. The Marches claimed Venetian-bred Carlo Crivelli, while neighbouring Umbria had Perugino, responsible for melancholy, soft-edged devotional paintings (sometimes executed in tandem with another Umbrian, Pinturicchio). Siena's masters included sculptor Jacopo della Quercia and

Ghirlandaio's Adoration *in Florence's Santa Trinità*

The Raphael Rooms in the Vatican Museum in Rome contain some superb frescoes

painters Sassetta and Giovanni di Paolo. Elsewhere, other artists of genius included Mantegna (Mantua), Correggio (Parma), Lorenzo Lotto (Lombardy), Tura (Ferrara), Melozzo da Forlì (Forlì), Pisanello (Verona) and Antonello da Messina (Sicily).

High Renaissance Much as three innovators tower over the Renaissance's formative years, so a trio of artistic geniuses dominate its maturity – the so-called High Renaissance – a period that begins at the turn of the 16th century with the painting of Leonardo da Vinci's *Last Supper* (in Milan). Elsewhere the end of Florence's artistic primacy was marked by Michelangelo (1475–1564), who left his Medici patrons to work in Rome, where papal patronage was to be the spur for the frescoes of the Sistine Chapel – perhaps the supreme achievement of western art. Another consummate genius lured to Rome was Raphael, born in Urbino, apprenticed to Perugino, and responsible for such masterpieces as the Vatican's *Stanze di Raffaello* (Raphael Rooms). Paragons of High Renaissance architecture included Bramante, Baldassare Peruzzi, Sangallo the Younger, Sansovino and the great Andrea Palladio (1508–80).

Mannerism Following the Sack of Rome by the troops of Emperor Charles V in 1527, Renaissance self-confidence gave way to the self-conscious and disquieting world of Mannerism, a genre – part-inspired by Raphael and Michelangelo – which put art above nature, style above substance, and flouted the conventions of scale, colour and composition. Its leading lights were Pontormo, Bronzino, Rosso Fiorentino, Benvenuto Cellini, Andrea del Sarto, Domenico Beccafumi (from Siena), Parmigianino (from Parma) and the sculptor Giambologna.

Venice Venice charted a course of its own during the Renaissance, its artists more concerned with colour and atmosphere than the Florentine preoccupations with line and composition. Early on, the Vivarini family (Antonio, Bartolomeo and Alvise) emphasised the city's debt to Byzantine art and the opulent courtly style known as 'International Gothic'. Another dynasty, the Bellinis, Giovanni Bellini in particular, marked the city's Renaissance heyday (together with Carpaccio). Venetian painting reached renewed heights during the High Renaissance with painters like Titian, Tintoretto, Paolo Veronese and Giorgione – the last as mysterious in his way as Piero della Francesca.

■ **Born in Rome, and nurtured by papal largesse, baroque – the artistic expression of Counter-Reformation optimism – may derive from the irregularly shaped pearls known in Italian as *perle baroche*. In the words of Luigi Barzini, it 'came to be used metaphorically to describe anything point-lessly complicated, otiose, capricious and eccentric'.** ■

Architecture Baroque's first star, Carlo Maderno (1556–1629), respon-sible for the façade of St Peter's, was soon outshone by the two giants of the period – Gianlorenzo Bernini (1598–1680) and Francesco Borromini (1599–1667). Bernini trans-formed the face of Rome, infusing everything – from fountains to St Peter's monumental piazza – with his exuberant *joie de vivre*. Borromini, his bitter rival, was more tortured and introspective (he eventually commit-ted suicide) but proved the more innovative – even more eccentric – architect. Lacking Bernini's sculptural skill, he was famous instead for his sophisticated geometry and exotic combinations of shapes (best seen in Rome's Sant'Ivo, San Carlo and Sant'Agnese).

Sculpture In sculpture Bernini knew no rivals, his genius apparent from an early age in such works as *Apollo and Daphne* and the *David* in Rome's Galleria Borghese (Italy's first impor-tant sculptures since Michelangelo's final works). His masterpiece, *The Ecstasy of St Teresa* (in Rome's Santa Maria della Vittoria) captures fully the period's emphasis on emo-tion and stylised drama, his own

Bernini's St Teresa, *pierced by the arrow of divine love*

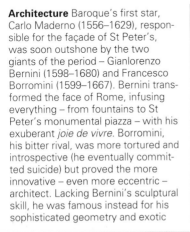

36

The powerful David *of Bernini in the Galleria Borghese*

Painting The baroque spawned two broad schools of painting, the first dominated by Caravaggio (1573–1610), whose vividly realistic works displayed virtuoso effects of light and shade (*chiaroscuro*), the second championed by the Carracci family (Ludovico, Annibale and Agostino), whose works signalled a return to the clarity of classical models. Ornate and illusionist ceiling frescoes were also a feature of the age, and in Pietro da Cortona (1596–1669) they found their chief exponent, best known for work in Rome's Palazzo Barberini (other masters of the art included Bernini's protégé G B Gaulli and Andrea Pozzo). Naples proved a hotbed of baroque endeavour, producing artists such as Luca Giordano, Salvator Rosa and Artemesia Gentileschi, one of Italy's finest woman painters.

passion for illusion and sensuality, and – above all – the intense spirituality of Teresa's ecstatic vision of God. Alessandro Algardi challenged Bernini briefly, but the period's other principal players operated outside Rome – in Turin (Guarini and Juvarra), in Lecce (Zimbalo) and in Catania, Noto and Ragusa in Sicily.

St Peter's, Rome. Above: the bal-dacchino; *below: the piazza*

■ **The last three centuries of Italy's artistic history are often written off as a sad anticlimax, yet Italian artists produced two new styles in neo-classicism and Futurism, and excelled in another (rococo). Today, Italian artists still manage to make Italy one of Europe's leading centres of fashion and design.** ■

The 18th century Art and architecture reacted in different ways to the baroque. While architecture turned away from its excesses to find refuge in neo-classicism, a return to the most basic of classical principles (notably in Rome), painting turned to the still more florid and opulent world of rococo, a sensually-obsessed style born in France that in Italy found its greatest expression in Venice. Though stripped of its political pre-eminence the city was still a wealthy, even decadent retreat, capable of producing and patronising artists such as Sebastiano Ricci, the great Giovanni Battista Tiepolo (1696–1770), and three leading landscapists, Francesco Guardi, Bernardo Bellotto and Canaletto (1697–1768). Neo-classicism's more restrained outlook found its way into painting, but was more marked in sculpture, as in the creamily erotic works of Antonio Canova (1757–1822).

The 19th century Neo-classicism continued its architectural march in the 19th century, but in painting it was largely outflanked by the Europe-wide Romantic movement, whose Italian trend-setter was Francesco Hayez (1791–1882) – almost the country's only notable artist for several decades. The middle of the century saw the emergence of the *Macchiaioli* (from the Italian *macchia* – spot or stain), a group of painters whose use of colour marked a reaction against the polish of neo-classicism and shared the modern outlook of the French Impressionists (leading artists included Lega, Fattori and Signorini). All were overshadowed by Amedeo Modigliani (1884–1920), the best known of Italy's more recent artists (though most of his life was spent in Paris).

The 20th century Art nouveau took a glittering hold in Italy, where it was known as *Lo Stile Liberty*; examples can still be seen in the galleries of Milan and the turn-of-the-century interiors of cafés in Turin, Trieste and elsewhere. In painting, Futurism – which was founded by Italians in Paris (in 1909) – aimed to capture and glorify the dynamism of the new mechanical age, its style pioneered by Umberto Boccioni (1882–1916), and developed by Gino Severini and Giacomo Balla. Elements of Futurism, fused with Cubist ideas, are found in the Surrealist works of Italy's last big 'name' in painting, Giorgio de Chirico (1888–1978).

Top: Canova's Three Graces. *Above:* Seated Man Leaning on a Table, *Modigliani*

39

CITY HIGHLIGHTS ◄ ◄ ◄ ◄ ◄

FORO ROMANO (ROMAN FORUM) *see page 44*

PANTHEON *see pages 44–45*

CASTEL SANT'ANGELO *see page 46*

MUSEI CAPITOLINI *see page 46*

MUSEI VATICANI *see pages 48–49*

COLOSSEO (COLOSSEUM) *see page 50*

SANTA MARIA MAGGIORE *see page 52*

FONTANA DI TREVI *see page 54*

PIAZZA NAVONA *see page 54*

SAN PIETRO *see page 55*

ROME

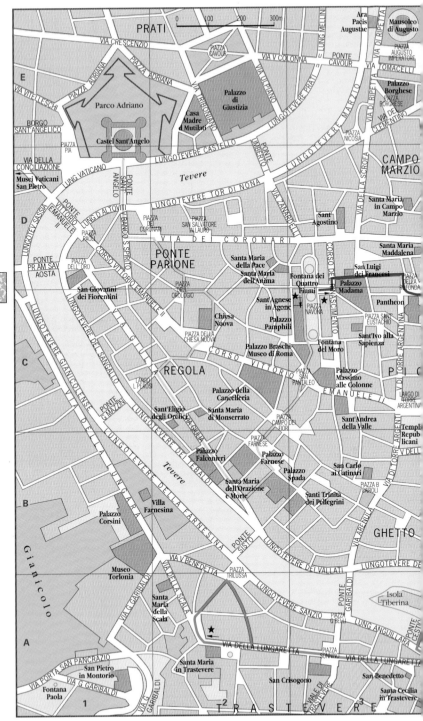

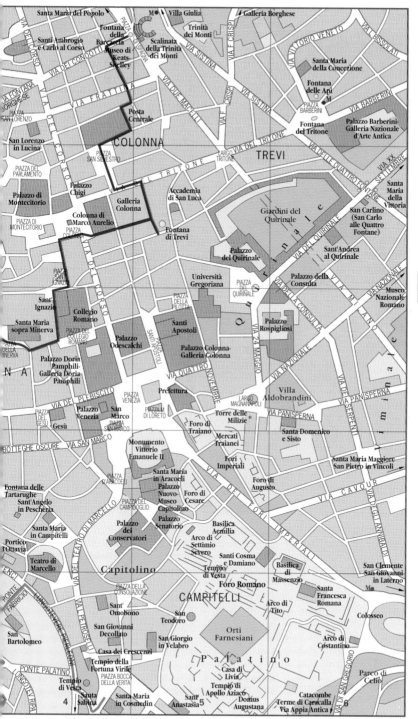

Santa Maria del Popolo
Villa Giulia
Galleria Borghese
Santi Ambrogio e Carlo al Corso
Fontana della Barcaccia
Museo di Keats-Shelley
Scalinata della Trinità dei Monti
Trinità dei Monti
Santa Maria della Concezione
Fontana delle Api
Posta Centrale
VIA FRATTINA
PIAZZA BARBERINI
Palazzo Barberini-Galleria Nazionale d'Arte Antica
San Lorenzo in Lucina
PIAZZA DEL PARLAMENTO
COLONNA
PIAZZA SAN SILVESTRO
VIA DEL TRITONE
TREVI
Santa Maria della Vittoria
VIA XX SETTEMBRE
Palazzo di Montecitorio
Palazzo Chigi
Accademia di San Luca
LARGO TRITONE
Fontana del Tritone
San Carlino (San Carlo alle Quattro Fontane)
PIAZZA DI MONTECITORIO
Galleria Colonna
Giardini del Quirinale
Colonna di Marco Aurelio
PIAZZA COLONNA
Fontana di Trevi
Palazzo del Quirinale
Sant'Andrea al Quirinale
Sant' Ignazio
Università Gregoriana
PIAZZA DEL QUIRINALE
Palazzo della Consulta
Museo Nazionale Romano
Collegio Romano
PIAZZA DELLA PILOTTA
Palazzo Rospigliosi
Santa Maria sopra Minerva
PIAZZA DEL COLLEGIO ROMANO
Santi Apostoli
PIAZZA DELLA MINERVA
Palazzo Odescalchi
Palazzo Colonna-Galleria Colonna
Palazzo Doria Pamphili-Galleria Doria Pamphili
VIA QUATTRO NOVEMBRE
Villa Aldobrandini
N A
VIA DEL PLEBISCITO
Prefettura
PIAZZA VENEZIA
Santa Domenico e Sisto
Fontana delle Tartarughe
Palazzo Venezia
San Marco
PIAZZA M. DI LORETO
Torre delle Milizie
VIA PANISPERNA
Gesù
PIAZZA SAN MARCO
Foro di Traiano
Mercati Traianei
Sant'Angelo in Pescheria
BOTTEGHE OSCURE
VIA SAN MARCO
Monumento Vittorio Emanuele II
Fori Imperiali
Santa Maria Maggiore San Pietro in Vincoli
Santa Maria in Campitelli
PIAZZA D'ARACOELI
Santa Maria in Aracoeli
Palazzo Nuovo-Museo Capitolino
Foro di Cesare
Foro di Augusto
VIA CAVOUR
Portico d'Ottavia
PIAZZA DEL CAMPIDOGLIO
Palazzo Senatorio
Basilica Aemilia
Teatro di Marcello
Palazzo dei Conservatori
Arco di Settimio Severo
Santi Cosma e Damiano
Basilica di Massenzio
San Clemente San Giovanni in Laterno
Capitolino
PIAZZA DELLA CONSOLAZIONE
Tempio di Vesta
Foro Romano
Santa Francesca Romana
San Bartolomeo
Sant' Omobono
San Teodoro
CAMPITELLI
Arco di Tito
Colosseo
PONTE FABRICIO
San Giovanni Decollato
San Giorgio in Velabro
Orti Farnesiani
Arco di Costantino
PONTE PALATINO
Casa dei Crescenzi
Tempio della Fortuna Virile
PIAZZA BOCCA DELLA VERITA
P a l a t i n o
Parco di Celio
Tempio di Vesta
Santa Sabina
Santa Maria in Cosmedin
Sant' Anastasia
Casa di Livia
Tempio di Apollo Aziaco
Domus Augustana
Catacombe Terme di Caracalla Via Appia Antica

41

Throw a coin in Rome's famous Trevi Fountain and legend has it you'll return to the city one day

Rome (Roma) We expect a lot of Rome – seat of empire, mother of civilisation, *caput mundi* (head of the world). It is the city of the Caesars, of romance, the city of the *dolce vita* and languorous sunny days, the city of endless art, of churches and museums, of fountain-splashed piazzas and majestic monuments to its golden age of empire. Sadly, it is also the city of uncontrollable traffic, the city of frenetic noise and confusion, the city of wanton crowds, obstinate bureaucracy and groaning inefficiency. Its 20th-century face is not a pretty one, and to get under its rumpled skin requires an oblique approach to sightseeing.

Seeing the city Head-on confrontation with Rome, however energetically you join battle, always leaves you the dispirited loser. Plan ahead, therefore, and neither attempt too much, nor tackle its streets in the heat of the afternoon. Avoid the temptation to join the trudge around the famous sights. Avoid St Peter's and the Sistine

Chapel; forget the Colosseum and the Pantheon, at least in the beginning. Reflect instead over a quiet *cappuccino* in Campo dei Fiori, the city's loveliest square. Forgo the Spanish Steps' aimless mob and climb to the Pincio Gardens for a view over the rooftops to St Peter's. Thus initiated you can prepare for the assault on the Vatican museums, or the stroll around the Forum; you can face the traffic and the chaos – and perhaps in time even come to enjoy them as dynamic aspects of a city that is struggling, as it has for centuries, to incorporate the present into its eternal past.

Layers of history Rome belongs to no single historical period. Its sights and quarters are a lavish medley of ancient, medieval, Renaissance and modern buildings, making it difficult to define areas, or to plan your sightseeing around a single epoch. In the earliest days Rome gathered around seven famous hills – the Aventino, Capitolino, Esquilino, Caelio, Palatino, Quirinale and Viminale. Later, Augustus created several *rioni*, a series of wards like Paris' *arrondissements*. Neither of these divisions, however, adequately defines the present city.

Areas of the city Piazza Venezia is now Rome's hub, a junction of streets that strike off to the four points of the compass. The *centro storico* (Historical Centre) is not, confusingly, the Forum and the ancient heart of Rome, but a warren of streets that made up the city's core from the Middle Ages to the last century. Contained between the Tiber and Via del Corso, it divides into a medieval quarter (north of Corso Vittorio Emanuele II) – centred on Piazza Navona and the Pantheon – and a Renaissance district (south of Corso Vittorio Emanuele II), centred on Via Giulia and Piazza Farnese. The latter contains the Ghetto, one of the city's most captivating areas (the streets east of Via Arenula). Across the river is **Trastevere** ('across the Tiber'). Once Rome's 19th-century slum – and still seedy in places – it is now generally a charming area, especially good for aimless wandering, restaurants and evening entertainment. To its north lies **Vatican City**, centred on St Peter's, an independent state under papal control. Near by stretch the leafy residential districts of Prati and Parioli.

Romulus and Remus This is the myth about Rome that everyone knows. It begins in the old Latin capital *Alba Longa*, where Amulius usurped the throne of his brother Numitor. To avoid rival claims Amulius forced Numitor's only daughter, Rhea Silvia, to become a vestal virgin. A visit from the god Mars left her pregnant with Romulus and Remus. Amulius cast the twins adrift in a basket, but the gods steered them safely to the Palatine, where a she-wolf cared for the pair until they were found by a shepherd. Told of their destiny by Mars they founded Rome in 753BC. The brothers could not agree whether to name the city *Rema* or *Roma* – but Romulus started building his walls regardless. Incensed, Remus jumped over them and was killed by his brother.

Weekend's itinerary

Saturday
Breakfast in Campo dei Fiori (walk: Ghetto–Isola Tiberina–Piazza Bocca della Verità–Campidoglio). *Morning*: Campidoglio, Forum, Colosseum, San Clemente (San Giovanni in Laterano). Lunch (walk: Colle Oppio–Foro Traiano–Fontana di Trevi). *Afternoon*: Fontana di Trevi, Santa Maria sopra Minerva, Pantheon, Piazza Navona (walk: Via dei Coronari–Via Governo Vecchio/shopping: Via Condotti, Via del Corso). *Evening*: walk/bus to Trastevere (Santa Maria in Trastevere, Santa Cecilia). Dinner in Trastevere.

Sunday
Breakfast in Piazza Navona (walk to Castel Sant'Angelo). *Morning*: (Castel Sant'Angelo), St Peter's, Vatican Museums. *Afternoon*: (walk: to Piazza del Popolo). Pincio, Piazza di Spagna.

Etruscan bronze of a she-wolf in the Capitoline Museum. The human twins were added later

Colonna Traiano

Trajan's Column was built in AD113 to celebrate Trajan's victories over the Dacians (tribes from present-day Romania). Its great spiralling frieze contains 2,500 figures and 18 huge drums of Greek marble. The reliefs have provided a wealth of information about Roman arms and modes of warfare.

Vestal Virgins

Vestal Virgins were the guardians of Rome's sacred flame. They were chosen, before they reached the age of 14, from Rome's leading patrician families. Up to 30 years were spent in service, after which they could retire on a state pension. The only man allowed in their temple was the Pontifex Maximus, or high priest. The title – 'Greatest Bridge Builder' – was adopted by the popes, hence the abbreviation *Pont Max* on many papal buildings.

Clever engineering

The Pantheon's remarkable dome, for centuries one of the world's largest, rests on brick-faced Roman-era concrete walls some 7m thick. Its lower drum starts the same width, becoming progressively thinner – and thus lighter – until it is a little over a metre thick at its apex. This helped lighten the dome's payload, an effect reinforced by using increasingly lighter materials towards its crown. Heavy travertine mixed with concrete is used at the base; less sturdy volcanic tufa midway, and feather-light pumice at the summit.

Roman Monuments

▶▶   **Ara Pacis Augustae**   *40E3*

Via di Ripetta

The 'Altar of Peace' was raised by the Senate in 13–9 BC to commemorate the victories of the Emperor Augustus. Its superb reliefs include mythological scenes and episodes from the altar's ceremonial consecration.

▶▶   **Arco di Costantino**   *41A6*
           (Arch of Constantine)

Piazza del Colosseo

The largest and best-preserved of Rome's ancient arches was raised to honour the victory of the Emperor Constantine over Maxentius in AD 312. Many of its reliefs were taken from earlier monuments, partly out of pragmatism, and partly to link the Emperor's regime to the glories of the past. The battle scenes, for example, show Trajan at war with the Dacians.

▶▶▶   **Castel Sant'Angelo** (see page 46)   *40E1*

▶▶   **Catacombe (Catacombs)**   *41A6*

Rome has over 800km of catacombs, the underground tombs of pagans and early Christians. The best are the **Catacombe di San Callisto** (*Via Appia Antica*) with 170,000 graves; others are the nearby **Catacombe di San Sebastiano,** and those of Domitilla and Priscilla.

▶▶▶   **Colosseo (Colosseum)** (see page 50)   *41A6*

▶▶   **Fori Imperiali**   *41B5*

Via dei Fori Imperiali

The five imperial fora were built by successive emperors after the Foro Romano and Palatino became too small. The best are the Foro di Augusto and Foro Traiano. The latter contains the great **Colonna Traiano**▶▶▶ (Trajan's Column) and the **Mercati Traianei**▶ (Trajan's Market).

▶▶▶   **Foro Romano (Roman Forum)**   *41A5*

The old heart of the Roman empire is crowded with the jumbled ruins of temples, basilicas and other buildings spanning 1,100 years – a wonderfully evocative place to wander in. Be sure to see the **triumphal arches of Tito and Settimio Severo**▶▶, the mighty **Basilica di Massenzio**▶▶▶, and the **Tempio di Vesta**▶▶▶ (Temple of the Vestal Virgins).

▶▶▶   **Palatino**   *41A5*

Via dei Fori Imperiali–Via di San Gregorio Magno

The Palatine hill was the first of the famous seven hills to be inhabited. In time it became the favoured residential district of Rome's élite, including emperors. Most buildings are now badly ruined, or buried under the beautiful 16th-century **Orti Farnesiani**▶▶ (the Farnese Gardens).

▶▶▶   **Pantheon**   *40C3*

Piazza della Rotonda

This, the grandest monument of Roman antiquity, built by Hadrian in AD 128, became a Christian church in 609 (one

reason for its remarkable state of preservation). The immense cupola was the largest free-standing dome in the world until as late as 1960.

► Teatro di Marcello 41B4

Via del Teatro di Marcello

When Augustus built this theatre in 11 BC it must have been as impressive as the Colosseum – which it closely resembled. Used as a fortress in the Middle Ages, it now stands bizarrely over-built with medieval houses.

► Terme di Caracalla 41A6

Via delle Terme di Caracalla

The Baths of Caracalla (AD 206) were not as large as the Baths of Diocletian (remains of which you can see around Piazza della Repubblica), but they were more luxurious and are far better preserved. They could accommodate 2,000 bathers, and many thousands more in the complex of sports and leisure facilities near by.

►► Via Appia Antica 41A6

Via Appia Antica

Rome's 'Queen of Roads' was built in 312 BC and connected the city with Capua and Brindisi in southern Italy. Today it still has many of its original cobbles (see below), and is lined with ancient tombs and catacombs. Much of the route is delightful to drive down or wander along – a little piece of countryside only a stone's throw from the city.

The classical splendour of the Pantheon

Coffee and ice cream
Immediately off the Pantheon's Piazza della Rotonda is **La Tazza d'Oro** (Via degli Orfani 84). By general consent it sells Rome's best cup of coffee. One minute's walk north is the **Gelateria della Palma** (Via della Maddalena 20), known for its 100-plus flavours of ice-cream.

The Ghetto
The area west of the Teatro di Marcello is the old Jewish Ghetto (created in 1555). The area contains some of the city's quietest and nicest back streets. Wander here during siesta or in the early evening. A good stroll is from Campo dei Fiori along Via Giubbonari and Via Portico d'Ottaviano to explore the picturesque streets of the Ghetto. Be sure, too, to see Bernini's delightful Fontana delle Tartarughe (Fountain of the Tortoises) in Piazza Mattei.

The cobbled surface of the 2,300-year-old Via Appia Antica

Elegance and force: the Ponte Sant' Angelo leading to the Castel Sant'Angelo

Museums & Galleries

►►► Castel Sant'Angelo   40E1
Lungotevere Castello
Built as the tomb of the Emperor Hadrian (AD 139), the great circular bulwarks of the Castel Sant'Angelo have been used over the centuries as prison, barracks, papal fortress and now a museum, interesting both for its precious works of art and the labyrinth of imperial tombs, state rooms and endless nooks and crannies that honeycomb the interior.

►►► Galleria Borghese   41E5
Villa Borghese-Via Pinciana
Only the Vatican offers a grander art collection than the Galleria Borghese. Its many highlights include Canova's *Paolina Borghese* and outstanding masterpieces by Bernini: *David, Apollo and Daphne* and *The Rape of Prosperine*. On the upper floor (closed for restoration) the paintings include Raphael's masterly *Deposition* and fine works by Caravaggio and Pinturicchio.

►► Galleria Nazionale d'Arte   41E6
Antica-Palazzo Barberini
Via delle Quattro Fontane 13
This is Rome's foremost picture gallery, most famous for Raphael's *La Fornarina*, but also home to paintings by Old Masters including Fra Angelico, Perugino, Filippo Lippi, Tintoretto, Holbein and El Greco. The sumptuous gallery's rooms are attractions in their own right, notably the tremendous **Gran Salone**►►►, dominated by Pietro da Cortona's exuberant ceiling frescoes.

►►► Musei Capitolini (Capitoline Museums) 41B5
Piazza del Campidoglio
Two museums face one another across Piazza del Campidoglio. **Palazzo Nuovo**►►► contains many masterpieces of classical sculpture, principally the *Dying Gaul*,

Paolina Borghese
Numerous myths attach to Canova's erotic statue of Paolina Borghese, doubtless because of the knowing sensuality of its subject – bare-breasted, hips half-draped in veils and a pose of haughty yet come-hither languor. Paolina was as slyly seductive in life as in art, and excited much gossip with her jewels, her clothes, her long line of lovers, the servants she used as footstools and the black attendant who carried her from the bath.

Capitoline Venus and *Amor and Psyche*. Sculptures in the **Palazzo dei Conservatori**►►, opposite, include the *Spinario*, the *Esquiline Venus* and the *Capitoline Wolf*. Upstairs, the **Pinacoteca Capitolino**►► has fine paintings by, among others, Caravaggio, Van Dyck and Titian.

►►► **Musei Vaticani** (see pages 48–9)　　　40D1

►► **Museo Nazionale Romano**　　　41D6
Piazza dei Cinquecento-Piazza della Repubblica (due to move to Palazzo Massimo off Piazza dei Cinquecento)
This museum incorporates part of the Terme di Diocleziano, the largest baths built in ancient Rome. The museum's vast collection – only parts of which are exhibited – includes numerous classical artefacts, most notably the **Ludovisi throne**, part of a 5th-century BC Greek altar.

►► **Palazzo-Galleria Doria Pamphili**　　　41C4
Via del Corso-Piazza del Collegio Romano 1a
Open: Tue and Fri–Sun 10–1
With over 1,000 rooms, this is one of Rome's largest palaces. Only part is open to the public, four large galleries crammed with paintings that include works by Titian, Raphael and Caravaggio. Its most famous canvas is a portrait of *Innocent X* by Velázquez. Guided tours offer glimpses of the palace's other private apartments.

►►► **Villa Giulia (Museo Nazionale Etrusco)** 41E5
Viale delle Belle Arti
This museum holds the world's most exhaustive collection of Etruscan art and artefacts. The villa in which it is housed is an attraction in its own right. Highlights include the *Sarcofago degli Sposi* (Sarcophagus of the Married Couple); the giant terracotta statues of *Apollo and Hercules*; the many urns and vases; and a panoply of jewellery, household utensils and other objects.

Museo di Palazzo Venezia
This modern museum occupies the first floor of the Palazzo Venezia (Via del Plebiscito). It houses splendid Italian, German and Flemish tapestries, and a miscellaneous collection of medieval art, sculptures, ceramics, jewellery and other artefacts.

Stroll
Walk from Piazza Navona to the Pantheon by way of the church of San Luigi dei Francesi, Piazza Sant'Eustachio and the church of Sant'Ivo alla Sapienza.

47

Inside the Galleria Borghese. Much of its collection was accumulated by Cardinal Scipione Borghese

Il Vaticano

■ **The Vatican City is an independent sovereign state in the heart of Rome. Although it has public museums, the rest of the 43-hectare principality hides behind high walls and is out of bounds to all but a privileged few.** ■

The Swiss Guard
The Vatican's 90-strong army is designed to protect the papal person. Recruited from Switzerland's four Catholic cantons, the guards must be aged between 19 and 25, be at least 1.75m tall, and remain unmarried during their tours of duty – which last anywhere between two and 20 years. Their striped uniforms, designed by Michelangelo, bear the medieval colours of the Medici popes (red, yellow and blue).

Vatican City About 200 people live and work in the world's smallest state (only 30 of them women); 800 'foreigners' commute in daily. The state is ruled by Europe's only absolute monarch, Pope John Paul II, and has its own judicial system, shops, bank, currency, post office, garages – even its own radio station and daily newspaper (the *Osservatore Romano*). Its official language is Latin.

Musei Vaticani (Vatican Museums) The museums, the largest in the world, include the Sistine Chapel, the Raphael Rooms and at least a dozen self-contained museums. The most important is the **Museo Pio-Clementino**, housing some of the greatest works of classical sculpture. The finest are in the Cortile Ottogono: the *Apollo Belvedere* and the incredible *Laocoön* group. The **Museo Gregoriano-Etrusco** contains some of Italy's best Etruscan artefacts, notably the *Mars of Todi* and *Head of Athene*. The **Pinocoteca** has Rome's greatest paintings, with works by Giotto, Fra Angelico, Filippo Lippi, Leonardo and Raphael.
The **Cappella di Nicolò V** contains sublime frescoes by Fra Angelico. Five dark rooms with outstanding frescoes by Pinturicchio (1492-5) form the **Appartamento Borgia**. The **Museo Gregoriano Profano** is a museum of pagan art, mainly classical sculpture, while the **Museo Missionario Etnologico** has a fascinating collection of artefacts brought together from missionary expeditions all over the world.

Raphael Rooms (Stanze di Raffaello) Raphael's frescoes, commissioned by Julius II in 1503, are one of the masterpieces of the Renaissance. The **Stanza della Segnatura** (Room II) is the most celebrated and was the first to be painted. Its four main frescoes are allegories of Theology, Philosophy, Poetry and Justice. The **Sala dell'Incendio** (Room I) was the last to be executed, by which time Leo X was pope. Raphael celebrated Leo's papal namesakes, painting the *Coronation of Charlemagne* (performed by Leo III); the *Oath of Leo III*; the *Battle of Ostia* (where Leo IV showed mercy to the defeated Saracens); and the *Fire in the Borgo*, where Leo IV (actually a portrait of Leo X) extinguishes a fire by making the sign of the Cross. Room III's frescoes describe episodes where Divine Providence has intervened to defend the Christian faith, notably Leo I (again Leo X in disguise) *Repulsing Attila the Hun*.

Cappella Sistina (Sistine Chapel) Michelangelo's frescoes in the Sistine Chapel are the pinnacle of European artistic achievement. The 930sq m ceiling (1508) took four years to complete, the artist lying recumbent most of the time to paint. The newly restored frescoes divide into nine sections, arranged chronologically. The first describe five

A Fra Angelico in the Vatican Museum

Side walls

The Sistine Chapel's side walls are often overlooked. These were painted in 1481–3 by leading artists such as Perugino, Botticelli, Pinturicchio, Piero di Cosimo, Ghirlandaio and Luca Signorelli. Many are collaborations. Panels on the left as you face the altar show scenes from the life of Christ, on the right scenes from the life of Moses.

key events from the Book of Genesis: *The Separation of Light and Darkness*; *The Creation of the Heavens*; *The Separation of Land and Sea*; *The Creation of Adam*; and *The Creation of Eve*. After them come: *The Fall and Expulsion from Paradise*; *The Sacrifice of Noah*; *The Flood*; and *The Drunkenness of Noah*. The *Last Judgement* on the rear wall was painted 20 years later, and shows Christ in the centre with the damned sinking to the right, the saved rising heavenward on the left. Around Him are the Virgin and saints.

Papal audiences

To join the 7,000 or so at papal audiences each Wednesday, apply for a ticket from the Prefettura della Casa Pontifica (through the bronze doors in the right-hand colonnade of Piazza San Pietro. *Open* Mon and Tue).

49

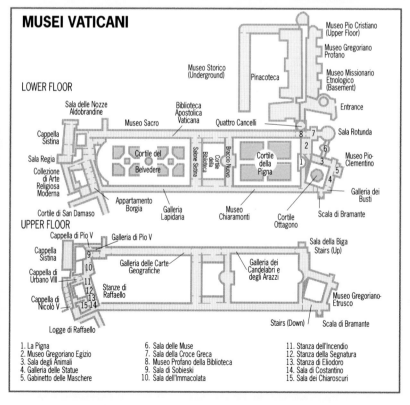

MUSEI VATICANI

Museo Pio Cristiano (Upper Floor)
Museo Gregoriano Profano
Museo Storico (Underground)
Pinacoteca
Museo Missionario Etnologico (Basement)

LOWER FLOOR

Entrance

Sala delle Nozze Aldobrandine
Biblioteca Apostolica Vaticana
Museo Sacro
Quattro Cancelli
Sala Rotunda

Cappella Sistina
Cortile del Belvedere
Salone della Biblioteca
Cortile della Biblioteca
Braccio Nuovo
Cortile della Pigna
Museo Pio-Clementino

Sala Regia
Collezione di Arte Religiosa Moderna
Appartamento Borgia
Galleria Lapidaria
Museo Chiaramonti
Cortile Ottagono
Galleria dei Busti
Scala di Bramante

Cortile di San Damaso

UPPER FLOOR

Cappella di Pio V
Galleria di Pio V
Sala della Biga Stairs (Up)

Cappella Sistina
Galleria delle Carte Geografiche
Galleria dei Candelabri e degli Arazzi

Cappella di Urbano VIII
Stanze di Raffaello

Cappella di Nicolò V
Museo Gregoriano-Etrusco

Logge di Raffaello
Stairs (Down)
Scala di Bramante

1. La Pigna
2. Museo Gregoriano Egizio
3. Sala degli Animali
4. Galleria delle Statue
5. Gabinetto delle Maschere
6. Sala delle Muse
7. Sala della Croce Greca
8. Museo Profano della Biblioteca
9. Sala di Sobieski
10. Sala dell'Immacolata
11. Stanza dell'Incendio
12. Stanza della Segnatura
13. Stanza di Eliodoro
14. Sala di Costantino
15. Sala dei Chiaroscuri

The Colosseum

■ **The most magnificent of Rome's ancient monuments was started by the Emperor Vespasian in AD 72 and was completed seven years later by his son, Titus. The Colosseum was inaugurated (in the taste of the times) with a gala in which no fewer than 5,000 animals were slaughtered in an afternoon, followed by over 100 days of continuous games and other entertainment.** ■

A trendsetter
An architectural and engineering marvel, the Colosseum's arena has provided the model for large stadia ever since. Over 50,000 spectators could leave their seats within minutes through the 76 numbered exits or *vomitoria*. On the upper levels, a huge moveable sailcloth (*velarium*) could be winched into place to shade spectators from the sun.

Both animals and gladiators remained below stage in the Colosseum before fighting in the arena above

On stage Contrary to myth, the stage was probably not used to kill Christians. It was, however, used for a variety of violent and decadent gladiatorial games (the Romans took the idea of gladiators from the Samnites and Etruscans, who used them originally to train soldiers for battle).

Men, women – even dwarfs – fought each other (and animals) to keep the crowds entertained. The arena could also be flooded to stage mock sea battles. Audiences often exercised the power of life and death. They could reply to a fighter's appeal for mercy (raising a finger on the left hand) with a waving of handkerchiefs (a reprieve), or with the notorious down-turned thumb. Survivors, if they were criminals, often had their throats cut anyway.

Days of ruin The games were finally outlawed in AD 438. Fires and earthquakes then began to take their toll on the arena. The clamps holding the massive travertine blocks were removed in AD 662–4, leaving the distinctive holes that punctuate the exterior today. Over the Middle Ages huge amounts of stone were pillaged to build the city's churches and palaces. Preservation only began in 1744 when the area was consecrated and a cross erected in memory of murdered Christians.

Churches

▶ **Gesù** *41C4*

Piazza del Gesù

The Gesù is the principal church of the Jesuits. Initiated by the movement's founder, Ignatius Loyola, it was designed by Vignola and Giacomo della Porta. Both its plan and façade (1575) were to be imitated in later churches all over Europe. The overwhelmingly rich interior has works of art by Bernini, Pozzo and Pietro da Cortona.

▶ **Sant'Andrea al Quirinale** *41D6*

Via del Quirinale

Sant'Andrea is a baroque jewel. It was designed by Bernini and was one of his favourite churches. Many of its ideas were unique at the time (1658–71), notably the two-columned portico and stretched-oval floor plan. The aristocratically elegant decoration largely relates to the martyrdom of Sant'Andrea (St Andrew).

▶ **San Carlino** *41D6*
(San Carlo alle Quattro Fontane)

Via del Quirinale

Bernini's great rival, Borromini, designed San Carlino (1634–8). It is another baroque masterpiece, but expresses the idiom in a completely different style from that of neighbouring Sant'Andrea. The interior is crammed with details, shapes and symbols, all bound with precise geometrical patterns. The same inspired use of space is found in the cloisters, also by Borromini.

▶▶ **Santa Cecilia in Trastevere** *41A3*

Piazza di Santa Cecilia

Santa Cecilia dates largely from 824, but the interior was disastrously remodelled between 1725 and 1823. Its gardens and 12th-century portico are still enchanting. The apse contains 9th-century **mosaics** and an altar canopy by Arnolfo di Cambio (*c* 1293). There is a fine statue of St Cecilia by Stefano Maderno (1600). The cloister has fresco fragments of Pietro Cavallini's important *Last Judgement* (1293).

▶▶▶ **San Clemente** *41B6*

Via di San Giovanni in Laterano

San Clemente comprises three distinct levels. The present church has the city's finest medieval interior (1130), with superb 12th-century mosaics, pulpits and frescoes by Masolino da Panicale (*c* 1428). The lower 8th-century church has faded (but important) early frescoes. Below it lie the ruins of a Mithraic temple, which are open to the public.

▶▶▶ **San Giovanni in Laterano** *41B6*

Piazza di San Giovanni in Laterano

San Giovanni (not St Peter's) is Rome's cathedral church. It was founded by Constantine in 313, and although much has now been restored, it still remains immensely impressive. The **cloisters▶▶▶**, with their Cosmati marblework, are one of Rome's loveliest spots. The much-copied octagonal **Baptistery▶▶▶**, adapted from 5th-century Roman baths, is the earliest in Christendom. The church was damaged by a terrorist bomb in 1993.

Santa Cecilia
Cecilia – *coeli lilia* (The Lily of Heaven) – was martyred around 303. The executioner's three axe blows – all he was allowed under Roman law – failed to remove her head. She survived for several days, converting many to the faith before dying of her wounds (Maderno's statue of her clearly shows the three sword cuts). Cecilia is the patron saint of music, having reputedly invented the organ ('to enlarge her prayer'), and sung during her execution.

Santa Cecilia in Trastevere, which contains a beautiful apse mosaic and works of art by Pietro Cavallini and Arnolfo di Cambio

Bocca della Verità
The 'Mouth of Truth' is a weatherbeaten stone face once used by the Romans as a drain cover. According to tradition, anyone suspected of lying would have their hand forced into the gaping mouth (*bocca*). If they were lying the mouth would shut, severing their fingers. A priest supposedly hid behind the stone to chop off the hands of those known to be lying. Oaths and business deals were sworn and settled here.

▶▶▶   San Luigi dei Francesi   41D3
Piazza di San Luigi dei Francesi
The French church of Rome (1589) contains a single great treasure, a chapel containing three paintings by Caravaggio (5th chapel on the left). All three deal with events from the *Life of St Matthew*, showing the painter's earthy realism and *chiaroscuro* techniques to virtuoso effect.

▶▶   Santa Maria in Aracoeli   41B5
Piazza del Campidoglio
This church occupies Rome's Holy of Holies – the crown of the Capitoline Hill that once housed the city's first *Arx* (Citadel) and Temple of Juno Moneta. Founded in the 6th century, or possibly earlier, the church has a dazzling interior with ancient columns, chandeliers and a quite magnificent wooden ceiling. Its main treasures are Pinturicchio's frescoes on the *Life of San Bernardino* (first chapel in the right-hand aisle) and, until it was stolen, the *Santo Bambino*, a miracle-working statue carved from an olive tree in Gethsemane.

Nightlife outside Santa Maria in Trastevere

Bernini's Elephant
Piazza della Minerva's famous statue of an elephant with a small Egyptian obelisk on its back was designed by Bernini for Pope Alexander VII. The inscription states that it takes the massive strength of the elephant to sustain the weight of true wisdom.

▶▶   Santa Maria in Cosmedin   41A4
Piazza Bocca della Verità
Though lacking great treasures, few Roman churches are as beautiful as Santa Maria in Cosmedin, one of the handful of medieval buildings in the city to have escaped the baroque. The portico contains the famous *Bocca della Verità* (see panel), while the sublime interior boasts a lovely pavement, pulpits and choir screens, faded patches of fresco and an 8th-century mosaic.

▶▶▶   Santa Maria Maggiore   41B6
Piazza di Santa Maria Maggiore
Rome's finest early Christian basilica, 5th-century Santa Maria is the largest and most important of the city's 80 churches dedicated to the Virgin. The interior is magnificent, graced with 40 ancient columns and mosaics from the 5th and 13th centuries. The Paolina and Sistina chapels are also outstanding.

▶▶ Santa Maria sopra Minerva 41C4

Piazza della Minerva

Rome's only Gothic church lies behind the Pantheon, built over (*sopra*) the ruins of a temple dedicated to Minerva. It contains many fine works of art. Filippino Lippi left frescoes in the Cappella Carafa, and there is a statue of *The Redeemer* by Michelangelo to the left of the altar. St Catherine of Siena, the Medici popes Leo X and Clement VII, and painter Fra Angelico are buried in the church.

▶▶▶ Santa Maria del Popolo 40E4

Piazza del Popolo

Bramante and Bernini designed much of this church, which contains superlative frescoes by Pinturicchio and two masterpieces by Caravaggio. The **Cappella Chigi▶▶▶**, commissioned by a Sienese banker, was designed and executed by Raphael. The choir boasts a pair of tombs by Andrea Sansovino.

▶▶ Santa Maria in Trastevere 40A2

Piazza di Santa Maria in Trastevere

This church provides the backdrop to Trastevere's liveliest piazza. At night its mosaic-covered façade (12th-century) is beautifully floodlit. Inside the solemn interior are more mosaics, the work of Pietro Cavallini (1290) and earlier Byzantine craftsmen. The ancient columns are from the Terme di Caracalla.

▶▶▶ San Pietro (St Peter's) (see page 55) 40D1

▶▶ San Pietro in Vincoli 41B6

Piazza San Pietro in Vincoli

The chains (*vincoli*) are the links which bound Peter in Jerusalem, and to which were later added those that shackled him in Rome's Mamertine prison. Both sets of chains, miraculously fused together, can be seen below the high altar. The church is renowned, however, for Michelangelo's monumental statue of Moses (1503–13), considered one of the sculptor's greatest works.

The sumptuous interior of Santa Maria Maggiore

Nero's Tomb
Santa Maria del Popolo was supposedly built on the site of Nero's tomb in 1099. The Virgin appeared to Pope Paschal II and ordered him to chop down a great walnut tree that had grown from the grave. Paschal obliged, then built a chapel. The Emperor's ghost reputedly wandered the area, making for the pyramid tomb which contained the remains of his wife. Today it is the stylish *Rosati* café, a fashionable spot now haunted by the city's artists and literati.

Stroll
From Piazza Santa Maria in Trastevere wend through the streets to the south and climb the Gianicolo hill for views over the city.

Piazzas: Barberini and Colonna
Piazza Barberini has two Bernini fountains, both commissioned by the Barberini – the Fontana del Tritone and Fontana delle Api. Piazza Colonna takes its name from the Colonna di Marco Aurelio (AD196), a column raised to celebrate Aurelius' military campaigns in northern Europe.

Of wedding cake and tortoises
Piazza Venezia is a vast square near the heart of Rome, dominated by the Monumento Vittorio Emanuele II (known to Romans today as the 'wedding cake' or 'typewriter'). Piazza Sant'Ignazio is noted for its architectural harmony, while Piazza Mattei harbours Bernini's touching Fontana delle Tartarughe (Fountain of the Tortoises).

Stendhal's syndrome
Beware of trying to see too much in Rome. There is a passage in Stendhal's *Journal* where he alludes to the symptoms brought on by an excess of culture: 'If the foreigner who enters St Peter's tries to see everything, he will develop a furious headache, and presently satiety and pain will render him incapable of any pleasure.'

Piazzas and Fountains

▶▶▶ Fontana di Trevi 40D5
Piazza Fontana di Trevi
Rome's most famous fountain lives up to expectations as it foams dramatically from a whole wall of the Palazzo Poli. Its central figure, Neptune, is flanked by figures representing a calm and stormy sea. The tradition is to throw a coin into the fountain if you wish to return to Rome. It is one of the city's main meeting places.

▶▶▶ Piazza Campo dei Fiori 40C2
This lovely square is as picturesque as any in Italy, with its colourful street market, crammed with stalls selling flowers, fish and mounds of fruit and vegetables. Take time to sit out at one of the cafés and enjoy the streetlife.

▶▶▶ Piazza Navona 40C3
Rome's social centre is Piazza Navona, an exhilarating spot thronged with life and edged with elegant ochre *palazzi* and outdoor cafés. Its contours match exactly the outlines of the Emperor Domitian's *circo* (stadium), built to hold games and horse-races in AD86. It was transformed in 1644 by Pope Innocent X. Bernini designed two of its fountains, the **Fontana dei Quattro Fiumi** (Fountain of the Rivers), and the **Fontana del Moro.**

▶▶▶ Piazza di Spagna 41E4
At the heart of Rome's best shopping area, and backed by the famous **Spanish Steps▶▶▶**, this colourful square rivals Piazza Navona and the Fontana di Trevi as the city's most popular meeting place. It is named after the palace of the Spanish ambassador to the Vatican. The **Museo di Keats-Shelley** is here, together with the eccentric **Fontana della Barcaccia▶**.

Piazza Navona: the heart of Rome

St Peter's (San Pietro)

■ The most famous church in Christendom and Catholicism's most important point of pilgrimage, St Peter's sees visitors from all over the world, drawn to the spot where St Peter was buried after his crucifixion in AD 64 or 67. Few remain unimpressed by the basilica's size and spiritual significance, though many perhaps come away disappointed by its chill interior and – for a church of such fame – its surprising lack of great art. ■

The first St Peter's was built in 326 by Pope Sylvester I with the backing of the Emperor Constantine. It was to survive until 1452, when Pope Nicholas V and then Julius II began to consider plans for a new basilica.

The new church Designs were drawn up by Bramante, then Antonio da Sangallo. Michelangelo, aged 72, was asked to correct mistakes, which he did by removing much of Sangallo's work and redesigning the dome. Carlo Maderno (1605) made more additions, and in 1637 Bernini was called in to act as the interior's chief architect.

Piazza San Pietro, Bernini's great square framing St Peter's

Highlights Inside, the overall impression is of size, with little of real artistic merit among the gloomy tombs, heavy marble and welter of baroque decoration. The exceptions are Michelangelo's *Pietà* (1499) behind glass at the beginning of the right aisle and Bernini's colossal bronze *baldacchino* (altar canopy) in the crossing. See also the two finest tombs, della Porta's for Paul III and Bernini's influential tomb of Urban VIII. They lie at the rear of the apse, flanking Bernini's *Cathedra Pietri*, designed to encase a chair reputedly used by St Peter to preach to the Romans.

Climb the dome for breathtaking views, and visit the piazza's tourist office to organise a trip to the crypt, where early Christian tombs possibly include St Peter's.

Entrances
The church's grand portico contains the famous Porta Santa (Holy Door), opened only every 25 years (on the right), and the main bronze doors (1433), one of the few treasures salvaged from the first basilica.

Walk Through Rome's piazzas to the Spanish Steps

For routes see map on pages 40–1

Trastevere Start from Piazza Santa Maria in Trastevere and take Vicolo delle Cinque to explore the quarter's pretty back streets. Return to the piazza and follow Via della Lungaretta to Piazza Piscinula. Cross to the Isola Tiberina to wander the island's promenades and see the church of San Bartolomeo. Head south for the Roman temples and church of **Santa Maria in Cosmedin** (page 52) in Piazza Bocca della Verità. Cross back to Trastevere and wind through the back streets to **Santa Cecilia in Trastevere** (page 51). Return to Santa Maria in Trastevere.

Piazza Navona–Castel Sant'Angelo
See the church of Sant'Agnese in Agone and Piazza Navona's fountains and walk to Piazza **Campo dei Fiori** (page 54). Stroll through Piazza Farnese (with detours to Palazzo Spada and Santa Maria dell'Orazione e Morte) and then follow Via Giulia before cutting up to the Chiesa Nuova (frescoes by Pietro da Cortona). Next door see Borromini's idiosyncratic façade for the Oratorio dei Filippini and his clocktower in Piazza dell' Orologio. Walk to Via dei Coronari and across the Ponte Sant'Angelo to **Castel Sant'Angelo** (page 46).

Piazza Navona–Piazza di Spagna
Walk to the **Pantheon** (page 44) via **San Luigi dei Francesi** (Caravaggio frescoes – see page 52). Then see **Santa Maria sopra Minerva** (page 53) and Sant'Ignazio (for Andrea Pozzo's ceiling frescoes) *en route* for Piazza Colonna and the Colonna di Marco Aurelio. Head for the **Fontana di Trevi** (page 54) and stroll through the grid of shopping streets around Via dei Condotti towards **Piazza di Spagna** (for the Spanish Steps, see page 54).

Accommodation

Where to look Rome has the range of accommodation you can expect of any great city, from squalid *pensioni* to palatial luxury hotels. The best part to stay in is around Piazza Navona, although it is an area with relatively few hotels. More establishments cluster around Piazza del Popolo and Piazza di Spagna, both pretty and reasonably central but a notch below the top hotels on Via Veneto and the area south of the Villa Borghese. The station hotels (on Via Magenta, Via Amendola, Via Principe Amadeo) are a cheap last resort. More salubrious *pensioni* are dotted around the outlying areas of Prati and Borgo (near the Vatican).

Prices and booking Rome lacks characterful hotels in the mid-range. The best in this bracket are booked up months in advance, so aim to reserve well ahead during the city's peak season (Easter to mid-October). Even off season (when booking is still recommended), prices in Rome are high, and you often get less for your money than elsewhere. Anywhere with a garage, though, is worth its weight in gold. It usually pays to take meals in restaurants, rather than opt for full or half-pension. Watch out for breakfast and air-conditioning supplements, and remember that prices vary even within a hotel – so ask to see a variety of rooms.

Tourist offices
Avoid the touts and the long queues at the station's tourist office if you need help finding accommodation. Try instead to use the booths at Fiumicino airport (tel: 06/6501 0255); at the Roma-Nord service station on the A1; the Roma-Sud Frascati service area on the A2; or the EPT office at Via Parigi 5, near Piazza della Repubblica (tel: 06/487 1270).

Guided tours
The best guided tours of the city are offered by CIT and American Express. Both offer a variety of (coach) itineraries, most of which last around three hours.

57

Noise and appearance You will never entirely escape the noise in Rome. Many hotels are double-glazed, but unless they are also air-conditioned you will need the windows open in summer. You can reduce the problem by avoiding Termini and the main thoroughfares in favour of back streets or hotels near the parks. Also ask for a room either away from the front of the hotel or facing on to a central courtyard. When choosing a hotel do not judge by the exterior, as many a crumbling façade conceals a sumptuous interior. Finally, if you arrive at Termini, the city's main railway station, it is possible that you will be approached by touts working for hotels. Only agree to accompany them as a *last resort*. Check prices and confirm *exactly* where the hotel is located.

Rome's Grand Hotel is one of the city's smartest hotels, and a favoured home from home for visiting VIPs and royalty

Food and drink

Wine

Rome's local wine is the amber-coloured bianco of the Castelli Romani. Frascati is the most famous version, though most varieties are fairly similar. Good wine bars to try include *Cul-de-Sac*, Piazza del Pasquino 73; the intimate *Enoteca Piccola*, Via del Governo Vecchio 75; and the relaxed *Enoteca Cavour*, Via Cavour 313. Also visit the *Enoteca Isabelli*, Via della Croce 76, a lovely shop where you can buy or drink wine.

Cafés and coffee

Rome's best cups of coffee are to be had at *La Tazza d'Oro*, Via degli Orfani 84 and *Sant'Eustachio*, Piazza Sant'Eustachio 82. Other famous bars include the 18th-century *Caffè Greco*, Via dei Condotti 86, a Roman institution; *Bernasconi*, Largo di Torre Argentina 1; *Columbia*, Piazza Navona 88; the trendy *Bar della Pace*, Via della Pace 5 (off Piazza Navona); and two bars on Piazza del Popolo – *Canova* and *Rosati*.

Pavement dining in Rome

What to eat Few things – perhaps only cars, football and families – come between Romans and a good meal. Eating out is all the nightlife many of them need, and a summer evening's meal *al fresco* can be one of Rome's most memorable experiences. The city's specialities may not always be appetising – things like tripe, brains, salt cod, veal (often inhumanely raised) and offal – but more common Italian staples can be found in most restaurants. Favourite pasta dishes include *bucatini all'amatriciana*, *spaghetti alla carbonara*, *fettucine*, *gnocchi* and *penne all'arrabiata*. *Stracciatella* is the classic soup, a clear broth with egg, pasta and cheese. The best known main course is *saltimbocca alla romana* (veal with ham and sage cooked in wine and butter). Grilled meats – lamb and beefsteak – are also common. Purple Roman artichokes are renowned, so too are asparagus and leaf vegetables like spinach and rocket (*rucola* or *rughetta*). The best puddings are simple desserts like ice-cream or mixed fruit salad (*macedonia*).

Where to eat Trastevere and the streets around Piazza Navona contain many restaurants, though few areas are without their quiet neighbourhood *trattorie* and pizzerias. It is often in these places, away from tourist areas, that you will enjoy your best (and most reasonably priced) meals. Rome has more than its share of deceptively smart restaurants where the food and the prices are equally appalling. At the other extreme, do not overlook bars as a source of cheap snacks, and bear in mind that Rome now has many fast-food outlets (there are large branches of McDonald's in Piazza di Spagna and Piazza della Repubblica). Tourist menus are as cheap as elsewhere, but the standard of food they offer is perhaps as low as anywhere in Italy.

The tradition of making lunch (*pranzo*) the main meal of the day is slowly dying out – though you can still indulge heavily between 1 and 3. In the evenings Romans eat dinner (*cena*) from around 8pm, a little earlier in pizzerias, a little later (and longer) in summer.

Shopping

Shopping districts Though not a shopping city to compare with London, Paris or New York, Rome still has much to satisfy the wealthy or discerning shopper. Best known for luxury goods, its silks, leather, jewellery, shoes and accessories are of the highest quality. The most exclusive shops cluster in the grid of streets around Via dei Condotti and Piazza di Spagna. Less expensive streets include Via del Corso, Via Nazionale and Via del Tritone, Via Cola di Rienzo and the areas around Campo dei Fiori and the Fontana di Trevi.

Fruit stall in the market in Rome's Campo dei Fiori

Markets Rome's most attractive food and vegetable market is in Piazza Campo dei Fiori. Piazza Vittorio Emanuele, however, is the city's main market, selling food and all manner of general goods. Via Andrea Doria runs it a close second (north of the Vatican Museums). Porta Portese is the city's most famous flea market (Sunday only), but there are few bargains and the crowds are appalling (be on special guard against pickpockets). Via Sannio next to San Giovanni in Laterano has a smaller junk and second-hand clothes market on Saturday.

Antiques
Antique shops with breath-taking pieces and prices to match concentrate on Via del Babuino and Via Monserrato. Via Giulia's stores specialise in furniture: those on Via dei Coronari offer items a touch below Via Babuino in cost and quality.

Leather goods Shoe shops almost outnumber food shops in Rome. For quality look on and around Via dei Condotti; for keen prices try Via Nazionale. Leather shops are similarly numerous. **Beltrami** (Via Condotti 84) and **Valextra** (Via del Babuino 94) have high-quality selections. For gloves you need visit only **Sergio di Cori** (Piazza di Spagna 53). For socks, tights and stockings try **Calza e Calze**, Via della Croce 78.

China, fabrics and linen
For china try *Ginori,* Via Cola di Rienzo 223 and Via del Tritone 177, or the 100-year-old *Cavatorta,* Via Veneto 159. For silks and fabrics visit *Bises* (Via del Gesù 91), *Meconi* (Via Cola di Rienzo 305) or *Galtrucco* (Via del Tritone 18–23). *Frette* (Piazza di Spagna 11) is famed for its household linens.

Department stores La Rinascente is Rome's grandest department store (with branches at Piazza Colonna and Piazza Fiume). **Coin** at Piazzale Appio is best for clothes and kitchenware (five minutes from San Giovanni in Laterano). **Standa** at Via del Corso 148 and elsewhere is cheap and popular; while **UPIM** in Via del Tritone, Piazza Santa Maria Maggiore and elsewhere has a full range of medium-quality goods at good prices.

Nightlife

Rome's *dolce vita* days are all but over, and nightlife for many Romans means a meal out or relaxing in a pavement café (though there are plenty of more active nightspots if you want them). Cultural entertainment is what you would expect of a capital city, though cinema and theatre hold relatively few rewards for non Italian speakers.

Concerts and recitals The Accademia di Santa Cecilia stages concerts by its own and visiting orchestras at Via della Conciliazione 4 (box office Via dei Greci 18, tel: 06/6880 1044). The **Accademia Filarmonica** (tel: 06/320 1752) holds a major recital series at the Teatro Olimpico, Piazza Gentile da Fabriano 17 (tel: 06/323 4890). The **Oratorio del Gonfalone** stages baroque and chamber recitals at Via del Gonfalone 32A (tel: 06/4770 4664 or 687 5952). A wealth of classical music can also be heard free of charge throughout the year in Rome's churches.

Music clubs Jazz and Latin clubs are especially popular in Rome. Latin features heavily at **Caffè Caruso** (Via Monte Testaccio 36), jazz at **St Louis**, Via del Cardello 13a.

Yes! Brazil is also great fun (Via San Francesco a Ripa 103). The best overall venue is **Big Mama** (Vicolo San Francesco a Ripa 18), with both jazz and blues; **Caffè Latino** (Via Monte Testaccio 96) and **Alexanderplatz** (Via Ostia 9) are also popular. Most places offer light meals as well as drinks and music.

Beer and bars Sitting at cafés until the small hours is a feature of Rome's summer nightlife. **Bar della Pace** (Via della Pace 5) is perhaps the most popular, the more exclusive **Hemingway** the most trendy (Piazza delle Coppelle 10). Pubs and beer halls (*birrerie*) are also well patronised. Try the **Fiddler's Elbow** (Via dell'Ormata 43, near Santa Maria Maggiore); **Tempera**, Via San Marcello 19 (behind Piazza Venezia); or Trastevere's buzzing **La Scala**, Piazza della Scala.

Discos and Nightclubs Discos and clubs are subject to sudden changes of fashion (and ownership), so consult *Trovaroma* for the places of the moment. Admission is often expensive and dressing up *de rigueur*. Longer-established places include **Piper** (Via Tagliamento 9) and **Black Out** (Via Saturnia18), both of which attract a young crowd. **Gilda** (Via Mario de'Fiori 97) and **L'Alibi** (Via Monte Testaccio 44–57) are celebrity spots.

Information

Newspapers like *La Repubblica* and *Il Messagero* contain daily nightlife listings. *La Repubblica's* Thursday edition also contains a free weekly listings magazine called *Trovaroma*.

Ticket agencies

Rome's leading agency is Box Office, Viale Giulio Cesare 88 (tel: 06 372 0215 or 372 0216); also at Via Del Corso 506 (tel: 06/361 2682). *Orbis* also has tickets for most events (Piazza Esquilino 37, tel: 06/474 4776).

Opera and ballet

Opera and ballet performances are held at the Teatro dell'Opera, on the corner of Via Torino and Via del Viminale. Tickets go on sale 2 days before a performance (box office Tue–Sat 10–1 and 5–7; tel: 06/6759 5721). Lavish outdoor opera performances take place in Piazza di Siena in the Villa Borghese in summer – tickets from the Teatro dell'Opera box office.

Yet another way to see Rome

Buses Rome's orange buses are run by ATAC. Most services start from Piazza dei Cinquecento, in front of the main station (Stazione Termini). You must buy tickets before boarding, at shops with an ATAC sticker or at the automatic ticket machines at major stops. Tickets are valid for any number of journeys during 75 minutes. You can get a day pass or a weekly tourist ticket (BIG) (also valid on the *metro*). Remember to board buses at the back and leave at the centre. Cancel tickets in the small machine near the rear doors. There is a patchy night service (*notturno*) on main routes.

Metro Rome's underground (*la metropolitana*) is fast and easy to use, but it has only two lines. **Line A** connects Ottaviano (north of the Vatican) to Flaminia (for Piazza del Popolo and the Villa Borghese), Piazza di Spagna (Spanish Steps), Piazza Barberini (for the Galleria Barberini), Termini, Vittorio Emanuele and beyond. **Line B** is useful for Piramide (Protestant Cemetery), Circo Massimo (the Aventino and Santa Sabina), Colosseo (Colosseum), Cavour (the Roman Forum) and Termini. Direct overground trains to Fiumicino airport leave from Termini railway station. Tickets are obtainable from booths at the main stations, or from machines (correct change essential).

Taxis It is hard to hail Rome's yellow cabs on the street. Most gather at ranks or can be called by phone (tel: 3875, 3570, 4994 or 8433). Useful ranks are at Piazza Venezia, Termini, Piazza San Silvestro and Piazza Sonnino (Trastevere). Use only metered yellow cabs (ensure the meter is running). Supplements are charged for phone call-outs; after 10pm; on Sundays; and for each piece of luggage.

Bicycle hire Despite Rome's traffic, bike rental outlets are springing up all over the city. There are concessions in Via del Corso, Piazza Navona, Viale del Bambino (Pincio), Piazza San Silvestro, Largo Argentina and near the Piazza di Spagna and Piazza del Popolo (Flaminia) metro stops.

Trains and stations
Most trains arrive and leave from Stazione Termini, Piazza dei Cinquecento (usually called 'Termini'). Queues for tickets are long, especially on Friday evening and Saturday morning. Afternoons are the quietest times. Be certain to validate all tickets in the yellow-gold platform machines prior to travel. You will be fined on board if you fail to do so. International tickets, ferries, reservations and couchettes are all dealt with by separate booths. Only a few trains use Tiburtina, Ostiense or Trastevere stations.

Useful bus routes
No 27 Termini–Via Cavour–Roman Forum–Colosseum; No 64 Termini–Via Nazionale–Piazza Venezia–Piazza Navona–St Peter's; No 81 Colosseum–St Peter's/Vatican Museums (Piazza del Risorgimento).

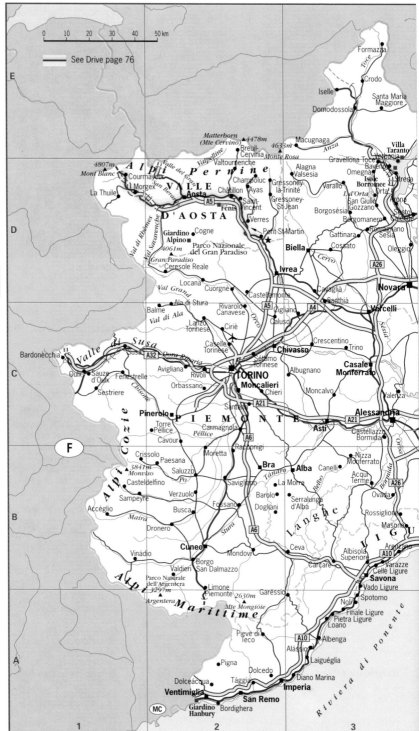

See Drive page 76

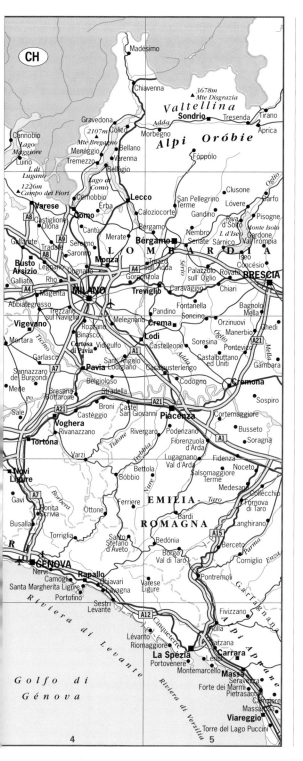

THE NORTHWEST

REGION HIGHLIGHTS ◄◄◄◄◄

AOSTA see page 65
CINQUE TERRE see page 66
GENOVA (GENOA) see page 67
**PARCO NAZIONALE DEL GRAN
PARADISO** see page 68
PORTOFINO see page 69
PORTOVENERE see page 69
**GIARDINO HANBURY
(HANBURY GARDENS)**
see page 73
TORINO (TURIN) see page 74
VALLE D'AOSTA see page 76
VALLE DI SUSA see page 77

THE NORTHWEST

Tourist information
Aosta: Piazza Chanoux 8
(tel: 0165/236 627).
Asti: Piazza Alfieri 34 (tel:
0141/530 357, 538 200 or 582
007).
Levanto (Cinque Terre):
Piazza Cavour (tel:
0187/808 125).
Genoa: Via Roma II (tel:
010/541 541).
Turin: Via Roma 226 (tel:
011/535 181); Porta Nuova
Station (tel: 011/531 327).

The Northwest The regions of Piemonte (Piedmont), Valle d'Aosta and Liguria have riches to offer every kind of visitor, with a combination of mountain scenery, seaside, fine food and historic towns.

Piemonte Cradled by the Alps on three sides, Piedmont – *piede dei monti*, or 'foot of the mountains' – is a region of mountains, vineyard-covered hills, crumbling castles and half-forgotten villages. Scenery is the spur for most visitors, principally the upland enclaves of Monviso, Gran Paradiso, and the Alpi Marittime. In the west, France's proximity colours culture, cuisine and language. At the same time, Piedmont produces such Italian staples as Fiat cars, vermouth and, that mainstay of Italian restaurants, breadsticks (*grissini*).

Torino (Turin), Piedmont's capital, is a refined, baroque city made prosperous by industry. North are the mountains of the Valle d'Aosta and south the rippling hills and vineyards around Asti and Alba, home of great wines like Barolo and Barbaresco.

Valle d'Aosta One of Italy's smallest regions, the Valle d'Aosta contains some of the country's most spectacular scenery. Its links with France were reinforced by the opening of the Mont Blanc tunnel in 1965, and increased trade has brought prosperity, along with busy roads and some light industry.

A journey through the Valle d'Aosta, the valley which scythes through the region and gives it its name, provides a fine introduction to the area's mountains and fairytale castles. Its focus, Aosta, offers Roman remains and a splendid cathedral. Almost any of the smaller nearby valleys offers wonderful views, stone-housed hamlets, Alpine meadows and ice-clear streams. The Val d'Ayas and Val di Gressoney are outstanding, but probably the most rewarding is the Val di Cogne, if only because it leads to Italy's premier national park, the Parco Nazionale del Gran Paradiso.

Scenic drives
(*Piedmont*) SS21
Cuneo–Vinadio–Argentera;
Cuneo–Valdieri–Parco
Naturale dell'Argentera;
Turin–Lanzo Torinese–Val
Grande–Val di Ala; SS460
Turin–Locana–Ceresole
Reale; (*Valle d'Aosta*) SS26
Pont-St-Martin–Aosta; SS
505 Pont-St-Martin–Val di
Gressoney; SS506 St
Vincent–Val d'Ayas;
(*Liguria*) SS530 La
Spezia–Portovenere;
La Spezia–Lerici–
Montemarcello.

Maritime Liguria With Genoa (Italy's largest port) as its capital and Christopher Columbus as its most famous son, Liguria is naturally a region dominated by all things maritime. Its beautiful coastline – the so-called Italian Riviera – divides into the Riviera di Ponente (west of Genoa) and the Riviera di Levante (east). Both are sheltered by the Ligurian and Maritime Alps, mountain walls which guarantee mild winters and a long growing season – resulting in the region's nickname of *Riviera dei Fiori* (Riviera of Flowers).

If you have time for only one sojourn on the coast make for the Cinque Terre, five tiny fishing villages wedged into the cliffs and mountains on the Riviera di Levante. If your itinerary is more leisurely, amble down the entire coast from Ventimiglia, stopping at Alassio, for its broad beach, or San Remo for its mixture of old world charm and tacky modernism. Drive inland to explore the hills, dotted with attractive, little-known villages, and visit the coast's most famous hilltowns, upmarket Portofino and Portovenere. Spend time in Genoa, a salty and industrialised port, of interest principally for its old quarter and collection of modest galleries.

► **Alba** 62B3

Austere and medieval Alba is renowned above all for its food and wine: wine in the shape of Barolo and Barbaresco (both red), and food in the form of truffles (*tartufi*), prised from the oak woods of the surrounding hills (see page 174). After sampling the town's food shops head for **San Lorenzo►**, the old cathedral, containing a finely carved and inlaid choir. Another church, **San Giovanni►** contains the town's most prized painting, the *Madonna delle Grazie* by Barnaba da Modena (1377).

► **Aosta** 62D2

Capital of the Valle d'Aosta, relaxed and largely French-speaking Aosta is a sedate and historic town whose lightly industrial fringe is redeemed by a tremendous mountainous backdrop. Its **Cattedrale►** is worth a look for its choir stalls and small museum housing a magnificent early 5th-century ivory diptych. The finest church, however, is **Sant'Orso►►**, renowned for its 11th-century crypt and the wonderfully carved columns of its cloister (1133). Also outstanding are the town's Roman remains.

►► **Asti** 62C3

One time rival to Milan, Asti is well worth a visit, and deserves to be known for more than Asti Spumante, its famous (if downmarket) sparkling wine. Most of its best monuments – towers, palaces and churches – are on or near the main street, Corso Vittorio Alfieri. The Gothic Duomo (1309–54) has a chequered façade of red and white stone, but is less interesting overall than the church of **San Pietro in Consavia►**, whose little circular baptistery dates from around the 12th century. Look, too, at **San Secondo►**, a looming Gothic church with numerous frescoes, the most noted a polyptych by Gandolfino d'Asti.

You could make an excursion to Albugnano, to see the **Abbazia di Vezzolano►►**, the finest Romanesque building in Piedmont (22km from Asti). Reputedly founded by Charlemagne, it has a remarkable 12th-century façade, magnificent carved rood screen and lovely cloister.

Sant'Orso church below the snow-capped mountains of the Valle d'Aosta

The wines of Piedmont
Piedmont produces some of Italy's most famous wines, from its noble, tannic reds, Barolo and Barbaresco, to semi-sweet and sparkling whites like Asti Spumante and Moscato d'Asti. Some other outstanding reds include Gattinara, Ghemme, Lessona, Barbera and Dolcetto d'Alba. Whites are less renowned, though Gavi is fashionable (if sometimes bland) and Arneis has a rising reputation.

Bagna cauda
Meaning literally a 'hot bath', *bagna cauda* is a type of Piedmontese fondue, a spicy dip made by simmering together a mixture of butter, olive oil, garlic, white truffle, anchovies and cream. It is a common wintertime dish all over the region.

THE NORTHWEST

Wines of the Cinque Terre
Cinque Terre Bianco is the basic white; Pigato and Vermentino are generally superior. Rossese and Dolceacqua are good reds. The best wine of all is the rare amber-coloured Sciacchetrà, made from semi-dried grapes. Dry versions are drunk as an aperitif, sweeter variations as a fine dessert wine.

Eating out
Take advantage of the Cinque Terre's often romantically situated restaurants to sample Liguria's culinary specialities. *Cacciucco* is a rich fish soup, *cappon magro* a fish and vegetable dish eaten in Lent; *burrida*, fish in a spicy sauce; and *ciuppin* a minced fish sauce. *Pansôti* are ravioli stuffed with ricotta cheese and chard, then topped with a walnut cream sauce. *Cima* is meat – usually veal – stuffed with vegetables, herbs, nuts, eggs and cheese.

Vernazza's pretty fishing harbour

►► **Cinque Terre** 63A5

The Cinque Terre (Five Lands) are five tiny seafront villages strung along one of the most dramatic stretches of the Ligurian coast. Each is a picturesque jumble of pastel-coloured houses gathered around a small fishing harbour (though tourists these days heavily outnumber fishermen). Above the huddle of houses, mountains covered in woods and lush vegetation provide a beautiful backdrop. Savage cliffs tumble to the sea on all sides, cut by terraces of vines and olives that date back thousands of years. Well-marked and panoramic paths follow the coast and criss-cross the hinterland.

Access to the region for centuries was possible only by sea, and even today some of the villages have no road links to the outside world. Boats connect them all, and this is a fine way of seeing the coast. The train, however, is the most practical way of moving from village to village. Any one of the villages makes a fine place to stop, though most people base themselves in **Levanto**, a town just to the north with plenty of hotels and services – as well as a fair amount of charm in its own right.

The villages Each of the villages has its own attractions, and if one palls, it is only a few minutes by rail to the next. From north to south you find **Monterosso**, the largest and perhaps least charming of the five, but with the biggest beach and most hotels. **Vernazza** is a tangle of tiny streets, alleys and arcades. **Corniglia** – the smallest – sits high above the sea, but has a long, if pebbly beach. **Manarola** is the jewel in the crown, clustered behind a sickle of sand and hemmed in by precipitous mountains. Its steep cobbled streets are the most charming in the area and the harbour still presents a rustic picture of bobbing fishing boats and seamen mending nets in the sun. **Riomaggiore** also sits behind a sliver of sand, and has a more generous range of accommodation than most of the villages.

The striped façade of Genoa's cathedral

► **Genova (Genoa)** 63B4

Italy's premier maritime city, Genoa receives relatively little attention from visitors, most of whom are put off by its lack of famous sights and by the grim suburbs which spread in a confused sprawl over the surrounding hills. Away from the vibrant – and sometimes sordid – waterfront, however, the *centro storico* (historic centre) is a medley of teeming streets, some best avoided after dark, but all a joy to explore. Public lifts and cog railways transport you around the city's confusing multitude of levels.

The proud city One of Italy's four great medieval maritime republics, Genoa in the 14th century claimed territories stretching from North Africa to Syria and the Black Sea. It became Europe's most densely populated city, nicknamed La Superba, 'The Proud', by the poet Petrarch.

Genoa's medieval trading prowess brought it great wealth, much of which went to build the imposing patrician palaces lining **Via Garibaldi**►►, one of Italy's most impressive streets. Most of the palaces are now offices or grand shops, but two house important art galleries: the **Palazzo Bianco**►► contains works mainly by Genovese masters, with additional pieces by Veronese, Pontormo and Filippino Lippi, plus an outstanding medley of Dutch and Flemish paintings; and the **Palazzo Rosso**►► offers canvases by Caravaggio, Dürer and Van Dyck, among others, and the masterpiece of Genoa's own Bernardo Strozzi, *La Cuoca*.

Other museums to hunt out are the **Museo Chiossone**►, home to Italy's foremost collection of oriental art, and the **Galleria Nazionale di Palazzo Spinola**►, crammed with furniture, sculpture and Renaissance paintings.

San Lorenzo►► is the city's cathedral, fronted by a fine black-and-white-striped façade. Inside, the Museo del Tesoro contains a collection of the gold and silverware for which medieval Genoa was renowned. Close by, make for **Piazza San Matteo**►► an outstanding ensemble of medieval buildings.

Cable cars
If you want views of the mountains without having to work for them, several ski-lifts and cable cars operate during the summer. One of the most convenient is the telecabina from Cogne, which climbs to Montseuc (2,100m) just a kilometre south of the town. A couple of little paths from its upper station offer easy strolls in the woods, or to the upper summit of Montseuc (2,333m).

▶▶   **Parco Nazionale del Gran Paradiso**   62D2

Italy's first ever national park is also its most spectacular. Ranged around the Gran Paradiso massif (4,061m) – the only mountain over 4,000m solely in Italy – the park started life as a hunting reserve for the Savoys in the 19th century. In 1919 the family donated the area to the state, thus helping to preserve not only the area's stupendous scenery, but also the ibex, a type of wild goat, for which the park is now best known. Snow-capped mountains, vast glaciers, verdant valleys and deep-green forests lie within easy reach of drivers and walkers alike.

Three valleys push into the park from the Valle d'Aosta – the Val di Rhêmes, Val Savarenche and Val di Cogne. Roads run up each one, offering superlative views and many opportunities for walks into the mountains. The best approach overall, though, is via the Val di Cogne, and its main centre, Cogne▶▶, just half an hour from Aosta. A pleasing little winter and summer resort, it has plenty of accommodation and makes a perfect base for the whole of the park. It is a particularly good launching pad for walks. For details of the best hike see 'Walking', pages 70–1.

The Gran Paradiso National Park has a wide variety of land-scapes, from barren mountain uplands to verdant flower-filled meadows

Just south of the village is the hamlet of **Valnontey**, a little too swamped by visitors for its own good, but home to the Giardino Alpino, a botanical garden that contains examples of much of the park's outstanding alpine flora. Come in June to see the flowers at their best, and if at all possible try a few walks up to mountain meadows to see them in their natural habitat. The same walks will almost certainly reward you with sightings of ibex, as well as the more numerous chamois and a range of smaller fauna and alpine birds. Around 3,500 ibex and some 6,000 chamois now thrive within the park's confines. Their numbers are giving slight cause for concern, as they have no natural predators: plans have been mooted to reintroduce wolves, perhaps even lynx, to re-establish a natural equilibrium.

▶   **Riviera di Levante**   63A4

The Riviera di Levante is the less developed and more spectacular half of the Italian Riviera. Like the Riviera di Ponente, however, it is a region where you have to choose carefully if you want to avoid over-priced or over-

popular resorts. Almost any town will suffice, though, if all you want is racy nightlife and noisy beachlife.

A general tour by road or rail rewards with glimpses of turquoise sea, tiny fishing villages and a romantic medley of cliffs and mountains. Pine forests plunge to pebbly beaches, interspersed with luxuriant and herb-scented swaths of *maquis*. The best section is the Cinque Terre (see page 66).

Moving east from Genoa, however, the first stop is Camogli►, little changed since Charles Dickens described it as the 'saltiest, roughest, most piratical little place'. Clustered around a pleasant harbour, it is quieter than many spots on the coast, full of steep streets, brightly painted houses, and dozens of *al fresco* restaurants. Beyond lies Rapallo►, once a fashionable Edwardian resort, now rather spoilt by modern building and the weight of summer tourists. People come to enjoy its mild climate, beaches with long promenades and its many cultural events.

From Rapallo or nearby Santa Margherita Ligure you can reach Portofino►►►, one of Italy's most beautiful but also most exclusive seafront villages. The country's rich and famous treat this as their personal playground, with the inevitable result that prices are high and the atmosphere exclusive. This said, the village's sheer prettiness makes it well worth a day trip. Escape the crowds by walking to the Castello di San Giorgio and the little church of San Giorgio just beyond. Most of the Portofino promontory is protected as a *parco naturale*, designed to preserve one of the few unspoilt stretches of the Italian Riviera (see panel).

A little further round the coast Sestri Levante► has one of the area's better beaches, the Baia di Silenzio, edged around one of the town's two large bays. Portovenere►► is almost as pretty as Portofino, but not as ruinously expensive. It has plenty of restaurants and bars, a ruined fortress and a beautiful sanctuary believed to stand on the site of a temple to Venus. Italians in the know make for Lerici► an attractive and unpretentious resort with sheltered beaches and an imposing 13th-century Pisan castle.

Portofino's colourful waterfront

Parco Naturale di Monte di Portofino
Portofino's hills are cloaked in *macchia* (like the French *maquis*), a thick vegetation of aleppo and maritime pines, and a fragrant undergrowth of herbs, juniper, heathers and cistus. Tranquil paths criss-cross the park's hilly interior. Boat trips from Portofino and Camogli offer views on to the often dramatic coastline.

The Golfo dei Poeti
The area around Lerici has been praised for its beauty for centuries, never more fulsomely than by Byron and Shelley, the two poets after whom the area – the Golfo dei Poeti – was named. In one noted incident, Byron swam from Portovenere across the Gulf to visit Shelley in San Terenzo, a quaint fishing village across the bay from Lerici. It was here in 1822 that Shelley started the fateful voyage to Livorno that ended in shipwreck and his death by drowning.

Walking in Northwest Italy

■ **Northwest Italy offers some of the country's best walking, from the high Alps of the Gran Paradiso National Park to the coastal cliffs of the Cinque Terre and Portofino peninsula.** ■

La Morra and Le Langhe
The lovely hilly countryside around Alba is known as Le Langhe, a region swathed in vineyards and dotted with castles and hilltop villages. La Morra is one of the finest, enjoying all-embracing views (hence its nickname, the *Belvedere delle Langhe*). It also boasts a wine museum and a series of walks which follow designated wine routes. Each path is colour-coded according to its destination and takes you past vineyards, wine cellars and rustic inns where you can sample the local vintages.

Explore the Italian countryside on foot

Hiking is not always easy in Italy. The Alps, however, benefit from well-marked trails and a range of up-to-date and readily available maps. This also applies to less well-known areas, foremost of which are the scarcely explored mountains of the Parco Naturale dell'Argentera in southwest Piedmont. Walking possibilities are endless throughout the Alpine areas of Piedmont and Valle d'Aosta. Below are a few of the finest to get you started.

Parco Nazionale del Gran Paradiso To explore this park buy the Kompass 1:50,000 map *Gran Paradiso-Valle d'Aosta* (No 86) or IGC *Parco Nazionale del Gran Paradiso* (No 3). The most popular walk in the area starts from Valnontey south of Cogne. From the village (1,666m) take trail 106/36 to the *Rifugio Vittorio Sella* (2,584m). The path climbs through pine woods, with grand views of the surrounding mountains and glaciers, as well as excellent opportunities of seeing ibex and chamois. At the *rifugio* take trail 39 south towards Lago di Lauson (2,656m) and follow it to the *Rifugio Sella Herbetet* and the head of the valley. Then walk down the valley on trail 33 back to Valnontey. Allow a full day for the walk, and try to avoid August and summer weekends, when the route is extremely popular.

Parco Naturale dell'Argentera This walk starts from Terme di Valdieri, a hamlet at the heart of the park (35km southwest of Cuneo in southern Piedmont). Use the IGC 1:50,000 map *Alpi Marittime e Liguri* (No 8). Pick up the N8 trail, which strikes west up the Valle di Valasco from immediately south of Terme di Valdieri (1,368m). Follow the well-made mule track to the upper part of the valley, which flattens out into one of the most beautiful upland meadows in the Alps (1,763m). At the small Savoy hunting lodge, the ruined *Casa di Caccia*, take the trail over the river and follow the main path into the mountains to the Lago di Valscura (2,274m). Then descend via trails N22, N20 and N18 to the *Casa di Caccia* and thus back to Terme di Valdieri. Allow a full day for the walk.

Parco Naturale del Monte di Portofino All sorts of marked walks, long and short, are possible on the Portofino promontory. The most popular depart from Portofino itself, whose tourist office has several maps and guides covering many local hikes. The neatest circuit, a marked trail, leaves the village and climbs to San Sebastiano (191m), continuing to Monte delle Bocche (516m) before dropping down to the little fishing village of San Fruttuoso. Here you can either take one of the regular boats back to Portofino, or walk back along a quite magnificent coastal path via Punta Carega and the Val

Ruffinale. You should allow four hours to follow the complete circuit from Portofino.

Cinque Terre Numerous paths have been marked and mapped around the Cinque Terre villages and their mountainous hinterland. Maps and details are available from all local tourist offices, and the Italian Alpine Club (CAI) produce their own 1:40,000 *Carta dei Sentieri delle Cinque Terre*, available in local bookshops. Trains linking all the villages mean you can easily return to base without having to retrace your steps. The most obvious walks link the coastal villages, traversing breathtaking scenery, often by means of precipitous terraces or thousands of tiny steps cut into rocks. Any stretch between two villages has its rewards, though it is also worth exploring the mountains to the rear, where paths run along the entire summit ridge (linked by transverse trails to the coast).

The Castello di Verres lies in the Valle d'Aosta, northeast of the Parco Nazionale del Gran Paradiso

THE NORTHWEST

San Remo's flower market
Every morning except Sunday, at around 6.30, traders gather in San Remo's Corso Garibaldi for one of Europe's largest flower markets. Over 20,000 tonnes of roses, carnations, mimosa and other flowers change hands here every year.

A scenic rail journey
The railway from Ventimiglia to Limone Piemonte is one of Italy's most scenic, passing through French territory as it climbs from the coast into the heart of the Alpi Marittime. An engineering marvel, the line was badly damaged in World War II and only reopened as late as 1979. Around 10 trains daily ply the route. The journey takes 70 minutes.

The palms of Bordighera
Bordighera has the unique privilege of supplying the Vatican with palms during Easter week, a tradition said to go back to 1586, and the raising of the Egyptian obelisk in front of St Peter's, Rome. The supporting ropes threatened to break, but a sailor from Bordighera shouted 'Water on the ropes', despite an order that the watchers should stay silent on pain of death. The pope, Sixtus V, awarded the village the palm concession in gratitude. Sadly, the story is probably a tall one.

Elegant San Remo's palm-fringed harbour

▶   **Riviera di Ponente**   62A3

The Italian Riviera's western portion stretches from Ventimiglia on the French border to Genoa. For the most part it is an unbroken chain of popular beach resorts, all far cheaper and more down-to-earth than their neighbours across the border.

Ventimiglia has a passable old quarter, but remains essentially a border town, crammed with dreary hotels, garages and duty free shops. **Bordighera▶▶**, beyond, is more refined, one of the first resorts to attract well-heeled British and European visitors in the 19th century. The beach is good and the historic centre still boasts a brace of medieval monuments.

San Remo▶ was once the Nice of the Italian Riviera, its mild climate, gardens and genteel charm the magnet for the cream of European aristocracy. These days its appeal combines ritz with kitsch, though the old town (La Pigna), flower market and palm-lined promenades are all worth an hour's exploration. The cable car up Monte Bignone also makes a good excursion, offering views on clear days as far as Cannes.

Diano Marina and Laiguelia are both functional, family-orientated resorts, overshadowed by **Alassio▶**, a large, affluent and lively town with the best beach in Liguria (over 3km of fine sand).

Albenga▶ only has a pebbly foreshore, but its old town is the most historically rewarding on the Riviera. Its chief draws are the 5th-century baptistery – Liguria's most important early Christian building – the cathedral, the Museo Igauno, the intimate Piazza dei Leoni and the Palazzo Peloso-Cipolla, whose Museo Navale Romano contains finds from a Roman galley sunk near by in the 1st century BC. The Museo Diocesano is also worth a quick visit for its tapestries and colourful medieval frescoes.

Finale Ligure▶ is among the Riviera's most pleasant spots, less crowded than Alassio. There is an interesting old-town area (Finalborgo) 2km inland. Little **Noli▶** is a picturesque resort-cum-fishing village, with a good beach and interesting Romanesque church, San Paragorio. Savona, the last town before Genoa, is a heavily industrialised seaport.

■ **The Hanbury Gardens (Giardino Hanbury) lie near the village of Mortola Inferiore, a distance of 6km from Ventimiglia. Founded in 1867 by Sir Thomas Hanbury, a wealthy English tea merchant, they were acquired by the Italian state in 1960, and now rank as some of the most important gardens in Italy.** ■

The Ligurian coastline has one of the mildest winter climates in the country. Flowers of all varieties flourish here even in February, a natural bounty that has been turned to commercial advantage by the region's market gardeners. All down the coast you see chequered fields of coloured blooms, or row upon row of cavernous greenhouses.

At Mortola Hanbury took advantage of the region's benign climate to produce Italy's largest botanical gardens, planting out over 5,000 species of plants and flowers from all corners of the globe. Many were exotic specimens from Africa and Asia, carefully acclimatised to grow alongside the staples of Mediterranean and Alpine flora. The palms, together with succulents and cacti, are particularly outstanding. These days the garden is past its prime, over three-quarters of the species having been lost over the years (restoration work, however, is currently in hand). Nonetheless it still remains worth visiting, particularly if you come armed with a picnic and prepared to spend the whole afternoon there.

At the gardens' centre is an extravagant Islamic-style mausoleum, Sir Thomas Hanbury's eccentric final resting place. From here the gardens fan out on steep terraces, a clever piece of design that constantly unfolds new vistas as you walk from level to level.

The gardens' partial ruin in places only adds to their atmospheric appeal, creating overgrown nooks and hidden corners among the more formal settings. The terraces fall away to the sea in a mixture of unkempt arbours and riotous pergolas, occasionally revealing an artificial grotto or crumbling fountain.

The gardens are open daily from 10 to 6 (until 4 off season): admission charges are high.

The Hanbury Gardens are among Italy's finest, their mild climate making them worth a visit throughout the whole year

Old world cafés

Turin is famous for its *fin-de-siècle* cafés. The best-known include *Caffè Torino*, Piazza San Carlo 204; *Caffè San Carlo*, under the arcades of Piazza San Carlo (opposite *Stratta*, the city's top chocolate shop); the intimate *Mulussano* in Piazza San Carlo; and *Baratti e Milano*, just off Piazza Castello in the gallery leading to Via Po.

Basilica di Superga

In 1706, King Vittorio Amedeo II, surveying from a hill outside Turin the French and Spanish armies that had been besieging the city, promised to build a basilica in honour of the Virgin if she came to the city's rescue. Turin was duly spared and the pledge fulfilled in the shape of the Basilica di Superga, one of Italy's most striking baroque buildings.

The old centre of Turin, capital of Piedmont

▶▶   **Torino (Turin)**   62C2

Piedmont's capital is a mixture of industrial hinterland – the domain of Fiat and Lancia – and a gracious city centre of gardens, arcades and boulevards. A quiet university town during the Middle Ages, it acquired a French flavour it has never entirely lost when the Savoys moved from Chambéry to establish their capital here in 1574. The city is oddly undervisited – dreary suburbs put people off – but the old core is well worth a morning's exploration.

The two main sights gather under one roof in Piazza San Carlo's Palazzo dell'Accademia delle Scienze: the **Museo Egizio▶▶**, generally considered the most important museum of Egyptian antiquities outside Egypt, and the **Galleria Sabauda▶▶**, an outstanding picture gallery built around the Savoys' family collection. Near by, visit the **Museo Nazionale del Risorgimento▶**, for more background on Turin's pivotal role in Italian unification.

A little to the north lies the traffic-choked Piazza Castello, home to a trio of easily seen sights. Most prominent is the **Palazzo Reale▶**, a Savoy royal palace crammed with gaudily decorated state apartments (guided tours), of less interest than the gardens to the rear, the Giardino Reale. Opposite stands the **Palazzo Madama▶▶**, fronted by a fine baroque façade. Inside is the Museo Civico dell'Arte Antica, an eclectic collection of glassware, ceramics, jewellery and paintings. On the square's north side the **Armeria Reale▶** offers one of the world's greatest collections of arms and armour. The **Duomo▶▶▶**, off Piazza Castello, is best known for the Turin Shroud (see opposite page). For an overall view, and if you have the requisite energy, climb the **Mole Antonelliana▶▶**, the towering 19th-century folly (once the world's highest building) that can be seen from all over the city.

The Turin Shroud

■ **Turin's cathedral contains one of the most famous – and most controversial – relics in Christendom: the *Sindone*, or Holy Shroud, the cloth reputedly used to wrap Christ after His crucifixion.** ■

The Turin Shroud is a 4m length of linen, unremarkable but for the fact that it contains an imprint of what the faithful claim is an image of the crucified Christ. It first made its appearance around the middle of the 15th century, when it was presented to Ludovico of Savoy in Chambéry. In 1578 it was brought to Turin by another member of the Savoy family, Duke Emanuele Filiberto.

It is only in the last few years that the Church has allowed rigorous scientific study of the shroud. The results have been double-edged. On the one hand three separate university teams – in Italy, Britain and the United States – have concluded, as a result of Carbon 14 dating, that the cloth is a forgery dating from between 1260 and 1390. On the other, they are unable to explain how the shroud's image, which is like a photographic negative, could have been created.

The shroud's image
A photographic replica of the shroud on display in the cathedral shows the face of a bearded man, complete with a crown of thorns, as well as front and rear images of a body displaying spear wounds, the marks left by a thonged whip and bruises compatible with carrying a cross.

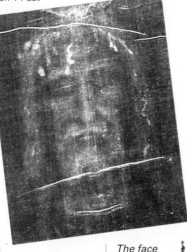

The face of Christ?

Housing the Shroud The *Sindone* is only brought out of hiding on very special occasions. The original is kept in the Cappella della Sacra Sindone, locked securely away in a silver casket, which in turn is hidden in an iron box, a marble coffer and a heavy urn on the chapel's main altar. Although Filiberto intended to build a new church to house the relic, his successors commissioned Amedeo di Castellamonte and then the more gifted Guarino Guarini (1624–83) to design a chapel within the cathedral (badly damaged by fire in 1997).

One of the baroque school's leading lights, Guarini has monuments built to his designs in places as far afield as Lisbon, Paris and Prague. The chapel in Turin, however, is perhaps his masterpiece; a consummate piece of baroque-mannerist frippery, notable for the exuberant excess of its unusual cupola.

Drive The Valle d'Aosta

See map on pages 62–3.

A spectacular drive through one of Italy's major Alpine valleys, full of castles, old stone villages and Europe's highest mountains, Mont Blanc, the Matterhorn and Monte Rosa.

Note: although this drive follows the valley floor, be sure to explore the minor roads which strike off into scenic side valleys along the way – Val di Gressoney, Val d'Ayas, Valtournenche and Val di Cogne.

Pont-St-Martin, gateway to the valley, is a fine old village, surrounded by vineyards and known for its 1st-century BC Roman bridge. Bard offers the first of the valley's castles, most of which were built by the Challant family who ruled the region for seven centuries. The stark fortress at Verres hoves into view soon after, perhaps less interesting than the castle at Issogne▶, a plain affair from the outside, but inside completely full of

fascinating apartments and period furnishings.

St-Vincent is a fashionable spa and home of one of Italy's largest casinos. Further west, **Fenis**▶▶ is undoubtedly the one castle to visit if you visit no other, a fairytale fortress of towers and turrets, its court, chapel and loggias covered in 14th-century frescoes.

Fairytale Fenis Castle

Aosta is the region's focus (page 65), an interesting town in its own right and a base for trips to the **Parco Nazionale del Gran Paradiso** (page 68) and **Valle del Gran San Bernardo** (page 77). Beyond it, castles come thick and fast, those at Sarre, St-Pierre and Avise – pretty villages all – particularly fine.

Round off a drive by taking the renowned cable car ride over Mont Blanc, the **Funivia del Monte Bianco**▶▶▶, which starts from La Palud, a hamlet 3.5km north of the resort town of Courmayeur. There are three stages; you can ride to 3,321m at Punta Helbronner, press on over the Géant Glacier, or cross right over the mountain to Chamonix over the French border.

Farming in the Valle d'Aosta

►► Val d'Ayas
62D2

The Val d'Ayas is one of the prettiest of the valleys that branch off the Valle d'Aosta: broad, heavily wooded and crowned by the colossal peaks of Monte Rosa and the Matterhorn (Cervino in Italian). Champoluc is the chief resort, departure point for mountain hikes and the cable car to Testa Grigia (3,315m), one of the most spectacular viewpoints in the Alps. Brusson, to the south, is a base for easier walks, the best the trail to the coronet of mountain lakes below Punta Valfredda (3hr 30min).

► Valle del Gran San Bernardo
62D2

Easily seen from Aosta (see page 65), this valley is best known for its pass and famous St Bernard dogs (see panel). Along its entire length, however, it is a scenic delight, well worth travelling for the ride alone. For still grander scenery, take the tortuous mountain road east of the valley into the wild reaches of the Valpelline.

► Val di Gressoney
62D3

So perfect an alpine valley it is almost a cliché, the Val di Gressoney is a vision of emerald-green meadows, snow-capped peaks, shimmering glaciers and geranium-hung wooden houses. Its inhabitants, the Walser, speak an obscure German dialect, having migrated here from the Swiss Valais in the 12th century. The main centres, Gressoney-St-Jean and trendier Gressoney-La-Trinité, offer plenty of hiking and skiing opportunities.

► Valle di Susa
62C1

The Valle di Susa lacks the drama of smaller alpine valleys, and is spoilt in places by light industry and its busy road and rail links. It has, however, one or two highlights, notably the dramatic abbey of **Sacra di San Michele►►►**, just west of the pretty lakeside village of Avigliana. **Susa►** features a scattering of Roman remains and several ancient churches. Close by, roads lead into glorious scenery, particularly around the nature reserves of Salbertrand and Orsiera-Rocciavré.

Bridge leading to the St Bernard Tunnel

The St Bernard Pass
The 2,469m pass has long been one of the Alps' most important routes, used by Roman legions, Celts, Charlemagne and Napoleon. Today, its chief attraction is the Hospice of St Bernard, founded in 1050. It is just in Switzerland, so take your passport. Part of the monks' vocation involved ministering to weary and snowbound travellers, helped by a uniquely robust type of dog. The souvenir shacks are stuffed with china, plastic and fluffy versions of the famous brandy-carrying St Bernard dog.

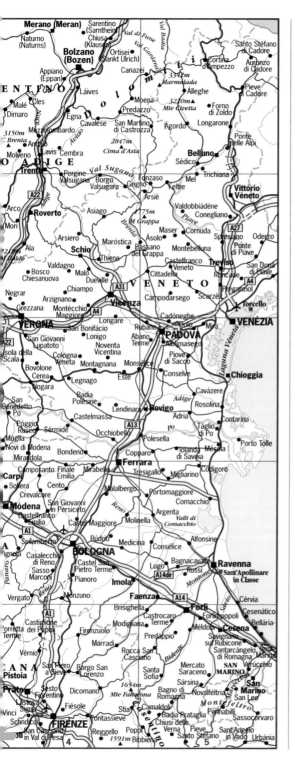

▶▶▶▶▶ **REGION HIGHLIGHTS**

BERGAMO: ACCADEMIA CARRARA *see page 82*

BOLOGNA *see page 82:* **SAN PETRONIO AND SAN DOMENICO**

COMO, LAGO DI *see page 83*

FERRARA *see page 84*

LAGO MAGGIORE *see page 87*

MANTOVA *see page 87:* **PALAZZO DUCALE AND PALAZZO TE**

MILAN *see page 88:* **DUOMO, ACCADEMIA BRERA,** *LAST SUPPER*

PARMA *see page 91*

PAVIA: *see page 91* **CERTOSA DI PAVIA**

RAVENNA *see page 92*

80

Tourist information
Bellagio: (Lake Como) Piazza della Chiesa 14 (tel: 031/950 204).
Bergamo: Viale Papa Giovanni XXIII 110 (tel: 035/242 226).
Bologna: Piazza Maggiore 6 (tel: 051/239 660).
Como: Piazza Cavour 17 (tel: 031/ 262 091 or 269 712).
Malcesine (Lake Garda): Via Capitanato del Porto 1 (tel: 045/740 0044).
Mantova: Piazza A Mantegna 6 (tel: 0376/ 328 253).
Milano: Via Marconi 1 (tel: 02/809 662); Stazione Centrale (tel: 02/669 0432).
Parma: Via Melloni 1 (tel: 0521/234 735).
Pavia: Via Fabio Filzi 2 (tel: 0382/22 156).
Ravenna: Via San Vitale 2 (tel: 0544/35 755).
Stresa: (Lake Maggiore) Via Principe Tomaso 70 (tel: 0323/30 150).

Lombardy and Emilia-Romagna Italy's richest regions are a perfect balance of city and countryside. Lombardy is divided between the plains of the Po and the mountains of the high Alps (Emilia-Romagna is mainly plain). Two cities lie at their heart: Milan, Italy's fashion and finance capital; and Bologna, ancient seat of learning and gastronomic *non pareil*. Elsewhere, scattered small cities combine medieval centres with industrial hinterlands. Immense agricultural riches spring from the plains, creating, sadly, unlovely landscapes. If it's fine scenery you want, head for the Italian Lakes, a dozen or more lakes that fill the great Alpine valleys north of Milan.

Milan Italy's capital by rights is Rome, but these days it could as easily be Milan (Milano), a major industrial centre, and a flourishing hothouse of fashion, design and high technology. Visitors often find its modern face less appealing than more obviously historic cities like Venice and Florence, yet the city's sights include a grand cathedral, the world-class Brera art gallery – and Leonardo's *Last Supper*. The city also makes a good touring base: the lakes and mountains are surprisingly close, and fascinating towns like Bergamo and Pavia – with its magnificent abbey – are less than an hour away.

The Italian Lakes Celebrated for centuries for their great natural beauty, the lakes these days are slightly sullied by people and pollution, but for the most part they remain a romantic medley of mountains, forests, lakeside villas and mild-weathered resorts. The big three – Como, Garda and Maggiore – are well known; slightly less frequented are Iseo and Orta. The latter, in particular, is still largely unspoilt by crowds and commercialism. Como takes most of the scenic plaudits, and Maggiore is a must, if only to visit the Isole Borromee (Borromean Islands).

You really need a car to do the lakes justice (though trains offer first-hand views of them all save Garda). If possible avoid July and August, and weekends in particular, when many of Lombardy's cities empty northwards

towards the region. Ideally, make base camp near a lake, then take boat trips to its other towns – by far the best way to see the scenery. Stresa is the best overall centre on Lake Maggiore; Como the best on Lake Como; and Malcesine the first choice on Garda. All these places are popular, of course, and smaller villages are always worth checking out. If in doubt, head north, away from the spots easily reached from Milan.

Cities Northern Italy's plains offer next to nothing in the way of scenery. Their tedium is relieved only by some of Italy's finest medium-sized cities, places that most people pass by as they rush to Florence or Venice. Lombardy's are perhaps the least known, and as a result can make surprisingly peaceful spots to while away a couple of days. Mantova is the best, a perfect medieval city in a strange, lagoon-circled setting. Cremona is a little too provincial, but attracts attention as the birthplace of the great violin-maker Stradivari. Bologna and Parma are the big draws in Emilia-Romagna, prosperous cities renowned for their cuisine and wide range of medieval monuments.

Rice and risotto It comes as a surprise to many people to see the vast paddy fields that spread over large areas of Piedmont and Lombardy. Rice – and not pasta – is the mainstay of the Milanese diet (the area is Europe's largest rice producer). No-one knows when or why cultivation started, though the theory is that the grain spread from Asia to Egypt and was then brought by Arabs to Sicily. The classic recipe for risotto uses rice fried with butter and onions, then cooked with stock, marrow and saffron (butter and parmesan are added before serving). Other versions include *Certosa*, with crayfish (invented by Carthusian monks); *Monza*, with sausage; *Comasco*, using perch; *Lomellina*, with frogs; and *alla pilota*, from Mantova, with salami. Do not worry if none of these takes your fancy – pasta is as popular here as it is everywhere else in Italy.

Bellagio, the jewel of Lake Como

Scenic railways
Europe's highest and most spectacular railway, the 'Red Train', runs from Tirano (near Sondrio) to St Moritz. Special tourist trains operate in summer, carrying observation cars for better views of the peaks and glaciers of the Bernina Alps. Almost equally spectacular is the 2-hour run through the mountains from Domodossola to Locarno.

Scenic drives
SS 229 Lago d'Orta; SS 337 Domodossola–Santa Maria Maggiore–Locarno; SS 659 Domodossola–Crodo–Formazza; (*Lake Como*) SS 340/SS 583 Como–Gravedona–Bellano–Lecco–Bellagio–Como; SS 38/SS 39 Sondrio–Aprica–Edolo; (*Stelvio National Park*) SS 300 Bormio–Santa Caterina–Ponte di Legno: (*Adamello Regional Park*) SS 345 Breno–Collio–Iseo.

The Colleoni chapel,
Bergamo

Donizetti
Gaetano Donizetti, master of *bel canto*, the style of virtuoso aria that characterised his operas, was born in Bergamo in 1797. Around 60 operas and 51 years later he also died there, riddled with syphilis and certifiably insane.

Eating and epithets
Bologna has many nicknames: *La Dotta* (The Learned), after the university; *La Turrita*, (The Turreted), after its towers; and *La Grassa*, (The Fat), after a cuisine widely considered Italy's finest. Besides *bolognese* sauce (or *ragù*), specialities include baloney (Bologna) sausage; *mortadella* (a kind of Italian luncheon meat); *tortellini*; and *tagliatelle*, reputedly invented for the wedding feast of Lucrezia Borgia and the Duke of Ferrara. The long, straw-coloured strands of pasta were said to have been inspired by the bride's flowing locks.

▶▶ **Bergamo**   78D2

Bergamo is in two parts: an old hill town, Bergamo Alta, and the more modern Bergamo Bassa. Most of the sights cluster in Bergamo Alta's Piazza Vecchia and the adjoining Piazza del Duomo. The French writer Stendhal thought the Piazza Vecchia 'the most beautiful place on earth ... the prettiest I have ever seen'. Gracious medieval buildings fill both squares, notably the Romanesque church of **Santa Maria Maggiore**▶▶, its riotously over-decorated interior distinguished by a magnificent wooden choir. Flanking the church is the even more impressive **Cappella Colleoni**▶▶▶, designed in 1476 for the Venetian *condottiere* Bartolomeo Colleoni by G A Amadeo (also responsible for Pavia's Certosa, see page 91). Its ceiling frescoes, by Tiepolo, depict the life of John the Baptist. Nearby, see also the **Baptistery**▶, and climb to the **Cittadella**▶ for fine views over the town.

Walk towards Bergamo Bassa on Via Pignolo to take in the **Accademia Carrara**▶▶▶, one of northern Italy's most important – and least-known – art galleries. Many of the greatest Italian masters are represented (Botticelli, Titian, Raphael), as well as other European 'greats'.

▶▶▶ **Bologna**   79B4

Capital of Emilia-Romagna, wealthy Bologna is known for its cuisine, its left-leaning politics, Italy's oldest university, and its mellow-bricked palaces and porticoes. It centres on Piazza Maggiore and Piazza del Nettuno, home to Giambologna's 1556 Fontana del Nettuno, the medieval Palazzo Comunale and **San Petronio**▶▶▶, one of Italy's greatest Gothic churches (note its portal in particular, by the Sienese sculptor Jacopo della Quercia). The nearby **Museo Archeologico**▶ has a wide-ranging collection, best seen in conjunction with the **Archiginnasio**▶▶, part of the city's original medieval university.

No trip to the city is complete without climbing the leaning Torre degli Asinelli, but leave time also for the **Pinacoteca Nazionale**▶▶, with its important collection including Raphael's famous *Ecstasy of St Cecilia*; **San Giacomo Maggiore**▶▶ for its Bentivoglio chapel; the Gothic church of San Francesco; Santo Stefano, a group of ancient churches; and the art-crammed **San Domenico**▶▶▶, with the Arca di San Domenico, the saint's sarcophagus, bearing sculpted decoration by Nicola Pisano and Michelangelo.

▶ **Brescia**   78D3

Lombardy's second city is disappointing, its historic centre tarnished by hideous Fascist architecture, its sights scattered around chill modern streets. **Piazza della Loggia**▶ has a delicately festooned Loggia, a palace designed in part by Palladio and Sansovino (1492–1570). The nearby Piazza del Duomo has two cathedrals, one drab, the other – the **Rotonda**▶ – a more interesting 12th-century affair. Via dei Musei contains several Roman remains, the excellent **Museo Romano**▶ and the Museo dell'Età Cristiana, a collection of early church art. The **Pinacoteca Tosio-Martinengo**▶▶ offers the works of mainly local artists (plus Raphael, Tiepolo and Tintoretto). But the city's masterpiece – Titian's *Annunciation* – can be seen in the church of **San Nazario**▶▶.

▶ **Como** *78D1*

Como, on the shores of Lake Como, is part elegant resort, part industrial town. Parks and bustling cafés line its lakefront promenades, all a stone's throw from the splendid 15th-century Renaissance-Gothic **Duomo▶▶**. Other fragments of old Como include San Fedele (once the town's cathedral), at the heart of the medieval quarter, and the Porta Vittoria, the late 12th-century city gate. Brave the industrial quarter of Como to see **Sant'Abbondio▶▶**, a beautiful 11th-century church, and leave time to ride the funicular to hilltop Brunate for views of the lake. When you tire of Como and its lake, you can drive 20km west, to **Castiglione Olana▶▶▶**, to see the Gothic Collegiata, with its superlative frescoes by Giotto's pupil Masolino da Panicale, and his even finer frescoes in the Baptistery.

▶▶▶ **Como, Lago di (Lake Como)** *78D2*

Edged by plunging mountains, Lake Como is the most dramatic of the Italian lakes. True, its waters are often polluted and its many resorts thronged by British and German holidaymakers, but this said, its lush surroundings, its villas and gardens and the views make a visit essential. The best thing to do is to take a tour of the lake by boat (special passes available at Como allow you to stop off where the fancy takes you). **Bellagio▶▶▶** is by far the most picturesque village (see panel), though Cernobbio, Tremezzo and Menaggio all have their charms.

Bellagio
Lake Como's jewel has been called the prettiest village in Europe. From its promontory, it looks out over both arms of Lake Como, commanding peerless views, and is best approached by boat from either Como or Menaggio. Wander the cobbled streets, almost too quaint for their own good, and visit the gardens of the Villa Melzi and Villa Serbelloni. The apse and capitals of San Giacomo, a 12th-century church, both have some good carvings. From the village you can also visit Varenna, with the Villa Monastero and its lovely garden.

The death of Mussolini
Lake Como's beautiful surroundings were the incongruous setting for the capture and killing of Mussolini by partisans in 1945, when the Fascist leader was attempting to flee to Switzerland. He was caught at a roadblock near Mezzegra (just south of Tremezzo). The partisan leader, Waltger Audasio tried to shoot Mussolini, but the Duce's mistress Claretta threw herself on the gun, which jammed. Audasio then took his driver's gun and shot Claretta before complying with Mussolini's last request to shoot him in the chest.

The Neptune Fountain, or Fontana di Nettuno (1556) is the work of local sculptor, Giambologna

▶ **Cremona** 78C2

A quiet provincial town, Cremona is synonymous with violins, and in particular with Antonio Stradivari (1644–1737), the greatest violin-maker of all time. Needless to say the town honours its most famous son with a museum, the **Museo Stradivariano▶**, complemented by the adjoining Museo Civico, both crammed with violins and miscellaneous memorabilia (as well as displays devoted to Roman Cremona).

Violins apart, Cremona can seem a little stultifying: too quiet to hold your interest for long. The Romanesque **Duomo▶▶** and medieval **Piazza del Comune▶▶**, however, are superb, and in the **Torrazzo▶▶** the town boasts the tallest medieval tower in Italy (112m).

Faenza's distinctive ceramics have been celebrated for their beauty for centuries

▶ **Faenza** 79B5

You visit Faenza, an otherwise melancholy town, for one thing: the vast **Museo Internazionale delle Ceramiche▶▶**, one of the most comprehensive ceramic collections in Italy. The town's pottery (faïence-ware), with its characteristic blue and ochre colouring, has been famed throughout Europe for over 500 years. Today it is still produced and sold in numerous workshops. The museum displays not only indigenous ware, but also pottery from many periods and many countries – from Roman majolica and Renaissance sculpture to the modern ceramic art of Picasso, Matisse and Chagall.

84

The violins of Cremona

Cremona's Andrea Amati produced the first modern violin in 1566, handing down his techniques to his son Nicolò, who passed them in turn to his pupils, Antonio Stradivari and Giuseppe Guarneri. Stradivari's career spanned 68 years, during which time he made an estimated 1,200 violins, violas, cellos, harps, guitars and mandolins. He reputedly kept instruments in his bedroom for a month before completion. In this way, he claimed, his dreams imparted 'soul' to his creations.

Between 800 and 1,000 violins annually are still produced in Cremona's 60 workshops (*botteghe liutarie*). Europe's foremost violin-making school, La Bottega, is also here.

▶▶ **Ferrara** 79B4

In its day, Ferrara – a lovely and unvisited town – could claim one of Europe's most dynamic Renaissance courts. Its driving force was the Este family, a dynasty who ruled and rebuilt the city over several hundred years. Their dynastic seat, the **Castello Estense▶**, still lords it over the town, worth seeing for its decorated apartments and atmospheric dungeons. Another Este retreat, the **Palazzo Schifanoia▶▶**, is noteworthy for its Sala dei Mesi, a roomful of fine frescoes illustrating the 12 months. Other worthy paintings, including works by Bellini and Mantegna, reside in the gallery of the early Renaissance **Palazzo dei Diamanti▶▶**. The **Duomo▶▶** contains a jewel of a museum, the Museo del Duomo, full of precious works of art. Sights apart, pleasure is to be had simply walking Ferrara's streets – Via delle Volte and the distinct medieval and planned Renaissance quarters in particular.

▶▶▶ **Garda, Lago di (Lake Garda)** 78D3

Garda is the largest of the Italian Lakes, its landscapes divided between gentle plains in the south and tree-covered hills and mountains in the north. Its most popular spot is **Sirmione▶▶**, enchanting off-season, tourist-choked in summer. The beautifully situated castle called **Rocca Scaligera►** is the most memorable sight (great fun to explore). Out of town you should also see the **Grotte di Catullo►**, the ruins of a Roman spa scattered over a hillside of ancient olive trees.

Midway up the lake's eastern shore, stop off at **Punta di San Vigilio►►**, by common consent the lake's prettiest spot. After enjoying its views and cypress-filled gardens, move on to **Malcesine►**, one of Garda's more sedate and appealing villages. Like Sirmione, it too has an evocative castle, though more people plump for the cable car ride to the 2,000m summit of Monte Baldo for its views and wealth of hiking opportunities. It is known as the 'Garden of Italy' for its exceptional botanical variety.

Riva del Garda► is the lake's best-known resort, a young and lively spot, though its crowds and commercialism weigh against its undoubted prettiness. Near by, visit the 95m waterfall, Cascata del Varone. Moving round to the lake's less ravaged western shore, drive into the hills above Limone sul Garda for a tiny network of scenic roads (via Vesio Pieve and Tignale). Views from the church of Madonna di Monte Castello (near Tignale) are especially good. **Gardone Riviera►►** was once the lake's most fashionable resort and still retains much of its erstwhile elegance. Near by stands the unmissable **Il Vittoriale degli Italiani** (see panel). **Salò►**, too, is worth a stop, a nicely situated town with a fine Gothic cathedral.

►   Iseo, Lago di   78D2

One of the quieter, second division Italian Lakes, Iseo has little to see but shares its neighbours' romantic beauty and mountainous surroundings. The west shore is quieter, served by small resorts like Sarnico, Tavernola and Riva di Solto. **Monte Isola►►**, an island in the centre of the lake, is known for its panoramic views.

Poetic eccentricity
The extraordinary villa called Il Vittoriale was presented by Mussolini to Gabriele d'Annunzio, larger-than-life poet, soldier, socialite and aristocratic womaniser. The gift was ostensibly in recognition of d'Annunzio's patriotism, but was also designed to keep him quiet (his claim to have eaten dead babies can hardly have helped the Fascist cause). The poet transformed the villa into a kitsch palace, filling it with souvenirs of his military, literary and amatory accomplishments. Furnishings include an embalmed tortoise, a bath surrounded by 200 pieces of bric-à-brac and a World War I bi-plane.

85

Sirmione is one of the prettiest and most popular towns on Lake Garda

Walking in Lombardy

■ **The plains of Emilia-Romagna have little to offer the walker, but hikes to suit all abilities await in Lombardy's Lakes region, the Alpine foothills and mountain fastness of the Stelvio National Park.** ■

Lago di Como On Como's western shore try the walk that starts from the hamlet of Breglia above the lakeshore town of Menaggio. The trail reaches the *Rifugio Menaggio* after about an hour and a quarter and from here several trails lead into higher terrain. The best option (weather allowing), is the path to Monte Bregagno (2,107m), a breathtaking viewpoint.

Lago di Garda Monte Baldo on Lake Garda's eastern shore has several easily accessible high-level walks (take the cable car from Malcesine or minor roads into the mountains from the lakeshore). The best follows the mountain's main ridge, heading for the *Rifugio Telegrafo* (2,150m). To plan this and other local walks use the Kompass map *Lago di Garda-Monte Baldo* (No 102).

Parco Nazionale dello Stelvio Italy's largest national park has over 1,500km of marked trails. The classic walk for first-time visitors is along the Valle dello Zebrù, a spectacular valley due east of Bormio, a town on the park's western flanks. Immediately to the south, the parallel Valle dei Forni has a great walk to the *Rifugio Branca* from Forni, with magnificent views of the Cevedale glaciers (use Kompass map *Ortles–Cevedale* (No 72).

Practicalities Walking is best in the Alps from June to September: the season is longer in the Lakes, where snow on low ground is less persistent. Most of the area is well-mapped, the most comprehensive coverage being provided by the 1:50,000 Kompass series. Tabacco maps are better, but cover fewer areas. Both brands are widely available on the spot, and in major bookshops in the UK and abroad. Tourist offices often have guides to easier walks, particularly in the Lakes.

Malcesine's cable car offers an easier way to see the views of Lake Garda

▶▶▶ Lago Maggiore (Lake Maggiore) 78D1

You need to pick and choose what you see on Lake Maggiore. Much of the shore is flat and factory-pocked, the mountains are distant, and the towns crowded. At the same time the villas, lush gardens and vestigial 19th-century elegance of the lake's resorts continue to draw visitors every year.

Refined **Stresa▶▶**, though busy, is the best centre. An international music festival takes place here annually in late August. A cable car runs from the town to Monte Mottarone for stunning views. Pick up boats at Stresa for the **Isole Borromee▶▶▶**, an exquisite archipelago of islands (worth seeing if you see nothing else in the Lakes). **Isola Bella**'s villa and gardens make it the most visited of the group (see panel), but neither **Isola Pescatori▶▶** nor the quieter **Isola Madre▶▶▶** should be missed. The town of Cannobio is a good place to stay: it has little to see, but is well connected by buses and ferries to other points on the lake.

More intimate **Baveno▶** was once patronised by Queen Victoria. **Villa Taranto▶▶** near Verbania is the most famous of all the Lakes' botanical gardens. Resorts further north and on the lake's eastern (Lombardy) shore have little to recommend them other than tranquillity. The best are **Cannero Riviera▶**, Ghiffa, Cervo and **Angera▶**.

▶▶▶ Mantova (Mantua) 78C3

Once past Mantova's grim outskirts you can see why Aldous Huxley described it as the most romantic city in the world. Surrounded by lakes (it is sometimes known as *piccola Venezia* – little Venice), the city has an evocative skyline of ancient towers, and an historic centre of almost theatrical medieval perfection.

Star turn is the astounding **Palazzo Ducale▶▶▶**, home of the Gonzagas, one of the Renaissance's foremost dynasties. In its day it was the largest palace in Europe. When it was sacked in 1630 80 carriages were required to remove the two thousand works of art contained in its 500 rooms. Be sure to see the Camera degli Sposi and its Mantegna fresco cycle, the palace's real treasure. The family's summer residence, the **Palazzo Te▶▶▶**, with its wonderful Giulio Romano Frescoes, is also unmissable.

Mantua's highlights continue with **Piazza delle Erbe▶▶**, a lovely central square; **Sant'Andrea▶▶**, an overblown Renaissance church; the Rotonda, a half-ruined 11th-century church; and the Torre della Gabbia and Broletto, medieval prison and town hall respectively.

Top: Isola Bella
Above: neighbouring Borromean island, Isola Pescatori

Isola Bella
The most captivating of the Isole Borromee, Isola Bella was no more than a barren rock until the 17th century, when Count Carlo III Borromeo decided to convert it into a garden paradise for his wife, Isabella. The ravishing island is spoiled only by the artificial grottoes, kitsch statues and appallingly decorated villa – described by Robert Southey as 'one of the most costly efforts of bad taste in all Italy.'

Milan's magnificent Gothic cathedral

Milanese food

Milan's gastronomic specialities include *polenta*, a type of maize-based porridge, a staple of northern Italy – trendy today, but overrated. More mouthwatering are breaded cutlets, *cotolette alla milanese* – Wiener schnitzel by another name (a legacy of Milan's period under Austro-Hungarian rule). *Risotto alla milanese* is also common, traditionally made with saffron and broth. *Panettone*, a Milanese cake with fruit and raisins, is a Christmas speciality now eaten all over Italy.

Local wines

The closest wine zones to the city produce Oltrepò Pavese and San Colombano. From further afield look for Pino and Rosso di Franciacorte; the fine white, Lugana; the reds Groppello, Buttafuoco and Barbacarlo; and the wines from the Valtellina, a high Alpine valley – Grumello, Valgella and Sassella.

▶▶▶ **Milano (Milan)**   *78D2*

There is little *dolce vita* in Milan: busy and work-orientated, Italy's capital of fashion and high finance is a slick and business-like city – and firmly European in outlook (a 'southern suburb of Paris', according to some, in contrast to Rome – a 'northern suburb of Cairo'). Pollution is a constant plague, while corruption scandals in the early Nineties rocked the city's political hierarchy. Modern in appearance as well as outlook, Milan is perhaps less fun to wander in than some cities – though its main sights are as compelling as any in the country.

The finest of these is the **Duomo▶▶▶**, Italy's largest Gothic building, and Europe's third largest church (after St Peter's and Seville cathedral). The exterior's forest of spires and intricate decoration – a 'poem in marble,' said Mark Twain – compensates for a disappointing interior. The highlight is a trip to the roof, a magical world of spires and turrets, with views – smog allowing – that extend as far as the Matterhorn.

West of the Duomo, stroll through the **Galleria Vittorio Emanuele**, a Belle Epoque arcade, to reach La Scala, Milan's famous opera house, and then Via Manzoni, one of the city's most fashionable and frenetic streets. Part way up it stands the **Museo Poldi Pezzoli▶▶**, a collection of antiques and paintings, the best of which are in the Salone Dorato (Golden Room). Antonio Pollaiuolo's *Portrait of a Young Woman* is here, one of Italy's most renowned portraits, together with works by Raphael, Mantegna, Botticelli, Giovanni Bellini and Piero della Francesca.

For the city's single most famous work of art, however, you need to trek across the city to the church of **Santa Maria delle Grazie▶▶▶**. Partly designed by Bramante, the church is a Renaissance tour-de-force, though few people give it more than a passing glance. Most are more keen to see Leonardo da Vinci's *The Last Supper*, on a wall of Santa Maria's old refectory (see page 90).

The colossal size of the **Castello Sforzesco** makes it the city's principal landmark after the **Duomo▶▶▶**. Built by the Viscontis, Milan's medieval overlords, and enlarged by their successors, the Sforzas, it became the seat of one of Europe's leading courts of the Renaissance period. Now its rambling inner courtyards house two middling art galleries: the **Pinacoteca▶▶** and **Museo d'Arte Antica▶▶**. The latter's collection is a mish-mash of sculpture, dominated by Michelangelo's unfinished last work, the *Pietà Rondanini*. The former includes a fresco cycle of scenes from Boccaccio's *Decameron*, a plethora of medieval *objets d'art*, and works by Mantegna, Crivelli, Giovanni Bellini and Filippo Lippi.

Ten minutes away is the **Accademia Brera▶▶▶**, one of Italy's top galleries, so rich it probably requires several visits to avoid artistic indigestion. Among the feast of paintings are Mantegna's famous *Cristo Morto* and Veronese's equally well-known *Supper in the House of Simon*. Other titbits include Raphael's *Marriage of the Virgin*, Piero della Francesca's *Pala di Urbino*, Giovanni Bellini's superlative *Pietà*, and works by Caravaggio, Carpaccio, Tintoretto, El Greco, Rembrandt and many more.

For still more art, visit the **Palazzo dell' Ambrosiana▶▶**, home to a fabulous 17th-century library, but of more general interest for a distinguished art collection which includes Botticelli's *Tondo* and *Madonna del Baldacchino*, Caravaggio's *Fruit Basket* (Italy's first still-life), Giorgione's *Page*; Leonardo's *Portrait of a Musician*; and the cartoon for Raphael's *School of Athens*.

If looking at pictures begins to pall, you could make for the most eminent of Milan's many churches, **Sant'Ambrogio▶▶▶**, founded in 379 by St Ambrose, Milan's first bishop and the city's patron saint. Most of the present structure dates from the 11th century. Inside, its chief treasures are a handsome pulpit, one of Italy's finest Romanesque works, the apse's 11th-century mosaic, and the sanctuary's 9th-century gold and jewel-studded ciborium.

Shopping
Milan is tops for high fashion, accessories and luxury goods. The big-name shops cluster in the so-called *Quadrilatero d'Oro* (Golden Quadrangle) – the area defined by Via Monte Napoleone, Via della Spiga, Via Borgo Spesso and Via Sant'Andrea. For more affordable prices you could do worse than visit *La Rinascente* in Piazza del Duomo, Milan's largest and oldest department store – and a city institution. Many of the glass-domed *gallerie* off Galleria Vittorio Emanuele have interesting, high quality shops.

89

High-class shopping in the Galleria Vittorio Emanuele

The Last Supper

■ **Asked to name the world's most famous paintings, many people would cite first the *Mona Lisa* and then perhaps another of Leonardo da Vinci's masterpieces – *The Last Supper*, painted in the refectory of Milan's Santa Maria delle Grazie.** ■

The search for Judas
The 16th-century art historian Giorgio Vasari tells us that the figure of Judas gave Leonardo great problems in the two years he worked on the painting. He scoured Milan's streets and prisons for models, casting around for someone with a face of sufficient venality. The result, said Vasari, was 'the very embodiment of treachery and inhumanity'.

90

Leonardo's vision of the beginning of Christ's agony is one of European art's best known images, yet in the flesh the faded and badly deteriorated surface of *L'Ultima Cena (The Last Supper)* makes for chastening viewing (Aldous Huxley called it 'the saddest painting in the world'). For all its decay, it remains a startling work, capturing the moment Christ announces He will be betrayed by one of His disciples.

Leonardo chose to apply oil and tempera to a dry surface, rather than the accepted fresco method of painting pigment on to wet plaster. This allowed him greater flexibility of tone and colour, but moisture soon began to corrode the painting. Over the centuries the fresco suffered further from cack-handed attempts at restoration. At one point, Santa Maria's monks gave up on the project altogether – and whitewashed part of the painting. On another occasion, Napoleonic troops billeted in the refectory used the fresco for target practice. In 1943 a bomb hit the building, destroying everything but *The Last Supper*.

Modern restoration techniques are now attempting to turn back the years. Amazingly, many of the fresco's details are still vivid, gestures and expressions captured in almost photographic detail. Look for the figure of Doubting Thomas and his raised finger; the hangdog profile of Philip, arms folded, fearful that he may be the betrayer; or Peter, partly blocked by the figure of Judas who is hurrying forward with his 30 pieces of silver.

The Last Supper
under restoration

▶ Modena
79B4

A long time rival to Bologna, Modena is a northern city in the classic mould: provincial and quietly prosperous, its outskirts industrial, its tight centre a medieval delight. Pride of place goes to the **Duomo▶▶**, a 12th-century Romanesque masterpiece, known for its tribuna (rood screen) and a lurching campanile, the **Torre Ghirlandina▶**. In the maze of appealing old streets near by, make a point of visiting the Palazzo dei Musei, home to three museums: the Biblioteca Estense, its prize exhibit the *Bibbio Borso*, a sumptuously decorated medieval Bible; the Museo d'Arte Mediovale e Moderna e Etnologia and the Galleria Estense, a gallery of paintings, many by local Renaissance masters.

▶▶ Orta, Lago di
78D1

Lake Orta's tranquil beauty is the perfect antidote to the commercialism and tainted charms of the larger Italian lakes. Its main centre, **Orta-San Giulio▶▶**, is a peaceful small town, a base for boat trips out to the **Isola San Giulio▶▶**. This is a dream of an island, its hamlet capital dominated by a brilliant white Romanesque church, the Basilica di San Giulio.

Around the lake the best of the gardens is the **Villa Junker▶** near Gozzano. For wonderful views, walk up the Sacro Monte above Orta San Giulio, or drive to Madonna del Sasso and Quarna, perched above the lake's western shore.

▶▶▶ Parma
78B3

Italy's most prosperous town, Parma is a monument to good living, with fine food (it is the home of Parma ham and Parmesan cheese), an excellent opera house and a wealth of elegant cafés and exclusive shops. The **Duomo▶▶▶** is one of the country's finest Lombard-Romanesque churches, distinguished by the 16th-century painter Correggio's great dome frescoes of the *Assumption of the Virgin*. Near by, the 12th-century octagonal **Baptistery▶▶▶** contains some of the most expressive Romanesque sculptures in Italy, a series of reliefs on the exterior and 12 carvings inside depicting the months of the year. Behind the Duomo, **San Giovanni Evangelista▶▶▶** boasts more superlative frescoes by Correggio. The Galleria Nazionale, the antiquities museum and the extraordinary Teatro Farnese are all housed in the vast **Palazzo della Pilotta▶▶**.

▶ Pavia
78C1

A neat day trip from Milan, Pavia – where kings and emperors were crowned in the Middle Ages – has a sleepy collection of medieval streets, with something of interest at every turn. Most of the sights in the city, however, are overshadowed by the nearby **Certosa di Pavia▶▶▶**, one of the most dazzling monasteries in Europe, set in a former hunting ground of the Visconti family and rich in Renaissance and baroque art. Nevertheless, do not miss two outstanding churches; **San Michele▶▶▶** and **San Pietro in Ciel d'Oro▶▶**, both eye-catching Romanesque masterpieces. The austere 14th-century **Castello Visconteo▶** also houses a trio of modest art and archaeology museums.

Ferrari
One of the world's most famous cars is made just outside Modena near the village of Maranello. Enzo Ferrari founded the Ferrari factory in 1945. Today it produces around 2,500 cars a year. Another famous marque, Maserati, also has a plant near the city.

91

Your table is ready in Parma's Piazza Garibaldi

The Empress Theodora
The career of Justinian's wife Theodora – featured in the mosaics of San Vitale in Ravenna – would make headlines in today's popular newspapers. Accounts of her life tell of a youth spent as a child prostitute and circus performer, followed by spells as a courtesan and performer in live sex shows. Something of a stir ran around court circles when Justinian picked her as Empress, a ripple of scandal that meant he had to wait until his disapproving mother's death before he could marry. Their reign, by all accounts, was one of rampant corruption.

Ravenna: Basilica di San Vitale

► **Piacenza** 78C2

Unassuming Piacenza stands in the shadow of better known cities like Parma and Cremona. Few people visit its sleepy medieval centre, still laid out on the gridiron pattern of the old Roman colony (the city marked the end of the old Roman road, the *Via Aemilia*). Piazza dei Cavalli, the central square, is dominated by the crenellated **Palazzo del Comune►►**, the council chamber of the medieval city. At its centre there stand two equestrian statues, frequently lauded as some of Italy's finest baroque sculptures.

►►► **Ravenna** 79B5

Most people come to Ravenna expecting only mosaics (see opposite page), and are surprised to find as appealing a small town as any in Italy. True, the mosaics are virtually the only things to see, but the centre's tangle of streets are a pleasure to wander. You might also spend a happy hour in **Piazza del Popolo►**, a square filled with outdoor cafés and noble medieval *palazzi*. Close by, be sure to visit the **Tomba di Dante►**, burial place of the famous medieval poet. He died in Ravenna in 1381 after being exiled from Florence, his home town.

► **Rimini** 149D5

Rimini is nirvana for beach enthusiasts who like their resorts big and brash (none come bigger – this is Europe's largest seaside town). Crammed with Italian families, and German and Scandinavian students, it is a by-word for sun, sea and sex, for dusk to dawn nightlife, and for huge, heavily commercialised beaches. Given all this, it remains surprisingly unsleazy – though it is not the place for quiet sunbathing. Smaller resorts in a similar mould run all the way down Italy's Adriatic coast.

The Mosaics of Ravenna

■ **Ravenna boasts the finest Byzantine mosaics in the world outside Istanbul, a legacy of its role as the capital of the Roman Empire during the 5th century. Its history made it a meeting place of eastern and western artistic trends.** ■

Honorius moved the seat of Empire to Ravenna around AD 403, prompted by Rome's stagnation and the town's proximity to *Classis*, the Romans' main port on the Adriatic coast. The city boomed and continued to thrive after the Empire's fall, first under the barbarian leaders Odoacer and Theodoric, and later as a Byzantine vassal ruled by the Emperor Justinian.

The main mosaics Far and away the most breathtaking mosaics – 'monuments to unageing intellect', in the words of W B Yeats – are to be found in the **Basilica di San Vitale**, a magnificent Byzantine-style church (built in 547) in the city centre. Two main strands can be identified in the mosaic panels, the first the obviously Byzantine scenes depicting Justinian, Theodora and their court, the second the more classically inspired episodes taken from the Old Testament. Both sets of mosaics date from as early as the 6th century.

Across the grassy piazza outside the church stands the **Mausoleo di Galla Placidia** (see

panel), a tiny chapel completely studded with marvellous mosaics of ethereal blues and glittering golds – one of the most intimate and most impressive buildings in Italy. The **Museo Nazionale**, near by, also boasts a fine collection of Roman, Byzantine and early Christian mosaics.

Galla Placidia
Galla Placidia was one of the most remarkable women in ancient Rome's history. Daughter of Theodosius, the father of Emperor Honorius, she was kidnapped when the Goths sacked Rome. Almost immediately she married Ataulfo, one of her kidnappers – who was promptly assassinated. She then sought refuge with her half-brother Honorius. Forced to marry Constantius, a Roman general, she contrived to have her husband made joint emperor with Honorius. Widowed again, she had her son, Valentinian III (aged six), made emperor (with herself as Regent). She died and was buried in Rome in AD 450, leaving open the question of who instigated her mausoleum in Ravenna.

93

Peacock mosaic in San Vitale

... and the rest The church of **Sant'Apollinare Nuovo** contains two further mosaic cycles. Both show processions, one of virgins and the other of martyrs, both gliding towards the altar against a beautifully evoked background of gold and green-leafed palms. On a smaller scale, the 6th-century **Oratorio di Sant'Andrea** contains mosaics from two eras; one sequence from the building's period as a Roman bath-house, the other a cycle executed when the building became a Christian baptistery.

Five kilometres from Ravenna, the church of **Sant'Apollinare in Classe** is about all that survives of ancient *Classis*. Consecrated in 549, its mosaics are as impressive as any in the city, particularly those in the apse of *The Transfiguration of Christ*.

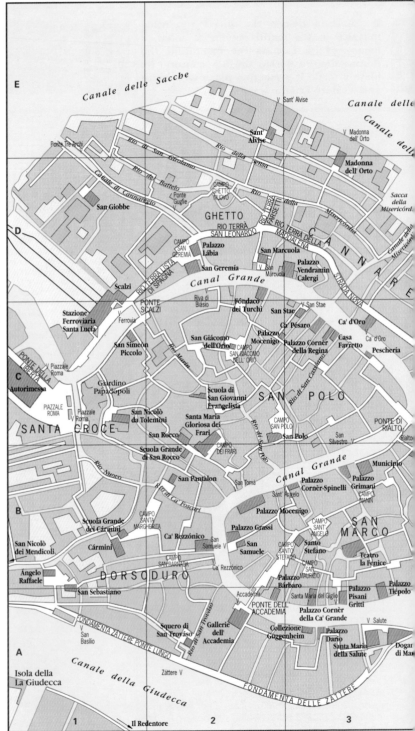

VENÉZIA - SESTIERI

Canale delle Sacche

PONTE DELLA LIBERTA

Navi

Nuova Isola
del Tronchetto

CANNAREGIO

Canal Grande

Stazione
Ferroviaria
Santa Lucia

SANTA CROCE

SAN POLO

DORSODURO

SAN MARCO

CASTELLO

Canale di Fusina

Canale della Giudecca

LA GIUDECCA

Isola di
San Gióryio
Maggiore

Murano

Burano

Canale delle Navi

Isola di
San Michele

Canale delle Fondamente Nuove

Isola di
San Pietro

Canale di San Marco

Isola
di
Sant'
Elena

Lido

0   1 km

Isola di
San
Michele

Cimitero

Fondamente Nuove

FONDAMENTE NUOVE

Gesuiti
(Santa Maria
Assunta)

Rio dei Gesuiti

V Fondamente Nuove

0   100   200   300 m

CAMPO DEI
SANTI
APOSTOLI

Santa Maria
dei Mirácoli

Fóndaco dei
Tedeschi

Santa Maria
Formosa

San Salvatore

Monumento
a Colleoni

Rio dei Mendicanti

Santi Giovanni e
Páolo (San Zanipolo)

CAMPO
SANTI GIOVANNI
E PAOLO

CAMPO
SANTA MARIA
FORMOSA

Palazzo Querini-
Stampália
e Pinacoteca

CASTELLO

V Ospedale Civile

Rio di San Giustina

San Francesco
della Vigna

Celestia

Scuola di San Gióргio
degli Schiavoni

Torre
dell'Orológio

Procuratie
Vecchie

PIAZZA
SAN MARCO

Campanile

Procuratie
Nuovo

Museo Civico Correr

Giardini
ex Reali

V San Marco

Basilica di
San Marco

Palazzo
Ducale

RIVA DEGLI SCHIAVONI

San Zaccaria

Ponte
dei Sospiri

San Giorgio
dei Greci

CAMPO
SAN ZACCARIA

Prigioni

Santa Maria
della Pietà

Rio della Pietà

San Zaccaria

Riva
Schiavoni

CAMPO
BANDIERA
E MORO

Santa Maria San Giovanni
della Pietà in Brágora

Arsenale

San
Martino

Museo
Stórico
Navále

Arsenale

San Blágio

Bacino di
San Marco

Canale di San Marco

Punta della
Dogana

San Giórgio V

San Giórgio
Maggiore

Isola di
San
Giórgio
Maggiore

San Pietro
di Castello

Teatro Verde

4   5

CITY HIGHLIGHTS ◀◀◀◀◀

BASILICA DI SAN MARCO
see page 100

SANTI GIOVANNI E PAOLO
see page 101

**SANTA MARIA GLORIOSA DEI
FRARI** *see page 102*

SAN ZACCARIA
see page 103

ACCADEMIA *see page 106*

PALAZZO DUCALE
see page 107

**SCUOLA GRANDE DI SAN
ROCCO** *see page 108*

**SCUOLA DI SAN GIORGIO
DEGLI SCHIAVONI**
see page 108

PONTE DI RIALTO *see page 109*

CANAL GRANDE *see page 110*

95

Chiesa della Salute

Venice (Venezia) Not everyone falls in love with Italy's most idiosyncratic city. Its decay can seem sinister, its crowds unendurable, its canals dark and its alleys claustrophobic. Yet there are few people who remain unmoved by it. No matter how you picture the city, be prepared for the reality to be stranger – and probably lovelier – than you imagined. It is no use pretending that you can do justice to its treasury of sights on a short visit. Most of the time it is best simply to wander at random, for Venice is as much a city of atmosphere as of museums and monuments.

A word of warning Visit Venice in the frenetic months of July and August and you risk coming away disappointed. Venice has no real off-season, but during these months the city becomes a travesty (crowds, high prices, packed hotels). Although it sounds like heresy, therefore, give careful thought to taking a room outside Venice in high summer – perhaps in Padua, Treviso or Verona – and making several day-trips by train. Leave cars behind – parking is a nightmare and long queues develop on the causeway from the mainland. Rail services are excellent, and link directly to the heart of the city. Follow this advice and it will save you money, hassle and time.

The city's origins The Venetian lagoon was probably first settled around the time of Christ. More sustained settlement took place during the barbarian invasions (when the lagoon became a safe haven). By the 6th century a loose confederation of communities had formed, initially under the firm hand of Byzantium (with its rule based in Ravenna), but by 726 under the autonomous control of an elected leader – the Doge. Trading links with the east soon brought great wealth, particularly during the Crusades, and by the 13th century the city owned territories stretching to the Black Sea (a domain 'one quarter and one half quarter of the Roman Empire'). These included a sizeable mainland empire (present day Veneto and beyond).

Arriving

Venice's main Marco Polo airport is at Tessera (13km), linked by ATVO buses (25 minutes) to Piazzale Roma (the end of the causeway joining Venice to the mainland). Treviso airport, 30km north of Venice, is the main airport for charter flights. Cars must be parked in the multi-storey car parks in Piazzale Roma or the Tronchetto (500m away). From here you must walk or take a water bus (*vaporetto*) to the rest of the city.

Conflict Venice's prestige inevitably led to conflict with the papacy and other leading European powers. The League of Cambrai, formed in 1508, united the major European powers against the city, an alliance the city withstood, but only at the cost of sacked territories and an exhausted treasury. In the east, the Ottoman empire had been an increasing threat since early in the 15th century. Even at sea, Venice faced competition, the opening up of the Americas having tilted world trade away from Venice's traditional eastern markets.

Decadence and decline The Sack of Rome in 1527 left most of Italy except Venice under the control of Charles V. Stranded on the country's periphery, the city declined, its fall hastened by the Turks, who continued to nibble away at its overseas empire. Napoleon demolished the moribund state in 1797, leaving the city to pursue its own decadent devices (casinos, brothels and endless festivities). It passed to the Austrians, who in moving their trade through Trieste, further quashed any hope of Venice's re-emergence. In this century tourism has developed apace (to 20 million visitors a year), as have the industrial towns of Mestre and Marghera on the mainland (responsible for reducing the city's population from 180,000 in 1945 to its present level of around 70,000).

Orientation Venice has six districts (*sestieri*), hundreds of canals, thousands of streets and *campi* and just one 'piazza' (Piazza San Marco). Addresses include the name of the relevant *sestieri* (see map, pages 94–5). The main canal, the Canal Grande, has only three bridges (at the railway station – the Scalzi – the Rialto and the Accademia). Often the best way of finding your way back to Piazza San Marco, the heart of Venice, is by *vaporetto* – so carry a map of the stops and routes.

Tourist information
The main tourist office is at the Casino del Caffè (tel: 041/522 6356), close to Harry's Bar on the waterfront by the Giardinetti Reali (2 minutes' walk from St Mark's). There are smaller and busier offices at Piazzale Roma (tel: 041/529 8711); Santa Lucia station (tel: 041/529 8711); Marco Polo airport (tel: 041/541 5887), and the Tronchetto car park. American Express is at Salizzada San Moisè 1471 (tel: 041/520 0844), useful for foreign exchange and a variety of organised guided tours.

Stroll – Riva degli Schiavoni
Running along the waterfront from the Palazzo Ducale, this is one of the most popular strolls in the city. Despite the crowds and occasional commercialism, it still makes an outstanding walk – particularly at sunset.

97

The Canal Grande

■ **Although Venetian painting followed the broad currents of Italian art, it always plotted a distinct course, influenced by ideas from East and West, and distinguished by an emphasis on colour, texture and the use of light to evoke atmosphere (in contrast to Florence's preoccupations with structure and perspective). The result was an artistic patrimony barely equalled by any city in the world. ■**

Sculpture

Venice differed from central Italy in its lack of indigenous sculptors or sculptural masterpieces (the Colleoni statue – see page 109 – is a notable exception and was sculpted by a Florentine, Verrocchio). Instead, the medium tended to be an integral part of larger architectural projects. Its principal exponents were Jacopo Sansovino, the Republic's foremost architect (who came from Rome in 1527), and Alessandro Vittoria, a member of Sansovino's workshop, who dominated Venetian sculpture in the latter part of the 16th century.

Where to see – Giovanni Bellini

The Accademia contains several Madonnas, a series of allegorical panels and a pair of altarpieces by Bellini. Elsewhere in the city the best of his work is to be found in San Zaccaria, San Pietro (Murano), Santa Maria Gloriosa dei Frari, Madonna dell'Orto and San Zanipolo.

Generations have tried – and failed – to find a precise meaning in Giorgione's mysterious painting, The Tempest

Byzantine and Gothic Venice's earliest artistic influences came from the east, fostered by the city's close political and commercial links with Byzantium. The greatest evidence of this is the Basilica di San Marco. Byzantine elements continue in the Gothic splendour of the Ca' d'Oro, and in the 14th-century paintings of Paolo Veneziano. In time the Orient's influence was married to the Gothic by Lorenzo Veneziano and Michele Giambono.

Early Renaissance painters The Renaissance was slow to take hold in Venice, but the city's artists – with a distinctive use of colour – moulded Renaissance tenets into a style of painting that was distinctly Venetian.

Some of Venice's most celebrated artists belonged to families that produced generations of painters. The first was the Vivarini family: Antonio (c 1419–80), his brother Bartolomeo (c 1430–91) and son Alvise (c 1445–1505). The most prominent were the Bellinis: father Jacopo (c 1400–70), a pupil of Gentile da Fabriano, and sons

Venetian art

The Miracle of the Cross on San Lorenzo Bridge *by Gentile Bellini, in the Galleria dell'Accademia*

The Istoria
Narrative fresco cycles, or *istorie*, were a distinctive part of the Venetian Renaissance. Although often concerned with lives of the saints, they also wove depictions of contemporary Venetian life into their narrative thread. Only three of the 10 cycles commissioned between 1475 and 1525 survive: the Accademia has two; Carpaccio's *St Ursula* and the *Miracles of the Relic of the True Cross* (executed by five artists, including Carpaccio and Gentile Bellini). The third, Carpaccio's *St George and St Jerome*, is in the Scuola di San Giorgio degli Schiavoni.

Gentile (*c* 1429–1507) and Giovanni (*c* 1430–1516), the latter among the greatest of all the Venetian painters. Gentile is known for his *istoria*, or narrative cycle, (see panel). Another artist involved in the genre was Vittore Carpaccio (*c* 1465–1526), famous for the colour and detail he brought to paintings depicting the Venice of his day.

High Renaissance Two pupils of Giovanni Bellini marked Venice's artistic zenith. Giorgione (1475–1510) is one of art's most mysterious figures. His poetic paintings are as enigmatic as his short life, their strange, unsettling qualities exemplified by *The Tempest* (in the Accademia). Tiziano Vecelli, known as Titian (*c* 1485–1576), is among the finest painters of any age, and is renowned for a robust style, brilliant colour and technical skill.

Initially in thrall to Titian, Tintoretto (1518–94) became his chief competitor. His dynamic paintings were more vivid and concerned with show than Titian's, where the sensuousness is expressive of an event's inner drama. Paolo Veronese (1528–88), by contrast, is less turbulent, his works harmonious blends of warmth, light and colour. Both artists worked on huge canvases, often playing visual games – juggling viewpoints and perspective – as they strove for drama and effect.

Self-portrait by Titian

Baroque and rococo Artistically, the 17th century was a fallow period, dominated by the baroque, a largely Roman preoccupation. In the 18th century, though, Venetian artists adopted rococo, a softer and riper style whose approach emphasised sensuality for its own sake. It was taken up by Sebastiano Ricci, Gian Battista Tiepolo and his son, Gian Domenico Tiepolo. They produced brilliant, almost decadent works, their trademark that of so many artists in Venice – dazzling use of colour. Venice's artistic last gasp came with Antonio Canal, called Canaletto (1697–1768) and Pietro Longhi (1702–85); both painted often frivolous or idealised portraits of Venice itself.

Where to see – Titian
Despite his long life and prodigious output, Titian is badly represented in his home city (many of his works were stolen by Napoleon and now form the cornerstone of the Louvre's fine collection). In Venice his greatest works are in Santa Maria Gloriosa dei Frari, the Accademia and Santa Maria della Salute.

Basilica di San Marco

■ A quite literally glittering repository of art and an extravagant mixture of differing architectural styles, the Basilica di San Marco is one of Europe's most exotic cathedrals as well as being Venice's single most famous building. ■

Four Horses
San Marco's most famous statues, the four gilded bronze horses that stood above the portal, are now kept inside the basilica to protect them from atmospheric pollution (the present incumbents are copies). No-one is certain whether the originals are 4th-century BC Hellenistic bronzes, or statues from a Roman triumphal arch cast seven centuries later. They were stolen from Constantinople by the Venetians during the Crusades.

The Pala d'Oro
Made in Constantinople in 976, this gold altar panel is encrusted with 300 sapphires, 300 emeralds, 400 garnets, 15 rubies, 1,300 pearls and countless lesser stones, figures, roundels and enamel plaques.

Origins The basilica was conceived to house the body of St Mark, the city's patron saint, stolen from Alexandria by Venetian merchants in 828. Completed in its basic form in 1094, the church was then embellished over nine centuries, creating a unique blend of Islamic, Byzantine and European art and architecture. The decoration is completely overwhelming – so it is best to pick your way through it selectively.

The exterior The most noteworthy details of the exuberantly decorated exterior are the Romanesque carvings of the main portal. In particular, look closely at the central arch's *Months and the Seasons* (1225) and the outer arch's *Trades of Venice*. The mosaics above the doorways describe the story of St Mark's abduction and the arrival of his body in the city (1260).

The interior Beyond the vestibule, or narthex, the main body of the basilica is dominated by 4,000 square metres of mosaics – a vast kaleidoscope of colour and Biblical anecdote dating mostly from the 12th and 14th centuries. Be sure also to see the Treasury, and its collection of gold and silverware; the rood screen (1394); the 10th-century pulpits; the icon known as the *Madonna di Nicopeia*; and – most important of all – the famous Pala d'Oro (see panel).

Part of the flamboyant façade of San Marco

Churches

All the churches described are outstanding, but if you are short of time the top three are the Basilica di San Marco, Santi Giovanni e Paolo (San Zanipolo) and Santa Maria Gloriosa (I Frari).

▶▶▶ Basilica di San Marco 95B4
Piazza San Marco
Venice's cathedral and finest church is most visitors' first port of call (see opposite page).

▶▶ Campanile di San Marco 95B4
Piazza San Marco
Venice's tallest building rises 99m above Piazza San Marco, offering panoramic views over the city, the lagoon and – on clear days – the distant Dolomites. The original tower collapsed in 1902, but was faithfully rebuilt over the next 10 years. At its base stands the beautifully decorated loggetta▶▶, built 1537–49 by Jacopo Sansovino.

▶▶ Madonna dell'Orto 94D3
Cannaregio
Tintoretto was a parishioner of this little church in the north of the city (and is buried here). Several splendid paintings by him decorate the walls, including *The Presentation of the Virgin* (in the right aisle), and *The Last Judgement* and *The Adoration of the Golden Calf* (both in the chancel). Other major paintings include Cima da Conegliano's *St John the Baptist* (first chapel on the right).

▶▶▶ San Giorgio Maggiore 95A4
Isola di San Giorgio Maggiore
This is one of Palladio's two Venetian masterpieces (the other is Il Redentore). The church occupies its own small island, the views from its courtyard and campanile some of the most celebrated in the city. The marvellous if austere interior is the setting for two Tintoretto masterpieces, *The Last Supper* and *Shower of Manna,* and his *Deposition* is in the Cappella dei Morti (right of the choir).

▶▶ San Giovanni in Bragora 95B5
Campo Bandiera e Moro, Castello
Vivaldi was once the organist in this Gothic church, rebuilt in 1475, whose paintings include the *Baptism of Christ* by Cima da Conegliano, the *Risen Christ* by Alvise Vivarini, and Bartolomeo Vivarini's lovely *Madonna.*

▶▶▶ Santi Giovanni e Paolo (San Zanipolo) 95C4
Campo Santi Giovanni e Paolo, Castello
Venice's largest church (built by the Dominicans in the 14th and 15th centuries) is renowned both for its sheer size and for the tombs of the 25 doges that are buried here. The best are the tombs of Pietro Mocenigo (on the entrance wall) and Michele Morosini (on the right of the chancel). Some other outstanding works of art include a polyptych by Giovanni Bellini, *St Vincent Ferrer,* and an altarpiece, *St Antony and Supplicants* by Lorenzo Lotto. The ceiling panels of the Cappella Rosario are by Veronese.

The imposing bulk of Santi Giovanni e Paolo (San Zanipolo in the Venetian dialect)

101

VENICE

▶▶ **Santa Maria Assunta (Gesuiti)**   95D4
near the Fondamente Nuove, Cannaregio
Fronted by a soaring façade, and obviously built to impress, this Jesuit church (1714–29) has a quite awe-inspiring interior, its pillars, pulpits and floor draped in what appears to be swathes of green and white damask. All the hangings, however, even down to the tassels and frills, are made from the most delicately carved marble.

▶▶▶ **Santa Maria Gloriosa dei Frari (I Frari)** 94C2
Campo dei Frari, San Polo
Known as I Frari (The Friars) after its Franciscan founders, this cavernous church is a treasury of exceptional paintings and sculpture. Its main glories are three of the greatest paintings in Italian art: Titian's *Assumption of the Virgin* (behind the high altar); his *Madonna di Ca'Pesaro* (second altar of the left aisle); and Giovanni Bellini's sublime *Madonna and Child with Saints* (in the sacristy). Elsewhere the church is loaded with paintings and sculptures that could occupy you for an hour or more. They include works by Donatello, Antonio Canova, Sansovino, Bartolomeo Vivarini and many more.

▶▶ **Santa Maria dei Miracoli**   95C4
Campo dei Miracoli, Cannaregio
One of the most exquisite small churches in Venice, the Miracoli is a miniature masterpiece of classical architecture. Elegant and refined in exterior form, its interior contains some of the city's most intricate decorative sculpture.

▶▶▶ **Santa Maria della Salute**   94A3
Dorsoduro
Salute means health, and this church was built as thanks for the city's deliverance from the plague of 1630, when 45,000 Venetians died. (A similar pledge 54 years earlier had resulted in the building of Palladio's Redentore.) Built on 100,000 wooden piles, the church occupies a prime position on the Grand Canal, making it one of the city's great landmarks. The sacristy contains several paintings by Titian and Tintoretto's *Marriage at Cana.*

▶▶ **San Pantalon**   94B2
Campo San Pantalon, Dorsoduro
A shortage of money left San Pantalon with an unfinished façade, a shortfall for which the interior more than compensates. Its ceiling – the city's most melodramatic – contains some 60 panels depicting a mass ascent into Heaven: *The Martyrdom and Apotheosis of San Pantalon.* It was painted by Antonio Fumiani between 1680 and 1704. The church's smaller paintings include Veronese's last work, *San Pantalon Healing a Boy*, and Antonio Vivarini's *Coronation of the Virgin.*

▶▶ **San Salvatore**   95B4
Campo San Salvatore, San Marco
A noted Renaissance church, San Salvatore contains several tombs, including that of Caterina Cornaro (see Asolo, page 118), and a pair of paintings by Titian; an *Annunciation* (right-hand wall) and a *Transfiguration* over the high altar.

*Marble drapery in
Santa Maria Assunta*

Il Redentore
Leading Italian architect
Andrea Palladio designed
only two churches in
Venice. One was San
Giorgio Maggiore (see
page 101), the other Il
Redentore, commissioned
in 1576 by the Senate to
mark the end of a plague.
Its prominent position on
the Giudecca and eye-
catching façade make it
one of the city's landmarks,
best seen across the water
from Dorsoduro.

San Stae
San Stae is close to a
vaporetto stop on the
Grand Canal, and at the
heart of a neighbourhood
of tiny squares and narrow
canals that sees relatively
few tourists. Its statue-
filled baroque façade is
one of the Grand Canal's
most striking sights.

►►► San Sebastiano   94A1
Campo San Sebastiano, Dorsoduro
Newly restored (though not always open), San Sebastiano
belongs almost entirely to Paolo Veronese, who is buried
in the church and who left in it the greatest single collection of his paintings. The best are: three ceiling panels
depicting the *Life of St Esther*; two paintings in the sanctuary, *San Sebastian* and *St Mark and St Marcellian*; the
walls of the *barco* (nuns' gallery); the painted organ doors;
and the ceiling panels of the sacristy.

►► Santo Stefano   94B3
Campo Francesco Morosini, San Marco
As well as being a handsome, highly decorated church,
Santo Stefano is notable for its Gothic portal, its 'ship's
keel roof' (like an up-ended wooden hull) – one of only
two in the city – and a calm, airy interior whose sacristry
contains late works by Tintoretto.

►►► San Zaccaria   95B4
Campo San Zaccaria, Castello
Massive San Zaccaria is chock-full of paintings, the most
celebrated Giovanni Bellini's *Madonna and Four Saints*
(second altar on the left). It is worth paying the small
admission fee to see Tintoretto's *Birth of John the Baptist*
(in the Cappella di Sant'Atanasio). The Cappella di San
Tarasio has three composite altarpieces by Antonio
Vivarini and Giovanni d'Alemagna (1443).

Campo San Zaccaria
The square outside San
Zaccaria has a chequered
past. San Zaccaria itself
was built as a shrine for
Zaccharias, father of John
the Baptist, who is buried
under the second altar on
the right. The convent
alongside was once notorious for its licentiousness.
Most of the nuns were
reluctant internees, incar-
cerated because of
parental pressure or
because their fathers were
too poor to provide
dowries.

The Lagoon

■ **Scattered across the 1,300 square kilometres of Venice's lagoon (the *Laguna Veneta*) are some 40 islands, many of them deserted, others home to sights that merit as much attention as the city itself.** ■

Getting there
To reach the islands of the lagoon, take the *vaporetti* from Piazzale Roma or the Fondamente Nuove: line 1 and line 4, a summer-only service known as the *turistico*, cross to the Lido; line 52 goes to San Michele and Murano; line 12 from the Fondamente Nuove takes in Murano, Burano and Torcello.

Burano▶▶ While Burano's menfolk attended to the fishing, the island's women spent hours making the famous Burano and Venetian-point lace. Traditionally each woman specialised in a single stitch (there are seven in all), passing the lace between one another during its creation. Today the island's many craft shops sell local and factory-made foreign lace. Before leaving, visit the **Scuola dei Merletti**, an interesting lace museum and school, and allow time to wander the village's streets of neat and brightly painted houses.

Lido▶ Ranged over the lagoon's largest sandbank, the Lido is a fully fledged seaside resort, once Europe's most fashionable (Thomas Mann's *Death in Venice* is set there) but now a more downbeat – and in places dingy – conglomeration of big hotels, crowded beaches and murky water. It is, however, worth taking the *vaporetto* here from San Marco for the sublime spectacle of the Venetian skyline – one of the world's great views.

Murano glass; not to everyone's taste, but certainly distinctive

Murano▶▶ Murano is a workaday and slightly down-at-heel place dedicated almost entirely to glass-blowing. The glass furnaces moved here from the city in 1291 as a precaution against fire. For centuries thereafter the island's craftsmen were European leaders in their field. Nowadays the streets are crammed with shops hawking glassware that is exquisite and hideous by turns. Be sure to visit the furnaces themselves to see glass being blown – entry to most is free (many lie along the Fondamenta dei Vetrai). To see examples of Murano glass past and present, and to learn about glass-making techniques, visit the glass museum, the **Museo Vetrario**. The church of **San Pietro Martire** has two good paintings: Veronese's *St Jerome* and Giovanni Bellini's *Madonna and Child*.

Torcello▶▶▶ The best day-trip from Venice, this rustic and peaceful little island is easily explored. Most people are here to see **Santa Maria Assunta**, Venice's first cathedral, home to magnificent 11th- and 12th-century mosaics, but the 11th-century church of Santa Fosca and the small Museo dell'Estuario are both also worth a visit.

Venice in peril

Subsidence Only a couple of decades ago subsidence threatened Venice with catastrophe. The main culprits were the water-hungry industries on the mainland, whose exploits lowered the water-table and threatened to undermine the city's foundations. Two large aqueducts to pipe water from mainland rivers saved the day in 1973.

Local subsidence, though, continues to be a threat. Most of the city's buildings rest on pilings driven into the mudflats of the lagoon – or in the case of poorer houses, shored up on a loose cement of rubbish and rubble. With the lagoon now subject to increasingly frequent low tides, air can reach the pilings and accelerate their rate of decay.

Flooding Floods in Venice are nothing new, but severe inundations in 1966, 1979 and 1986 have made them the focus of the city's planners. Winter flooding is caused by strong southeast winds and seasonally high tides. Recently they have grown more frequent – not, research shows, because of global warming, but through human interference in the lagoon over the last century in the form of land reclamation and the deepening of channels.

Solutions The solution is to be a tidal barrier built across the lagoon's three main entrances. Opinion of the boom's likely efficacy is divided and many conservationists argue it does not address the city's basic problems: the more general but ultimately more critical ones of a declining population, slowly stagnating lagoon, and the choice between preserving Venice for the Venetians – more housing and industry – and turning the city into an historical fossil preserved for profit and posterity.

The flood of 1966
On 4 November, 1966, Venice's sea walls (*murazzi*) were breached by the combined effects of gale-force winds, an earth tremor and two successive high tides, and the city found itself under a metre of water. There were no injuries and no paintings lost (unlike Florence, flooded on the same day).

Air pollution
Smog is another problem. Sulphur dioxide from mainland factories combined with the lagoon's humid and salty air produce an intensely corrosive cocktail. The conversion of domestic heating systems from oil to gas has lessened the problem, but local industry still pumps 50,000 tonnes of toxins into the atmosphere annually.

Water pollution
Venice's sewage is treated, but most of its sinks and baths empty straight into the lagoon. For years the cleansing effects of daily tides and the work of natural biological agents (marine life) preserved the ecological equilibrium. The increased use of phosphate-rich detergents and fertilisers, however, has upset this – some £175 million was spent on the problem in 1988, but the building of the barrier, which will further disturb tides, does not augur well for the lagoon's health.

You may need water-proof footwear on even the sunniest days in Venice

Grand Canal palaces
Numerous *palazzi* not mentioned in the gazetteer line the Grand Canal, several with literary connections. From San Marco west some of the more eminent include the Pisani-Gritti, home to English critic John Ruskin in 1851; Palazzo Corner, designed by Sansovino; Palazzo Barbaro, where Henry James wrote *The Aspern Papers*; the Palazzo Mocenigo, once home to Lord Byron; Corner-Spinelli and Palazzo Grimani, both stately Renaissance piles; and Vendramin-Calergi, where Wagner died in 1883 (home of the Casino).

Stroll – Dorsoduro
Walk on the waterfront along Fondamenta delle Zattare for lovely views across the lagoon to the Giudecca. Finish at Santa Maria della Salute.

Museums & Galleries

►►► Accademia   94A2
Campo della Carità, Dorsoduro
The Accademia is Venice's greatest art gallery, a superlative collection of Venetian paintings, many gathered from churches and palaces around the city. Masterpieces by all Venice's painters adorn its walls, the highlights of which include Giovanni Bellini's *Madonna Enthroned* and Carpaccio's *The Presentation* (Room II); Mantegna's *St George*, Giorgione's *Tempest* and some of Bellini's *Madonnas* in Rooms IV–V; Titian's *St John the Baptist* (Room VI); three Veronese masterpieces in Room XI; six 18th-century *Scenes from Venetian Life* by Longhi (Room XVII); and two narrative fresco cycles – *The Miracles of the Relics of the Cross* (Room XX) and Carpaccio's *The Legend of St Ursula* (Room XXI). There is just one Canaletto (in Room XVII).

►► Ca' d'Oro e Galleria Franchetti   94C3
Canal Grande, Cannaregio
Named after the now-vanished gilding (*oro* – gold) that covered its elaborate façade, this is Venice's most famous *palazzo*, currently home to a well-presented and varied art collection. Its showpieces are Mantegna's *St Sebastian* and A Vivarini's polyptych of *The Passion*. There are also lesser pieces by Titian, Giorgione and Tintoretto, and numerous rewarding works by less prominent artists and sculptors.

Inside the Doge's Palace

▶ Ca' Pesaro   94C3
Canal Grande, Santa Croce
A highpoint of Venetian baroque, this 17th-century Grand Canal palace is as worth seeing for its original interior as for the pair of modest museums under its roof – the Museo Orientale (oriental art), and the Galleria d'Arte Moderna (works from past Venice Biennales).

▶▶ Ca' Rezzonico e Museo del   94B2
Settecento Veneziano
Canal Grande, Dorsoduro
This palace's 'Museum of 18th-century Venice' evokes the splendour of the city's last great flowering through magnificently decorated rooms crammed with tapestries, furniture, costumes, silks, brocades, lacquerwork – even a contemporary puppet theatre and chemist's shop. You may find the trappings gaudy, but the frescoes of the Tiepolo family and the touching Venetian scenes by Longhi and Guardi merit the entrance fee alone.

▶▶▶ Collezione Guggenheim   94A3
Calle Cristoforo, Dorsoduro
Millionairess Peggy Guggenheim's gallery – housed in an 18th-century **palazzo** on the Grand Canal – has one of the world's most important collections of modern art. Rooms are arranged by style (Dadaism, Cubism, Surrealism) and contain all 20th-century art's top names.

▶▶ Museo Civico Correr   95B4
Piazza San Marco
This is Venice's main historical museum, a vast and generally fascinating showcase for documents, weapons, coins, ducal regalia and a wealth of miscellania relating to the city over the centuries. Some knowledge of Venetian history is needed to get the most from the exhibits. The fine art gallery upstairs is second only to the Accademia.

▶▶ Museo Storico Navale
(Naval Museum)   95B5
Campo San Biagio, Castello
Housed near the Arsenale (the Republic's old naval base), this museum is the best collection of all things maritime in Italy. With plenty of background on gondolas, the displays range from models of galleys used against the Turks to manned torpedoes from World War II.

▶▶▶ Palazzo Ducale (The Doge's Palace)   95B4
Piazzetta San Marco
The Doge's Palace was the seat of power in Venice for almost a thousand years, but most of the present building dates from the 15th century.

You need at least a morning to do the palace justice (arriving early helps avoid the crowds). Be sure to tarry over the main entrance (Porta della Carta) and courtyard; the staircase (Scala dei Giganti): the Anticollegio, with paintings by Titian and Veronese; and the Sala del Maggior Consiglio, the council chamber, famous for Tintoretto's huge oil painting, *Paradiso*. The Bridge of Sighs and prisons are also superb.

The Bridge of Sighs
The famous Ponte dei Sospiri links the Palazzo Ducale with its prisons (the name supposedly comes from the sighs of condemned prisoners). For the most part the prisons harboured only petty criminals (Casanova was imprisoned here in 1755 for 15 months). Hardcore convicts were kept in the less salubrious Piombi (the Leads), under the palace's roof, or in the Pozzi (Wells), 18 dark and dank cells in the palace's bowels.

107

The Bridge of Sighs, reputedly named after the sighs of condemned prisoners

VENICE

Campo Santa Margherita
This square, ringed by 14th-century houses, is the social heart of the Dorsoduro district. It has an attractive food and vegetable market, and lots of relaxed bars, haunts of students from the university. Near by is the Scuola Grande dei Carmini, rich in Tiepolo frescoes.

The Scuole
The *scuole* of Venice were religious confraternities administered by wealthy Venetians as charities for the needy. The main ones took their names from their patron saints, or from the nationality of their founders. Many acquired tremendous prestige, reflected in their works of art, among the most remarkable in Venice.

San Rocco
The *scuola* of San Rocco was always chiefly concerned with the relief of the sick – as was its patron, San Rocco (or St Roch). The saint was held especially useful in cases of bubonic plague, an illness from which he was saved by divine intervention. Paintings all over Italy (and especially in Venice) often show him pointing to a plague sore on his thigh.

►► Palazzo Mocenigo 94C2
Salizzada San Stae, Santa Croce
Once owned by one of Venice's grandest families, this palace's nine rooms must still look much as they did in their 18th-century heyday. Each is richly gilded and painted, and decorated with period furniture and Murano glass chandeliers.

► Palazzo Querini-Stampalia 95B4
Campiello Querini, Castello
The splendour of this 16th-century **palazzo** suggests the scale of Venice's former wealth and power. Its 20 rooms contain the art collection and furnishings of one of the city's leading 18th-century families. The paintings are not the city's best, but there are one or two persuasive works, notably the chronicles of Venetian life by Pietro Longhi, Giovanni Bellini's *Presentation in the Temple* and some popularist – if inept – portrayals of *Venetian Festivals* by Gabriele Bella.

►►► Scuola di San Giorgio degli Schiavoni 95B5
Calle Furlani, Castello
Schiavonia (the name refers to Slavs) was what Venetians called Dalmatia, a coastal strip along the eastern Adriatic, and a dominion of the Republic for centuries. The *scuola* established by the city's resident Slavs contains Vittore Carpaccio's poetic frieze of frescoes illustrating the lives of St George, St Tryphon and St Jerome (the patron saints of Dalmatia).

►►► Scuola Grande di San Rocco 94B2
Campo San Rocco, San Polo
'One of the three most precious buildings in Italy', said John Ruskin of San Rocco, grandest of the city's *scuole*. He was referring to Tintoretto's series of over 50 visionary Biblical scenes that took 23 years to complete. The paintings were executed after the artist had won the commission in a bitterly fought competition.

Start your exploration in the Sala dell'Albergo, almost one wall of which is covered in a magnificent *Crucifixion*. Pictures on its entrance wall depict scenes from The Passion (1567). In the main upper hall, painted later (1581), the wall panels contain New Testament scenes, the ceiling inventive Old Testament episodes. There are more Tintorettos on the ground floor (1587) and in the neighbouring church of San Rocco.

The Torre dell'Orologio, Piazza San Marco

Landmarks

► Arsenale 95B5

Ride *vaporetto* No 52 and you pass through the arch and flanking towers that mark the entrance to the Arsenale. This vast naval dockyard in the east of the city was where the great ships of the Venetian empire were built and berthed. Most of the old basins and docks are now deserted, or used by the Italian navy, but glimpses from the outside still evoke their past scale and splendour.

►►► Monumento a Colleoni 95C4
(Colleoni Statue)

Campo Santi Giovanni e Paolo, Castello

Bartolomeo Colleoni, a native of Bergamo, served Venice as one of its leading *condottieri*, or mercenaries, from 1448. At his death he left a portion of his wealth to the state, on condition a statue of him be raised in front of the Basilica di San Marco. The Republic took the money, but cheated by erecting the statue in front of the Scuola di San Marco. In the statue itself, however, they did Colleoni proud, commissioning the Florentine sculptor Andrea Verrocchio to produce one of the masterpieces of Renaissance sculpture (1481–8).

The Rialto
Venice's earliest settlers were drawn to the stable land and defensive position on the Grand Canal's *rivo alto* (high bank). In time the area (and name) developed into the Rialto, the city's commercial heart. In the 'Bazaar of Europe', textiles, precious stones, silks, spices and exotica from the Orient were traded. Europe's first state bank opened here in the 12th century, and finance flourished – as did prostitution. The Rialto still has a busy market, concentrated on the Ruga degli Orefici (souvenirs), Campo San Giacomo (fruit and meat) and Campo Battisti (fish).

109

►►► Ponte di Rialto (Rialto Bridge) 94C3

The Rialto Bridge with its three pedestrian walkways and two rows of shops is one of the city's best-known landmarks. Built between 1588 and 1591, it replaced a wooden bridge whose central portion could be raised to allow the passage of ships (many paintings, like Carpaccio's *Miracles of the True Cross* in the Accademia, show what this and earlier bridges looked like).

►► Torre dell'Orologio (Clock Tower) 95B4

Piazza San Marco

Crowds invariably gather around this curio, a brightly enamelled clock-face and 'digital' clock linked with automata. The face indicates the hours, phases of the moon and movement of the sun through the signs of the zodiac. Two bronze figures of Moors strike the hours.

The elegant Rialto Bridge, once the only crossing of the Grand Canal

Walking in Venice

■ In a city as beautiful and free of cars as Venice, walking is the perfect way to get around. Almost all of the city offers magnificent walks and strolls. But remember that Venice's great pleasure is escaping the crowds to lose yourself in its labyrinth of alleys and canals, so treat the suggestions below as no more than starting points. ■

Venetian words
An open space (piazza) in Venice is called a *campo*, *campiello* or *campazzo*. Alleys are *calle*, *calletta* or *callesella* (occasionally *ruga*, analogous to the French *rue*). A *ramo* is the branch of a *calle*. *Salizzada* refers to the first alleys paved with stone; *fondamenta* (or *riva*) means the path alongside a canal (used as the 'foundation' for the canal's buildings). A canal is a *rio*; a *rio terra* is a canal which has been filled in.

Canal Grande Venice's single best excursion is not a walk at all, but a boat trip on one of the *vaporetti* which ply up and down the Grand Canal (Nos 1, 82, 83, or 84). Buy one of the many guides or maps devoted solely to the canal to identify its key buildings (there are 200 separate palaces alone). Boats make frequent stops if you want to see anything on the way.

Piazza San Marco In and around Piazza San Marco you can wander between some of the city's most famous sights – the Basilica di San Marco, Campanile di San Marco, Palazzo Ducale, Museo Correr, Libreria Sansoviniana and the Ponte dei Sospiri ('Bridge of Sighs').

The west Start at the Accademia and head west towards the Fondamenta Gheradini, home to a lovely fruit and vegetable market, and then make for the Scuola Grande dei Carmini, San Pantalon, the Scuola Grande di San Rocco and Campo San Polo. Then move north toward the Grand Canal (and a boat to the centre) via Campo San Giacomo dell'Orio and the churches of San Giacomo and San Stae.

The east Eastern Venice is one of the city's quieter areas. Start at Campo Santa Maria Formosa and its eponymous church, just northeast of Piazza San Marco. Then take in Santi Giovanni e Paolo and its lovely square and Colleoni monument. Proceed to San Francesco della Vigna, the Arsenale, the Museo Storico Navale and the Scuola di San Giorgio degli Schiavoni.

The Ghetto Venice's was the world's first ghetto (the word comes from the word *getar*, to found, or *geto*, foundry, after the metal-working industry that dominated the area until 1390). Jews were segregated here from 1516. The district's low, crowded houses are distinctly different from the rest of the city. Its heart is in Cannaregio, north of Rio Terra San Leonardo.

Taking the weight off their feet: visitors outside St Mark's

Transport and shopping

Getting about The *vaporetto*, or water bus, is the principal means of travelling Venice's canals (*motoscafi*, or motor launches, are similar but quicker). The system is initially confusing, but you soon get the hang of the numbered routes. The city map (pages 94-5) shows the main stops, each of which usually has a ticket office, route maps and timetable. Tickets can also be bought in shops with an ACTV sign (the public transport company). Tickets cost a flat fare, though if you are making several journeys buy 24- or 72-hour tourist tickets, or a discounted 10-ticket block (a *blochetto*). A special ticket for visiting Murano, Burano and Torcello is also available (the *Biglietto Isole*). Remember to date-stamp your ticket at each pier before boarding. Tickets must be bought for large pieces of luggage. Services run about every 10 minutes. Seats in the prow are the most coveted spots – offering the best views.

Walking – the city's only other means of transport – is helped by yellow signs giving directions to the main destinations. Given Venice's complexity, no map is totally accurate: Hallweg, Falk, FMB or Kummerly and Frey are the best.

Shopping Venice has always been a city where goods are bought and sold. These days, the vast number of visitors means prices are inflated and much of its merchandise little more than tourist tat. This said, shops can still be found selling the quality crafts for which the city has traditionally been renowned – fabrics, glass, leather, metalwork, paper and woodwork. The island of Burano is especially known for its lace, Murano for its glassware – though much can be horribly kitsch. Metalwork and woodwork (furniture) shops are found around Campo San Barnaba. For the most distinctive of Venetian souvenirs – carnival masks and hats – visit **Tragicomica**, Campiello dei Meloni, San Polo and **Mondonovo** (Rio Terra Canal, Dorsoduro 3063, just off Campo Santa Margherita).

The most fashionable shopping areas are the Mercerie – the streets between Piazza San Marco and around the Rialto bridge. The busiest area is the Strada Nova, leading from the railway station to the heart of the city.

The gondolier still provides the most romantic – if most expensive – way of seeing Venice

111

Hiring a gondola
Gondola fares are governed by a tariff – though few gondoliers adhere to this, so confirm the price *and* duration of a trip before setting off. Rates are doubled between 8:00 at night and 8:00 in the morning. Useful tips are to take rides in the late afternoon, when the Grand Canal is less crowded, and to start from a station on the Canal (as rides on the lagoon are more choppy).

Traghetti
As the Grand Canal has only three bridges, it can often save time to use the *traghetti* (two-man gondola ferries) which cross the canal between special piers (at several points). Fares are very cheap – you pay the boatman directly. Visitors usually sit, but Venetians like to stand for the short crossing.

Carnival masks make stylish and unusual souvenirs

Accommodation

Alternatives to Venice
Price and availability of accommodation can be a problem in Venice, and though it may not be an ideal arrangement, you might consider seeing the city as one or more day-trips from a base in nearby towns. Padua (see page 124) and Treviso (see page 125) are good options, both less than half an hour by train from Venice.

Many visitors willingly pay extra for a room with a canal view

Booking and high season Venice has around 200 hotels. While most are well run, a few have become slovenly, taking for granted the constant flow of visitors that fills the city virtually year round. It is almost essential to book a room in advance during July and August, and wise to do so for the rest of the high season – which runs from mid-March to late October. Christmas and Easter must also be reckoned peak periods – together with the two weeks of Carnevale in February.

Prices Hotel rates are generally higher than in Rome or Florence, which in the upper price brackets puts them among the highest in western Europe. Off-season rates can be far more reasonable – but this is when many hotels close. It is now often impossible to avoid paying for a breakfast, whether you take it or not, and charges for air-conditioning – a definite boon in summer – can be hefty. Relatively few hotels have restaurants, but where they do, half-board deals often involve unappetising dinners (and you lose the chance to eat out).

Finding a room
If you arrive without a room, head straight for one of the tourist offices run by the AVA (the Venetian Hoteliers' Association). They have kiosks at the Santa Lucia railway station, Marco Polo airport, or the Autorimessa Comunale in Piazzale Roma. The queues may be long, but each will find you a room, taking a L10,000, L20,000 or L30,000 deposit according to the category of hotel (deductible from your first night's bill).

Rooms Because of the constraints imposed by planning regulations, Venice's old hotels often have a wide variety of rooms – so ask to see several before parting with any money. Rooms with canal views often command a premium, worth paying if it avoids a dark and miserable back room. Singles are notoriously bad, so lone travellers might consider taking a double room in a cheaper hotel. Lounges and communal spaces can be restricted in all but the grandest hotels.

Noise and location The best hotels lie on the Grand Canal near San Marco; the cheapest in the streets around the railway station off Rio Terra Lista di Spagna. Wherever your hotel, be certain when booking to find its exact location (and remember you may need to carry your luggage). Even without cars, Venice has its share of nocturnal traffic. Church bells and pedestrian chatter can also reverberate noisily in narrow streets. Dorsoduro is one of the quieter areas.

Restaurants Mass tourism has not been good for Venetian cuisine. Restaurant prices are high, cooking unimaginative and service indifferent. This said, good restaurants can be found – usually in the upper price bracket – and even an average meal can be made memorable by a waterfront setting. As a general rule, places away from San Marco and in the quieter eastern and northern parts of the city, are good areas to search out cheaper and more authentic *trattorie*.

If you are watching your budget, most restaurants offer a *menù turistico*, a set price menu. Quality and quantity, however, are usually inferior to eating *à la carte*. Most places, large or small, close once a week, often on Sunday or Monday.

Cafés and bars Given Venetian prices, cafés and bars are more than ever the great standby if you want cheap snacks and sandwiches on the hoof. Between-meals nibbles in the city are known as *cichetti*, typically including *polpette* (meatballs), *carciofi* (artichoke hearts), eggs, anchovies and *polipi* (baby squid). All are traditionally washed down with *un ombra*, a glass of wine – literally a 'shadow', from the idea of coming out of the sun for light refreshment. For a one-off treat, indulge yourself in one of the city's more famous and venerable bars (see panel).

Venetian cuisine Fish and seafood form the basis of Venice's cuisine, as prawns, squid and octopus in *antipasti*, in fish soups (*zuppa di pesce*), or as Murano crabs (*granseola*), *sarde in saor* (marinated sardines), *baccalà* (salt cod) and *seppioline nere* (cuttlefish cooked in its own ink). *Risotto* is the first course *par excellence*, whether with seafood, vegetables, or ingredients like snails, tripe and quails. *Bigoli* is a local pasta, often served with a tuna (*tonno*) sauce. Thick soups are also popular, especially *pasta e fagioli* (pasta and beans). Cornmeal *polenta* is another staple, often an accompaniment to the famous *fegato alla veneziana* (calves' liver and onions).

Wine
Good local wines include Friulian whites like Tocai and Pinot Bianco and reds like Merlot, Refosco and Raboso. The best tipple is *prosecco*, a delicious, light sparkling wine. It is cheap and available in any bar – simply ask for *un prosecco*.

Bars – The Top Three
Venice's most famous café is *Florian* in Piazza San Marco, opened in 1720 and patronised ever since by the famous and notorious – Proust, Wagner and Casanova included. Prices here, and at its competitor, the less pretty but equally notorious *Quadri* opposite, are stratospheric – but worth it for a once-in-a-lifetime treat. Much the same goes for the legendary *Harry's Bar*, Calle Vallaresso, San Marco.

One of the world's great settings for an al fresco *meal*

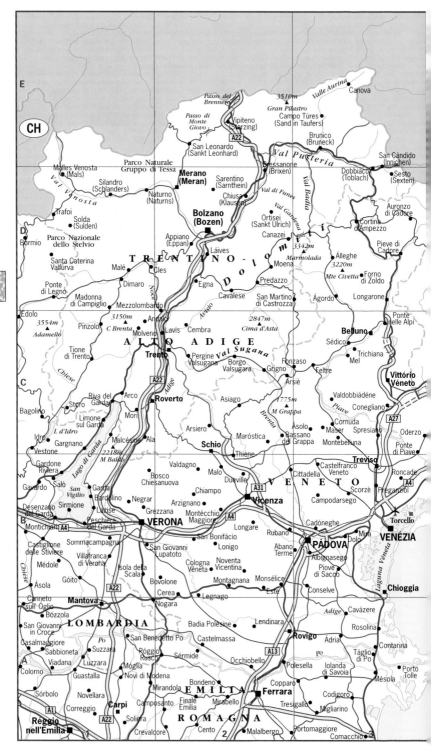

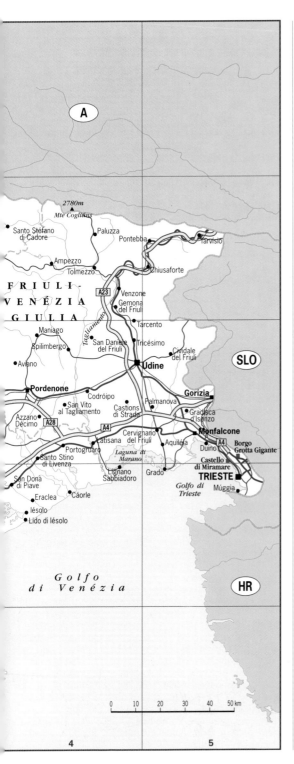

REGION HIGHLIGHTS ◄◄◄◄◄

AQUILEIA *see page 118:*
THE BASILICA

CIVIDALE DEI FRIULI
see page 120

DOLOMITES *see page 120*

**GRANDE STRADA DELLE
DOLOMITI (DRIVE)**
see page 121

PADOVA (PADUA)
see page 124

TRENTO *see page 125:*
DUOMO

TRIESTE *see page 126*

VERONA *see page 128*

VICENZA *see page 130*
**TEATRO OLIMPICO,
PALLADIAN PALACES**

The Northeast Venice exerts such a pull that few visitors escape its clutches to explore the rest of northeast Italy – the regions of the Veneto, Trentino-Alto Adige and Friuli-Venezia Giulia. Yet in many ways this is a region whose attractions are among the best of their kind. Among its landscapes are the Dolomites, the most spectacular mountains in Europe. Architecturally, it contains the villas of Andrea Palladio, one of the most influential of all architects. Padua has one of Italy's great fresco cycles, and Verona is undoubtedly among the country's finest Roman and medieval cities. Ethnically, too, the region is fascinating, a melting-pot of Italian, Slav and German-speaking peoples. Even some of Italy's most famous wines originate in the northeast – notably the ubiquitous Soave and Valpolicella.

The Veneto Modern-day Veneto is the heartland of Venetia, the mainland territories ruled by the Venetian Republic between the 14th and 18th centuries (though Venetia's domain also included much of present-day Friuli-Venezia Giulia). Like most northern regions it divides neatly into plain, low hills and mountains. The plain is prosperous and densely populated, which means sightseeing involves braving swathes of industry and modern housing. Any unpleasantness, however, is worth enduring to see Verona, Shakespeare's setting for *Romeo and Juliet*, and as beautiful today as it must have been when the play was written. Vicenza, too, deserves a day's visit, mainly for its Palladian architecture and wonderfully prosperous and tight-knit little city centre. Padua, by contrast, is disappointing, though its modern horrors should be overlooked for as long as it takes to see Giotto's frescoes and the Basilica di Sant'Antonio. Few places stand out among the lesser towns, though Asolo provides a restful retreat from the bustle of the cities.

Trentino-Alto Adige This strange, multi-cultured hybrid is a region where unresolved historical problems have come home to roost. Southern Trentino (capital Trento) is Italian-speaking, while Alto Adige, or Sudtirol (capital Bolzano) is mainly German-speaking. Alto Adige was ceded to Italy at the end of World War I, having previously been part of the Austro-Hungarian Empire. As a result, everything here has more than a tinge of the Teutonic. Ethnic differences have led to inevitable tensions (including acts of terrorism), though a large measure of autonomy has, in the main, kept the lid on nationalist ambitions.

While the disputes are generally out of sight, the region's bilingualism and brisk efficiency are immediately noticeable. Most of the area's pleasures, however, are those which transcend cultural differences. Trento and Bolzano both have their charms (along with Merano), but it is the mountains of the Dolomites which provide the region's main attraction. Their magnificent scenery can be enjoyed by road or rail, but hiking (and skiing) facilities are so outstanding it would be foolish not to attempt a little walking.

Alto Adige's cuisine has a decidedly Teutonic flavour. Be prepared for *knödel* (dumplings), often in a clear broth (*suppe*); *wienerschnitzel* (breaded veal cutlets); *sauerkraut*; *blau forelle* (mountain trout); *speck* (a special ham); *gröstl* (a meat, onion and potato pie); goulash; and – of course – the ubiquitous apple strudel. Delicatessens

---

Tourist information
Bolzano: Piazza Walther 8 (tel: 0471/970 660).
Cividale del Friuli: Largo Boiani 4 (tel: 0432/731 398).
Padua: (Padova) Railway Station (tel: 049/875 2077).
Trento: Via Alfieri 4 (tel: 0461/983 880).
Trieste: Via San Nicolo 20 (tel: 040/369 881) and Railway Station.
Verona: Palazzo del Municipio, Via Leoncino 61 (tel: 045/592 828).
Vicenza: Piazza Matteotti 12/Piazza del Duomo 5 (tel: 0444/320 854).

Scenic drives
(*Veneto*) SS48/SS51 around Cortina d'Ampezzo; SS203 Belluno–Agordo–Cortina d'Ampezzo; SS141 Bassano del Grappa–Monte Grappa; (*Trentino*) SS612 Trento–Cembra–Cavalese–San Martino di Castrozza; SS421/SS237/SS239 Mezzolombardo–Andalo–Molveno–Tione di Trento–Madonna di Campiglio; (*Alto Adige*) SS241/SS48 Bolzano–Canazei–Cortina d'Ampezzo; SS508 Bolzano–Val Sarentina–Vipiteno; SS44 Vipiteno–Passo di Monte Giovo–Merano; SS621 Brunico–Valle Aurina–Canova.

are full of excellent cheeses, pickles, hams and sausages. Bakeries have many types of black and rye bread, as well as Viennese-type pastries (be sure to try *krapfen*, a cake with jam and whipped cream). Do not despair if you want pasta, as most 'conventional' Italian culinary staples are usually also available.

Friuli-Venezia Giulia This region is more ethnically jumbled than Trentino-Alto Adige, comprising a cocktail of Italian, Slavic and central European cultures that fills Italy's extreme northeastern corner. A potentially fascinating area, its peripheral position puts it beyond the ambitions of most visitors. Its coastal plains are not much to look at (though the lagoons have a beauty of sorts), but two of the little towns – Aquileia and Cividale del Friuli – can hold their own with any in Italy. The old Austro-Hungarian port of Trieste has a unique old-world atmosphere and makes a perfect base for local excursions.

Piazza delle Erbe, the social heart of Verona

117

THE NORTHEAST

Caterina Cornaro
Caterina Cornaro was a scion of one of Venice's most powerful families. Through marriage she became queen of Cyprus, but was eventually duped by Venice into abdicating. In return she received Asolo, where she lived and held court for 30 years. In 1509 she was forced out by Emperor Maximilian, and fled to Venice, where she died a year later.

Grado
Isolated in the heart of the Venetian lagoons (11km from Aquileia) is Grado, a wonderfully atmospheric place. The town's centrepiece is Sant'Eufemia, a church which has changed little since it was built in 579, its highlight a 6th-century mosaic floor. Grado is also a beach resort, with enormous beaches, warm water and safe bathing (the town's name comes from its gently graded shoreline). Boats run here from Trieste (four per week), a lovely way to visit the town.

Villa Barbaro
The Villa Barbaro at Maser, northeast of Asolo, is not only one of Palladio's finest villas, but also contains a virtuoso group of frescoes by Veronese, considered one of Italy's finest examples of *trompe l'oeil*.

▶▶　　**Aquileia**　　　　　*115C5*

Today Aquileia is a sleepy agricultural town. Little at first glance suggests it is the region's most significant archaeological site. In its day, however, its trading links and defensive position made it the fourth most important Italian city in the Roman Empire (after Rome, Milan and Capua). By the 4th century, it was also a patriarchate, a region ruled by a bishop-prince, or patriarch.

The first patriarch, Teodoro, built a sumptuous **basilica▶▶▶** in 313, remodelled in the 10th century and now – despite damage from earthquakes – the region's most impressive medieval building. Its most breathtaking feature is a vast mosaic floor, considered among the world's finest early Christian mosaics. Almost as noteworthy are the Cripta degli Scavi, a crypt containing parts of the 4th-century church; the tombs of several patriarchs; and the crypt's 12th-century frescoes.

Elsewhere there are numerous **Roman remains▶▶**, together with two pithy museums – the **Museo Paleocristiano▶** and **Museo Archeologico▶**.

▶▶　　**Asolo**　　　　　*114C3*

Asolo is a romantic medieval hill town, full of churches and tiny squares, and set in the Dolomites' bucolic foothills. Of all the Veneto's small towns, it is perhaps the most beautiful, and its wooded and villa-studded countryside the most charming. It lends its name to an Italian verb, *asolare*, meaning to pass one's time in pleasant aimlessness.

The actress Eleonora Duse was born in Asolo in 1859, notorious as much for her tempestuous love affairs as for her performances. She frequently retreated to the town to escape gossip and scandal, and after her death in Pittsburgh during an American tour was returned to her birthplace to be buried. The **Museo Civico▶** houses many mementoes of her, together with memorabilia connected with the English poet Robert Browning, one of the town's other notable inhabitants.

▶　　**Bassano del Grappa**　　　　　*114C2*

Formerly renowned for its school of painting, this town in the foothills of the Alps is now better known for its colourful pottery and – as its name suggests – a noted *grappa* (a type of *eau de vie*). Local-born painter Jacopo Bassano (1516–92) dominates the **Museo Civico▶**, which includes his famous *St Valentine Baptising St Lucilla*. More famous still is the town's covered wooden bridge, the much rebuilt 13th-century **Ponte Coperto** or **Ponte degli Alpini▶**.

▶　　**Belluno**　　　　　*114C3*

Belluno's old town occupies a lofty position high above the confluence of the Ardo and Piave rivers. To the west it is framed by the saw-toothed mountains of the Dolomiti Bellunesi, the most southerly and least explored of the Dolomite ranges. For the rest, the town is full of old arcaded streets, ancient fountains and Renaissance *palazzi*. **Piazza del Duomo▶** is the most beautiful of the squares, the Venetian-style Palazzo dei Rettori the best known of the palaces. The Gothic church of **Santo Stefano▶**, the Museo Civico and the elegant Piazza delle Erbe are also worth a visit.

► **Bolzano (Bozen)** *114D2*

Capital of the mostly German-speaking Alto Adige, Bolzano is a congenial base for exploring the Dolomites (see pages 120–1). Over the centuries it has been controlled by the Counts of Tyrol, the Habsburgs, the Austrians and the Bishops of Trento. Its Gothic **Duomo►** (repaired after World War II) neatly combines modern altars with fragments of medieval fresco. Its carved spire and green-tiled roof are eye-catching, but less interesting than the fine sandstone Gothic pulpit and famous *Porta del Vino* (Wine Door). This is embellished with vines and peasants tending their vineyards, commemorating a special licence granted to the church to sell wine in 1387.

Elsewhere, the **Chiesa dei Domenicani►** contains the town's best paintings, several 14th-century Giottoesque frescoes. Also visit the **Chiesa dei Francescani►**, known for its carved altarpiece and gracious frescoed cloisters. The **Museo Civico►** offers archaeological fragments and an excellent folklore section, with wood carvings, costumes, old household objects and several reconstructed interiors. Take the *funivia* (cable car) to Soprabolzano (literally 'over Bolzano'), whence a tiny tramway takes you 7km to the hamlet of Collalbo and the 'Earth Pyramids', a bizarre rock 'forest' of eroded spires and pinnacles.

Monte Grappa
From Bassano del Grappa take the winding mountain road 31km north to Monte Grappa, whose 1,775m viewpoint offers some of the grandest panoramas in the area.

Castello Rancolo
You can visit one of several castles in the Val Sarentina north of Bolzano. Castello Rancolo (13th- to 19th-century) is the nearest and most impressive, with guided tours of its rooms, many of which are decorated with 15th-century frescoes.

119

Above: market day in Bassano del Grappa
Left: elegant traditional houses in Bolzano

Drive
One of the best of the many scenic drives near Bolzano is the SS508, which follows the Val Sarentina to Vipiteno (65km).

What's in a name
The Dolomites are so-called because of the dolomite rock, or magnesium limestone, which is their main constituent. The rock itself was named after the 18th-century French geologist Diendonne Sylvain Guy Tancrède de Gratet de Dolomieu.

The Tre Cime di Lavaredo with the Rifugio Locatelli (refuge) beneath

▶▶ **Cividale del Friuli** *115C5*

Important as one of the few places in Italy where there is some tangible record of the Lombards (see panel), Cividale is a lovely place, filled with a tangle of medieval streets, ancient bridges and interesting churches.

The 15th-century **Duomo**▶▶ boasts several remarkable works, including an embossed early 13th-century *pala*, or silver altarpiece. Off the right aisle, the Museo Cristiano contains the octagonal *Baptistery of Callisto*, commissioned in the 8th century by Cividale's first bishop-patriarch and made from 5th-century Lombard fragments of marble and stonework. Alongside stands the *Altar of Ratchis*, carved in 749, and one of the few surviving masterpieces from the Lombard era.

To the Duomo's left, the **Museo Archeologico**▶▶ houses Lombard weapons, tools and jewellery, but the town's finest monument to the era is the **Tempietto Lombardo**▶▶, an old temple whose carved stucco arch is a peerless example of Lombard sculpture.

The coming of the Lombards
The Lombards swept into Italy after the fall of the Roman Empire. A Teutonic warrior race, they had descended from Scandinavia to occupy the Danube. They came south in AD568, under their king, Alboino. The entourage included 40,000 men, women and children, supported by a huge retinue of slaves, wagons and livestock. They established three Italian dukedoms, the first of which had Cividale as its capital (the other two were Pavia, in Lombardy, and Spoleto, in Umbria).

▶▶▶ **Dolomiti (The Dolomites)** *114D2*

No other European mountains approach the scenic spectacle of the Dolomites, a group of 30 or so self-contained massifs in a wide arc from Lake Garda to the Austrian border. Set apart from the rest of the Alps by their geology, they are ancient coral reefs that have been compressed, uplifted and weathered. This largely explains the incredible crags and rock pinnacles which are their hallmark, and the peculiar, pinky-orange limestone that forms most of the massifs.

Many mountain roads offer views unparalleled in Italy (see page 121) but it would be a shame to come here and not attempt a little walking (see pages 122–3). On a first visit, the best way to get to grips with the area is to concentrate on one or two massifs. The most famous is the **Dolomiti di Brenta**▶▶▶ in the west, with Madonna di Campiglio as the best base. Several massifs are also easily accessible from Bolzano (Sciliar, Puez-Odle) and from Cortina d'Ampezzo (Sesto, Cristallo, Marmarole and Fanes-Sennes-Braies).

THE GREAT DOLOMITES ROAD

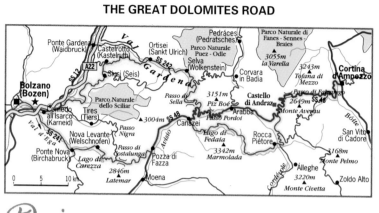

Drive **La Grande Strada delle Dolomiti**

La Grande Strada delle Dolomiti – the Great Dolomites road – was opened in 1909 to link Bolzano with Cortina d'Ampezzo and runs for 110km through some of the most spectacular mountain scenery in Europe. You can add many scenic options to this itinerary, especially if you make the return loop to Bolzano.

From Bolzano the road enters the Val d'Ega, a corridor of gorges and waterfalls that offers thrilling views of the Catinaccio and Latemar massifs. Mountain-cradled Lago di Carezza is one of the road's more famous viewpoints. The road then continues over high passes, skirting thick forests and wild countryside, and constantly unfolding breathtaking vistas as it hairpins towards Canazei. Here the SS641 offers a tortuous alternative to the Strada, breasting the Marmolada massif, glaciers and Lago di Fedaia before the last leg to Cortina d'Ampezzo.

The Passo Sella with Sassolungo in the background

121

■ **Anyone who loves mountains and the activities associated with them will be entranced by the Dolomites. They offer an unbeatable combination – stupendous scenery, hikes to suit every ability and some of the best skiing in Europe.** ■

Monte Civetta walk
Start from the village of Alleghe, 39km southwest of Cortina (use the SS638 and SS203 roads). Take the path from the village to the *Rif. A Tissi* via Lago Coldai and *Rif. Sonino* (tremendous views of Civetta's huge rock walls). For a longer walk continue from *Tissi* south to *Rif. Vazzoler* and thus to Listolade on the SS203 (15km south of Alleghe). Use Kompass map *Alpi Bellunesi* (No 77).

The Passo di Giau, La Gusela

Walking

On no account should you come here without tackling at least one walk. It need not be difficult: there is ample choice between easy low-level strolls and more demanding high-level walks. Towns and starting points are often high up, so even what look like 'mountain climbs' are often easier than they first appear. Access to all the main centres is easy; maps are excellent and widely available; paths are well-marked and well-trodden; and accommodation is cheap and plentiful. Refreshment stops (*rifugi*) are rarely more than an hour apart, and there are numerous cable cars to take the sting out of the longer ascents.

The only problem is knowing where to start. Numerous guidebooks are published, and tourist offices have lists of walks. The best approach is to settle on one massif and a single base, and start with a recognised 'classic'. At the same time, you should not take the mountains lightly. Go equipped with boots or stout shoes, carry some food and

water, and take adequate warm clothes and wet weather gear: weather can change quickly at high altitudes.

Dolomiti di Brenta Use Madonna di Campiglio (1,500m) as your base. It offers plenty of accommodation, and numerous circular walks you can complete in a day. The easiest is to take the Grostè ski lift to *Rif. G Graffer* (2,348m) and follow trail 316 to the *Rif. Tuckett* (2,272m). From here you can follow paths 317 or 328/318 back to Madonna. Alternatively, walk from Madonna to *Rif. Vallesinella* (an easy hour's stroll on trail 375) then climb to the *Rif. Brentei* (317/318), one of the Dolomites' most popular refuges. For a longer walk, continue on path 318 up the spectacular Val Brenta Alta towards *Rif. Pedrotti*. Double back the same way to the *Brentei*, or drop to the Val Brenta and back to Madonna on trail 323 or 391 (all walks are marked on the Kompass map *Dolomiti di Brenta* No 73).

Dolomiti di Sesto This is the easternmost Dolomite massif. Cortina is a good overall base, but Sesto or Dobbiaco are the closest villages to the best known walk, which follows path 5/102 up the Val Fiscalina from San Giuseppe (south of Sesto) to the *Rif. Locatelli* with extraordinary views of the much-photographed Tre Cime di Lavaredo (see illustration on page 120). Paths 101/104 give closer views of these peaks and longer walks. There is another, easier approach to the Tre Cime from *Rif. Auronzo* to the south (reached by road from Cortina). The Tabacco map *Cortina-Dolomiti di Sesto* (No 1) covers the whole area.

Skiing

In the Dolomites, the choice of both skiing runs and resorts is almost endless. Even the tiniest of villages has some runs, together with shops, hotels and outfitters.

The main centres for skiing are perhaps **Cortina d'Ampezzo**, east of Bolzano in the heart of the mountains, and **Madonna di Campiglio**, west of Trento, on the fringe of the Dolomiti di Brenta. Both towns are crowded and decidedly up-market, but offer all the trappings of top-class international resorts.

For similar facilities – but in cheaper and less chic surroundings – try the resorts in the Val Gardena (such as **Ortisei Canazei**), or in the **Val Badia** south of **Brunico** (itself one of several modest resorts in the Val Pusteria). There are also good cross-country options (*sci di fondo*), two of the best centres being Ortisei and Dobbiaco in the Val Pusteria.

Accommodation

Almost every hamlet in the Dolomites has a superb range of accommodation. Most is aimed at skiers, which means that summer rates are immensely competitive. Hotels are comfortable and of higher overall quality than in much of Italy. Do not be afraid to spend a night in a mountain refuge – they are not the preserve of hardened mountaineers. Accommodation is in dormitories, but they are snug and friendly places. Most open daily from June to September. Details from tourist offices.

Skiing in the Dolomites at Vigo di Fassa

Settimane Bianche
Ski resorts' bargain periods are known as *settimane bianche* (white weeks). They usually fall in January and February when slopes are at their emptiest and snow conditions are often unreliable. Prices on passes and accommodation are reduced.

THE NORTHEAST

124

Excursion from Merano
The tiny church of San Procolo lies in the hamlet of Naturno in the lovely Val Venosta (15km west of Merano). It contains exceptional wall paintings from the 8th century – the oldest in the entire German-speaking world. The trip is best combined with a drive into the Tessa mountains, an Alpine massif northwest of Merano. From Naturno, pick up the road west of the hamlet which strikes north up the Val di Senales. This provides a breathtaking 25km route into the mountains.

▶▶ **Merano (Meran)** 114D2

Sedate, mountain-ringed Merano is a fossil from a bygone age, full of *belle epoque* memories, leftovers from the turn of the century, when its mild climate, thermal springs and 'grape cure' made it a favoured spa with monied Europeans (the cure – reputedly used since Roman times – involves a two-week diet of fresh grapes). Among the many parks and promenades, the most famous is the **Passeggiata d'Inverno e d'Estate▶**, a path by the banks of the River Passirio. Above the town is the Passeggiata Tappeiner, a path which winds through gardens and vineyards offering views of Merano and its valley.

The town centre is at its best around Via dei Portici, where rustic houses sit alongside more recent neo-classical and art-nouveau buildings. Near by are the Gothic **Duomo▶** and ivy-clad **Castello Principesco▶** – the main things to see – together with a handful of churches and the modest Museo Civico. But Merano, is mainly a place to relax in, preferably – if you can afford the cures – at the **Terme**, the largest of the town's spa facilities.

The condottiere Gattamelata rides proudly outside St Antony's basilica, Padua

▶▶▶ **Padova (Padua)** 114B3

Padua is an ugly city, worth enduring for two unmissable sights. The **Cappella degli Scrovegni▶▶▶** is home to one of Italy's greatest fresco cycles: Giotto's 32-panel series of paintings on the lives of Christ and the Virgin Mary (1303–9). Like the artist's cycle in Assisi (see page 168), it marked a turning point in Western art, introducing a fluency and naturalism into painting that departed from the formality of Byzantine art.

In the **Basilica di Sant' Antonio▶▶** is buried St Antony of Padua, one of Italy's most revered saints (patron saint of the lost and found). Outside the church stands the famous statue of Gattamelata, a noted Venetian *condottiere*. Inside, are Donatello's bronze reliefs illustrating the life of St Antony; high altar figures of the Madonna and Saints (also by Donatello); St Antony's votive-filled chapel; and the 14th-century frescoes in the Beato Luca and San Felice chapels.

► **Trento (Trent)** *114C2*

Italian-speaking capital of Trentino, Trento is best known for the Council of Trent, a meeting of the Catholic hierarchy between 1545 and 1563 which debated ways to turn Europe's rising tide of Lutheranism. Its opening and closing sessions took place in the **Duomo►►**, heart of the present town, whose austere nave contains an unusual arcaded stairway, traces of old fresco and a modest copy of Bernini's *baldacchino* in St Peter's, Rome. Outside, on the east wall, look for the church's famous 'knotted columns', a memorial to the skill of the town's medieval masons. Alongside the Duomo, the Palazzo Pretorio contains the **Museo Diocesano►**, a small museum displaying 16th-century Flemish tapestries, carved altarpieces and painted chronicles of the Council of Trent.

Elsewhere, Trento is nicely uncommercialised, and a pleasure to wander through for an hour or so. Via Belenzani, with its rows of Renaissance *palazzi*, is the most singular street. As you explore, try to take in the church of Santa Maria Maggiore and the **Castello del Buonconsiglio►►**, for centuries the home of Trento's prince-bishops. Inside, it houses the Museo Provinciale d'Arte and the *Ciclo dei Mesi*, a lovely 15th-century fresco cycle depicting the months of the year.

Trento's prince-bishops
From the 13th century Trento's bishops enjoyed considerable power, revelling in the unique position of being able to act as the Papacy's representatives in clerical matters and as arbiters for the Holy Roman Empire in secular affairs. This even-handedness was one reason the Council of Trent was held in the town. Their autonomous balancing act continued for 800 years, ending when the Habsburgs secularised the principality in 1802.

125

► **Treviso** *114B3*

Drawn away by Venice's siren call, few people have much time for Treviso. Yet its old centre is an alluring mixture of canals, frescoed façades, shady porticoes and medieval fragments. The Dominican church and seminary of **San Nicolò►►** is the main monument, filled with frescoes and decorated tombs. The **Duomo►**, which has paintings by Tintoretto and others, is also diverting, while **Via Carlo Alberto►**, heart of an appealing market district, is the best single street to wander for its own sake. Also explore the central Calmaggiore area, with many old *palazzi*, the Peschiera (Fish Market) and two excellent museums: the **Museo Civico►**, with works by, among many others, Titian and Bassano, and the **Museo della Casa Trevigliana►**, a gorgeous 14th-century house and museum of applied arts.

For wine-lovers, the wine roads known as Strada del Vino Rosso and Strada del Vino Bianco (the 'Red' and 'White' wine roads respectively) start from Conegliano, just 23km north of Treviso, with plenty of opportunities to sample wine.

An evocative glimpse of Treviso

THE NORTHEAST

Trieste's old harbour was once one of the most important ports in the old Austro-Hungarian Empire

Miramare
The most popular excursion from Trieste is to Miramare, a beautifully situated castle built for Archduke Ferdinand Maximilian between 1856 and 1870 (located 7km north of the city). It is a marvellously kitsch and eclectic building (open to the public), though Triestini prefer to come here for the beaches.

Grotta Gigante
Borgo Grotta Gigante, 15km from Trieste, is near the largest publicly accessible cave in the world. The Grotta Gigante can reputedly accommodate St Peter's, Rome, with room to spare (it is 107m deep by 208m wide).

▶▶   **Trieste**   *115B5*

Trieste has little to see, if truth be told, but it rates as one of northern Italy's most atmospheric and distinctive cities (it also has lovely surroundings and a rugged coastline). At the crossroads of three cultures, its character and appearance have been shaped by Italian, Slavic and middle-European influences. Once the chief port of the Austro-Hungarian Empire, its most tangible memorials relate to this golden age – notably several neo-classical districts and a handful of wonderful turn-of-the-century coffee houses (**San Marco** in Via G Battisti and **Tommaseo** in Piazza Tommaseo are the most famous).

From earlier times, you could visit **San Giusto**▶▶, the Romanesque-Gothic cathedral (with its origins in the 6th century), filled with frescoes and some outstanding 12th-century mosaics. Close by, the Museo di Storia e d'Arte▶ chronicles the city's history from Roman times (the city was the Roman port of Tergeste). It is easily seen in conjunction with the **Museo Sartorio**▶, a series of gloomily decorated rooms redeemed by a noted ceramics collection and some 270 Tiepolo drawings. You should also climb to the Castello (1470–1630) for its views and small museum of weapons and armour.

▶   **Udine**   *115C4*

Once a bastion of the Roman Empire's northern frontier, Udine is today one of Italy's more urbane and airy little towns. At its heart lies the monumental **Piazza della Libertà**▶▶, dominated by the Palazzo del Comune, one of many buildings around the town to bear a Venetian stamp (the town was ruled by Venice from 1420 to 1797). To the south, the main attractions of the **Duomo**▶ are several paintings by Giovanni Battista Tiepolo, a painter who also left frescoes in the **Oratorio della Purità**▶ and **Palazzo Arcivescovile**▶.

Be sure to climb to the 16th-century **Castello**▶ from the Piazza della Libertà (you pass the lovely Loggia del Lionello *en route*). Paintings in the castle's museum include works by Tiepolo, Caravaggio, Carpaccio and Bronzino. Also leave time for San Francesco, a neat little Renaissance church, and for the collection of Friulian crafts, costumes and folk art in the **Museo Friuliano delle Arti e Tradizioni Popolari**▶.

Opera

■ **Opera's emotional drama and sensuality are perfectly suited to the Italian temperament – 'more heart than mind', said Giacomo Puccini – and there is nowhere better to enjoy a performance than in Italy itself, whether under the stars in Verona's amphitheatre or in one of the country's many great opera houses.** ■

Opera's roots lie in the traditional Italian mystery plays, the *maggi*, and the madrigal comedies of the 16th century. The composer Jacopo Peri produced the first *opera in musica*, literally a 'work in music', in 1600, a performance of *Euridice* to mark the marriage of Maria de' Medici to Henry IV of France. This and other early pieces were little more than spoken recitals with a light musical backing. The first composer to use a full orchestra was Claudio Monteverdi (1567–1643), whose *La Favola d'Orfeo* (1607) is held to be the first operatic masterpiece.

The first public opera house, the Teatro di San Cassiano, opened in Venice in 1637, followed by others all over the country. By 1700 there were 17 in Venice alone. About 2,000 new operas were staged during the 18th century.

The golden age Opera's 19th-century golden age was heralded by the almost simultaneous arrival of Rossini, Donizetti and Bellini. All enjoyed success at an early age, were often in fierce competition, and burnt out quickly, the first two dying relatively young (Rossini's last triumph came at the age of 40). Italian opera's greatest genius was perhaps Verdi. The son of a semi-literate peasant, Giuseppe Verdi (1813–1901) wrote such masterpieces as *Rigoletto* (1851), *La Traviata* (1853), *Aida* (1871) and *Otello* (1887).

Harsh critics
In the 18th century, Italian audiences were notorious for their rowdiness and uncompromising criticism. Charles Dickens noted their 'uncommonly hard and cruel character' and thought them 'always to be lying in wait for an opportunity to hiss'.

127

Giacomo Puccini
The curtain fell on the golden age with the death of Verdi's successor, Giacomo Puccini, responsible for many highlights of the operatic canon, such as *La Bohème* (1896), *Tosca* (1900) and *Madame Butterfly* (1904).

The Roman Arena in Verona, scene of a summer opera season

Opera in the amphitheatre
Even if you are no fan of opera, seeing a performance in Verona's Arena is an unforgettable experience. The season runs throughout July and August, when the city is crowded and accommodation difficult to find. You can get tickets from the box office (Arch 6 of the Arena); from the *Ente Lirico*, Piazza Brà 28 – or from touts outside the Arena (who sell at little over face value). Most seats are unnumbered, so arrive early – the build-up is fun anyway – and be sure to hire a cushion and bring a sweater.

The pleasing exterior of Verona's Duomo

Romeo and Juliet
Shakespeare's Capulets and Montagues were based on true families (the Cappelli and Montecchi). Their feuds were also real enough, though the characters of Romeo and Juliet are fictional inventions. Nonetheless, it is hard to resist the so-called *Casa di Giulietta* (Juliet's House) on Via Cappello. The house and courtyard are pretty and there's even a balcony, though, as Arnold Bennet pointed out, it is 'too high for love, unless Juliet was a trapeze artist, accustomed to hanging downwards by her toes'.

'There is no world without Verona walls, /But purgatory, torture, hell itself./ Hence – banished is banish'd from the world – And world's exile is death...'

William Shakespeare (*Romeo and Juliet*).

▶▶▶ **Verona**   *114B1*

Verona is one of northern Italy's loveliest and most artistically alluring cities. You should try to spend several days here – a couple seeing the city sights and soaking up the atmosphere, and a few exploring nearby towns like Vicenza, Padua and Mantua. Verona's picturesque centre, evocatively set on the fast-flowing Adige river, is scattered with Roman and medieval remains together with churches, monuments and a labyrinth of old streets – every bit as romantic as when Shakespeare chose Verona as the setting for *Romeo and Juliet*.

In the centre Collect your wits and start a tour in Piazza Brà, the city's mammoth main square. It holds the 1st-century AD **Arena▶▶▶**, one of the largest surviving amphitheatres of the Roman world. Built to hold 20,000 spectators, it still provides the stage for the city's famous summer opera season (see panel). You need not pay for a performance, however, to see its interior, nor to enjoy the cityscape from its upper tiers.

Via Mazzini▶, the centre's elegant main street, leads to a far more intimate square: **Piazza delle Erbe▶▶**, the city's heart and social meeting place. Renaissance palaces and medieval townhouses surround it on all sides, echoing to the bustle and commotion of a colourful fruit and vegetable market.

Alongside it lies one of Italy's most magical piazzas, the **Piazza dei Signori▶▶▶**, once the city's chief public *piazza*, hence its trio of 12th-century civic buildings: the Loggia del Consiglio, a council meeting chamber; the Palazzo del Governo, seat of Verona's medieval rulers; and the

Palazzo della Ragione, a Gothic ensemble whose **Torre dei Lamberti**►► offers dizzying views of the city.

In its lower corner are the **Arche Scaligere**►►►, among the most accomplished Gothic funerary monuments in Italy. They are the tombs of the Scaligeri, principally Cangrande I ('The Big Dog'), a protector of Dante and patron of the arts. His grinning figure looks down from the equestrian statue atop his tomb, distinct from other clan members, whose canopied graves lie behind a wrought-iron palisade (decorated with ladders, the family's emblem and a pun on their name – *scala* means 'ladder').

Going north Not far away is Sant'Anastasia►, Verona's largest church, the focus of the city's most captivating medieval quarter. Here, too, is the **Duomo**►, distinguished by its exterior carvings and Titian's *Assumption* (first altar on the left). Behind the church, cross the river for the **Teatro Romano**► – a ruined Roman theatre – and the modest Museo Archeologico. Above the museum, climb the steps to the Castel San Pietro to enjoy one of the city's best viewpoints. **San Giorgio in Braida**►, just to the west, is worth a look for the *Martyrdom of St George* by Veronese.

Going west More paintings await in the Castelvecchio►►►, a fortress and former Scaligeri seat, now home to the Museo Civico d'Arte. Before you reach its paintings, the castle's maze of courtyards, chambers and passages is a fascinating diversion in its own right. Foremost among the artworks are Madonnas by Pisanello, Carlo Crivelli and Giovanni Bellini; Tiepolo's *Heliodorus*; and Tintoretto's *Nativity* and *Concert in the Open*. Behind the castle the evocatively fortified Ponte Scaligero (1355) crosses the river to Piazza Arsenale, part of a large city park where you can escape the rigours of sightseeing. Wander north and recross the river and you come to **San Zeno Maggiore**►►►, widely regarded as northern Italy's most magnificent Romanesque church. Exterior details to admire include the ivory-coloured façade; the huge rose window and its *Wheel of Fortune*; the reliefs of the main portal; and the extraordinary 12th-century bronze panels of the door. Inside, frescoes cover many surfaces, overshadowed by Mantegna's compelling *Madonna and Saints* above the high altar.

The splendid tomb of Cangrande I

129

THE NORTHEAST

Villa Valmarana ai Nani
Hundreds of villas scatter
Vicenza's countryside.
Some of the best – like the
Villa Valmarana – are only
a stone's throw from the
city. Valmarana is known
for its fresco cycles by
Giambattista and
Giandomenico Tiepolo,
poetic and cheerful depictions of classical stories
and idealised country life.

Villa Cordellina-Lombardi
This villa near Montecchio
Maggiore, 13km southwest
of Vicenza, has further
notable frescoes by
Giambattista Tiepolo.

Basilica di Monte Berico
This gaudy 17th-century
basilica commemorates
two apparitions of the
Virgin, held to signal
Vicenza's deliverance from
plague in 1426. Pilgrims
throng its interior, but for
lay visitors its lures are its
views of the city and two
exceptional paintings:
Montagna's *Pietà* and
Veronese's handsome
*Supper of St Gregory the
Great.*

*Setting up shop:
craft fair in Vicenza's
Piazza dei Signori*

▶▶▶ **Vicenza**   *114B2*

Vicenza is a showcase for the architectural acumen of
Andrea Palladio (see opposite), who over many years
designed or restructured most of the city's finest buildings. Otherwise, it is a wealthy city, grown fat on the back
of a booming electronic sector, Italy's largest textiles
industry, and the printing business.

Piazza dei Signori▶, site of the old Roman forum and
still the city centre, contains the **Basilica▶▶▶**, Palladio's
first project and the building with which he made his reputation. Its tremendous colonnades buttress the earlier
Palazzo della Ragione, a medieval law court whose crumbling exterior had defied all previous attempts at repair.
The **Loggia del Capitanio▶** opposite is also by Palladio,
though never completed. Before leaving the square, enjoy
the sights and sounds of Piazza delle Erbe's fruit and
flower market and take a drink in the Gran Caffè Garibaldi,
an old-world coffee-house overlooking the Basilica.

Corso Andrea Palladio▶▶, the centre's main street, is
lined with palaces, some by Palladio, some by Vincenzo
Scamozzi, his chief disciple: the best are Bonin-Thiene (No
13); Capra (No 45); Pagello (No 47); Thiene (No 67);
Braschi (No 67); the **Palazzo del Comune▶** (No 98); and
the **Palazzo da Schio▶**. To complete a Palladian tour, visit
the **Teatro Olimpico▶▶▶**, Europe's oldest indoor theatre
and perhaps Palladio's finest work. The tourist office
alongside has information on the architect's villas around
Vicenza, and other city-centre palaces like the Valmarana-
Bragna and Porta-Festa. The most famous of all Palladio's
villas is on the outskirts of town. **La Rotonda** was a pleasure pavilion whose elegance of design was widely
copied, particularly in the United States.

No visit is complete without seeing the church of **Santa
Corona▶▶**, site of two sublime paintings: Veronese's
The Adoration of the Magi and Giovanni Bellini's *The
Baptism of Christ.* The **Museo Civico▶** houses works by
Veronese, Bassano, Montagna and Tintoretto.

■ **Andrea Palladio was among the most important Italian architects of the 16th century. Through his reworking of classical idioms he became one of the most influential figures in the development of Western architecture.** ■

Born in Padua in 1508, Palladio was apprenticed to a sculptor at an early age. At 16 he moved to Vicenza and enrolled in the guild of bricklayers and stonemasons. He soon found employment as a mason in a workshop specialising in monuments and decorative sculpture. He later became the protégé of Count Giangiorgio Trissano, a humanist poet and scholar, who guided his studies, directing him to the works of ancient Roman architects like Vitruvius (active 46–30BC). During this period Palladio probably met Alvise Cornaro, the architect responsible for importing the Roman Renaissance style into northern Italy. He also came into contact with Vicenzan high society, whose leading pillars were to employ him to design their palaces and country villas. He embarked on the first of these – the Villa Godi – in 1540.

The legacy of Rome In 1541 and again in 1547 Palladio visited Rome, studying not only the works of Rome's High Renaissance masters – men like Bramante and Peruzzi – but also the city's Roman antiquities, whose classical forms were to inspire much of his work. The fruit of his studies appeared in the variety and proportional subtlety of the many palaces he built over the next 30 years. Of the many classical conceits which informed his buildings, perhaps the most distinctive was the use of the ancient Greco-Roman temple front as a portico (as in La Rotonda).

Another visit to Rome in 1554 produced *L'Antichità di Roma*, which for 200 years remained the standard guidebook to Rome. Even more influential still were *I Quattro Libri dell'Architectura* (1570), four books which together form perhaps the most important architectural treatise ever published.

The last years After 1570 Palladio was preoccupied with church design in Venice, producing Il Redentore, San Giorgio Maggiore and the façade of San Francesco della Vigna. Remarkably, he never received a civic or private commission from the city. His last work was Vicenza's Teatro Olimpico in 1580, the year of his death.

Top: La Rotonda, near Vicenza
Above: Palladio's Venetian masterpiece: San Giorgio Maggiore

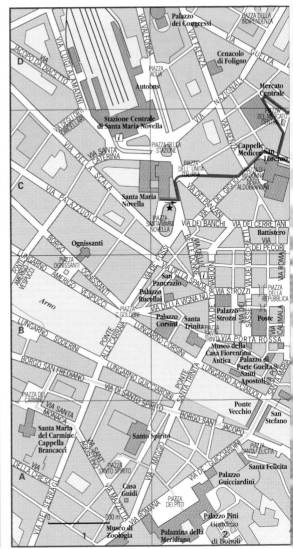

Above: Florentine monk, a link with the past
Below: Florence's unmistakable roofscape

FLORENCE

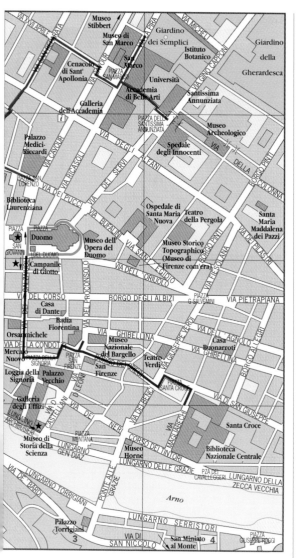

133

CITY HIGHLIGHTS ◄◄◄◄◄

BATTISTERO *see page 137*
DUOMO *see page 137:*
CAMPANILE, THE DOME
SAN LORENZO *see page 138*
SANTA CROCE *see page 138*
SANTA MARIA DEL CARMINE
see page 139
SANTA MARIA NOVELLA
see page 139
BARGELLO, MUSEO
NAZIONALE DEL *see page 140*
GALLERIA DELL'ACCADEMIA
see page 140
GALLERIA DEGLI UFFIZI
see page 140
PONTE VECCHIO *see page 143*

Florence (Firenze) Tuscany's main attraction is as a city-sized shrine to the Renaissance. Florence's churches, palaces and museums are crammed with enough fine art to last a lifetime. Its streets, on the other hand, are surprisingly dour, hunched up with dark *palazzi* and filled with traffic and tourists. One or two notable exceptions aside, therefore, it is a city where your time is best spent indoors, either poring over paintings or swooning over sculpture. Not that the city is without its visual appeal. Few sights are as impressive as a first view of Piazza del Duomo, the Ponte Vecchio or the Piazza della Signoria. But these are aberrations – more points of departure than places to linger. Florence has cafés for relaxation, and gardens, of course, but head for Siena if you want atmospheric streets and medieval charm.

Festivals
Florence's foremost event
is the **Maggio Musicale
Fiorentino**, one of Europe's
leading festivals of opera
and classical music
(April–early July). The
Estate Fiesolana, a festival
of chamber and symphonic
music, is held at Fiesole
(June–late August). ***Box
Office*** at Via della Pergola
10r has information on all
events (tel: 055/242 361).

134

Tourist information
The main tourist offices
are at Via Cavour 1r (tel:
055/290 832), north of the
Duomo, and at Chiasso dei
Baroncelli 17r (near Piazza
della Signoria); tel: 055 230
2124.

Highlights Piazza della Signoria offers the Palazzo Vecchio and the Loggia della Signoria (or Loggia dei Lanzi), Piazza del Duomo the Duomo and Baptistery, while Piazza della Repubblica, situated between the two, is a 19th-century square on the site of the Roman forum. From these central piazzas it only takes a matter of minutes to reach the city's three great galleries: the Uffizi (paintings) and the Bargello and Museo dell'Opera del Duomo (sculpture).

Churches Where Florence's galleries chronicle the Renaissance in its entirety, its churches tend to be monuments to particular artists. Most contain individual works of genius: San Marco (Fra Angelico); San Lorenzo (Michelangelo); Santa Croce (Giotto); Santa Maria del Carmine (Masaccio and Masolino); and Santa Maria Novella (Masaccio, Ghirlandaio and Filippino Lippi). Other buildings offer similar one-off attractions – Michelangelo's *David*, housed in the Accademia, for example, or the sculpture-filled façade of Orsanmichele. And just when you thought it was safe to venture outdoors, there is the city's second-ranked picture gallery – the six-museum complex of the Palazzo Pitti across the Arno, surrounded by the Boboli Gardens.

Origins Ancient *Florentia* was reputedly founded in 59 BC by Julius Caesar (though there was an earlier Etruscan settlement in the hills at nearby Fiesole). Florence emerged from the Dark Ages as an independent city state, prospering through banking and trade in wool and textiles. It was ruled first by mercantile elements (the Primo Popolo); it later passed to the guilds (the Secondo Popolo) and in 1293 to the quasi-republican Signoria (a council drawn from the major guilds).

Guelph and Ghibelline Florence's rise to power, however, was blighted by the Guelph and Ghibelline conflicts that affected many Italian city states (fights between supporters of the Pope and Emperor respectively). Often these were a cover for local rivalries, the most famous of these being the divisions in the Guelph camp between 'Black' and 'White' factions (Dante belonged to the latter, and with many others was expelled from the city in 1302).

The Medici A single family emerged triumphant from Florence's conflicts – the Medici, a banking dynasty founded by Giovanni de' Medici. They were to control Florence – and later Tuscany – for over three centuries. Their power reached its zenith under Giovanni's son Cosimo, and Cosimo's grandson Lorenzo il Magnifico (1449–92), under whose enlightened patronage the city became the engine room of the Renaissance. Influence slipped when Lorenzo's son, Piero, surrendered to the French in 1494, leaving the way open for Savonarola, a charismatic monk who held the city in thrall until executed by the Papacy in 1498.

Last of the Medici The family returned in 1512 with reduced power, only to be removed again in 1527 when Charles V overran Rome (ousting Clement VII, a Medici pope). They were back again just three years later, and under another (distantly related) Cosimo declared themselves Grand Dukes of Tuscany in 1569. The last of the Medici died in 1737, and the city passed by treaty to the future Francis I of Austria. Bar 15 years of Napoleonic rule, it remained under Austrian control (with nominal independence) until Italian Unification in 1860. The city was capital of Italy from 1865 to 1871.

The view from Florence cathedral's dome

■ **Italy's many ghosts include the poets, painters and men of letters lured by what Keats called a 'beakerful of the warm south'. The years between about 1720 and 1790 marked the halcyon days of the Grand Tour, a trip round several European cities, culminating in Rome and Naples, without which no gentleman's (rarely lady's) education was complete.** ■

Top: Thomas Cook's first tour poses for a group photograph in the ruins of Pompeii

Modern visitors
The Grand Tour's turning point came in 1864 when a Mr Thomas Cook ran the first package tour from London to Naples. He provided food, travel, entertainment and accommodation for some 50 people, thus sounding the death knell of travel in the grand style, and ushering in the era of mass tourism.

With at least 50 million visitors a year, tourism is now among Italy's top money-earners, a boon and a bane for residents and, perhaps, for foreigners too, now left with only scraps of the old Italy captured in the poems, paintings, letters and journals of travellers past.

Early visitors After those who came for plunder and pillage, Italy's earliest visitors were pilgrims, drawn by Rome's shrines and churches. Their greatest incursion occurred during the Holy Year proclaimed by Boniface VIII in 1300. Although doubtless designed to line papal coffers rather than provide spiritual solace, Boniface's offer of plenary indulgences attracted some two million visitors.

Pilgrims continued to outnumber tourists until about the 16th century, when gentlemen of substance turned to Italy to add the final polish to their courtly and cultural education. Castiglione's famous book *Il Cortegiano* (The Courtier) was translated and became a bible of behaviour for English courtiers. However, this was also the period in which Italy acquired its reputation for intrigue, corruption and diabolic debauchery.

Paradise of exiles By the 18th century, Italy had come to be seen either as a museum of the past, or as a country where foreigners could cast off their inhibitions and indulge in its more sensuous diversions. Some came for art and inspiration; some sought escape, others health; and many felt the lures of love and lust, hundreds being emboldened by the idea of a warm climate stimulating the passions.

However, the journey to the promised land turned out to be fraught with incident and difficulty. Joseph Addison arrived at Calais and fell into the harbour; Casanova was sexually molested by a policeman; and Tobias Smollett, perhaps the most miserable man ever to travel, found dirt

and disappointment at every turn. Goethe wisely observed that 'every foreigner judges by the standards he brings with him'. Italy worked its spell on countless others, among them Milton, Montaigne, Rubens, Turner, Veláz-quez, Poussin, Tennyson, Liszt, Melville, Nietzsche, Browning, Mark Twain, Henry James.

San Giorgio from the Dogana, sunrise, *painted by JMW Turner on his visit to Venice*

Churches

▶▶▶ Battistero (Baptistery) *133C3*
Piazza San Giovanni
The 11th-century Baptistery is most famous for its bronze doors, whose creation is generally considered to mark the start of the Florentine Renaissance. The south (entrance) doors – cast in 1326 by Andrea Pisano – were already in place when the 20-year-old Lorenzo Ghiberti won a competition to design the others in 1401. The north doors have panels illustrating the Life of Christ; the east doors show Old Testament scenes. Inside are a lovely marble floor; a 13th-century mosaic ceiling; and Donatello and Michelozzo's tomb of the anti-pope John XXIII (a landmark of early Renaissance sculpture).

▶▶ Campanile *133C3*
Piazza San Giovanni
'The model and mirror of perfect architecture', said Ruskin of the Duomo's bell-tower, begun in 1334 to a design by Giotto. It was finished by Andrea Pisano and Francesco Talenti, and decorated with reliefs by Pisano, Donatello and Luca della Robbia (most of the originals are now in the Museo dell'Opera del Duomo). Climb the 414 steps to the top for the vertiginous views – George Eliot did, and found her 'muscles much astonished at the unusual exercise'.

▶▶▶ Duomo (Santa Maria del Fiore) *133C3*
Piazza San Giovanni-Piazza del Duomo
The cathedral was started in 1296 to a design by Arnolfo di Cambio, but only consecrated in 1436, after contributions by several architects, notably Filippo Brunelleschi, whose magnificent dome is one of the miracles of medieval engineering. The interior is spartan; its only major works of art are newly restored frescoes in the dome by Vasari and two equestrian frescoes: a portrait by Uccello of *Sir John Hawkwood*, a famous English mercenary, and a study of *Niccolò da Tolentino*, by Andrea Castagno.

The Gates of Paradise
According to myth, Michelangelo described the Baptistery's east doors as 'so beautiful they are worthy to be the Gates of Paradise'. Their name may actually come from the fact that the district between the Baptistery and Santa Reparata was known as *Paradiso*. Lorenzo Ghiberti included a self-portrait in the frame of the left-hand door. He is the bald, smiling man – the fourth head from the top of the right-hand band. The original doors are being replaced by copies, the restored originals going to the Museo dell'Opera del Duomo.

Baptisms
Every 25 March (New Year's Day in the old Florentine calendar), it was the tradition for all children born in the city over the last 12 months to be brought to the Baptistery for a mass baptism. This made it both the civic and religious symbol of the city.

The Duomo, Florence

The Annunciation
Until the end of the 18th century the Florentine New Year began on 25 March, the festival of the Annunciation – hence the popularity of paintings of the Annunciation and of the church of Santissima Annunziata, a fashionable spot for society weddings. The festival is still marked by a large annual fair in Piazza Santissima Annunziata.

Michelangelo's Tomb
Michelangelo's body was brought back from Rome in 1574 and buried in Santa Croce following a magnificent memorial service in San Lorenzo. His tomb is immediately on the right of the church as you enter. Michelangelo is said to have chosen this spot personally. The reason? – On the Day of Judgement, when the graves of the dead fly open, the first thing he would see would be Brunelleschi's dome on the Duomo.

Santa Croce's 19th-century façade

Mercato Centrale
Be sure to visit this market near San Lorenzo, the largest covered food hall in Europe (built in 1874). It is a fantastic medley of fruit, vegetable, meat and fish stalls, plus all manner of bars and specialist food shops (tripe, pasta, olive oil etc). It is open Monday–Saturday 7–2 and also Saturday 4–8pm. The streets around it are crammed with stalls selling cheap bags, belts, shoes and clothes.

►► **Orsanmichele**   *133B3*
Via dei Calzaiuoli
Built originally as a granary, Orsanmichele became a trade hall for the city's guilds and later a place of worship. Each guild commissioned a piece of sculpture for the church's exterior, eliciting works from artists such as Ghiberti, Verrocchio and Donatello. Inside is a large, highly ornate marble **tabernacle** by Andrea Orcagna (1355–9).

► **Santissima Annunziata**   *133 D4*
Piazza Santissima Annunziata
Several of this church's frescoes repay a visit, chiefly Andrea del Castagno's powerful works (first chapel on the left) and the paintings of Pontormo, Rosso Fiorentino and Andrea del Sarto (in the entrance atrium).

►►► **Santa Croce**   *133A4*
Piazza Santa Croce
Florence's most famous church is renowned for its frescoes and the tombs of some of the city's most illustrious personalities. The key frescoes are two cycles by Giotto, painted in the Peruzzi and Bardi chapels right of the altar. One has scenes from the life of St Francis, the other episodes from the lives of St John and John the Baptist. The frescoes near by are by Taddeo Gaddi and his son. Among the church's 270 tombs are shrines to Machiavelli, Michelangelo, Galileo, Rossini and Dante (the last is empty, as Dante was exiled from Florence and is buried in Ravenna).

Donatello has two exceptional works on display in the church, a relief of the Annunciation and a wooden Crucifixion.

If you revel in Renaissance architecture, make sure you pay a visit to Brunelleschi's Cappella dei Pazzi, which is a masterpiece of the genre.

▶▶▶ San Lorenzo 132C2
Piazza San Lorenzo

Founded in the 4th century as the city's first cathedral, San Lorenzo later became the parish church of the Medici. Most people come here for the **Cappelle Medicée**, the family's mausoleum (entered via a separate entrance behind the church). It contains four tombs, two of them sculpted by Michelangelo: one for Lorenzo (grandson of Lorenzo the Magnificent), carved with reliefs representing *Dawn and Dusk*, the other for Lorenzo the Magnificent's youngest son Giuliano, decorated with figures representing *Night and Day*. Michelangelo also designed the Biblioteca Laurenziana, an extraordinary Medici library (located in the cloister off the main church).

▶▶▶ Santa Maria del Carmine 132A1
Piazza del Carmine

This church contains Masaccio's famous Brancacci fresco cycle, one of the great Renaissance masterpieces. Masolino da Panicale started the cycle in 1425, and was joined by Masaccio (then aged 22), first as an assistant, later – when his genius became apparent – as an equal. The paintings were a turning-point in Renaissance art, demonstrating innovative use of perspective, increased drama and naturalism, and a virtuoso handling of light and space. They were completed by Filippino Lippi 60 years after Masaccio's untimely death (at the age of 25).

▶▶▶ Santa Maria Novella 132C1
Piazza Santa Maria Novella

Santa Maria Novella's gloomy interior hides several of Florence's foremost frescoes, most notably Masaccio's 1428 *Trinity*, one of the first Renaissance paintings to master the principles of perspective. Crowds gathered at its inauguration, unable to believe a painting could create a 'recession' in a solid wall. The Cappella Strozzi is lavishly frescoed by Filippino Lippi, and the apse contains frescoes by Domenico Ghirlandaio. Ensure that you see the richly decorated **cloisters▶▶**, the Chiostro Verde, with frescoes by Paolo Uccello, and the Cappella degli Spagnuoli.

▶▶▶ San Miniato al Monte 133A4

Florence's finest Romanesque church perches above **Piazzale Michelangelo▶▶**, – a stunning vantage point that offers some of the city's most memorable panoramas. If you do not fancy the walk up the hill, take the regular No 13 bus from the station or Piazza del Duomo. The beautiful multicoloured façade dates from the 11th century, its pediment crowned by an eagle, a symbol of the guild entrusted with the church's well-being. The interior is distinguished by the unusual raised choir and large crypt, by an old pulpit and fragments of inlaid pavement (1207) and by the walls' 15th-century frescoes.

Art lesson
'All the most celebrated sculptors and painters since Masaccio's day have become excellent and illustrious by studying their art in this chapel.'
Giorgio Vasari on the Brancacci Chapel.

San Miniato
San Miniato (St Minias) belonged to a Christian community that settled in Florence in the 3rd century. After his martyrdom (he was beheaded), his corpse is said to have carried his severed head across the Arno to the site of the present church.

Stained glass in Santa Maria Novella

FLORENCE

Italy's most famous gallery, the Uffizi. Most of its contents were left to the city by the Medici family

Palazzo del Bargello

The building housing the Bargello's collection was once home to the *Podestà*, the city's chief magistrate, its courtyard the site of numerous executions. It was the Florentine custom to paint the condemned prisoners – artists as eminent as Botticelli undertook the commissions – whose portraits were hung on the palace's exterior walls. The building took its present name in the 16th century, when the chief of police – the *Bargello* – took up residence.

David's deformities

Michelangelo's *David* was originally destined to reside in front of the Duomo. It was intended as a piece of public sculpture, not a gallery exhibit, which explains its deliberate deformities – the huge head, overlong arms and overlarge hands – all of which serve to increase its monumental effect.
Started when the artist was 26, it took three years to complete, and when finished was the largest statue sculpted since Roman times.

Art Galleries

▶▶▶ Bargello, Museo Nazionale del   133B3

Via del Proconsolo 4
Italy's pre-eminent collection of Renaissance sculpture starts in style, opening with four Michelangelo masterpieces, including a serene *Apollo*, before moving on to the flamboyant art of Cellini and Giambologna. The first floor highlights include famous works by Donatello, and reliefs by Ghiberti and Brunelleschi, which took first and second place in the competition to design the Baptistery doors.

▶▶▶ Galleria dell'Accademia   133D3

Via Ricasoli 60
Most visitors come here for one thing – Michelangelo's *David*, the most famous male nude in the history of art. The gallery contains six other figures by Michelangelo – a *Pietà*, an unfinished *St Matthew*, and *Four Slaves*, the latter still deliberately 'imprisoned' in their stone.

▶▶▶ Galleria degli Uffizi   133A3

Piazzale degli Uffizi
Some of the world's best-known Renaissance paintings are here. Three majestic altarpieces by Cimabue, Duccio and Giotto open proceedings, followed by six rooms of Sienese and Gothic art. Then come the familiar names: Room VII (Fra Angelico, Paolo Uccello and Piero della Francesca); VIII-IX (Pollaiuolo and Filippo Lippi); and X-XIV (Botticelli). Later rooms include canvases by Leonardo da Vinci, Michelangelo, Raphael, Caravaggio and many more.

Museums & Palaces

▶▶ **Casa Buonarroti** 133B4
(Michelangelo Museum)

Via Ghibellina 70
Michelangelo never lived in this house, which belonged to his nephew, and its jumble of memorabilia includes only two accredited original works: the *Madonna della Scala*, his earliest known sculpture (executed when he was just 16), and the *Battle of the Centaurs*, carved not long afterwards. He is also credited with a *Crucifix*, discovered in Santo Spirito in 1963.

▶▶ **Museo dell'Antica Casa Fiorentina** 133B2

Via Porta Rossa 13
The museum occupies the Palazzo Davanzati, part of which has been furnished and decorated to suggest the appearance of a 14th-century Florentine house. Its rooms range from a typical kitchen to a frescoed bedchamber, all filled with fascinating period detail, including art, furniture, fabrics, tapestries, lace and domestic objects from the 14th to 18th centuries.

▶ **Museo Archeologico** 133C4

Via della Colonna 36
The Archaeological Museum's rambling collection embraces Greek, Roman and Egyptian objects, but is of most interest for its Etruscan exhibits. It suffered terribly in the 1966 flood, and ongoing restoration work means many of its treasures are still not on show.

Markets
Two of Florence's markets lie close to the Casa Buonarroti: Piazza dei Ciompi's Mercato delle Pulci, the city's flea market, and the Mercato di Sant'Ambrogio, a rumbustious food market missed by most tourists.

Stroll – Giardino dei Semplici
Close to San Marco and the Archaeological Museum is the Giardino dei Semplici, created by Cosimo I as a medicinal and botanical garden in 1545. A peaceful spot for a stroll, it retains its original layout, with medicinal herbs, Tuscan plants, flowers and shady avenues. The entrance is at Via La Pira 4.

141

▶▶▶ **Museo dell'Opera del Duomo** 133C3

Piazza del Duomo 9
The sculpture collection is drawn from works removed from the Duomo, Campanile and Baptistery. On the ground floor are reliefs from the cathedral's first façade (the present façade is a 19th-century addition).

Upstairs (after passing a *Pietà* by Michelangelo), you can see two masterly sculptures by Donatello – the *Prophet Habakkuk* and *Mary Magdalene* – and two *cantorie* (choir lofts), one also by Donatello and the other by Luca della Robbia. In the last room stand several of Ghiberti's original bronze panels from the Baptistery doors, together with a silver altarpiece by Pollaiuolo and Verrocchio.

Sculpture in the Museo dell'Opera del Duomo

FLORENCE

Museo Stibbert

One of the city's more off-beat museums lies 1km north of San Marco at Via Stibbert 26. Its 64 rambling rooms contain a 50,000-piece private collection, ranging from snuffboxes to paintings, but best known for one of the world's greatest assemblages of armour and militaria.

Henry James on Fra Angelico:

'He apparently never received an... impression of evil; his conception of human life was a perpetual sense of sacredly loving and being loved...'

Filippo Lippi

Filippo Lippi (1406–69) was a notorious womaniser – despite his monastic calling. Vasari said he was 'so lustful that he would give anything to enjoy a woman he wanted ...and if he couldn't buy what he wanted then he would cool his passion by painting her portrait'. On one occasion, Cosimo de' Medici – despairing of a commission ever being completed – locked him in the studio of the Palazzo Medici, only for Lippi to escape down a rope of knotted sheets.

Loggia della Signoria

Many of the statues outside the Palazzo Vecchio are copies – not those in the nearby Loggia della Signoria, however, an open loggia which contains two great originals: Benvenuto Cellini's bronze *Perseus* and Giambologna's *Rape of the Sabine Women*.

Part of the grounds behind the Medici's vast Pitti Palace

►►► Museo di San Marco (Fra Angelico Museum)   133D3

Piazza San Marco 3

Cosimo de' Medici rebuilt the monastery of San Marco for the Dominicans in 1437. During the work, Fra Angelico – himself a Dominican monk here from 1436 to 1447 – frescoed much of the building, creating the paintings as a hymn to God. The peaceful ex-monastery is now a veritable memorial to this most sublime of Renaissance painters. The Ospizio dei Pellegrini (Pilgrims' Hospice) near the entrance contains around 20 works, mostly collected from churches around Florence. The Sala Capitolare (Chapterhouse) across the cloister conceals a powerful *Crucifixion*, but Fra Angelico's single greatest work, the *Annunciation*, is on the stairs leading to the monks' dormitory cells, all 44 of which contain Biblical vignettes frescoed by the artist and his assistants.

► Museo di Storia della Scienza (History of Science Museum)   133A3

Piazza dei Giudici 1

This fascinating little museum, recently overhauled, explores the technological side of the Renaissance and the period's close links between art and science. It includes antique clocks and instruments, a reconstructed alchemical laboratory, surgical and anatomical models, and much material connected with Galileo.

►► Palazzo Medici-Riccardi (Medici Palace)   133C3

Via Cavour 1

This monolithic Renaissance palace was designed for Cosimo il Vecchio in 1444 and enlarged two centuries later by its new owners, the Riccardi family. Two windows in the ground floor arches are attributed to Michelangelo, and were copied in numerous *palazzi* around the city. The only part of the Medici wing to survive is the chapel, which contains limpid frescoes of *The Journey of the Magi* by Benozzo Gozzoli, a pupil of Fra Angelico (its figures are portraits of members of the Medici family). A first-floor gallery has a painting by Filippo Lippi, for whom Cosimo established a workshop in the palace.

▶▶ **Palazzo Pitti** 132A2

Piazza de' Pitti

The Pitti family commissioned this colossal palace around 1460 in an attempt to outdo the Medici – only for the Medici to buy them out in 1541. It now houses six separate museums. Of these the Galleria Palatina is by far the most important, though its impact would be greater if the paintings were better hung and the rooms less labyrinthine. Nonetheless, its highlights include 11 Titians and 14 Raphaels, a good selection of works by Andrea del Sarto, and paintings by Perugino, Caravaggio, Velázquez, Rubens and Van Dyck.

▶▶ **Palazzo Vecchio** 133B3

Piazza della Signoria

What this palace lacks in grace it makes up for in grandeur. Its imposing bulk and sturdy campanile loom over Florence's main piazza. Started in 1299, it was built to house the *signoria*, the city's ruling council, selected from Florence's seven major guilds. Most of its public apartments are worth a look, particularly the Salone dei

Museo di Zoologia

This museum (also known as *La Specola*) is a stone's throw from the Palazzo Pitti (at Via Romana 17). Most visitors come for the *Cere Anatomiche* – Anatomical Waxworks – open only Tuesday and Saturday 9–noon). It contains over 600 models made between 1775 and 1814, ranging from entire corpses to arms, legs and organs, each minutely dyed and detailed to reveal nerves, muscles and blood vessels. The most famous room shows four wonderfully graphic tableaux of Florence during the plague.

Cinquecento, full of statues and second-rate frescoes by Vasari. Off the *Salone* lies the Studiolo, a tiny masterpiece of Mannerist decoration. The Sala dei Gigli features frescoes by Ghirlandaio and a newly restored *Judith and Holofernes* by Donatello.

▶ **Ponte Vecchio** 132A2

This bridge and its picturesque huddle of overhanging shops is one of the city's most familiar landmarks. It was built in 1345, and its shops once included butchers, grocers and blacksmiths, all of which were removed in 1593 on the orders of the Medici Ferdinand I. The bridge contained a private corridor between the Medici offices in the Uffizi (*ufficio* – office) and the family's palace (the Palazzo Pitti). Unfortunately for the shopkeepers he objected to slabs of meat and other produce not fitting for the ducal passage. Since then the bridge has been the preserve of jewellers and goldsmiths.

Top: Ponte Vecchio Above: buildings on the 14th-century bridge

Walking in Florence

■ **Florence's occasionally gloomy streets are not as appealing to wander through as those of some other cities, but almost any itinerary takes you to churches, palaces, art galleries and museums of immense individual interest.** ■

Stroll – Giardino di Boboli
The Boboli gardens behind the Palazzo Pitti have innumerable peaceful corners for quiet strolls or leisurely picnics. Above the garden looms the Forte di Belvedere, from where there are unforgettable panoramas of the city. Access to the Belvedere is possible from the Costa San Giorgio, a lane behind Santa Felicita

A dramatic corner of Santa Maria Novella

Piazza del Duomo A wander around Piazza del Duomo and the adjacent Piazza San Giovanni introduces you to three of the city's landmarks – the Duomo, Battistero and Campanile. Stroll along the cathedral's southern exterior and you come to the Museo dell'Opera del Duomo.

Piazza della Signoria to Santa Croce From Piazza del Duomo follow Via dei Calzaiuoli, Florence's main street. Stop off at Orsanmichele, and in Piazza della Signoria, the city's main square. The piazza contains the Palazzo Vecchio and Loggia della Signoria (and the Uffizi is near by). Heading east you can then take in the Bargello and some of the attractive streets that lead to the church of Santa Croce.

Santa Maria Novella to the Museo di San Marco Start at the church of Santa Maria Novella. Cross Piazza dell'Unità Italiana to its east and take Via del Melarancio to San Lorenzo and the Cappelle Medicée. See the Palazzo Medici-Riccardi before cutting up to look around the Mercato Centrale, Florence's busy covered market. Then head north to see Sant'Apollonia and Andrea del Castagno's important but surprisingly little known fresco of *The Last Supper*. The Galleria dell'Accademia and Museo di San Marco lie a short distance east.

If you have time this walk can also encompass a trio of more minor sights around Piazza della Santissima Annunziata: the Museo Archeologico, Santissima Annunziata and the Spedale degli Innocenti.

Oltrarno This walk takes in some of the city's quieter reaches south of the River Arno. Start either at the Museo di Storia della Scienza or the Ponte Vecchio. Pop into the church of Santa Felicita to see one of Florence's greatest Mannerist masterpieces, Pontormo's *Deposition*, and then walk west to see Santo Spirito and Santa Maria del Carmine. Finish at the Palazzo Pitti and Giardino di Boboli (see panel).

Transport and shopping

Getting about Walking is the most practical way to see Florence – most of the city's sights are close together and traffic is restricted in the city centre. Orange ATAF **buses** can be used to cover larger distances, or to visit outlying spots like San Miniato al Monte. Most services stop in Piazza del Duomo (see panel – Useful Bus Routes). Tickets are valid for 70 or 120 minutes (for any number of journeys). They must be bought before boarding and are available from *tabacchi* or automatic machines around the city; 24-hour passes are also available. A few buses displaying a sign of a hand holding a coin have ticket machines on board which accept change.

If you are **driving**, the *zona a traffico limitato* (ZTL) – the city centre traffic restrictions – will prevent you taking your car into the centre between 7:30am and 6:30pm Monday to Friday. You can usually enter to unload luggage at hotels but must then leave the restricted zone and park elsewhere. The main car parks are Fortezza da Basso (behind the train station); Piazza Vittorio Veneto; Piazza del Carmine; Piazza Piave; Piazza Mentana; and Piazza Santa Maria Nuova. All become busy and all are pay car parks.

Quality does not come cheap in Florence

Shopping Florence is a good shopping centre, particularly known for its **leather goods**. The most exclusive stores, including the big-name designer boutiques, are concentrated on Via dei Tornabuoni and its two smaller tributaries, Via Strozzi and Via della Vigna Nuova (**Gucci** among them, which was founded in Florence). Borgo Ognissanti is also crammed with top-quality shops. For slightly cheaper clothes and leatherware visit the market stalls around San Lorenzo, or the **Leather Guild**, Piazza Santa Croce 20r, one of several outlets in Florence where you can watch craftsmen at work.

Jewellery is also of a high standard, with many shops on and around Ponte Vecchio (though prices are high – and beware the fakes sold by some of the street traders). For **antiques** visit Via Maggio, Borgo Ognissanti or the riverside streets like Lungarno Corsini. Speciality **food** shops can be found around the Mercato Centrale. For wines and liquors try **Biagini**, Via dei Banchi 57, off Piazza Santa Maria Novella.

Useful bus routes
No 7 Station–Duomo–Fiesole;
No 10 Station–Duomo–Museo di San Marco;
No 13 Station–Duomo–Piazzale Michelangelo–San Miniato;
No 15 San Marco–Via del Proconsolo–Ponte alle Grazie–Palazzo Pitti–Piazza Santo Spirito–Piazza del Carmine–Fortezza da Basso.
Maps and timetables are available from the ATAF office at Piazza del Duomo 57r.

Bicycle hire
Bicycles (and scooters) can be hired from several points in the city. Try **Bicicittà** outlets at Piazza Pitti, Fortezza di Basso and Via Alamanni (opposite the train station).

Farmacia S M Novella
Be sure to visit this shop, an original monastic pharmacy almost unchanged since the 16th century. It is as famous for its furniture and décor as its products, which include special soaps, face-creams, medieval cures and Dominican herbal remedies. *Via della Scala 16.*

Marbled paper
Florence is one of the few places you can find marbled paper, a craft brought to Venice from the Orient in the 12th century. The oldest outlet (1856) and *the* place to buy is **Giannini**, Piazza Pitti 37r – though it is also the most expensive.

Department stores
Upmarket **Coin** is at Via dei Calzaiuoli; mid-range **Standa** at Via Panzani 31; and bottom-of-the pile **Upim** at Via degli Speziali 3–23.

Accommodation

Hotel agencies
As well as the ITA agency you might try **Florence Promhotels**, Viale A Volta 72 (tel: 055/570 481) and **Toscana Hotels 80**, Viale Gramsci 9 (tel: 055/247 8543). Both take telephone and postal bookings.

A Room with a View
The *pensione* which features in E M Forster's well-known Florence-set novel is the **Jennings-Riccioli**, Corso Tintori 7 (tel: 055/244 751) – though restoration has removed much of the atmosphere evoked in the book. The hotel in which the film of the book was shot was the **Quisisana e Ponte Vecchio**, damaged by a terrorist bomb in 1993, and now, sadly, closed.

Picnics
Picnics cut cost and make pleasant outings. Buy food from *alimentari* or markets like the Mercato Centrale, Sant'Ambrogio (in Piazza Ghiberti near Santa Croce) or Piazza Santo Spirito. Then retire to the Semplici or Boboli gardens, or squares like Santissima Annunziata or Santa Croce.

Florence is undeniably one of Europe's tourist meccas, and although it has well over 400 listed hotels, it is a city where high-season accommodation is at a premium. If you arrive late in the day during July and August, you may well find it difficult to secure a room in almost any category of accommodation.

Ideally, of course, you should book well in advance, but all is not necessarily lost even if you turn up without a reservation. Florence has several agencies who find rooms at a set price for a small commission (which can usually be deducted from your first night's bill). Vacant rooms may only be available on the outskirts of the city, so make sure that you know where your hotel is and how to get to it.

Informazioni Turistiche Alberghiere (ITA) is the best-known of these agencies (see also the panel on this page). They have two year-round offices: one is inside the train station, open daily 8:30am–9pm (tel: 055/282 893) while the other is in the AGIP service station at Peretola on the A11 motorway west of the city (tel: 055/440 790). Seasonal offices (operating between April and October) are located at the Fortezza da Basso (tel: 055/471 960) and the Chianti-Est service area on the A1 motorway.

Choosing a hotel Most budget hotels are near the station (on Via della Scala, Via Nazionale and Via Faenza). Some – but not all – are fairly grim, and certain areas are best avoided at night. The district around Ognissanti has some of the more plush hotels. The quietest spots are in Oltrarno (where there is also more chance of rooms). The residential area around the Teatro Comunale is also a good base (Corso Italia).

Do not judge a hotel by its exterior, for plain façades on gloomy *palazzi* often conceal wonderful Renaissance interiors. Atmospheric and charming villa and palace hotels are widespread in the city centre. Rooms can vary greatly within a building, so ask to see a variety. Noise is as much a factor as it is in any Italian city.

The terracotta pantiles of a Florentine roofscape

Food and drink

Florence likes to claim it introduced cooking to the French – when Catherine de' Medici took a clutch of Florentine chefs to Paris on her marriage to the future Henry II of France. The city's cooking is now wholesome and down-to-earth, centred around basic ingredients like olive oil, top-quality meat and fresh vegetables. Restaurant prices are a little over the odds, as you would expect in a tourist town, but the overall quality is usually reliable and occasionally exceptional. Florentines eat a touch earlier than some – around 12.30 for lunch, 7.30 for dinner. As a general rule, cheap places cluster around the station, the top spots on the main streets, and the quieter *trattorie* in Oltrarno.

Anyone at all interested in Tuscan food should be sure to visit the Mercato Centrale, a superb covered food market located on Via dell'Ariento near San Lorenzo.

Specialities Florence's most famous dish is the ubiquitous *bistecca alla Fiorentina*, a thick, heavily-seasoned Val di Chiana steak grilled over an open fire. Opening shots in a meal are likely to include *crostini* (toasts covered in truffle, olive or liver paste) or strong hams and salamis (boar sausage is common – *salsiccia di cinghiale*). First-course favourites are thick soups like *ribollita* (literally 'reboiled'), *pappa al pomodoro* and *panzanella*, all variations on a theme of vegetables, pulses, oil and bread. The city's most traditional dishes are today rather scarce – things like tripe, pumpkin soup, cocks' combs and kidneys – though they can still be found.

Drinking The best place to sample wine is in a traditional *vinaio*, or wine-shop, which – like most bars – often also sells sandwiches and snacks (see panel). Chianti is the obvious local tipple, but most big Tuscan wines are usually available – Brunello, Vino Nobile and others. Outdoor cafés are not as big a feature as in some cities, but they exist, together with several famous, but rather touristy bars living on past reputations.

Taking a break in Piazza della Signoria

Bars and cafés
Piazza della Signoria's *Rivoire* is the city's classiest café, closely followed by Piazza della Repubblica's grand but more sterile **Gilli, Giubbe Rosse** and **Paszkowski**. **Giacosa**, Via de' Tornabuoni 83r, is good (and claims to have invented the Negroni cocktail). **Robiglio**, Via dei Servi, and **Manaresi**, Via de' Lamberti 16r, both claim to serve Florence's best cup of coffee. **Caffè**, Piazza Pitti 11–12r is a lovely old-world spot. For a perfect *vinaio* visit **Vini e Panini**, Via Cimatori 38r.

Ice-cream
Florence's – some say Italy's – best ice-cream is found at **Vivoli**, Via Isola delle Stinche 7r (between the Bargello and Santa Croce). Follow the crowds.

Enoteca Pinchiorri
This is among Europe's finest restaurants. The wine list matches the quality of the cooking – over 80,000 bottles of fine Italian and French wines. Prices are stratospheric, but for a one-off treat this cannot be beaten. Via Ghibellina 87 (tel: 055/242 777).

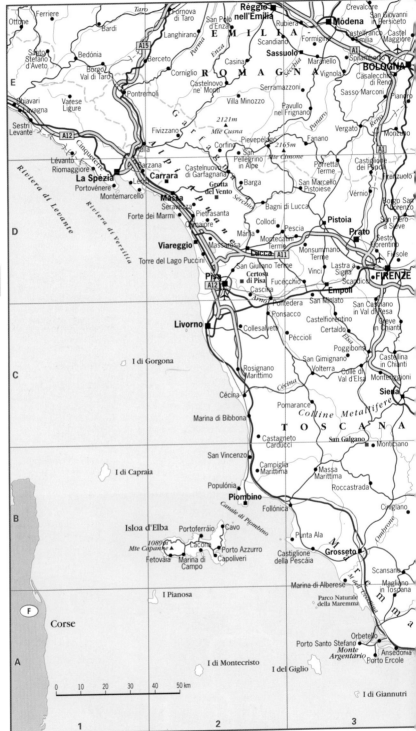

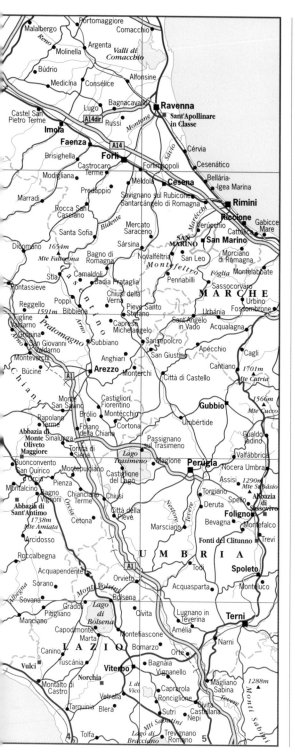

REGION HIGHLIGHTS ◄◄◄◄◄

AREZZO *see page 152:*
SAN FRANCESCO

CORTONA *see page 153:*
MUSEO DIOCESANO

LUCCA *see page 156*

MONTE OLIVETO MAGGIORE
see page 157

PIENZA *see page 158*

PISA *see page 158*

SAN GIMIGNANO
see page 159

SIENA *see page 160:*
THE CAMPO, DUOMO

SOVANA *see page 163*

Tuscany (Toscana) In exploring Florence – with all its treasures – you barely scratch the surface of Tuscany's artistic heritage. Almost every town in Tuscany boasts attractions that could occupy a day's sightseeing. Siena deserves at least that, its calm medieval ambience the perfect foil for Florence's frenetic tourist-filled streets. Little-known Lucca is as graceful a town as any in Italy, often overlooked in favour of Pisa, curiously lacklustre once you have seen the Leaning Tower and its surrounding ensemble. Lofty Volterra, too, has its medieval moments, but is better known for its fine Etruscan museum. Arezzo might be ignored altogether, but for its great frescoes, while nearby Cortona seduces with its fine position and atmospheric streets. Pienza and Montepulciano, too, are both as attractive for their own sakes as for any outstanding art and architecture they offer.

The villages The siren call of Tuscany's towns leaves little time for its villages. No trip to the region, though, would be complete without a visit to San Gimignano and its famous towers, still an evocative sight despite thousands of summer visitors. Fewer people find their way to Sovana, well off the beaten track, but well worth a trip for its charm, churches and Etruscan tombs. Near by, Sorano and Pitigliano complete a fine trio of villages. South of Siena are more villages (see Drive, page 155), most notably Montalcino – famous heart of the Brunello wine region. In this same area, lost in lovely countryside, stand three beautiful abbeys – Sant'Antimo, San Galgano and Monte Oliveto Maggiore.

The landscapes Chianti encapsulates for many people Tuscany's archetypal landscape. There is more to the region, however, than just vineyards and soft, rolling hills. In the far north, for example, rise the mountains of the Orecchiella and Alpi Apuane, famed for their marble and their scenic splendour. Caught between them is the green valley of the Garfagnana. Along much of the coast stretches the Maremma, an often melancholy but

Tourist information
Arezzo: Piazza della Stazione (tel: 0575/377 678).
Cortona: Via Nazionale 42 (tel: 0575/630 557).
Lucca: Piazza Verdi (tel: 0583/419 689).
Montepulciano: Via Ricci 9 (tel: 0578/757 442 or 758 787).
Pienza: Palazzo Civico, Piazza Pio II (tel: 0578/749 071).
Pisa: Piazza del Duomo 8 (tel: 050/560 464).
Siena: Piazza del Campo 56 (tel: 0577/280 551).
Volterra: Via Turazza 2 (tel: 0588/86 150 or 87257).

nonetheless evocative plain edged with low hills. One corner contains the Monti dell'Uccellina, a glorious pocket of coastal landscapes protected by the Parco Naturale della Maremma. South of Siena lie the *crete*, the region's strangest landscape, bare clay hills chequered with prairies of rippling wheat. In the east are the Casentino, Mugello and Pratomagno, all Chianti's scenic equals, but all still largely unexplored by foreign visitors.

Eating Italians who should know better dismiss Tuscans as *mangiafagioli* – bean eaters. The region's cuisine may be simple, but it is hearty and varied, based on excellent olive oils and the finest ingredients. Meals often start with *crostini* (small pieces of toast with liver, olive or tomato pastes), followed by soups like *ribollita* (a thick bread, bean and vegetable broth). Meat dishes include *lepre* (hare); *arista* (pork loin with garlic and rosemary); *pollo alla diavola* (grilled, marinated chicken); and the famous *bistecca alla fiorentina* (a steak grilled over charcoal). Meats often appear *alla cacciatore* ('in the way of the hunter'), simple roasts in a rich sauce of tomatoes, garlic and olives. Wild boar and game birds are also common. For dessert you might find *zuccotto* (sponge cake with cream and chocolate) or *panforte* (a spicy cake of nuts and candied fruit from Siena). Many menus also offer *cantucci*, small almond biscuits traditionally served at the end of a meal with Vin Santo (see below).

Wine Chianti needs little introduction, a wine of infinite variety and quality, sometimes sublime, often insipid. Of greater repute is Brunello di Montalcino and its younger cousin, Rosso di Montalcino. Almost as famous is Vino Nobile di Montepulciano, at its best one of Italy's more majestic reds. Less well-known are the excellent Carmignano, Pomino, Cercatoia (from Lucca) and Morellino di Scansano. Whites include the impeccable Villa Antinori Bianco, the rare Torricella, and variable Vernaccia di San Gimignano. The semi-sweet Vin Santo (Holy Wine) is a famed dessert wine, though its quality is inconsistent.

Scenic drives
SS146/SS451 Montepulciano–Pienza–San Quirico–(Montalcino)–Buonconvento–Monte Oliveto Maggiore; SS222 (*Chiantigiana*) Siena–Castellina in Chianti–Greve–Florence; SS68 Volterra–(San Gimignano)– Colle di Val d'Elsa; SS70/SS208 (Florence)–Pontassieve–Poppi–Camaldoli–Bibbiena–Chiusi della Verna; SS324 Castelnuovo di Garfagnana–San Pellegrino in Alpe–Pievepelago–San Marcello Pistoiese–Pistoia.

Scenic railways
For a look at the Garfagnana and its mountains, ride the little branch line from Lucca to Aulla (two hours). For a plodding journey around the *crete*, some of the region's most distinctive scenery, take the trains from Siena to Grosseto.

Miniature garden in Castellina in Chianti

TUSCANY

Antiques fair
One of Italy's leading antiques fairs, the *Fiera Antiquaria*, takes place in Arezzo's Piazza Grande on the first Sunday of every month. Prices are not for the nervous.

Part of The Legend of the Holy Cross *by Piero della Francesca in Arezzo's San Francesco church*

The Piero della Francesca Trail
To see more famous Piero della Francesca paintings drive 25km east of Arezzo to Monterchi. The village contains his *Madonna del Parto*, the only image of the pregnant Madonna in Italian art. Another 13km on, the Museo Civico in Sansepolcro houses the *Resurrection* and the *Madonna della Misericordia*, as well as several other more minor works.

▶▶ **Arezzo**   *149C4*

An otherwise unexceptional provincial town, Arezzo is distinguished by one of Tuscany's most famous fresco cycles – Piero della Francesca's *Legend of the Holy Cross* in the church of San Francesco▶▶. The frescoes, created between 1452 and 1466, tell the story of the cross used to crucify Christ, and represent one of the largest collections of this enigmatic artist's work (see panel for other noted paintings by him to be seen near by). Elsewhere, the town offers the **Pieve di Santa Maria▶▶**, an attractive Romanesque church with a striking façade and a high altar polyptych by Pietro Lorenzetti, a *Madonna and Child with Saints* (1320). Behind the church rises the **Piazza Grande▶**, a dramatically sloping medieval square, best known for the apse of Santa Maria (see above), which backs on to the square, and the superb carved 1434 doorway by Bernardino Rossellino on the Palazzetto della Fraternità dei Laici in the piazza's northwest corner. Above the square sits the **Duomo▶**, which contains another Piero della Francesca fresco, *Mary Magdalen*. Alongside stands some lovely stained glass and the tomb of Guido Tarlati, perhaps designed by Giotto. The **Fortezza Medicea▶** is a good spot for picnics, and provides a belvedere for views over the hills of the Casentino.

▶ **Casentino**   *149D4*

The Casentino is one of Tuscany's hidden corners. A large, mountain-ringed basin, it embraces the Arno's upper reaches – an undulating agricultural region – and the huge tracts of one of Italy's wildest primeval forests, the **Foresti Casentinesi▶▶** (a proposed national park). Most of the little villages have something of interest, and away from the slightly spoilt valley floor the upland roads are a scenic delight. **Poppi▶** is a picturesque village, centred on a 13th-century castle and fine 12th-century abbey, the Badia di San Fedele. Beautifully situated **La Verna▶** near Chiusi della Verna has a monastery founded by St Francis – it was here that he received the stigmata (a breezy walk behind it leads to La Penna (1,283m) for some fine views). The village of Caprese Michelangelo, birthplace of the great artist whose name it bears, lies just 12km south.

▶▶ **Chianti** *148C3*

Chianti's vineyards and wooded hills form the quintessential Tuscan landscape. They also form a veritable 'Paradise of Exiles' for hordes of foreign ex-pats, an influx that has undoubtedly spoilt certain hilltowns (in summer at least). Other villages – Radda in Chianti and Gaiole in Chianti, for example – are tarnished by a surprising amount of light industry. The region's real pleasures, therefore, are to be found in driving the back roads, exploring the smaller villages and sampling wine at any one of several hundred vineyards open to the public. **Greve in Chianti**▶ lies at the heart of Gallo Nero ('Black Cockerel') country; the consortium of this name is responsible for some of the region's better wine. The village holds a large wine fair every September, and is chock-full of wine shops (the best is Piazzetta Santa Croce's Enoteca di Gallo Nero). Elsewhere, one of the most interesting *cantinas* to visit is the Castello di Brolio at **Brolio**▶.

▶▶ **Cortona** *149C4*

Legend claims hilltop Cortona to be older than Troy, though today the town's appearance is medieval, with old churches and ancient corners dotted around its precipitous cobbled streets. The Renaissance church of **Santa Maria del Calcinaio**▶▶, one of the finest in this part of Italy, stands out as you approach. Piazza della Repubblica forms the town centre, close to the **Museo dell'Accademia Etrusca**▶▶, a fine little Etruscan museum, and to the **Museo Diocesano**▶▶▶ a small but superlative gallery which contains Fra Angelico's *Annunciation* and *Madonna and Child*.

Strada Chiantigiana
For a representative slice of Chianti scenery follow the *Strada Chiantigiana*, the name given to the SS222 road from Siena to Florence. Designed as a *Strada del Vino* (Wine Road), it also cuts through some of the region's less spoilt countryside by way of Castellina and Greve in Chianti.

Wine
Chianti was the world's first officially designated wine-producing area. In 1716 Cosimo III defined the boundaries within which vineyards could claim the *Chianti* name. Now there are seven separate wine-producing zones and over 7,000 registered vineyards. As a result, Chianti is not one wine, but many, with great variety in taste, type and quality. Standards have improved recently, with the best wines most often found in the *Chianti Classico* (*Gallo Nero*) and *Chianti Rufina* zones. Better Chiantis mature at between four and seven years. Recent vintage years have been 1985 and 1986.

The Piazza della Repubblica in the hilltop town of Cortona

Elba and Napoleon

Napoleon spent nine months in exile on Elba in 1814–15. During his brief sojourn as prince of the island (a concession by the British), the erstwhile emperor revamped Elba's iron ore mines, cleared its land, modernised agriculture, and restructured its education and legal systems. Intrigue and unrest in France, however, persuaded his future still lay elsewhere. After escaping from the island he embarked on the 'Hundred Days' that were to culminate in Waterloo.

154

Capraia

Capraia, largely a nature reserve, is by far the most appealing of the several small islands off Tuscany's coast (it is linked by ferry to Livorno and Portoferraio). There is only one small town, Capraia Isola, busy in summer, sleepy off-season. Footpaths criss-cross the mountainous interior, and boat trips operate around the rocky coastline.

Portoferraio on Elba

▶▶ Elba, Isola di   *148B2*

Elba is a world unto itself within Tuscany, hardly a part of the region at all. Its excellent white-sand beaches, limpid waters and lush interior landscapes attract a flood of visitors (over a million in August alone). **Portoferraio▶▶** is the capital, reached by ferry from Livorno and Piombino on the Tuscan mainland. **Marina di Campo▶** on the south coast has the largest beach, but is also the island's biggest and brashest resort. The beautiful part of the island centres on its highest point, Monte Capanne (1,019m), close to two lovely hilltowns – Poggio and **Marciana▶▶** – and on the spectacular cliff scenery of the west coast. In the southeast corner, **Capoliveri▶▶** provides access to a string of small popular resorts.

▶ Forte dei Marmi   *148D2*

Forte dei Marmi was once the main port for exports of marble from the Alpi Apuane. Today it is the most up-market town on the Riviera della Versilia, the string of beach resorts that lines the Tuscan coast north of Pisa. Palm-lined boulevards and a first-rate beach are hardly enough to explain why the town has such an exalted reputation (and prices). It is, however, a favoured holiday retreat for writers and artists, and a good base for excursions into the Alpi Apuane to the east.

▶ Garfagnana   *148D2*

North of Lucca, the Garfagnana embraces the Serchio valley and the staggering mountain ranges of the Alpi Apuane and the Orecchiella. Its towns are undistinguished, though **Bagni di Lucca▶** preserves something of the romantic beauty which attracted Byron, Browning and Shelley in the 19th century. **Barga▶▶** has a Romanesque gem in its cathedral. The Grotta del Vento, about 9km west of Barga, is Tuscany's most spectacular cave. In the **Orecchiella▶▶** drive the magnificent mountain roads to San Pellegrino in Alpe with its **Museo della Campagna▶▶**, an outstanding ethnographic museum.

SOUTH OF SIENA

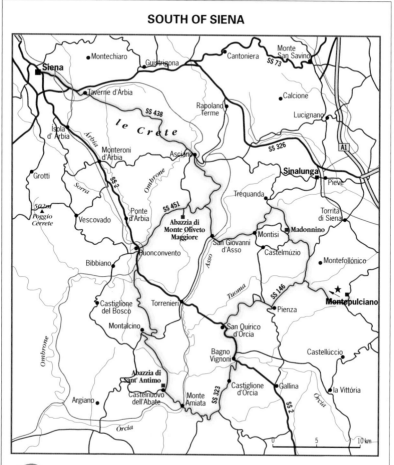

Drive Through Tuscany's heart

A glorious drive which takes you through the heart of the Tuscan countryside, visiting vineyards, abbeys, Roman baths and historic hill-towns.

Start in **Montepulciano** (page 158), and after a look round take SS146 west to **Pienza** (page 158), an essential stop, then drive down to **San Quirico d'Orcia▶** for its Romanesque church, the Collegiata. Just south, detour to **Bagno Vignoni▶▶** to see the sulphurous hot springs in the village square. Continue past the hilltop village of Castiglione d'Orcia to the romantic ruined abbey of **Sant'Antimo▶▶**.

After **Montalcino** (page 157), wind down to Buonconvento, home to an excellent art gallery, the **Museo d'Arte Sacra▶▶**. Climb through beautiful countryside to the wonderfully situated and remote **Abbazia di Monte Oliveto Maggiore** (page 157). Continue to Siena (SS438) or return by country roads to Montepulciano.

Note: you can start this drive from Siena, taking the SS326 towards Sinalunga, then the SS438 to Asciano, a gorgeous road through the *crete* (bare, deeply fissured hills that characterise the landscape south of Siena).

Lucca is Tuscany's most likeable town after Florence and Siena. Its Roman grid of streets is enclosed by tree-lined **walls**►► – which you should walk for the views – and dotted with palaces, museums and Romanesque churches.

San Michele in Foro►►► is the most beautiful of the churches, its muted interior overshadowed by perhaps Italy's most intricate and inspired façade. Home to more precious works of art is the **Duomo di San**

*Façade of Lucca's
San Michele church*

Certosa di Pisa
You can visit this fascinating 14th-century Carthusian monastery from either Pisa or Lucca (21km). Guided tours show you the frescoed main church, 11 tiny chapels and the cloister, with its three-room suites of cells and gardens. Monks lived here in solitude and silence except on Sundays, when they were permitted to speak and eat together. Note the message above the gate as you leave: *Egredere sed non omnis*: 'Leave, but not entirely', addressed to monks sent on missions into the outside world.

Martino►►►. The main portal has carvings by Nicola Pisano, while the nave is dominated by the Tempietto, a gaudy octagon built to house the *Volto Santo*. This highly venerated icon is supposed to be a true effigy of Christ carved at the Crucifixion (it is probably a 12th-century fake). Off the right aisle lies the 15th-century **tomb of Ilaria del Carretto** by Jacopo dell Quercia, one of Italy's most exquisite Renaissance masterpieces. To the left of the duomo in the square stands the Museo della Cattedrale, a fine little collection of art and artefacts.

San Frediano►► stands in the town's northern reaches, distinguished outside by a 13th-century mosaic, inside by a beautiful 12th-century font and a fresco cycle by Amico Aspertini. Near by is the **Piazza del Anfiteatro**►►, a medieval square built in and around the old Roman amphitheatre.

Lucca's museums and galleries are not exceptional: the **Pinacoteca Nazionale**► is as interesting for its extravagantly decorated rococo rooms as for its paintings, but best for art-lovers is the **Museo Nazionale Guinigi**► with good paintings, sculptures, furniture and applied arts. The birthplace of composer Giacomo Puccini, Via di Poggio 30, houses a small museum of Puccini memorabilia.

▶▶ Maremma 148A3

The Maremma stretches from Pisa to the border with Lazio, an area of empty, often melancholy countryside that for centuries has been covered in marsh and wild tracts of *maquis*. Drainage of the region was started by the Etruscans (and finished by Mussolini). Vestiges of its ancient landscapes, however, are preserved in the sublimely beautiful **Parco Naturale della Maremma▶▶**, well worth a visit. The park headquarters are at Alberese, from where a special bus takes you into the park (private traffic is banned from the area).

Tuscany's finest beach lies north of the park, the almost completely uncommercialised **Marina di Alberese▶▶▶**. More developed resorts include **Porto Ercole▶** and **Porto Santo Stefano▶**, up-market spots on Monte Argentario, a mountainous promontory close to the Laguna di Orbetello (some of Italy's best bird-watching territory). To the north are **Punta Ala▶**, a chic, purpose-built resort, and **Castiglione della Pescaia▶**, a moderate resort and fishing village.

Inland, **Massa Marittima▶▶** offers a perfect medieval piazza, with one of Tuscany's best small cathedrals. Other more far-flung villages well worth exploring are Sovana (see page 163), clifftop Pitigliano, Roccalbegna and Castagneto Carducci.

▶▶ Montalcino 149B4

A lovely, if unassuming hilltown, Montalcino produces one of Italy's most prestigious red wines – Brunello di Montalcino. The often busy *enoteca* in the Rocca (castle) is one spot to sample it (the ramparts offer the bonus of good views). No visit to the town is complete, however,

Vineyards
Two outstanding vineyards can be visited around Montalcino: the Fattoria dei Barbi (7km to the southeast), which also has a renowned restaurant attached, and the Villa Banfi (18km southwest), the area's largest and most modern producer.

Abbey of Sant'Antimo, south of Montalcino

without a drink of some sort in the **Fiaschetteria Italiana**, a wonderful 19th-century café in Piazza del Popolo. Around the town, which is well worth an hour's stroll, there are also several little churches and an excellent new Museo Civico.

▶▶▶ Monte Oliveto Maggiore, Abbazia di 149B4

No monastery can be more beautifully situated than Monte Oliveto Maggiore, founded in the 14th century by the Olivetans, or 'White Benedictines', a breakaway group who strove to return to the simple ideals of the Benedictine order. Its great treasure is a 36-panel fresco cycle on the life of St Benedict, by Il Sodoma and Luca Signorelli. The wooden choir of the main church is also outstanding.

Sant'Antimo
The 12th-century Benedictine abbey of Sant'Antimo (10km south of Montalcino) ranks high in Tuscany's pantheon of Romanesque buildings. Its setting, frescoes and carvings are delightful; on Sunday mornings a small group of French Cistercians often celebrate Mass with a Gregorian chant.

TUSCANY

The Leaning Tower of Pisa

▶▶ **Montepulciano**　　　　　　149B4

Hilltop Montepulciano is a perfect blend of medieval, Renaissance and baroque ingredients. As added spice it has the further attraction of Vino Nobile di Montepulciano – the 'king of wines'. An important Renaissance church, Sangallo's **San Biagio**▶▶, stands just outside the walls. Within them, Piazza Grande's ancient *palazzi* compete for attention with the **Duomo**▶▶, known for its Michelozzo sculpture and a sublime altarpiece by Taddeo di Bartolo. There is also a small civic museum. Be sure to climb the tower of the Palazzo Comunale for its views, and to explore the quiet back streets, as seductive as any in Tuscany.

▶▶ **Pienza**　　　　　　149B4

Pienza is a planned Renaissance town, created by Pope Pius II (and named after him) out of Corsignano, the village of his birth. The transformation began under Bernardo Rossellino in 1459, the architect responsible for most of the town's buildings. It was cut short by Pius' death, but not before the consecration of the **cathedral**▶▶▶, a handsome pile with a redoubtable wooden choir and five altarpieces executed by the leading Sienese artists of the day. More paintings (and papal vestments) are displayed in the **Museo Civico**▶ to the cathedral's left. The **Palazzo Piccolomini**▶▶, future seat of a new museum, contains richly appointed papal apartments and offers sweeping views from its courtyard. Churches worth a glance include San Francesco and the **Pieve di Corsignano**▶▶.

▶▶▶ **Pisa**　　　　　　148D2

Pisa's world-famous **Leaning Tower**▶▶▶ needs no introduction. A surprising number of visitors, however, overlook the other magnificent buildings in Piazza del Duomo – otherwise known as the *Campo dei Miracoli* (Field of Miracles). The tower was intended as a campanile for the **Duomo**▶▶▶, a stunning creation famous for its pulpit (by Giovanni Pisano) and paintings by Cimabue and Ghirlandaio. Pisano's father, Nicola, sculpted an equally fine pulpit in the **Baptistery**▶▶▶ near by. In the cemetery, or **Camposanto**▶▶, look out for the Cappella Ammannati's frescoes illustrating *The Triumph of Death* (many other paintings were lost as a result of considerable bombing during World War II). The **Museo dell' Opera del Duomo**▶▶ is something of a mixed bag of sculpture and paintings. The **Museo delle Sinopie**▶ contains sketches for the Camposanto's vanished frescoes. It is worth remembering that a single ticket is available to see all Piazza del Duomo's main sights.

▶▶ Pistoia 148D3

Pistoia's quiet provincial demeanour conceals a superb medieval interior. Its heart is the **Piazza del Duomo▶▶**, site of several stern *palazzi*, the Gothic Baptistery and the 12th-century Duomo. The cathedral boasts possibly the greatest piece of silverware in Italy, the Dossale di San Jacopo. Started in 1287 and not completed until the late 15th century, this amazing altarpiece weighs over a tonne and features 628 sculpted figures. Of the town's many churches, two deserve special attention: **San Giovanni Fuorcivitas▶▶** and **Sant' Andrea▶▶**, the latter home to a pulpit by Giovanni Pisano, a masterpiece of Italian Gothic sculpture.

▶▶ San Galgano, Abbazia di 148B3

San Galgano may not be Tuscany's best preserved building – the roof has collapsed and the nave is a grassy square – but it is by far its most romantic and atmospheric. Founded in 1218 by the Cistercians, it was for a period Tuscany's leading monastic centre. Be sure to walk to the nearby **Chiesetta di San Galgano▶▶**. The effort is rewarded by fine views and fragments of 14th-century fresco.

▶▶▶ San Gimignano 148C3

Few places look as thoroughly medieval as San Gimignano. Its famous crop of towers – a 'Renaissance Manhattan' – together with its art-filled churches make it one of the most popular excursions from Florence or Siena. Suffer the crowds to climb the Torre Grossa in Piazza del Popolo, one of the town's 14 surviving towers (out of an original 72). Also battle into the **Collegiata▶▶▶**, beautifully and comprehensively frescoed by three separate artists, including Taddeo di Bartolo. Also leave time to visit the **Museo Civico▶▶**, which is full of interesting Gothic and Renaissance paintings. Climb to the Rocca (castle) for its views, and to the church of **Sant'Agostino▶▶** for Benozzo Gozzoli's fresco cycle on the life of St Augustine.

Pistols
Pistoia was one of Italy's most violent medieval towns – Michelangelo called its inhabitants 'enemies of heaven' – which makes it only fitting that it should be responsible for the word 'pistol'. A *pistole* was originally a dagger, but the name came to be used for the small firearms made in the town during the 16th century.

Vernaccia di San Gimignano
Once one of Tuscany's greatest white wines, Vernaccia vintages are these days pale imitations of their former selves. Pale and flowery wines have largely replaced the aged, golden wine of times past. Good wines are still produced, however, notably by Falchini and Teruzzi & Puthod.

159

San Gimignano, a medieval jewel, is celebrated for its beautiful skyline

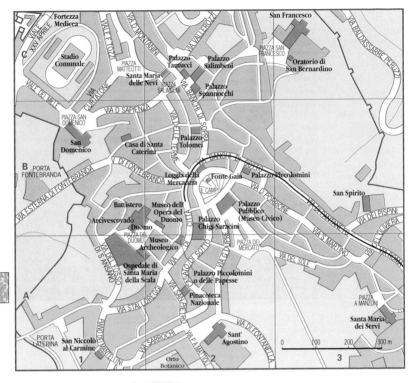

▶▶▶ **Siena** *148C3*

Florence's long-term historical rival is still its main rival for the attentions of visitors. Siena is the medieval city *par excellence*, more intimate and, for many who get to know it, ultimately more appealing than the Tuscan capital, notwithstanding all the latter's artistic bounty.

The Campo, Siena's magnificent heart

The Campo Siena's heart is the sloping semicircular Campo, Italy's greatest square and scene of the famous Palio (see page 162). At its lowest edge stands the Palazzo Pubblico►►►, long Siena's town hall, but also home to the Museo Civico. Numerous paintings line its walls, none more famous than two frescoes attributed to Simone Martini in the Sala del Mappamondo: a *Maestà* (1315) and the *Portrait of Guidoriccio da Fogliano*, a lovely courtly image of a *condottiere* on horseback.

Almost equally notable are the frescoes in the next room, the Sala dei Nove: Ambrogio Lorenzetti's *Allegories of Good and Bad Government*, panels which most entertainingly illustrate the consequences of good and bad government. If you can face the 503 steps, climb the adjacent **Torre del Mangia**►► next door for all-embracing views of the town. Before leaving the square, pay through the nose at least once for a drink at one of its many cafés – worth it just to enjoy the piazza and all its myriad comings and goings.

Monteriggioni
This unmissable village, 12km north of Siena on the SS2, rivals San Gimignano as the most evocative and complete medieval ensemble in Tuscany. Its fame rests on its perfectly preserved 13th-century walls, a formidable set of fortifications which look out from their unspoilt hilltop site over the surrounding countryside.

Siena's cathedral
Below: dome and campanile; bottom: interior

161

The Cathedral A short walk away the decorated façade of the Duomo►►► makes an exuberant introduction to a still more impressive interior. Of particular note are the inlaid marble pavement, Nicola Pisano's great pulpit, Donatello's bronze pavement (north transept), and the Piccolomini altar, partly sculpted by Michelangelo. Above all, though, see the Libreria Piccolomini (off the left aisle), with Pinturicchio's recently restored frescoes on the life of Pope Pius II (Aeneas Piccolomini). The baptistery, below the east end of the cathedral, contains one of Siena's leading Renaissance treasures, a baptismal font decorated with bronze panels by Donatello, Lorenzo Ghiberti, Jacopo della Quercia. Opposite the Duomo, do not miss the **Ospedale di Santa Maria della Scala**►►► and its superb church and fresco cycles.

More paintings Behind the Duomo, the **Museo dell'Opera del Duomo (Cathedral Museum)**►► contains the greatest of all Sienese paintings, a *Maestà* by Duccio (1311). For a full résumé of the city's art, however, visit the **Pinacoteca Nazionale**►►►, which is crammed with paintings by – among others – Duccio, Simone Martini, Pietro and Ambrogio Lorenzetti, Sassetta and Bartolo di Fredi.

■ **Siena's Palio is no mere tourist attraction. This horse-race, run twice yearly in the Campo, is not only Italy's most spectacular festival, it is also a symbol of the intense rivalries that still rage between the town's medieval *contrade*, or districts.** ■

Special events

Of the 600 or so Palios run since the 17th century – a second annual race was created in 1639 to be run each 16 August – around 60 have been held to celebrate special events. In 1809, races took place to mark Napoléon's victorious return to Paris; in 1849 to celebrate the opening of the Siena–Empoli railway; in 1945 to mark the end of World War II; in 1947 to record the sixth centenary of St Catherine's birth; and in 1969 to acknowledge the first lunar landing.

162

Origins The Palio has taken place almost every year since medieval times (though the custom may well go back further). It takes its name from the *pallium*, a banner embroidered with an image of the Virgin and presented to the race's winner. Originally run through the town's streets, the pageant moved to the Campo during the 16th century.

The *contrade* Siena has 17 *contrade* (districts), each with its own flag and heraldic motif (usually an animal), as well as its own church, museum and social centre. (At one time there were reputedly 59 *contrade*.) Allegiance to the *contrada* of your birth is still absolute – after a conventional baptism, children are baptised again in their *contrada* fountain. Each *contrada* holds an annual parade, and the *alfieri*, the famous flag-throwers, can often be seen practising in the streets.

Only 10 *contrade* may take part in the race, so lots are drawn to make the selections. Horses are also drawn by lot, though *contrade* select their own jockeys, many of whom are drawn from the *butteri*, the traditional cowboys of Tuscany's Maremma region. Other representatives of the *contrade* well in evidence are the flag-bearers, drummer, captain, grooms and pages.

Anything goes in the world's most colourful horse-race

The race The races are run on 2 July and 16 August, but the days beforehand are filled with numerous processions and pageantry. Trial races are run, parties held, and – most importantly – the horses are blessed in church (dung produced in the church is taken as a good omen). Meanwhile, jockeys can be bribed or ambushed before the race, and alliances are forged and broken between different *contrade*. Huge bets ride on the result. In the race itself, which lasts just 90 seconds, anything goes except interfering with a rider's reins. Despite the obvious dangers, no-one – supposedly – has ever been killed, thanks, say the Sienese, to the protection of the Virgin Mary (in whose honour the race is run). Even if you are not in Siena on race-day – when the town is hugely crowded – national television broadcasts the race live.

▶▶▶ Sovana 149B4

Tiny Sovana is as historically interesting a village as you will find in Italy. For centuries it was controlled by the Aldobrandeschi, a noble clan who held sway over much of the region. The election of a family member, Hildebrand, as Pope Gregory VII in 1073, brought it great wealth (reflected in buildings now out of all proportion to the village's size).

There is just one street, and one tiny square, Piazza del Popolo. On its left side stands **Santa Maria▶▶▶**, a glorious Romanesque church, remarkable for its frescoes and 9th-century ciborium (altar canopy). Along a country lane lies the **Duomo▶▶▶**, whose 8th- to 12th-century interior contains fascinating early carvings and a wonderfully intimate crypt. The countryside around the village is scattered with hundreds of **Etruscan tombs▶▶**, notably the Tomba della Sileno, Tomba del Sireno and **Tomba Ildebranda▶▶**, considered Tuscany's finest single tomb.

▶ Viareggio 148D2

Viareggio – Tuscany's 'Biarritz' – is almost Florence-on-the-Sea, kids and Italian families flocking here in summer from the region's landlocked capital. In the 19th and early 20th centuries it was a fashionable resort, vestiges of its heyday still visible in the town's famous Liberty and art-deco buildings. It is still a relatively sedate spot, with the Versilia coast's best facilities and beaches.

▶▶ Volterra 148C3

Dark, Etruscan Volterra dominates a strange, empty countryside from its magnificent hilltop position. **Piazza dei Priori▶▶**, the town's central square – of stage-set medieval perfection – is dominated by the Pisan-style Duomo and baptistery, the former noted for its pulpit and *The Magi,* a 15th-century fresco by Benozzo Gozzoli. For more paintings, pay a visit to the **Pinacoteca Comunale▶**, the star of which is Rosso Fiorentino's extraordinary *The Descent from the Cross,* a particularly good example of the Mannerist genre. Fans of Etruscan craftsmanship and culture should also visit the **Museo Etrusco Guarnacci▶▶**, one of Italy's major archaeological museums. Also wander the town's outskirts to see its many Roman remains, the *balze* – deeply eroded cliffs and gullies – and the shady gardens of the pleasant **Parco Archeologico▶**.

Sovana's sisters
Sorano and Pitigliano are sister villages to Sovana. Sorano is approached by roads cut through solid walls of tufa (volcanic rock) and fringed by hundreds of niche-like Etruscan tombs. Landslides have undermined the village, which has a strange, deserted air, but plenty of medieval corners remain. Pitigliano is dramatically situated on a steep-sided tufa crag. Etruscan tombs, ancient caves and old wine cellars honeycomb the cliff, and though there is little to see, the streets are peaceful and, as in Sorano, the views delightful.

Some of Volterra's extensive Roman remains

UMBRIA AND LE MARCHE

Umbria Umbria has emerged from Tuscany's shadow, no longer its poorer sister, but a beautiful and varied region in its own right. Its narrow borders harbour a dozen or more hilltowns, each crammed with treasures. Its pastoral countryside has earned the title *il cuore verde d'Italia* (The Green Heart of Italy). It is also Italy's mystical heart, the birthplace of St Benedict and St Francis.

The hilltowns Umbria's hilltowns are the highlight of any visit to central Italy. Pinky-stoned Assisi, birthplace of St Francis, is a medieval jewel (though earthquakes in 1997 severely damaged the town). Perugia, its more stern neighbour, has a warren of dark medieval streets and countless churches and galleries. Orvieto possesses Italy's finest Gothic cathedral. Spoleto and Gubbio (the 'Umbrian Siena') are both delightful medieval towns. Lesser and less-visited places also have their charms, notably Todi, the epitome of a hilltown; Spello, steep and sleepy; and Montefalco, a lofty belvedere with a smart little art gallery.

The countryside Part of Umbria's charm is its soft, gentle countryside. Some is spotted with light industry, but off the main roads the region is a picture of pastoral perfection – all olive groves, oakwoods, vineyards and silver-hazed hills rolling into the distance. Lago Trasimeno provides a watery contrast close to Perugia, while in the east a wild counterpoint is provided by the Valnerina and Monti Sibillini. The unspoilt scenery around Norcia – the equal of any in Italy – contains the Piano Grande, one of the country's most poetic landscapes.

Le Marche (The Marches) There are those who see the Marches following the tourist-filled track of Tuscany and Umbria. Virtually unknown, it has all the ingredients for a popular holiday destination – scenery, beaches and historic towns. Its landscapes vary from the mountains of the Apennines to the jumbled hills and valleys near the coast.

Vineyards carpet the slopes up to Assisi

REGION HIGHLIGHTS ◄ ◄ ◄ ◄

ASCOLI PICENO *see page 167*
ASSISI *see page 168*
GUBBIO *see page 170*
ORVIETO *see page 171*
PERUGIA *see page 173*
PIANO GRANDE *see page 175*
SAN LEO *see page 175*
SPOLETO *see page 176*
URBINO *see page 177*

Violin workshop in Ascoli Piceno

Scenic drives
(*Umbria*): SS209 Terni–San Pietro in Valle–Triponzo–Visso; Visso–Castelluccio–Piano Grande–Norcia; Spello–Monte Subasio–Assisi; SS79 bis Orvieto–Todi; (*Marche*): San Leo–Carpegna–Pennabilli–SS258–Sansepolcro; SS78 Ascoli Piceno–Amandola–Sarnano.

Urbino is unmissable, thanks to its great Ducal Palace, while San Leo and Ascoli Piceno are lesser spots of which any region would be proud. On the coast there are outstanding resorts, notably around Monte Conero and Ancona.

Gastronomy Umbria's gastronomic credentials are almost unknown to foreigners. It is one of only two areas in the country where truffles are found in abundance (the other is around Alba in Piedmont). These strange delicacies have been prized since Roman times for their aromatic, not to mention aphrodisiac qualities. They grace the dishes of many restaurants, especially around Norcia and Spoleto. In Norcia, too, you can eat wild boar, together with Italy's most celebrated salamis, and the miniature lentils of Castelluccio.

The Marches' best-known speciality is Ascoli Piceno's delicious *olive all'ascolana* – hollowed-out green olives stuffed with minced meat and fried in olive oil. Its other great delicacy is *vincisgrassi*, a rich lasagne filled with *prosciutto*, cream and black truffles. Up and down the coast, there are also at least seven different versions of *brodetto* (fish stew). Each town claims the perfect recipe. Ancona's is most famous, perhaps because it contains 13 types of fish. South of Monte Conero the broth is thickened with flour, saffron is used, and slices of bread are toasted. To the north, flour is omitted, vinegar is added, and the bread is eaten untoasted and rubbed with garlic.

Wine Tuscany for a long time outranked Umbria in wine as in much else, but Umbria is now at least the equal, and often the superior of its neighbour. The wines of Torgiano's Lungarotti, the Rubesco Riserva in particular, are among the most distinguished in Italy. Other Umbrian wines are like the region itself – subtle and understated – none more so than the vintages of Montefalco. Try the rare Sagrantino, Rosso di Montefalco and Grechetto (the classic Umbrian white), preferably from producers like Adanti, Caprai and Benincasa. Also look out for Antinori's Cervaro della Sala (which has the potential to become one of Italy's great whites). More humble but still acceptable tipples include Orvieto (white) or Colli Altotiberini (red).

► ▓▓▓ **Ancona**   *164C3*

Ancona is a busy and unattractive port, worth a call only to see the Romanesque church of **San Ciriaco►►** and the newly-refurbished **Museo Nazionale delle Marche►►**, a wide-reaching archaeological collection of palaeolithic and Roman remains.

The town takes its name from the Greek *ankon* (elbow), probably after **Monte Conero►►** to the south (11km). This wild promontory is the only land formation to disturb the ruler-straight coastline that runs for hundreds of kilometres from the Venetian lagoons to the Gargano peninsula. You can explore its rugged interior by walking from several centres, or by driving one of two scenic roads to the churches of Santa Maria di Portonovo and Badia di San Pietro. To see its spectacular cliffs and seascapes take boat trips from Portonovo, Sirolo or Numana, three popular and picturesque resorts on the so-called **Riviera del Conero►**.

►► Ascoli Piceno 164B3

After Urbino, Ascoli Piceno is the Marches' most enticing historic town. Much of its centre still conforms to the layout of the old Roman colony, built after the defeat of the *Picini*, an early Marchese tribe. At its heart lies **Piazza del Popolo►►►**, whose ensemble of medieval buildings creates one of Italy's loveliest squares. Admire it over coffee from the art-deco surroundings of the Bar Meletti, then take a closer look at the Palazzo del Popolo and the church of **San Francesco►►**. To the south stands the **Duomo►**, whose prize exhibit is a 10-panelled altarpiece by Carlo Crivelli, a Venetian artist who is also represented in the **Pinacoteca Civica►►** near by.

The most picturesque part of town (with many medieval watchtowers) lies at the top of Via del Trivio above the River Tronto (walk down Via della Luna for the best views). The area harbours the Gothic church of San Pietro Martire and the more appealing SS Vicenzo ed Anastasio, an 11th-century church built over a primitive 6th-century crypt.

Tourist information
Ascoli Piceno: Piazza del Popolo (tel: 0736/253 045).
Assisi: Piazza del Comune 12 (tel: 075/812 450 or 812 534).
Gubbio: Piazza Odersi 3–5 (tel: 075/922 0790 or 922 0693).
Perugia: Piazza IV Novembre 3 (tel: 075/572 3327 or 573 6458).
Orvieto: Piazza del Duomo 24 (tel: 0763/ 341 772 or 342 562).
Spoleto: Piazza Libertà 7 (0743/220 311).
Urbino: Piazza del Rinascimento 1 (tel: 0722/2613 or 0722/2441).

Ascoli Piceno's beautiful Piazza del Popolo

167

San Damiano
This church lies in a secluded spot amid olive groves, preserving the humility and mystical atmosphere usually associated with St Francis, but absent in much of the town. It was here that the saint received his calling from God, and where he composed his famous *Canticle to the Sun*. St Clare also lived here and the smoke-blackened church, cloister and refectory are little changed from her day. (The church is a pleasant 15-minute walk from Assisi.)

St Francis's Tomb
St Francis was buried in great secrecy to prevent his remains being stolen or desecrated (medieval relics had enormous spiritual and financial value). His tomb was so well hidden that it was only discovered in 1818 after almost two months of excavations.

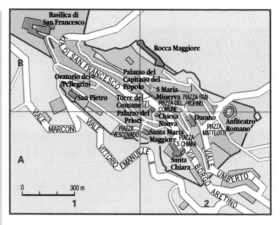

▶▶▶ **Assisi**   *164B2*

A series of earthquakes in late 1997 severely damaged the lovely medieval town of Assisi and subsequently closed its première sight, the **Basilica di San Francesco▶▶▶**, (St Francis's burial place). At the time of writing, it was estimated that it would reopen in the year 2000. The basilica housed many treasures, some of which have been damaged beyond repair. The walls of the sombre, atmospheric Lower Church were covered in frescoes and decorative motifs: including Simone Martini's frescoes of the life of St Martin; the ceiling vaults above the high altar (by Giotto and assistants); and Pietro Lorenzetti's powerful *Deposition* and *Crucifixion*. The walls of the Upper Church were covered by one of Italy's most famous fresco cycles, Giotto's *Life of St Francis* in 28 huge panels. The **Museo-Tesoro della Basilica▶▶**, rich in paintings and precious objects, is to the rear.

The Basilica of St Francis contains the saint's tomb and superb frescoes by Giotto and others

Other sights Elsewhere, see **San Pietro▶**, an expertly restored 11th-century Romanesque church; **Oratorio dei Pellegrini▶**, a lavishly frescoed 15th-century pilgrims' hospice; **Piazza del Comune▶▶**, the town's central square, on the site of an old Roman forum, with the 1st-century Tempio di Minerva; the Basilica di Santa Chiara, St Clare's burial place; and the **Duomo▶**, dull inside, but fronted by a glorious Romanesque façade. From the Duomo walk up to the restored Rocca Maggiore (castle) for mouth-watering views.

Saints

■ **Umbria is Italy's mystical heart, the** ***terra dei santi*** **– land of saints. The region was the birthplace not only of Francis and Benedict, founding fathers of Western monasticism, but also of a multitude of lesser saints including St Clare, St Rita and St Valentine.** ■

Light and landscape Few would deny the strange mystical light that illuminates Umbria's grey-hazed hills. Nor would many dispute the soft-edged beauty of the region's countryside – a landscape that epitomises pastoralism and seems made for peaceful introspection. Could it be that these abstract qualities have helped nurture the region's wealth of saints and mystics?

History Umbria's history and position also have a bearing on its preponderance of saints. One of the Romans' most important consular roads, the *Via Flaminia*, cut through the region, not only linking Rome with the Adriatic, but also providing a conduit for eastern monks and other early Christians fleeing persecution. Umbria's green hills were the first place they came to, many settling in the region's woods and caves, perfect sanctuaries in which to pursue lives of monastic contemplation.

St Benedict Tiny Romanesque churches all over Umbria mark the graves of the region's holy men and women. Each town had its bishop – who was invariably sanctified – each village its saint (or saints). The caves of three such early hermits can still be seen at Sant'Eutizio, a Benedictine abbey north of Norcia. It was through contact with these men – St Spes, St Fiorenzo and St Eutizio – that Norcia's St Benedict (480–547) found his vocation. This apparently minor event was of incalculable importance, for it led ultimately to the creation of the Benedictine Order. (Benedict, incidentally, is the patron saint of Europe.)

St Francis More than 600 years were to elapse before the birth of Umbria's other great saint, St Francis (1182–1226). A humble but revolutionary spirit, he took Christianity back to its basic principles – 'poverty, chastity and obedience'. Among his many followers was St Clare, who formed the Poor Clares, the Franciscans' female wing. Like many orders which sprang from Umbria's soil, it spread throughout Europe and survives to this day. (Francis is the patron saint of Italy.)

Montefalco
Nowhere shows Umbria's preponderance of saints better than Montefalco, a little village that produced eight saints. You can see the 3rd-century bones of San Fortunato (abbey of that name) and the mummified bodies of Illuminata and Chiarella (church of Sant'Agostino) and St Clare (convent of Santa Chiara).

St Francis of Assisi with one of his animal friends

Porte della Morte

Gubbio's famous 'doors of death' are narrow, bricked-up doors wedged into many of the town's medieval façades. They were supposedly used to carry a coffin out of the house. Having been tainted by death, it is said, they were then permanently sealed. In fact, their purpose was probably defensive, the narrow entrance behind the door being easier to defend than the main doors. The best examples are in Via dei Consoli.

Monte Ingino

A visit to this hill above Gubbio is a must: walk up the path behind the Duomo or take the cable car from Porta Romana. There are great views and you can see the *ceri*, large wooden 'candles' used in the Corsa dei Ceri, a 900-year-old pageant held on 15 May.

Wine

Orvieto's fertile volcanic soils partly account for the high reputation of its wine, once so prized that architects working on the Duomo were happy to be paid in it. These days newer and drier Orvietos rank less highly, though the old-style *Orvieto abboccato* is making a comeback through such wines as Decugnano dei Barbi's Pourriture Noble and Bigi's Vigneto Orzalume. Other good producers are Antinori, Dubini and Barberani.

► **Bevagna** 164B2

Plain-bound Bevagna, ancient *Mevania*, until recently a serene backwater sitting within medieval walls, is noted principally for its central **Piazza Silvestri►►**, one of Italy's most perfect medieval squares. On it stand two exquisite Romanesque churches, San Michele and San Silvestro. To one side a monumental staircase leads up to the 13th-century Palazzo dei Consoli. A series of earth tremors in late 1997 severely damaged the town.

Near Bevagna are medieval Foligno, which survived World War II bombs only to be hit by an earthquake in 1997, and the 11th-century Abbazia di Sassovivo with Umbria's finest cloister.

Taking it easy in Gubbio

►►► **Gubbio** 164C2

Umbria has few sights more enchanting than Gubbio's old streets, orange-tiled houses and mountain-backed setting. Start a tour just below the old town in Piazza di Quaranta Martiri, where the church of **San Francesco►►** has an engaging fresco cycle (1510) by Ottaviano Nelli, one of Umbria's earliest important painters. Opposite stands the **Loggia dei Tiratori►**, Italy's best-surviving example of a now rare type of building: wool was stretched out under its arches to dry evenly away from the heat of the sun.

Up in town, interest centres on the vast **Palazzo dei Consoli►►►**, a looming 14th-century palace (and bell-tower) that houses a small art gallery and museum. The latter is noted for the Eugubine Tablets, seven 2nd- to 1st-century BC bronzes inscribed in Latin and Etruscan. Nearby, the **Duomo►** and **Palazzo Ducale►** are worth a glance, so too the churches of Sant'Agostino and Santa Maria Nuova, both with more paintings by Ottaviano Nelli.

►► **Montefalco** 164B2

Known as the *Ringhiera dell'Umbria* (Balcony of Umbria) for its expansive views, Montefalco (the Falcon's Mount) is a delightful, somnolent village with a maze of medieval streets and alleys. The new art gallery in the church of **San Francesco►►►** is exceptional, built around Benozzo Gozzoli's superlative fresco cycle, *The Life of St Francis*. Two other churches deserve a look for their paintings – Sant'Agostino► and Sant'Illuminata►.

▶▶ Norcia   164B2

Norcia's stolid mountain- and market-town atmosphere comes as a surprise after the more bucolic charms of Umbria's western hilltowns. Although short of sights, it is an agreeable place and, for gourmets, one of the culinary capitals of Italy. Famous for its cheeses and truffles, it also has the reputation for producing the country's best sausages and salami (so widespread is its fame that a butcher's shop elsewhere in Italy is often called *Un Norcino*). Shops around the main square, Piazza San Benedetto, sell all manner of delicacies, from 'mules' testicles' to the ubiquitous boars' heads.

The square also contains the town's most notable buildings, namely the Castellina , a redoubtable papal fortress (1563), and the church of **San Benedetto▶**, reputedly built over the birthplace of St Benedict. Just off the square is a temple to Umbrian and Norcian cuisine, the wonderful old medieval hotel and restaurant, the **Grotta Azzurra**.

Words of praise
Pope Leo XIII described Orvieto's Duomo as the 'Golden Lily of Italian cathedrals'; the historian Jacob Burckhardt considered it the 'greatest polychrome monument in the world'.

Orvieto's great Gothic cathedral glimpsed down a side street

▶▶ Orvieto   164A1

Orvieto's celebrated crag, or *rupa* – the rim of an ancient volcano – attracted the Etruscans (who called it Volsinii), and later the Romans. These days it is perhaps Italy's finest Gothic **Duomo▶▶▶** which lures the invading hordes. The cathedral's awe-inspiring façade alone took over 300 years to complete, and employed 33 architects, 152 sculptors, 68 painters and 90 mosaicists. Started in the 13th century, it was built to celebrate the Miracle of Bolsena (in which the host being used in a Mass at nearby Bolsena dripped blood on to the altarcloth). Inside is Luca Signorelli's *Last Judgement* (1504), one of the great Italian fresco cycles, and a wealth of lesser paintings by local 14th-century artists.

The rest of the town is less impressive, but it is worth allowing an hour or so to see the sights. These include the frescoed church of **San Giovenale▶▶**; the church of **San Andrea▶**; the Museo del Duomo's eclectic collection (currently closed); the Museo Faina's Etruscan artefacts; the Etruscan tombs; and the **Pozzo di San Patrizio▶▶** (St Patrick's Well) an impressively engineered 16th-century well cut into the rock on which Orvieto stands.

Drive The heart of Umbria

A short drive which links six hilltowns and climbs over Monte Subasio – wild uplands with immense views – before dropping to Assisi.

The direct drive north from **Spoleto** (page 176) to Trevi on the SS3 is not pretty. For a better taste of Umbria's pastoral countryside follow the minor mountain roads to Montefalco via either Castel Ritaldi or Giano dell'Umbria (the more scenic route if you have time).

Otherwise, start in **Trevi**, (page 177), which with Todi is perhaps Umbria's most spectacularly sited hilltown. Then cross the plain to **Montefalco** (page 170) allowing a good hour for its churches, views and art gallery. As a possible diversion, take in **Gualdo Cattaneo►**, another perfect little hill village. Drop down to sleepy **Bevagna** (page 170) for its square and Romanesque churches, and then circumvent Foligno on your way to **Spello** (page 175). Allow an

hour or so to see Pinturicchio's frescoes and the town's medieval streets, churches and Roman remains.

North of Spello follow signs to **Collepino►**, an isolated hamlet, then cut back to take the well-made gravel road over Monte Subasio. In spring the mountain is smothered in orchids, narcissi and other wildflowers. Views from the top – the road reaches 1,200m – are exceptional. As the road drops to **Assisi** (page 168), visit the Eremo delle Carceri, a beautifully situated Franciscan monastery. If you do not want to take the gravel road, use the main SS3 to Assisi, or the minor road from Collepino to Assisi via **Armenzano►**.

Trevi, proud on its hilltop above the Vale of Spoleto

▶▶ **Perugia** 164B1

Perugia's industrial outskirts are unappealing, but once you are in the old centre, Umbria's capital is as attractive as any of the region's hilltowns. Much of Perugia is closed to traffic, so leave your car in one of the big peripheral car parks and ride the escalators (*scala mobile*) to the centre. Alternatively, park at the railway station and take a bus to Piazza Italia on Corso Vannucci. Corso Vannucci contains most of the sights, a bustling street, crowned by Piazza IV Novembre, the **Duomo▶** and **Fontana Maggiore▶▶▶**. The fountain, one of Italy's loveliest, was sculpted by Nicola and Giovanni Pisano. Palazzo dei Priori, a gaunt, grandiose medieval pile, is home to the **Galleria Nazionale dell'Umbria▶▶▶**, a rich art gallery which documents the development of Umbrian art. The paintings include canvases by Perugino and Pinturicchio, as well as works by non-Umbrians like Fra Angelico and Piero della Francesca. More fine frescoes by Perugino reside in the **Collegio del Cambio▶▶**. Close by lies the **Sala del Collegio della Mercanzia▶**, a 15th-century chamber lined with superlative wooden panelling.

Walk down **Via dei Priori▶** to see the **Oratorio di San Bernardino▶**, adorned with bas-reliefs by Agostino di Duccio. Then visit the Arco di Augusto, an Etrusco-Roman arch, and the outlying churches of Sant'Agostino and Sant'Angelo▶. Across the town, **San Domenico▶** boasts an exceptional Gothic tomb, while its cloisters house the **Museo Archeologico Nazionale dell'Umbria▶**. Beyond it lies Perugia's grandest church, the sumptuously decorated **San Pietro▶▶**.

Perugia, capital of Umbria, retains its medieval heart

Pasticceria Sandri
Perugia's most atmospheric bar is at Corso Vannucci 32, a turn-of-the-century Viennese-style café with lots of brass, wood panelling and frescoed ceilings. Try some of the town's nationally renowned Perugini chocolates. The best place to sample Umbria's wines is the *Enoteca Provinciale*, Via Ulisse Rocchi 16.

▶ **Pesaro** 164D2

Pesaro's 4km of beaches make it a popular package-holiday destination, but the influx of visitors does little to tarnish the town's stylish appearance. Behind the elegant white-stucco hotels of the waterfront stands a pleasant old centre, its most enticing street the porticoed Corso XI Settembre. Of the sights, the **Museo Civico▶▶** stands out, mainly for Giovanni Bellini's glittering polyptych, *The Coronation of the Virgin*. It also has a fine ceramics section – the fame of Pesaro's majolica once rivalled that of Faenza (see page 84).

Rossini
Opera composer Gioacchino Rossini was born in Pesaro in 1792. His home at Via Rossini 34 has a small museum and his works are performed during the town's summer festival.

■ **Weight for weight, truffles are the world's most expensive foodstuff. They have been prized for their earthy and aromatic flavour since Roman times (when they were believed to have been formed by lightning striking the earth). They are subterranean fungi of the class *Ascomycetes*, part of the *Tuber* genus.** ■

174

Sagre
You may come across a truffle *sagra* in an Umbrian town or village. This is a festival held to celebrate the truffle harvest (similar festivals take place in honour of many products of the Italian countryside, such as wine, fruit, vegetables – even sausages).

What, where and why Truffles are unable to carry out photosynthesis, and therefore live symbiotically with certain forest plants (using their chlorophyll). Anything from the size of peas to footballs, they thrive best in calcareous soils, and amid oak and hazel woods. Numerous other factors influence distribution, however, notably climate and drainage – one of the reasons why commercial production has proved something of a Holy Grail.

Finding truffles Dogs, rather than sows, are now used to hunt truffles (sows are attracted by the truffles' perfume, which closely resembles the musky pheromones of the male pig – unfortunately the sows often become uncontrollably excited when close to the truffle). In order to keep the valuable find secret, a truffle hunter will generally dig only at night. Equipped with torch and trowel, he searches in the spot where his dog sniffed out the truffles earlier in the day.

Types and uses Italy has two key truffle areas – near Alba, in Piedmont, and in Umbria around Norcia and Spoleto. Each has its specialities, for there are at least nine types of edible truffle – though only six are well known and commercialised. Restaurants usually serve them grated over pasta or omelettes (*frittate*). Shops sell truffle paste, or truffles preserved under oil (at a price). The real thing is rare, so beware of substitutes.

Umbrian truffles Umbria's most common truffle is the black winter truffle (*tartufo nero*), gathered from a few centimetres underground between mid-November and mid-March. The white truffle (the Alba, or Acqualagna truffle), is found as much as 50cm underground (from 1 October to 31 December). The rarer *scorzone*, or summer truffle, occurs near the surface (1 May to 30 November), rather like the prized *bianchetto* or *marzulo* truffle (15 November to 15 March). Musk and *uncinato* are the other two varieties.

▶▶ Piano Grande 164B2

In the Monti Sibillini, east of Norcia, lies one of the strangest and most magical landscapes in Europe. The Piano Grande is a vast upland plain, 1,200m high and covering 40 sq km, surrounded by barren whale-backed mountains. In spring the plain is smothered in poppies, buttercups and narcissi, as well as rarities like tulips, orchids and fritillaries. Walking opportunities are excellent, and the surrounding slopes form an ideal playground for hang-gliders.

Hang-gliders line up for take-off on the Piano Grande

▶▶ San Leo 164D1

Although less famous than nearby San Marino, San Leo is by far the more attractive destination. Machiavelli thought its castle▶▶ – hung on a vast cliff – Italy's greatest military fortress, and Dante used it as a model for the landscapes of *Purgatorio*. The little village below has a lovely cobbled square, on which lies a rude 9th-century Pieve▶▶, or parish church, and a Romanesque Duomo▶.

▶ San Marino 164D1

The little independent republic of San Marino trades ruthlessly on its rather bogus autonomy. According to tradition it was created around AD300 by a stonemason fleeing religious persecution (with him was Leo, founder of nearby San Leo). This makes it the longest surviving republic in Europe – its status was acknowledged even by Napoleon. It still has its own mint, postage stamps and international football team. From afar, its tremendous hilltop setting is inviting; close to, the streets are crammed with tourists and souvenir shops. Only the views merit the trip up here.

▶▶ Spello 164B2

Spilling down the lower slopes of Monte Subasio, Spello's pinky-stoned medieval houses present an alluring picture from the Vale of Spoleto. Built as a colony on the *Via Flaminia*, the old Roman road between Rome and the Adriatic, it still preserves a modest crop of Roman monuments. The best are two gateways, the Porta Venere and the Porta Consolare, the town's old entrance (be sure to try the award-winning ice-cream of the **gelateria** across the road, opposite the Porta Consolare). Midway up the street the church of **Santa Maria Maggiore▶▶** harbours a fresco cycle by Pinturicchio to rank with his masterpieces in Rome and Siena's Libreria Piccolomini. Higher still, two little churches are worth a peek – Gothic **Sant' Andrea▶**, dark and atmospheric, and baroque San Lorenzo.

Excursion from Spello
Follow signs from Spello's northern gateway to La Baita or Collepino for access to Monte Subasio. The views are magnificent, and there is plenty of opportunity for walking over the mountain's open grassy ridges.

Enchanting Spello

175

*Below: frescoes in
Todi's cathedral
Bottom: Todi has a
dramatic situation*

▶▶▶ Spoleto 164B2

Spoleto becomes many people's favourite Umbrian town.
During the 7th century it was the capital of the Duchy of
Spoleto, one of the Lombards' three Italian dukedoms.
Before that it was a pre-eminent Roman colony and one of
the ancient Umbrians' main citadels (traces of their 6th-
century BC walls are still visible).

The largely modern lower town contains a trio of worthwhile churches: **San Gregorio**▶; San Ponziano (notable for
its crypt and Romanesque façade); and 4th-century **San
Salvatore**▶▶▶, one of Italy's oldest churches. In the
upper town, picturesque **Piazza del Mercato**▶ is the spot
for a *cappuccino* before taking in its nearby sights – the
crypt of **San Ansano**▶ with 6th-century frescoes; the Arco
di Druso, a Roman triumphal arch; and **Sant'Eufemia**▶▶▶,
the town's most celebrated Romanesque church and
adjoining **Museo Diocesano**▶▶. Unmissable are the
Duomo▶▶▶, central Italy's loveliest, and the **Ponte delle
Torri**▶▶▶, a monumental 14th-century bridge and aque-
duct. The Duomo's star turn is Filippo Lippi's apse frescoes. If you cross the *Ponte*, you can walk above Spoleto's
breathtaking wooded gorge, or stroll to **San Pietro**▶▶,
whose façade's Lombard-Romanesque sculptures are
considered some of Italy's finest.

▶▶ Todi 164B1

Todi is the rising star of Umbrian hilltowns, a small market
centre at heart, but increasingly well known to Italians and
foreigners alike. Its position is phenomenal, perched
proudly above the Tiber on a great pyramid of a hill. Three
sets of concentric walls – Etruscan, Roman and medieval
– centre on **Piazza del Popolo**▶▶, a matchless ensemble
of medieval palaces crowned by the plain-faced elegance
of the Romanesque **Duomo**▶▶. **San Fortunato**▶▶ is the
town's premier church, its airy interior hidden behind an
unprepossessing façade. A stroll through the tranquil
public gardens takes you alongside **Santa Maria della
Consolazione**▶▶▶, considered by many Italy's most
perfect Renaissance church.

► **Trasimeno, Lago (Lake Trasimeno)** *164B1*

Trasimeno, the largest lake on the Italian peninsula, is only moderately pretty, but is nonetheless popular with campers, beach-addicts and watersports enthusiasts. **Passignano►** is the busiest resort. The nicest all-round spot, however, is **Castiglione del Lago►►**. Here you can swim off sandy beaches, or take boat trips to **Isola Maggiore►**, the prettiest of the lake's three islands. North of the lake, roads around the mountains offer quiet drives and marvellous views: **Castel Rigone►** is the best little village to make for.

► **Trevi** *164B2*

Trevi's glory is its position, perhaps the most impressive of any Umbrian hilltown. The tidy medieval centre is a delightful area to wander through, its little alleys known for their intricately patterned cobblestones. The **Duomo►** retains a Romanesque shell (the interior is baroque). The small **Pinacoteca►** has good Umbrian paintings, but the town's best art is Perugino's pictures in **San Martino►** and **Madonna delle Lacrime►**.

►►► **Urbino** *164C2*

Urbane and majestic, Urbino is one of the least known of Italy's great Renaissance cities. Raphael and Bramante were both born here, and in the 15th century the court of Duke Federico da Montefeltro became one of the most civilised and sophisticated in Europe. Federico's extensive and elegant **Palazzo Ducale►►►** is home to the **Galleria Nazionale delle Marche►►►** with two mysterious masterpieces of Piero della Francesca: *The Flagellation* and the *Madonna di Senigallia*. Almost as alluring are Raphael's *La Muta*, Uccello's *Miracle of the Host*, and Titian's *Resurrection* and *Last Supper*. Among the rooms, Federico's personal study stands out – the tiny Studiolo, renowned for its *intarsia* (inlaid wood).

Lake Trasimeno

Olive oil
Although less well known than the oils of Tuscany, Umbria's olive oil is prized by Italians, particularly that of Trevi and the Vale of Spoleto. You need not buy fancy bottles: the widely available *Monini* oils are some of the best.

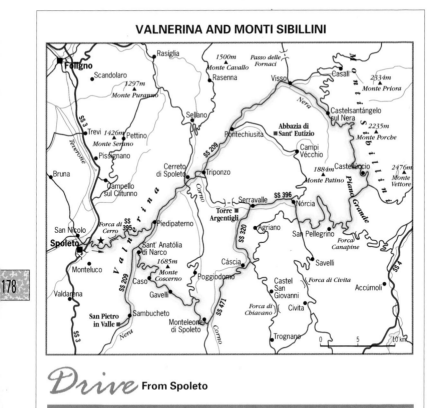

VALNERINA AND MONTI SIBILLINI

Drive **From Spoleto**

Historic Spoleto

A scenic drive through one of central Italy's most enchanting valleys, followed by mountain roads through the Monti Sibillini and across the wild Piano Grande.

Start in Spoleto and negotiate the twisting SS395 to Piedipaterno (fine views). Follow the Nera River on SS209 towards its source at the quiet market town of Visso, sometimes through gorges and mountains, elsewhere through farmland and water meadows. You then climb to the village of **Castelluccio**, one of Italy's highest settlements (1,490m), and cross the eerie desolation of the Piano Grande before dropping on a snaking road to **Norcia** (page 171). The gentler terrain from here takes in Cascia, birthplace of St Rita. More mountains, pastoral countryside and half-forgotten hill villages follow – Monteleone di Spoleto, Caso and Gavelli. Few tourists ever see this exceptional countryside, and the roads are likely to be deserted.

At **Sant' Anatolia di Narco**, if you have time, detour south before returning to Spoleto. Just after the hamlet of **Sambucheto** watch for the sign to San Pietro in Valle. The 8th-century monastery church is important as one of the few surviving memorials to the Lombards.

Walking in Umbria

■ **Umbria is unusual for central Italy in having several marked trails and sufficiently detailed maps to make hiking a possibility. There are three main areas: the Monte Cucco park; Gualdo Tadino; and the Monti Sibillini National Park.** ■

Parco Naturale del Monte Cucco This park protects a lovely tract of limestone mountains east of Gubbio. For information visit the Centro Nazionale di Speleologia, Corso Mazzini 9, Costacciaro (on the SS3, 50km north of Foligno). They issue a 1:16,000 map of the 30 marked trails in the area (Kompass sheet No 664 is also useful). The most popular routes begin in the Val di Ranco: trail 1 climbs to the 1,566m summit of Monte Cucco via Pian delle Macinarie: trail 2 is the descent (round trip 4 hours). Another favourite is the walk along the Valle delle Prigioni from Pascelupo to Pian di Rolla (4-hour round trip).

Gualdo Tadino Gualdo Tadino is on the SS3, 33km north of Foligno. Several marked paths push into the hills east of the town, all marked on the Kompass 1:50,000 map *Assisi-Camerino* (No 665). The most dramatic climbs the Valle del Fonno gorge, returning via the Passo della Sportella (5km: four hours). Another popular route follows the pilgrim trail up Monte Serra Santa (1,423m), reached on the extremely well-worn trail No 122. From the summit you can drop into the Valle del Fonno or follow a path south along the ridges of Monte Nero and Monte Penna. A track drops to Gaifana (5km south of Gualdo), or you can continue on the main ridge to Nocera Umbra (via Monte Alago).

Parco Nazionale dei Monti Sibillini This national park offers some of the best walking in central Italy. You can choose between high mountain routes or easy strolls around the Piano Grande. Numerous trails are marked on the Kompass 1:50,000 map *Monti Sibillini* (No 666). The most ambitious of these climbs Monte Vettore (2,476m) from the road at Forca di Presta. Several paths radiate from Castelluccio: try the pastoral stroll up the Valle di Canatra, or the exhilarating ridge walk along the western rim of the Piano Grande (via Poggio di Croce and Monte Vetica).

The Vale of Spoleto: there are several marked paths (red-and-white waymarks) around Spoleto

From Umbria into the Marches
On the eastern flanks of the Parco Nazionale dei Monti Sibillini (the Marches side) the classic walks are from the village of Foce to Lago di Pilato, a spectacular hike up a steep-sided valley, and the climb to Monte Sibilla from Montemonaco.

179

Assisi
A few paths have been marked from Assisi. The best day's walk follows trail No 50 from the Porta Cappuccini and Rocca Minore, climbing over Monte Subasio via the Eremo delle Carceri, and dropping down to Spello.

LAZIO AND ABRUZZO

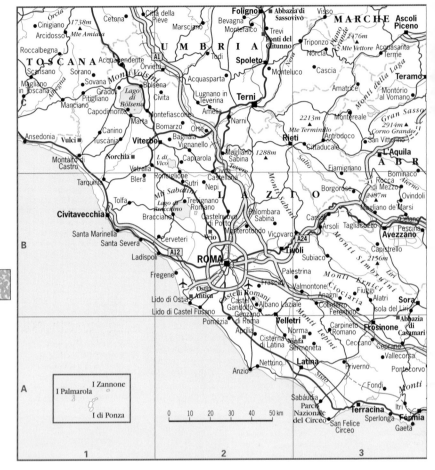

REGION HIGHLIGHTS ◄◄◄◄◄

CERVETERI *see page 186*
TARQUINIA *see page 187*
GRAN SASSO D'ITALIA
see page 188
TIVOLI *see page 189*
OSTIA ANTICA *see page 190*
PARCO NAZIONALE
D'ABRUZZO *see page 194*

Lazio and Abruzzo Rome cannot help but overshadow Lazio and Abruzzo. There is so much to see in the city you might easily overlook its neighbouring regions altogether. But after a few days seeing the capital's sights, it makes sense (if only for a change) to use Rome as a base for day-trips into Lazio. Further afield, greater relief from Rome's maelstrom awaits in the mountains of the Abruzzo, one of Italy's wildest and least spoilt regions, and the unexplored haunt of wolves and the country's last brown bears.

Lacklustre Lazio After the grandeur of Rome, Lazio can seem a trifle anticlimatic. In the north, its melancholy hills are redeemed only by Bolsena and its lake and the nature reserve around Lago di Vico, its featureless coastal plains by the Etruscan sites at Cerveteri and Tarquinia. Other historic centres are few and far between, some of the best attractions being provided instead by the villas and gardens such as Caprarola and the Villa Lante in the countryside around Viterbo.

Lake Bolsena, with its islands and Etruscan sites, is one of Lazio's most attractive areas

Take a trip to the Villa d'Este to see its dazzling water gardens

To the south the countryside is more inspiring, from the tiny Circeo national park with lovely coastal landscapes to the limestone heights of the Ernici and Simbruini mountains (see Subiaco, page 193). Parts of the coast have decent resorts, principally Sperlonga, and if you are feeling more adventurous, the island of Ponza – a great favourite with holiday-making Romans – has yet to be discovered by most foreign visitors. Few of the region's towns merit a special journey – with the notable exception of those you can see from Rome.

Excursions from Rome Most of the incursions you want to make into Lazio are best made as day-trips from Rome. Of these the most enticing is Tivoli. Here you can see the Villa d'Este, with some of Italy's loveliest gardens, and the ruins of the Villa Adriana (Hadrian's Villa), the largest villa ever built in the Roman Empire. More imperial echoes await in Ostia Antica, Rome's old seaport, a collection of ruins as impressive as any in Rome itself. Palestrina, too, has fine old remains, together with a good museum and tremendous views. Panoramas are also part of Frascati's appeal, the most famous and easily accessible of the Castelli Romani, a coronet of towns in the volcanic hills south of Rome.

All these trips can be made by public transport, not to be scorned given Rome's appalling traffic problems. The

most distant attractions you can see in a day are probably Cerveteri and Tarquinia's Etruscan tombs (not to mention their museums, and the smaller Etruscan sites at Sutri, Blera and Norchia). The best of the more remote prospects are the mountains as well as the Benedictine monasteries of Subiaco.

St Benedict's monastery, in the mountains around Subiaco

Scenic drives

(*Lazio*): Viterbo–Lago di Vico–Caprarola–Ronciglione; SS411 Arsoli– Subiaco– (Filettino)– Campocatino– Fiuggi.

(*Abruzzo*): Abruzzo National Park SS83 Alfedena–Opi–Pescasseroli–Gioia dei Marsi & SS479 Sulmona–Scanno–Villetta Barrea; SS5/5bis Sulmona–(Secinaro)–Celano–Rocca di Mezzo–L'Aquila; SS80/A 24 L'Aquila–Montorio al Vomano–L'Aquila; SS17bis L'Aquila–Campo Imperatore.

Scenic railways

The main Rome–Pescara line has a picturesque section between Avezzano and Sulmona. The Abruzzo's small branch lines are tempting to ride for their own sake. The short line from Sulmona to L'Aquila, for example, (and its cotin uation to Rieti) runsthrough good countryside. The best trip of all is from Sulmona to Castel di Sangro, which climbs high into the mountains on the eastern flank of the national park.

Seaside Lazio Southern Lazio's best beaches are at Sperlonga, Gaeta, Sabaudia and San Felice Circeo. Rome's seaside resorts – Lido di Ostia, Fregene and Ladispoli – are not recommended, being largely crowded and polluted. To the north, Santa Severa and Santa Marinella have reasonable beaches and pretty pinewood surroundings. Huge, undeveloped beaches stretch out from the hamlet of Chiarone, where Lazio meets Tuscany. Abruzzo's pleasantest seaside towns are Pineto (22km north of Pescara) and Vasto (68km south of Pescara).

Sun umbrellas line up on Santa Marinella's popular beach

Abruzzo Few people venture into the Abruzzo's desolate interior, despite road and rail links that put it within easy reach of Rome. Yet its rewards are immense, particularly if you are in search of wild mountains and villages where life is still harsh and strangers a novelty. Roads lead to the heart of the Abruzzo National Park, which has plenty of well-organised trails and interesting villages, and to the Gran Sasso d'Italia, the highest point on the Italian peninsula. Good paths in both areas allow endless hiking opportunities (see page 194), but there are also plenty of routes into the mountains for drivers. If you are driving, it is rewarding to explore the roads around the Abruzzo's three other great massifs – the Maiella, Monte Velino and the Monti della Laga (see Scenic Drives panel).

The region is not solely about mountains, however, for as well as any number of remote hill villages, the Abruzzo has a couple of bracing towns which are interesting spots in their own right. Sulmona was the birthplace of Ovid (and where confetti was invented), while L'Aquila contains a neat little museum and several captivating churches.

Molise Molise is a tiny region lodged south of the Abruzzo (until 1963 it was part of the old Abruzzi region). Gentler than the Abruzzo, the Matese mountains are still wild and impressive. Towns and villages are less interesting, though Termoli on the coast is a reasonable beach resort, and Isernia has a good archaeological museum. Around Isernia there is lovely rolling hill country.

Tourist information
L'Aquila: Piazza Santa Maria Paganica (tel: 0862/410 808).
Subiaco: Via Cadorna 59 (tel: 0774/85 397).
Sulmona: Corso Ovidio 208 (tel: 0864/53276).
Tarquinia: Piazza Cavour 1 (tel: 0766/856 384).
Tivoli: Largo Garibaldi (tel: 0774/21 249).
Viterbo: Piazza Caduti (tel: 0761/304 795).

LAZIO AND ABRUZZO

Early morning in the food market in L'Aquila

Ninety-nine
Emperor Frederick II reputedly created L'Aquila in 1242 by amalgamating 99 local castles and villages. The town has had a fondness for the number ever since. The town hall bell chimes 99 times at 9:09pm, and near the station stands the Fontana delle 99 Cannelle, a 99-spouted fountain.

Est! Est!! Est!!!
Est! Est!! Est!!! is a wine from the Bolsena region. A bishop is said to have instructed his retainer to search out taverns with the best wine and indicate his choice by chalking 'Est' ('It is here') on the relevant hostelry. When he reached Montefiascone, the wine was so good he excitedly scrawled Est! Est!! Est!!!. The satisfied bishop is buried in Montefiascone, reputedly having died from over-drinking.

► **Alatri**   *180B3*

Alatri's medieval appearance belies its antiquity, for its gateways, Cyclopean walls and mighty fortified **acropolis►►** date back to the 6th century BC. The ramparts offer impressive views and the streets are filled with medieval monuments, the most noteworthy being Santa Maria Maggiore, famous for its 14th-century wooden sculpture of the Madonna of Constantinople. While in the area, visit nearby **Anagni►**, another medieval town, renowned for its magnificent Cattedrale.

► **L'Aquila**   *180C3*

The Abruzzo's capital was for centuries the second most important town in southern Italy after Naples. Today on first acquaintance it appears dour and depressing. Further exploration reveals a lively mountain town that combines medieval and modern in equal measure. Your first port-of-call should be the castle's **Museo Nazionale d'Abruzzo►►**, the Abruzzo's foremost museum, a fascinating pot-pourri of exhibits ranging from a stuffed mammoth to displays of sacred art, local pottery, and the cream of the region's paintings. Close by stands **Santa Maria di Collemaggio►►**, the Abruzzo's premier piece of church architecture, known for its arched portal and intricate pink-and-white marble façade. The church of **San Bernardino►►** contains the tomb of San Bernardino of Siena, who died in the town (the Sienese visit L'Aquila on his feast day, bearing gifts of Tuscan oil).

►► **Bolsena, Lago di**   *180C1*

Lake Bolsena is the largest volcanic lake in Italy. One of the best trips locally is the boat ride out to **Bisentina►►**, one of the lake's two islands (the other is Martana – both are probably remnants of the old volcanic crater). Bisentina offers not only views and scenery, but also Etruscan tombs, a Farnese family villa and five quaint little chapels. Boats run from **Capodimonte►**, an attractive resort that pushes into the lake on a castle-tipped promontory. Other towns in the fertile hills around the lake include **Gradoli►**, at the heart of a large wine region, Etruscan **Montefiascone►** and medieval **Bolsena►**, a relaxed and likeable place that makes the best overall base for excursions around the lake. Civita, 15km east of Bolsena, is an eerie and half-deserted ghost-town in a lunar landscape.

► **Caprarola**   *180C2*

Easily seen in conjunction with Viterbo and Lago di Vico (see page 193), Caprarola is a little village almost entirely given over to the **Palazzo Farnese►►**. One of the high points of 16th-century mannerism, it is a building, said Stendhal, 'where architecture married nature'. Created as a castle in 1520, it was completed as a Farnese palace in 1559 by Vignola, one of the leading architects of his day. Many rooms are closed to the public and others are missing their period furniture. Several features, however, still stand out, notably Vignola's famous monumental stair-case (the Scala Regia) and the beautifully-frescoed Sala del Mappamondo. Outside there is a large park and two gardens – a south-facing summer garden and an east-facing winter terrace.

▶ **Castelli Romani** 180B2

The 13 villages of the Castelli Romani are descendants of the medieval castles built by the popes and Rome's leading patrician families. They nestle in the Albani hills south of Rome. Although they provide welcome relief from Rome's heat and hassle, many have been spoilt by wanton modern building, but much of the wooded surroundings, and lakes like Albano and Nemi, remain worth seeing; they serve as favourite destinations for Sunday-lunch excursionists from Rome. **Frascati**▶ is the most famous of the villages, thanks to its wine and villas. Castel Gandolfo is well known, mainly as the pope's summer residence. **Rocca di Papa**▶, **Grottaferata**▶ and **Albano Laziale**▶, however, are the most picturesque *Castelli*.

▶▶ **Circeo, Parco Nazionale del** 180A3

The smallest of Italy's national parks, Circeo was created to preserve a portion of the Pontine marshes following Mussolini's 1930s reclamation projects. It is a wonderfully diverse patchwork of lakes, coastal dunes, and forests. Wild boar and fallow deer roam the woods, and the wetland areas are renowned for their resident and migrating species of birds. Walking opportunities are myriad, and you can take boat trips around the lakes and lagoons.

Frascati
Frascati's famous and unassuming white wine is the mainstay of simple Italian restaurants the world over. In the Middle Ages, the Albani's foresters built huts of *frascata*, the brushwood that gave Frascati its name and the wine its symbol: the *frasca*, or branch, hung over the doors of taverns when the new vintage was ready.

185

Information
Parco Nazionale di Circeo's information centre is at Via Carlo Alberto 107, Sabaudia (tel: 0773/511 386). It provides a detailed and useful map. Many of the park's gentle marked trails fan out from the centre itself. For a more challenging morning's hike climb Circeo's one high spot, Monte Circeo (448m), a wooded and rocky promontory whose summit affords magnificent views over the park.

Capodimonte on Lake Bolsena. Boat trips on the lake start from here

■ **The Etruscans are one of the most enigmatic and mysterious of ancient civilisations. At their height between 800 and 400 BC they controlled much of central Italy (*Etruria*) through a twelve-strong confederation of cities.** ■

Death and life
'Death…to the Etruscans was a pleasant continuance of life, with jewels and wine and flutes playing for the dance. It was neither an ecstasy of bliss, a heaven, nor a purgatory of torment. It was just a natural continuance of the fullness of life. Everything was in terms of life…the things they did, in their early centuries, are as natural and easy as breathing.' D H Lawrence, *Etruscan Places*.

Norchia
The ruins of Etruscan *Orcia* lie west of Vetralla, 30km east of Tarquinia off the SS1bis. As well as several monumental tombs, some with great sculpted façades, the village has a silent medieval castle and 12th-century parish church, San Pietro.

History Where the Etruscans came from is one of history's great conundrums. Most evidence points to a mixture of seafarers and indigenous tribes whose ethnic links were with Asia Minor, and whose trading ties were with Greece. One reason for their shadowy past is depressingly banal – their cities were made almost entirely of wood, so that almost nothing of them remains. The culture's finest memorials are what has been found in their tombs, and this has given the Etruscans a reputation as a gloomy and introspective race. In truth, they seem to have been a lively and imaginative people, with highly developed social, cultural and political systems.

The Etruscan legacy Another reason we know relatively little of the Etruscans is that the Romans deliberately set out to absorb – and then obscure – the culture of their predecessors. Etruscans were probably Rome's earliest settlers (and even provided its earliest kings). Much of their alphabet and language passed into Latin (and thus into other European tongues). The Romans also inherited many of their gods and divinities, their rituals and divinations, even their circuses and gladiatorial games. Much of this assimilation had taken place by the 3rd century BC, by which time Rome had defeated most of the Etruscan cities.

Museums and monuments Grandiose monuments to the Etruscans lie scattered all over ancient *Etruria*, from the stone-cut amphitheatre at Sutri to the vivid wall-paintings of Tarquinia. Most of the smaller artefacts have been removed from tombs (or *necropoli*), for the Etruscans (like the Egyptians) left the dead with all they would need in the afterlife. Almost every Etruscan site, large or small, has a museum to display them, but their prize exhibits have gone to the Vatican museums and Rome's Villa Giulia (see page 47). These are the world's finest Etruscan museums, so if possible visit them before exploring the Etruscan sites.

Cerveteri Cerveteri, ancient *Kysry* (Roman *Caere*), was one of the leading Etruscan cities, its pre-eminence based on mineral riches and long-established trading prowess. Over 5,000 tombs lie in the **Necropoli della Banditaccia**, laid out as streets and houses to create a literal 'city of the dead'. Only 50 or so have been excavated (though many have been ransacked over the centuries).

No clue to its occupant remains in this empty Etruscan tomb

Some are curious pillboxes carved from the living rock, others earth-covered tumuli that ripple over the surrounding countryside. Of the 12 show tombs – all near the site's entrance – try to see the *Tomba dei Capitelli* and the *Tomba dei Letti Funebri*. Round off a visit with a trip to the Museo Nazionale Cerite, a modest collection of Etruscan artefacts housed in Cerveteri's 16th-century Castello Orsini.

Tarquinia In its day Tarquinia boasted a population of 100,000 and was probably the Etruscans' cultural and political capital. Now it is a strangely drab and half-derelict town, only redeemed by its museum and tombs, the most famous of any in Italy. The **Museo Nazionale** offers a small but pithy collection, its centrepiece, a pair of winged terracotta horses, perhaps the most beautiful Etruscan sculpture in existence. Its other exhibits include the inevitable funerary urns, some scintillating jewellery, and several tombs reconstructed to house their wall paintings under controlled conditions.

The 6,000 original tombs honeycomb the Monterozzi plateau east of the town. To protect their delicate frescoes, however, only a handful are open to the public at any one time (to guided tours). Their Hellenistic-style paintings span around 500 years, the earliest concentrating on mythical and ritualistic scenes, the later on the social (and sexual) context of Etruscan daily life.

Sutri About 18km southeast of Vetralla (on the SS1bis), Sutri is one of the more rewarding of the lesser Etruscan sites. A picturesque medieval town, it occupies a narrow rocky ridge – the type of site favoured by the Etruscans for their cities. Its overgrown amphitheatre was carved from the living rock (and seated 6,000 people).

Boxers on an Etruscan vase

In the city of the dead, Cerveteri

LAZIO AND ABRUZZO

Olive terraces backed by the snow-covered Gran Sasso ridge

Walking
Although it is easy to tour the environs of the Gran Sasso by car, there are numerous straightforward walking opportunities. For maps and information visit L'Aquila's tourist office in Via XX Settembre 8 (or the regional office in Piazza Santa Maria Paganica 5 – tel: 0862/410 808). Also helpful is the Italian Alpine Club (CAI) office at Via XX Settembre 15 (open weekdays 6–7pm).

Albergo Campo Imperatore
This hotel is famous as the place where Mussolini was imprisoned after the Italian surrender in 1943. He was sprung from the remote eyrie in a daring aerial raid, and taken north by the Germans to establish the puppet Salò Republic.

Abbazia di Casamari
Take in the Abbey of Casamari as part of a car tour of southern Lazio (it lies just west of Isola del Liri, 42km west of Montecassino). Founded by the Benedictines in 1035, rebuilt in 1140 and now fully restored, it is a fine example of French-inspired Cistercian-Gothic architecture. The church (1217) is the three-star highlight, though all the abbey's old components are of interest (these include the cloister, pharmacy, refectory and chapter-house).

▶▶ Gran Sasso d'Italia *180C3*

At 2,912m, the Gran Sasso d'Italia (Big Rock of Italy) is the highest point on the Italian peninsula (Etna in Sicily and many Alpine peaks are higher). Thousands of walkers and climbers are attracted to its slopes, drawn by its magnificent snow-capped ridges and the famous **Campo Imperatore▶▶**, a vast mountain-ringed upland plain.

Access is easiest from L'Aquila. It is only 20km on the A24 motorway to the turn-off at Assergi and the hamlet of Fonte Cereto (1,120m). Here there are a couple of hotels, a restaurant and a cable car (*funivia*) which takes you to the **Albergo-Rifugio Campo Imperatore** (2,130m), the starting point for most walks. It can also be reached by driving across the Campo Imperatore on the SS17bis (27km from Fonte Cereto). The easiest of the hikes – no more than a two-hour round trip – is trail No 10 to Monte della Scindarella (2,233m). The classic walk is trail No 3, which goes close to the summit (Corno Grande).

▶ Montecassino *181A4*

The huge bulwarks of the abbey of Montecassino can be seen from miles around. Its superlative position was perhaps the reason St Benedict chose it as the headquarters for the Benedictine movement in 529 (though legend said he was guided here by three ravens). For centuries it was one of the most important monasteries in the Christian world, disseminating the Benedictine ideal. It has been rebuilt many times, most notoriously after the entire building – except the crypt – was destroyed by Allied bombing on 15 February 1944. As the Nazis' regional headquarters it was an essential target, yet the abbey's destruction has been a cause for controversy ever since. The old buildings have been faithfully rebuilt, though almost inevitably the reconstruction is a sterile and soulless affair. The war cemeteries are much-visited, and the views – from the middle cloister in particular – are exceptional.

■ **Many visitors to Rome take time out from the sights of the capital to visit Tivoli. The crowds and endless cavalcade of tour buses are a small price to pay for the Villa d'Este, Italy's most famous gardens, and the Villa Adriana, the ruins of the Roman Empire's greatest imperial palace.** ■

Villa Adriana (Hadrian's Villa) Tivoli, ancient *Tiber*, was known for its travertine marble – from which much of imperial Rome was built – and as a retirement home for Rome's most prosperous citizens. It had so many villas, wrote Horace, that 'the Tibertine soil no longer has ploughland'. The greatest, the Villa Adriana, is about 5km from the present town. Started in AD125, it was built to Hadrian's own design, his intention to recreate some of the outstanding buildings he had seen during his travels. Work eventually took 10 years, the villa and its gardens extending over a site larger than Imperial Rome itself – making it the Empire's largest and costliest palace.

To make sense of the ruins, study the model near the entrance, an attempt to reproduce the villa's original appearance. Simply wandering the lovely site, full of trees and secluded corners, is a pleasure in itself, but make a special point of seeing the Teatro Marittimo, a colonnaded palace built in the middle of an artificial lagoon.

The Villa d'Este The Villa d'Este started life as a convent, but in 1550 was converted into a country retreat for Cardinal Ippolito d'Este, the son of Lucrezia Borgia and the Duke of Ferrara. The villa now is a rather shabby affair, overshadowed by its gardens, whose fountains and formal terraces rank as some of the most beautiful in the world.

Their main attractions are the *Viale delle Cento Fontane* (Avenue of a Hundred Fountains), and two outstanding individual fountains: Bernini's elegant *Fontana di Biccierone* and the *Fontana dei Draghi* (Fountain of the Dragons), built for Pope Gregory XIII, whose symbol was a short-tailed dragon. All the gardens' byways repay exploration, but be sure to find the little path leading to the *Rometta*, a model of Rome. Also leave time to see Tivoli's third – and often overlooked – villa, the **Villa Gregoriana** (see panel).

Villa Gregoriana
The Villa Gregoriana is Tivoli's third and least-known sight, centred on a pair of waterfalls and a deep-cut gorge of lush vegetation. The Grande Cascata, the larger of the falls, was created when the River Aniene was diverted in 1831 by Pope Gregory XVI to protect Tivoli from flooding. The smaller falls, designed by Bernini, are at the narrow head of the gorge. You can walk down a pretty path to the bottom of the 60m deep canyon.

189

Water is the dominant feature in the gardens of the Villa d'Este

▶▶ **Ostia Antica** *180B2*

Once ancient Rome's port, Ostia Antica is now Italy's best-preserved Roman town after Pompeii (its ruins are as good as any in Rome itself). The setting is lovely, with the ruins scattered among vines and wildflowers, the paths shaded by elegant stands of parasol pines.

The colony started life as a fishing village at the mouth (*ostium*) of the Tiber, but grew as the Empire expanded, trading a host of commodities with the furthest-flung imperial outposts. In the end the weight of trade exceeded the port's capacity. Coupled with the constant accumulation of silt, this led to Ostia's decline and the building of a new port, *Portus Romae* (near present-day Fiumicino).

The sprawling site centres on the Decumanus Maximus, the old main thoroughfare, from which innumerable streets branch off. Each is filled with theatres, temples, workshops, houses and the famous *horreae*, old warehouses used principally to store grain. Equally interesting are the many *insulae*, old Roman four- and five-storey apartment blocks.

190

The ruins of Ostia Antica, ancient Rome's most important port

▶ **Palestrina** *180B2*

Present-day Palestrina is largely medieval in flavour, but it rests over the ruins of *Praeneste*, an important Etruscan site founded in the 7th century BC. The city was famous for the Tempio di Fortuna Primogenia, which was the seat of an ancient cult and important oracle. The temple was enlarged under the Romans in the 4th century BC, the exact scope of the complex only coming to light after bombing during World War II.

The current town is still built on a series of vast terraces, which correspond to the levels of the original temple, fragments of which lie dotted around the streets. Most of the temple treasures have been removed to Rome's Villa Giulia or to Palestrina's own Museo Nazionale Archeologico Prenestino. Among the latter's many busts, reliefs and funerary headstones, the star turn is the outstanding 1st-century BC *Mosaic of the River Nile*, a detailed narrative which describes the story of the river from its source to its delta.

SOUTHERN LAZIO

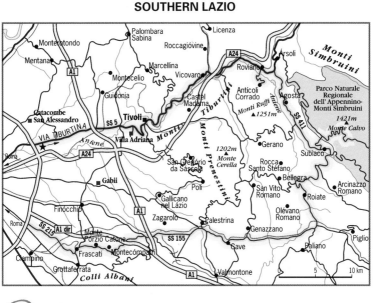

Drive **The Roman countryside**

A tour which encompasses pretty pockets of countryside and the most interesting towns within striking distance of Rome.

Make your way from Rome on the Via Tiburtina, not an attractive road – but few in the city's environs are – and see the Villa Adriana and Villa d'Este at **Tivoli** (page 189). Press north and make the short detour to **Anticoli Corrado▶** an unspoilt hilltown, and then follow country roads through the prettiest portion of the journey to **Subiaco** (page 193). Spend time seeing the Benedictine monuments and, if time allows, explore the wild mountains of the Monti Simbruini to the east.

Monti Simbruini For centuries the Simbruini mountains have supplied Rome with drinking water (their name means 'heavy rain'). They are now part of the Apennines Natural Park. By car you can explore the park's Zompo waterfalls; the Piano di Campoli (one of the region's many impressive karstic plains); and the

scenic road from Subiaco to Jenne and Vallepietra, which has fine views over the Aniene gorge, one of the park's several deep ravines. Wind through the hill country to the south to **Palestrina** (page 190), birthplace of the great 16th-century composer who took his name from the town, then return to Rome by way of **Frascati▶** and the Colli Albani.

Medieval Anticoli Corrado, with its wonderful hilltop setting

Ferries to Ponza
Daily ferries run year-round from Formia and Terracina on the Lazio coast (more frequently in summer). Journey time is 2 hours 30 minutes. Faster hydrofoils run from the same ports in high season, and from Anzio, with connections from Ponza to Ischia and Naples. Connections to Ventotene, the archipelago's other main island – flatter, smaller and less verdant – run daily from Formia and Ponza (except Sunday).

San Benedetto monastery, on a rocky ridge above Subiaco

►►   Ponza, Isola di   *180A1*

Romans – but not foreigners – have discovered Ponza, the largest island of the Pontine archipelago off the coast of southern Lazio. Ferries sail to Ponza Town, a beautiful fishing village of pastel-coloured houses curved around a small harbour. Most people wanting to swim, however, pass over its small beach in favour of Chiaia di Luna, a slender crescent of sand about ten minutes' walk away. To escape the summer crowds, you could take small boats from the port to more secluded coves like Spiaggia Santa Lucia. You can also hire bikes and scooters, and a regular bus connects with La Forna, the island's other sizeable village.

►►   San Clemente a Casauria   *181B4*

Among the Abruzzo's finest medieval buildings, this Cistercian abbey was founded in the 9th century and restored in the 12th century, creating a beautiful example of transitional Romanesque-Gothic architecture. The splendid portico ushers you into an interior whose simplicity is disturbed only by an elaborate pulpit. Other treasures include a 13th-century Paschal candelabrum and a ciborium taken from an early Christian sarcophagus. The crypt is the most striking feature to survive from the earliest church.

San Clemente is situated just off the A25 motorway near the Torre de' Passeri exit (30km north of Sulmona). If it is locked apply to the warden in the house near by.

►   Sperlonga   *180A3*

Southern Lazio's most beautiful tract of coastline stretches between Gaeta and Sperlonga. The latter is the area's nicest and most fashionable resort, its white-washed houses perched high on a rocky promontory. Although it fills up in summer, there is plenty of room on the beach, and if the hotels are full you should find beds at nearby **Terracina ►**, another likeable little resort.

▶▶ Subiaco 180B3

St Benedict retreated to caves around Subiaco in the 5th century, where he composed his famous *Rule*, one of the cornerstones of Western monasticism. Of 12 monasteries founded in his wake, only two survive. The **Convento di Santa Scholastica**, 25 minutes' walk from the town, has been largely restored, though the beauty of its three cloisters remains unsurpassed; 15 minutes further, the **Convento di San Benedetto** contains the saint's original cave, the *Sacro Speco*, which is adorned with numerous 14th-century Sienese frescoes. Subiaco itself is a winsome little hilltown.

▶ Sulmona 181B4

Sulmona is a bracing mountain-ringed town, ideal as a base for exploring the country around L'Aquila and for excursions into the Abruzzo national park (see pages 194–5). It was the birthplace of both Ovid, the great Roman poet (43 BC–AD 17), and confetti (see panel). Its particular sights are few, but the streets are appealing in themselves. Before you start exploring, take time out in Piazza XX Settembre's **Gran Caffè**, a lovely turn-of-the-century bar. Then see the **Annunziata▶▶**, a mixture of church, palace and poorhouse; the Gothic Fontana del Vecchio; the Duomo's 12th-century Byzantine relief; and the doughty portal of **San Francesco delle Scarpe▶**.

▶ Vico, Lago di 180C2

Lago di Vico is a secret little lake in the crater of an old volcano, surrounded by the forest-covered slopes of the Monte Cimini. The area is a nature reserve, with lots of lovely short walks, and a scenic drive, the **Via Ciminia▶▶**, which traverses the old crater's summit ridges.

▶ Viterbo 180C2

Historic towns in northern Lazio are thin on the ground, which is perhaps why Viterbo has a reputation out of all proportion to its appeal. A favoured retreat for numerous medieval popes, today it is a gloomy town, best seen quickly before moving to some of the sights near by (the Villa Lante, Bomarzo and Lago di Vico). Most of its old buildings lie on **Piazza del Plebiscito▶** and **Piazza San Lorenzo▶▶**, both fine medieval squares, and in the picturesque quarter around Via San Pellegrino.

Confetti
Real *confetti* are sugared almond confections bound with wire and ribbons into elaborate flowers. They have been made in Sulmona since the 15th century. Since then they have played a part in weddings the world over. These days, of course, coloured paper is thrown, though traditional white *confetti* are still used at Abruzzese nuptials.

193

Vaulted cloister of Santa Scholastica monastery, near Subiaco

Beauty...
Sacheverell Sitwell called the Villa Lante, in Bagnaia, 5km east of Viterbo, 'the most lovely place of the physical beauty of nature in Italy or in all the world'. Its grounds contain some of Europe's most beautiful Renaissance gardens. The formal gardens are seen by guided tour, but you are free to wander in the adjoining parkland.

...and the beasts
In Bomarzo, 12km north-east of Bagnaia, are Lazio's most extraordinary gardens, the Parco dei Mostri (Monster Park), designed in 1552 by the Duke of Orsini. Grotesques, moss-covered sculptures and huge, fantastical stone creatures give the effect of a surreal 16th-century theme park of fantasy and horror. Though commercialised, the garden is worth the high admission.

■ **The Abruzzo National Park is central Italy's natural jewel, a superbly administered wilderness area that provides wonderful hiking country and a refuge for wolves and brown bears as well as a host of other flora and fauna.** ■

Information

For information on the park, visit Pescasseroli's central information office (tel: 0863/91 955) and the large park centre/museum close by. Opi, Barrea, Villetta Barrea and Civitella Alfedena also have smaller, summer-only information centres.

Abruzzo national park, one of Europe's last great wildernesses

The lie of the land Most of the park's 40,000ha comprise a jumbled collection of Apennine mountain massifs. Most reach about 1,800m, though the highest point is Monti della Meta (2,247m). The Sangro valley cuts through their heart, scattered with the area's only villages – Barrea, Villetta Barrea, Civitella Alfedena, Opi and Pescasseroli. All of these have a handful of hotels and campsites. The most developed spot is Pescasseroli, home to the park's main museum and information centre. Old ways still predominate hereabout: national costume is sometimes seen, sheep farming flourishes, and you are as likely to encounter old men bringing firewood from the forests on donkeys as you are to meet tractors.

History Italy's environmental protection record is generally poor, but in the Abruzzo national park it can claim one of the best-administered parks in Europe. It started life – like many Italian parks – as a royal hunting reserve. This was dismantled in 1877 and an embryonic park created in its place in 1917. Most of the real work, however, has been done in the last 20 years. Early opposition has largely been overcome through initiatives to promote the local economy. A fine balance has been struck between the range of facilities – such as excellent marked paths – and the need to protect the wilderness in its natural state.

Walking The park has over 150 numbered and well-marked trails of all standards, most of them marked on the park's own 1:50,000 map, available from park centres. Perhaps the most popular is the 5-hour round trip from Civitella Alfedena to the Valle delle Rose (trail 1). Sightings of the park's 500-plus chamois are almost guaranteed. There are easy strolls in the Canala valley

immediately north of Pescasseroli, and in the Val di Fondillo east of Opi (one of the park's loveliest and most popular areas). Near Pescasseroli try trail B2 (to Monte di Valle Carrara, 2½ hours), or C3 to the Valico di Monte Tranquillo (2½ hours). Another favourite is the 2-hour hike from Barrea to Lago Vivo, or the walk in the Camosciara – another pretty area – to the Belvedere della Liscia (2 hours).

Flora The park claims over 1,200 species of plants and trees (and 267 types of fungi). Around two-thirds of its area is covered in ancient forests of beech and maple (beautifully coloured in autumn), interspersed with ash, hawthorn and hornbeam, and blossom-bearing trees like wild apple, pear, cherry and blackthorn. Spring ushers in swaths of asphodels, crocuses, gentians and snowdrops, easily seen on even the shortest walks, followed by wild orchids and rarities like endemic irises and Apennine edelweiss.

Wolves Italy has an estimated 150–200 wolves. Their numbers are increasing all the time, despite constant human harassment and the ever-increasing threat from feral dogs (the country has 800,000 wild dogs, which interbreed with wolves and challenge them for their food sources). The park has perhaps 15–20 individual wolves in the wild, plus several that are kept in special reserves near Civitella Alfedena and Pescasseroli. These are used for study and to preserve the thoroughbred characteristics of the Apennine wolf.

Bears The park's most jealously protected fauna are Italy's last Apennine brown bears (*Ursus arctos marsicanus*). Although descended from Alpine forebears, the Abruzzo's bears have developed enough indigenous features to be classified as a sub-species (named after the *Marsicano*, the generic name for much of the park, deriving from the Marsi, one of the area's earliest tribes). Bears were common until the 16th century, and bounties were still paid on every bear killed until as recently as 1915. About 80–100 are thought to survive, and numbers are gradually increasing. Sadly, the possibility of a sighting is minimal.

Chamois
The beautiful and graceful chamois are some of the most easily seen of the park's 40 species of mammal. Like the park's bears they are descended from Alpine ancestors, but have developed individual characteristics which allow them to be considered a sub-species (*Rupicapra rupicapra ornata*). The Valle delle Rose above Civitella Alfedena is one of their favoured haunts. Many of the park's 500-strong herd are being introduced into other parts of the Abruzzo.

Birds
Over 300 species of birds have been spotted within the national park. The park centres (and park map) identify areas where you are likely to see particular birds – notably the 10 or so pairs of golden eagles that nest in the region.

The Apennine brown bear clings precariously to existence in the national park, while numbers of wolves are steadily increasing

CAMPANIA

Campania To the Romans Campania was *campania felix* (the happy land), a sort of dream holiday destination – all views, fine wines, sunny skies and bountiful countryside. It is hardly surprising, therefore, that some of the country's greatest ancient sites are here. The Greek temples at Paestum look much as they must have done 2,000 years ago; so, too, do the remarkable Roman cities of Pompeii and Herculaneum, buried and preserved for posterity by the ash and mud of erupting Vesuvius – Goethe's 'peak of hell rising out of paradise'. Visitors still come to Campania in droves, to see the ancient sites certainly, but also to enjoy the unrivalled coastal scenery of the Sorrentino peninsula and the islands of Capri and Ischia.

Naples Nowhere is quite like Naples. On first acquaintance it appears a sort of hell, a sprawling, teeming city, the epitome of the urban nightmare. Many people leave at the earliest opportunity. Many more, intimidated by its reputation, avoid it altogether. The Neapolitans, however – some of the wiliest and liveliest Italians going – like to say that you hate the city after a day, love it after a week, and never want to leave after a year. It is well worth testing the theory, perhaps not over a year, but certainly over several days. With your valuables safely hidden, and your courage in both hands, wander the streets, visit one of Europe's finest museums, and – perhaps most importantly – sample pizza in the city where it was born.

Island idylls History's hedonists have long luxuriated on Campania's famous islands. Tiberius, for one, built a dozen villas on Capri to indulge his sexual whims. Later

REGION HIGHLIGHTS ◄◄◄◄◄

AMALFI *see page 199*
POMPEII *see page 201*
CAPRI *see page 204*
ISCHIA *see page 204*
ERCOLANO (HERCULANEUM)
see page 205
NAPOLI (NAPLES)
see page 206:
MUSEO ARCHEOLOGICO
NAZIONALE
PAESTUM
see page 208
POSITANO *see page 208*
RAVELLO *see page 209*
AMALFI COAST *see page 211*

Positano, a jewel of the Amalfi coast

CAMPANIA

Scenic drives
(*Amalfi Coast*): SS145/
SS163 Sorrento–Positano–
Amalfi–Salerno; (*Monti
Alburni*):SS19/SS488
Battipaglia–Sant'Angelo a
Fasanella; (*Cilento coast*):
SS267/SS 447 Agropoli–
Acciaroli–Pisciotta–
Palinuro–Camerota;
(*Cilento interior*): SS447a
Camerota–Foria–Laurito–
Rofranoo–Sanza–Torterell
a–Sapri.

Tourist information
Amalfi: Corso delle
Repubbliche 27
(tel: 089/872 619).
Benevento: Via N Sala 31
(tel: 0824/ 21 947).
Capri: Piazza Umberto
(tel: 081/837 0686).
Naples: Piazza del Gesù
(tel: 081/551 2701).
Pompeii: Via Sacra 1
(tel: 081/850 7255).
Ravello: Piazza Vescovado
13 (tel: 089/857 977).
Sorrento: Via L de Maio 35
(tel: 081/807 4033).

residents have included entertainer Gracie Fields, dancer Rudolph Nureyev, and droves of artists and writers. These days day-trippers make up the bulk of the bon viveurs, diminishing the island's social cachet but unable to tarnish its incomparable beauty. Brave the throng to share in the lotus-eating, and leave time, perhaps, to visit the region's other islands – Ischia and tiny Procida – less beautiful, just as crowded, but equally seductive.

Campanian coasts Where Grand Tourists once visited the Bay of Naples, package tourists now settle for the Sorrento peninsula – Italy's most renowned stretch of coastline. White-washed towns like Amalfi, Positano and Ravello rear up high above a turquoise sea, fringed by plunging cliffs and a stunning mountainous backdrop. Crowds flock to the region as they do to the islands – though its beauty is one which commercialism cannot taint. The area's main town, Sorrento, is less striking and often busy with package tours, but nonetheless makes an appealing and convenient base. You might also want to explore the Cilento, Campania's less sybaritic coastline, a long arc of cliffs, beaches and small resorts that skirts the mountains near the Calabrian border. See it after Paestum, and use Santa Maria di Castellabate as a base.

Pasta and pizza Two culinary staples originated in Campania – the pizza, and that most archetypal of pastas, spaghetti. Naples *is* the pizza's homeland (so ignore the kill-joys who claim it was created earlier elsewhere). The classic Neapolitan versions are *napoletana* (tomatoes, anchovies and mozzarella) and *Margherita* (created for Italy's first queen, using basil, tomato and mozzarella to suggest the colours of the Italian flag). Be sure to try a pizza in one of the city's old *pizzerie* such as Da Michele or Trianon da Ciro. Alternatively, buy it by the slice (*pizza taglia*). Other local specialities are: the famous *insalata caprese* (Capri salad) – slices of tomato and mozzarella; fish and seafood, mussels (*cozze*) and clams (*vongole*) in particular (though watch your wallet, as seafood can be expensive).

Pizza made in the traditional wood-fired oven

▶▶▶ Amalfi   *196B2*

Formerly one of the Mediterranean's leading seapowers, Amalfi is the largest town on Italy's most breathtaking coastline. Although it can often be dreadfully congested, its hotels and restaurants are generally more affordable than many in the area.

Poised romantically between the mountains and the sea, the town's narrow streets and dark passageways weave among monuments which testify to its former grandeur. The Romanesque **Duomo▶▶**, dominating the central square from the top of a large flight of steps, shows more than a hint of Saracen influence, even stronger in the adjoining **Chiostro del Paradiso▶▶** (Cloister of Paradise), full of palms and voluptuously intertwined twin columns.

Amalfi is known for its high-quality paper, and you can visit Europe's oldest working paper mill, as well as a small paper museum, the Museo della Carta. The **Museo Civico▶** houses the *Tavole Amalfitane*, a codex of maritime law which held sway over the entire Mediterranean until 1570.

199

Amalfi's highly decorated Duomo

▶   Benevento   *196C2*

Benevento was bombed heavily in World War II, and its centre – despite a certain atmospheric appeal – still has a battered and half-built feel. Nonetheless it remains one of the more interesting towns of the Campanian interior. The best sights are Roman, notably the 2nd-century AD **Arco di Traiano▶▶** (also known as Porta Aurea) and the ruins of the 20,000-seat **theatre▶**. Also worth at least a glance is the church of Santa Sofia, part of a Benedictine abbey founded by the Lombards in 760. Its cloisters hold the **Museo Sannio▶**, a collection of Roman antiquities.

▶   Campi Flegrei   *196B1*

The 'fiery fields', west of Naples, are the Phlegrean Fields of classical myth, Homer's and Virgil's entrance to Hades. They are also the Elysian Fields, long eulogised for their transcendental beauty. Nearby Naples has largely put paid to the beauty, though one or two spots repay a visit, and there are still signs of the volcanic activity that gave the region its name.

■ **Vesuvius (Vesuvio) is neither the world's highest nor most dangerous volcano, but the catastrophic eruption which buried Pompeii and Herculaneum has made it one of the most famous. 'Many a calamity has happened in the world,' wrote Goethe, 'but never one that has caused so much entertainment to posterity as this one'.** ■

The big bang On 24 August AD 79 Vesuvius had been belching smoke and debris for several days. Early that morning, however, its basalt plug collapsed, unleashing the full force of the volcano. A huge cloud blotted out the sun, raining dust, stone and lava on to the surrounding countryside. Pompeii was buried within hours, some 2,000 of its inhabitants killed by falling rocks and asphyxiating gases (many of its 20,000 population had already left). That evening, the volcano's internal walls disintegrated, sending further torrents of ash over the town (Herculaneum was engulfed at this point by a flood of superheated mud). Only late on 26 August did a feeble light return to the region.

Vesuvius today What you see today when you look up at the volcano from Naples is actually the truncated cone of Monte Somma (1,132m). Vesuvius proper (1,277m) rises from its floor, a cone largely created by the eruption of AD 79. Vesuvius has erupted around a hundred times since that fateful morning, the last in 1944. This works out at a strike rate of around once every 20 years, so the next cataclysm is long overdue. When it arrives Naples will be in the firing line – which makes it odd that there are no contingency plans to deal with an eruption.

Statistically, Vesuvius' next eruption is overdue, but if you are still interested in peering down into the crater of the famous volcano, it is easily reached

Reaching the crater There are several ways to get a closer look at Vesuvius. The easiest is to take the Circumvesuviana, a railway which runs in a broad circle around the volcano (2 hours). Alternatively, you can take the railway as far as Ercolano, where six SITA buses daily leave the station for the cafés and souvenir shops at Vesuvius' former chairlift station (*seggovia*). You can also drive to this point (or take a taxi from Ercolano – but fix a price first). From here it is a 30-minute climb to the summit (wear stout shoes). Views into the crater and over Naples are breathtaking. You can walk around the crater (2 hours), but watch out for the crumbling paths and rickety fences.

FOCUS ON *Pompeii*

■ Pompeii's fate was the archaeologists' fortune, for the volcanic eruption of AD 79 which buried it left posterity not only the world's finest surviving Roman town, but also an unparalleled insight into the minutiae of 1st-century life. An instant in the city's existence was captured by the disaster that overwhelmed its people. ■

History Pompeii (Pompei in Italian) was never as famous in its own time as it is today. It started life in the 6th century BC as a Greek trading post. After falling to the Samnites, it became a thriving Roman colony. Much was damaged by an earthquake in AD 63, the remainder obliterated by Vesuvius 16 years later. The city remained forgotten until around 1600, when the study of ancient texts suggested its existence. Excavations began in 1748 and have since revealed most of the site.

Sightseeing The site is huge, and even spending a day here still leaves many stones unturned. Some houses are little more than foundations, and after a time one ruin looks much like another, so be selective. Also be sure to see Naples' Museo Archeologico, which contains most of the site's moveable treasures.

The civic buildings Almost the first area you encounter (at the site's western entrance) is the **Forum**, the centre of Roman civic life. Its surviving buildings include the **Basilica** (a business centre and law courts), market place, and temples to Apollo, Venus, Jupiter and Vespasian. In the **Antiquarium** close by are body casts taken from the volcanic ash, figures whose contorted shapes graphically illustrate the horror of that fateful morning. Beyond the forum lie the **Terme Stabiane**, the town's earliest bath-houses. Still preserved are swimming pools, men's and women's sections, even small niches in the changing room for clothes. Alongside runs **Vico del Lupinare**, one of the main red-light districts. A small brothel at one end has several bed stalls and frescoes describing the services on offer.

More salutary performances took place in the 5,000-seat **Teatro Grande** and the smaller indoor **Teatro Piccolo** (or *Odeon*). The 20,000-seat **Anfiteatro**, built in 80 BC, is Italy's oldest surviving amphitheatre, and one of the most complete in the Roman world.

Casa dei Vetii This is Pompeii's best-preserved and most artistically rewarding house. Once the home of two wealthy merchants, it possesses the

201

Waiting for the visiting hordes at Pompeii

Past visitors
When Charles Dickens visited Vesuvius, he was carried to the summit in a litter borne by 15 attendants. In 1765, James Boswell noted sourly in his diary: '… on foot to Vesuvius. Monstrous mounting. Smoke: saw hardly anything'.

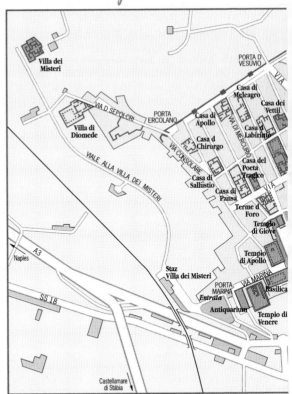

Pompeii possesses one of the most complete of all Roman amphitheatres

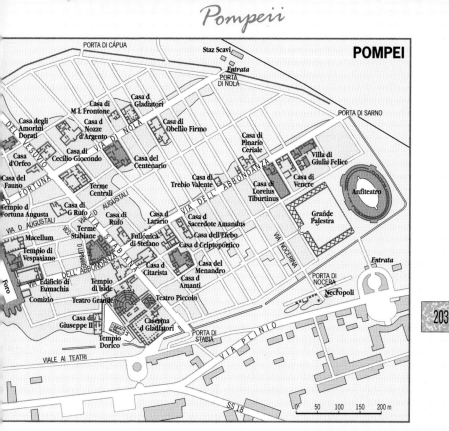

POMPEI

site's finest wall paintings. The frieze of the cupids is of special note. The vestibule contains the famously well-endowed Priapus, not to mention a roomful of explicit erotica (usually closed). Phallic symbols appear all over Pompeii, probably attempts to ward off the evil eye.

Three houses The largest of the town's houses is the **Casa del Menandro**, a patrician villa with a lovely peristyle and many appealing frescoes. Other noteworthy homes include the Casa del Fauno, source of many of the finest paintings in Naples' museum; and the **Casa di Loreio Tiburtino**, an elegant mansion whose structure is typical of many of the town's grander homes. In its courtyard, or atrium, stands the *impluvium,* a basin for collecting rainwater. To the rear spreads the peristyle, an open area of columns and fountains. Around it extend the house's private apartments.

Vesuvius, now quiet, broods over the ruins of Pompeii

Dogs and Dionysus Other well-kept houses include the Casa degli Amorini Dorati, Casa di M L Frontone, Villa di Giulia Felice and Casa del Centenario. You might hunt out the **Casa del Poeta Tragico**, a middle-class home built in Pompeii's final days. It is known for the sign above its door – *Cave canem* – 'Beware of the Dog'. Some 15,000 graffiti have been found around Pompeii, many salacious, others political or cultural. Finally, be certain to visit the **Villa dei Misteri**, for beautiful frescoes describing the initiation of women into the Dionysiac mysteries.

Capri practicalities
Boats and hydrofoils run year round to Capri from Sorrento and Naples (Molo Beverello). During the summer there are also connections from Ischia and towns along the Amalfi coast. Buses link the island's main centres (including the Blue Grotto). Accommodation is limited in July and August (reservations essential). Capri's reputation for high prices is deserved. To save money, use Sorrento as a base: a couple of day-trips at most are enough to see the island.

The Blue Grotto
Capri's most famous sight – La Grotta Azzurra – is an overrated, frustrating and extortionate experience. First you have to pay for a boat to take you from Marina Grande; then you cough up an entrance fee; then you pay for a small boat to whisk you in and out of the turquoise-hued grotto. You are better off taking the more rewarding two-hour boat trips around the whole island.

The lovely island of Capri has attracted pleasure-seekers since Roman times

▶▶▶ **Capri** 196B1

Capri's legendary beauty attracts day-trippers by the thousand. Most people come to indulge in a little lotus-eating – Augustus called the island *Capri Apragopolis* (City of Sweet Idleness) – which means lazy walks, lovely views, and sipping drinks from flower-decked terraces.

Boats dock at Marina Grande, from where you can take a funicular to the village of **Capri**▶▶▶, whose central *piazzetta* is the place to see and be seen. Near by, visit the Certosa San Giacomo, a crumbling monastery, and the Giardini di Augusto, gardens with tremendous views of the coast's cliffs. Below, the steep Via Krupp leads to Marina Piccola, the best place to swim (though it becomes uncomfortably crowded in summer). **Anacapri**▶▶ is the island's other main village, linked by chairlift to Monte Solaro (596m), a belvedere for views over the island.

▶ **Caserta** 196C1

Caserta's Palazzo Reale is Italy's largest royal palace (1,200 rooms, 1,790 windows and 94 staircases). The so-called 'Versailles of Naples' was begun in 1752 for the Bourbon King Charles III and finished 20 years later. Size for its own sake, however, is the palace's most impressive feature. Its apartments – though suitably painted, stuccoed and decorated – are insipid and uninspiring affairs. The gardens, by contrast, are enchanting. Caserta Vecchia (Old Caserta), a medieval village, is situated 10km to the north.

▶▶ **Ischia** 196B1

Although this island is less pretty and less chic than Capri, Ischia's spas, beaches and hot springs still make it much-frequented. The southern shores are nicest, around the villages of Fontana and **Sant'Angelo**▶▶, and the old volcanic peak, **Monte Epomeo**▶▶, is well worth climbing for the views. The town of **Ischia**▶ divides into Ischia Porto, the tourist centre, and Ischia Ponte, the less commercialised fishing village. Its only real sight is the Castello, an old Aragonese fortress.

Herculaneum

■ **When Vesuvius erupted in AD 79 it destroyed at least two towns. Although Pompeii is the better known, nearby Herculaneum (Ercolano) is almost equally as interesting – and its size makes it an easier place to visit.** ■

Origins Whereas Pompeii was a thriving commercial town, Herculaneum was a chic residential suburb, built to take advantage of the area's sea breezes and magnificent views. Houses here belonged to wealthy patrician families, and were built as sophisticated villas a cut above the town houses of Pompeii's business class. The wave of superheated mud that swept over the town in AD 79, however, was no respecter of class or property, and it entombed the town until its rediscovery in 1709. Excavations began in earnest in 1927, but since then less than half the site has been revealed.

The site Herculaneum lies at the seaward end of modern Ercolano's main street. Allow about two hours to see its highlights. On the whole it is better preserved than Pompeii, though there are fewer communal spaces or impressive civic buildings. Instead it preserves its Roman grid plan, based on two main streets – the *Cardine IV* and *Decumano Inferiore*. Only about 15 of the houses are open at any one time, though attendants may open others for a small tip. Among the public buildings, note the **Terme**, with its benches and basins intact (plus separate warm, hot and cold rooms); the *palaestra* (gymnasium), dominated by a lovely fountain; and the remnants of the 2,500-seat theatre.

The Casa dei Cervi
The house which best evokes Herculaneum's luxurious past is the Casa dei Cervi (House of the Deer), by virtue of its elegant gardens and its statues: one of a drunken Hercules (Ercolo), the town's legendary founder, the other of two groups of deer being hunted by dogs.

Herculaneum, risen from the mud of Vesuvius

▶▶ **Napoli (Naples)** *196B1*

Naples is a place which arouses fierce passions. On the one hand it is chaotic and crime-infested (guard your valuables), racked by pollution, poverty and grinding inefficiency. On the other it is the most Italian of cities (and yet unlike anywhere in Italy) – the place where family, food and religion reign as strongly as ever; the place that gave birth to the pizza, Sophia Loren and *O Sole Mio*; a city that was once so beautiful it formed the culmination of the Grand Tour.

To enjoy it you need to keep an open mind, but even if you take one look and want to leave, you should brave the city streets to see the **Museo Archeologico Nazionale▶▶▶**, one of Europe's greatest museums (see opposite page). Otherwise, sights are few. However, eating and soaking up atmosphere are as much a part of the Naples experience as sightseeing.

What to see Start a tour near the waterfront with the Castel Nuovo, (or Masdio Angioino) built in 1279 by Charles of Anjou (related to the French monarchy) and refurbished by Alfonso I of Aragon as a royal palace two centuries later (the Aragonese were an illegitimate branch of the Spanish monarchy, rulers of Naples until succeeded in 1734 by the Bourbons). Behind it lies the **Teatro San Carlo▶▶**, one of Europe's grandest opera houses (open to guided tours).

Among the churches, the **Duomo▶** is less than arresting, notable only for the phials of San Gennaro's blood and fragments of a basilica founded by Constantine in AD324 (Santa Restituta). Nearby **San Lorenzo Maggiore▶** is a fine Gothic church, and **Santa Anna dei Lombardi▶** offers excellent pieces of Renaissance sculpture.

The city's most worthwhile sight (after the museum) is the picture gallery of the **Palazzo Reale di Capodimonte▶▶** to the north of the city. Most Italian masters are represented, including Raphael, Michelangelo, Botticelli, Giovanni Bellini, Filippino Lippi, Simone Martini and many more.

Staying Avoid the offers of hotel touts and the mainly grim hotels near the station (around Piazza Garibaldi). Better budget options cluster between Piazza Dante and the Duomo. Further out, the up-market hotels congregate in the Mergellina district on the western side of the Bay of Naples.

Naples' grand arcade, the glass-domed Galleria Umberto I

■ **Naples' Museo Archeologico Nazionale is among the finest archaeological museums in Europe. Its collection covers classical sculpture, finds from Campania's ancient sites, as well as the finest artefacts and wall paintings taken from Pompeii and Herculaneum.** ■

The museum's exhibits are poorly labelled and whole sections are often closed – though even if you see only a fraction of what it has to offer you should come away satisfied. Invest in an English-language guide if you want to be thorough – they are on sale at the ticket office.

The ground floor The ground floor is devoted mainly to sculpture, the bulk of it from the Farnese collection, established in the 17th century by one of Rome's leading patrician families (mostly from sites in Lazio and Campania). Its most astounding pieces are the *Farnese Hercules*, a triumphant muscular figure, and the *Farnese Bull*, the largest sculptural group to have survived from antiquity (restored after its discovery by Michelangelo). Both came from the Terme di Caracalla in Rome.

Other outstanding works include the famous *Javelin Thrower*; the Augustan-era *Eurydice and Hermes*; the *Venus Callipyge* (literally 'Venus of the Beautiful Bottom'); and a figure of *Doyphorous* from Pompeii, one of the most accomplished Roman copies of a Greek original.

The upper floors Many upper floor rooms are devoted to mosaics and wall paintings, the majority removed from either Pompeii or Herculaneum. Among the mosaics look in particular for the *Battle of Issus*, a wonderfully realistic tableau showing Alexander the Great in battle with the Persians. Also hunt out the *Seascape* (a squid attacking a lobster), the *Street Musicians*, *Sorcerers* and *The Meeting of the Platonic Academy*.

Smaller exhibits
Leave plenty of time to study some of the smaller exhibits, too. Other rooms contain a wealth of artistic objects and household items from Pompeii. Two famous examples are the Tazza Farnese, a cup of veined sardonyx, and a 115-piece table service from the Casa del Menandro. Elsewhere, pieces of gladiatorial equipment – helmets, swords and trumpets – compete for attention with everyday items like shoes, pans, even dates, olives, onions and cakes.

For and against
Naples and its archaeological treasures have evoked different reactions over the years. In 1869, the writer Henry James remarked, 'I conceived at Naples a ten-fold deeper loathing than ever of the hideous heritage of the past'. Yet, in 1645, the diarist John Evelyn described Naples as the 'most magnificent city in Europe', while Goethe in 1787 wrote that 'Naples is a paradise: everyone lives in a state of intoxicated self-forgetfulness, myself included.'

Maiden gathering flowers, *wall-painting from Stabiae*

CAMPANIA

Shelley and Paestum
Part of Paestum's attraction is the site's beautiful setting. The poet Shelley wrote: 'The effect of the jagged outline of the mountains through groups of enormous columns on one side, and on the other the level horizon of the sea, is inexpressibly grand.'

►►► Paestum   196A2

Poseidonia was founded by the Greeks in the 6th century BC and renamed *Paestum* when it became a Roman colony in 273 BC. Among other things, it was famous for its roses and violets – Virgil mentions them – which were used in a lucrative scent industry. After falling into virtual abandonment in the 9th century, the site was rediscovered in the 18th century. Today it is dominated by three honey-coloured temples, among the greatest surviving Greek temples of antiquity.

The best-preserved is the **Tempio di Nettuno►►►**, (actually dedicated to Hera) built in the 5th century BC and often considered the greatest surviving Doric temple of antiquity. Despite its age only the roof and a few interior walls are missing. Alongside it stands the so-called **Basilica di Hera►►**, larger but more ruined than its neighbour (its nine-column width makes it broader by three columns than the Parthenon). Somewhat apart rests the **Tempio di Cerere**, built around 500 BC. The colony's Roman monuments are less impressive – piles of rubble in most cases – though the excellent on-site museum fills in many of the gaps. Its most celebrated exhibits are a statue of Zeus; many 6th-century BC metopes (friezes); eight bronze hydrias (water vessels); and several rare painted Greek panels.

The superb Temple of Neptune at Paestum

►► Positano   196B2

Few places are as picturesque as Positano, a pyramid of whitewashed houses spilling down from the mountains to the sea. Despite its small size it is one of the most monied and exclusive resorts on the Amalfi coast. This generally makes hotels an expensive proposition, but there are plenty of cafés and restaurants in which to while away an idle afternoon (as well as a couple of popular little beaches). Nearby **Praiano►►** is even smaller than Positano, but rapidly beginning to match it for prices and popularity.

► **Procida, Isola di** *196B1*

Tiny Procida is less varied and spectacular than Capri or Ischia. It is, therefore, less popular, which means the possibility of swimming and eating in relative peace and quiet. Ferries and hydrofoils run here from Ischia, Pozzuoli and Naples (Mergellina). Chiaiolella has the most attractive of the beaches, while the islet of Vivara's peaceful olive groves are the nicest places to walk.

►►► **Ravello** *196B2*

'Closer to the sky than the seashore', wrote André Gide of Ravello, an enchantingly beautiful small town whose lofty setting (350m) offers stupendous views of the Amalfi coast. Panoramas aside, Ravello's main attractions are quiet lanes and two magical, romantic villas. The **Villa Cimbrone**►► is known for its wild gardens, lush and full of overgrown arbours and lichen-covered terraces. They shelter Ravello's loveliest spot – a belvedere providing unrivalled views of the coast. The **Villa Rufolo**►►is slightly less spectacular, a Saracen-Romanesque building begun in the 11th century. Home over the centuries to several popes, its most famous guest was Richard Wagner, who used its gardens as the inspiration for his opera *Parsifal*.

Ravello's Duomo, a smart 11th-century church renovated in 1786, has fine bronze doors (1179) – modelled on those of Amalfi's cathedral – cast with 54 scenes from the Passion. Inside are two pulpits from the 12th and 13th centuries, decorated with mosaics and reliefs. There is also a small museum of antiquities.

Otherwise in Ravello there is little to do – one of its charms. It is also relatively quiet: being away from the coast, it has fewer visitors than Amalfi and Positano, and most of the trippers have left by mid-afternoon, making Ravello a tempting place to stay.

Top: Ravello
Above: pulpit, Ravello cathedral

► **Salerno** *196B2*

Salerno is a dusty, modern, ramshackle city, most famous as the site of the Allied landings of 9 September 1943. Its workaday atmosphere and scant sights do little to entice visitors, though its position makes it a convenient base for exploring Amalfi, Positano and Ravello. The small medieval quarter is worth a few minutes for the **Duomo**►, whose bronze doors and inlaid pulpits (1173) resemble those of Amalfi and Ravello. The adjacent Museo del Duomo contains an early medieval altar-front, embellished with 54 ivory panels, the largest work of its kind.

Grotta di Smeraldo
About 13km along the coast road from Positano to Amalfi is the Grotta di Smeraldo, named after the eerie emerald glow that bathes its stalagmites and stalactites. An escalator takes you to the grotto from the road, or drive to Amalfi and take a boat (trips every two hours).

CAMPANIA

Terra di Lavoro
Northwest of Capua
stretches the Terra di
Lavoro, literally the 'Land
of Work', long one of
Campania's prime agricul-
tural regions. It is perhaps
best known for its herds of
water buffalo, which yield
the milk that makes Italy's
finest mozzarella cheese.

Excursions in the Cilento
The Cilento's rugged interi-
or is scarcely explored, but
almost any drive along its
remote roads offers
numerous scenic rewards.
Try in particular the mountain roads in the north
around the Monti Alburni;
the desolate road from
Laurito to Padula (on the
A3 motorway); the SS18
from Vallo di Lucania to
Scario; and the short
SS447 loop from Palinuro
to Centola and Camerota.

*Sorrento, boats
at rest*

▶   **Santa Maria Capua Vetere**   *196C1*

The approaches to Capua are unprepossessing – endless
impoverished and semi-derelict suburbs – making it hard
to believe that during Roman times this was the second
most important city in Italy after Rome. Invading Arabs
destroyed the old city around AD 830. Its **amphi-
theatre▶▶**, once second only in size to the Colosseum, is
these days in a fairly poor state of preservation: most of
the seats and arches have collapsed – only the network of
tunnels around the arena remains largely intact. Close by
lies Italy's finest surviving **Mithraeum▶▶**, a temple to the
Persian god Mithras. Its underground chamber has a
vaulted ceiling painted with stars. Modern Capua, about
4km away, offers the **Museo Campano▶**, which houses
archaeological finds from the ancient city. The **Duomo**,
destroyed in 1942, has been rebuilt, but a 9th-century
campanile survives.

▶   **Santa Maria di Castellabate**   *196A2*

Santa Maria is one of several small resorts which cling to
the coast of the **Cilento▶▶**, a wild mountainous region
recently added to the list of Italy's proposed national
parks. A low-key place, the village gathers around a small
harbour, a clean, golden beach stretching away to the
north. **San Marco▶**, 3km south, is another picturesque
fishing village, dead in winter, but buzzing with life in summer. The region's spectacular coast road (the SS267-447)
links with other resorts, most notably Acciaroli and cosmopolitan **Palinuro▶**. You might also take a look at the
rather patchy Roman ruins at *Velia*, close to the village of
Marina di Velia.

▶▶   **Sorrento**   *196B1*

Sorrento is popular with package tourists (80 per cent of
whom are British). It is easy to see
why, for the town is an attractive and
unpretentious place, perfectly placed
for excursions to Pompeii and
Herculaneum (via the Circumvesuviana railway), and for trips to Amalfi,
Positano and Ravello – there is a
local bus service. Boats run around
the Sorrento peninsula to these
towns, and in summer also ply regularly to the islands of Capri and
Ischia.

    The great pleasures of Sorrento
itself are its lush, shady gardens
and its views. The belvedere
behind the Museo Coreale is a
favourite viewing point, and there
are few sights to equal a dramatic
Sorrento sunset. You can swim
locally at nearby Marina Grande,
at Regina Giovanna (on Punta del
Capo), or the Villa di Pollio, a
small park with old Roman ruins.
Otherwise there is little to do but
relax in the sunshine – something for which the town is
tailor-made.

THE SORRENTO PENINSULA

Drive **The Amalfi Coast**

This drive takes in the Amalfi Coast, Italy's most spectacular stretch of coastline, and its dramatically situated towns and villages.

Start from the end of the A3 motorway spur at Castellammare di Stabia, just a few kilometres east of Naples and Pompeii, and then follow the coastal road (the SS145) to **Sorrento** (page 210). Notice the tangle of roads beyond Massa Lubrense which lead to the tip of the peninsula. Beyond Sorrento continue on the SS145, climbing to the ridges of the craggy

mountains (the Monti Lattari) that form the peninsula's rocky backbone. The next 40km past **Positano** (page 208), **Praiano** and **Amalfi** (page 199) are some of the most breathtaking of any road in Europe. Just past Amalfi head inland to **Ravello** (page 209), and then either loop further inland to climb the slopes of Monte Cerreto, or return to Amalfi to pick up the SS163 coast road to Vietri sul Mare and **Salerno** (page 209).

The popular resort of Sorrento, on the dramatic Amalfi Coast

THE DEEP SOUTH

Tourist information
Bari: Piazza Aldo Moro 33
(tel: 080/524 2244).
Lecce: Via XXV Luglio
(tel: 0832/248 092).
Matera: Via di Viti de
Marco 9 (tel: 0835/333 541).
Taranto: Corso Umberto
113 (tel: 099/453 2392).
Trani: Via Cavour 140
(tel: 0883/588 825).
Tropea: Piazza Ercole
(tel: 0963/61 475).
Gargano: (Vieste)Corso
Lorenzo Fuzzini 8 (tel:
0884/707 495).

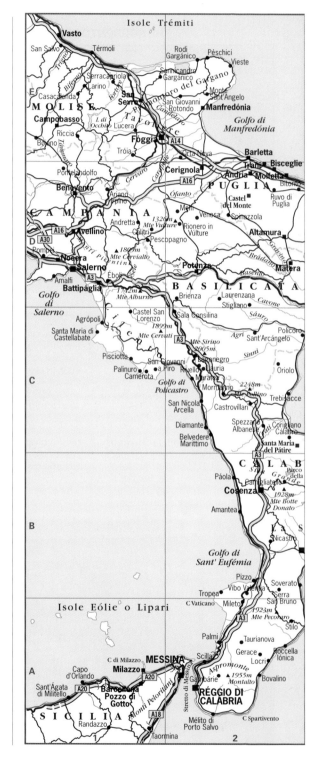

REGION HIGHLIGHTS ◄◄◄◄◄

BARI *see page 215*
CASTEL DEL MONTE
see page 215
GARGANO *see page 216*
LECCE *see page 217*
MATERA *see page 221*
ALBEROBELLO *see page 223:*
THE *TRULLI*
TARANTO *see page 224:*
MUSEO NAZIONALE
TRANI *see page 225*
TROIA *see page 225*

THE DEEP SOUTH

Frederick II
In the south you can't get away from Frederick II (1197–1250), Holy Roman Emperor and among the great personalities of the Middle Ages. Contemporaries called him *Stupor Mundi* (Wonder of the World), dazzled by his accomplishments in the fields of war, literature, science and mathematics. He left many monuments in Apulia, most notably the mysterious Castel del Monte.

Magna Graecia
The south's main Greek colonies were: (Basilicata) Metaponto; (Apulia) Otranto, Gallipoli and Taranto; (Calabria) Crotone, Reggio di Calabria, Locri and Sibari (home to the luxuriously living Sybarites). Today little remains of any of the cities, though artefacts excavated from their sites fill many regional museums, notably in Taranto and Reggio di Calabria.

Apulian wines
Apulia rivals Sicily as Italy's largest producer of wine and table grapes, yet although renowned for centuries, few of its wines are known outside the region. Many are used for blending, or for making vermouth. The outstanding vintages include Torre Quarto, Favonio (red or white), Castel del Monte; Donna Marzia (red or white); Copertino (the *riserva* in particular); Locorotondo, the region's best white; and Rosa del Golfo (produced by Giuseppe Calò), widely regarded as among Italy's finest rosés.

The Deep South Calabria, Basilicata and Apulia are the heart of the south – an area cut off for centuries by history and geography from the rest of Italy. Despite considerable efforts, it is still poorer and more backward than northern Italy, an imbalance worsening with the north's apparently increasing antagonism.

The south, with relatively little in the way of art or monuments, still evokes in atmosphere the Mediterranean Italy of old. Its landscapes are unspoilt, its villages age-old and many places never see a tourist. Its downside lies in a Byzantine bureaucracy, a decaying infrastructure, and a shortage of tourist facilities. But approach the south in the right spirit and it has much to recommend it, not least the fact that it costs less for eating and sleeping.

History The Greeks colonised all three regions, establishing cities in what become known as Magna Graecia (Greater Greece). The Romans were less influential, though Brindisi – connected to Rome by the Via Appia – became one of their most important links with the East. The Arabs and Byzantines held sway in the Dark Ages and influenced the region's architecture (Basilicata takes its name from *basilikos*, the name of the Byzantine administration). They were succeeded in the 11th century by the Normans, and later by the Swabians (Emperors), most notably Frederick II (see panel) and the Angevins (French). For centuries thereafter the south stagnated under the Spanish.

Calabria The 'toe' of the Italian boot, though bereft of any special artistic treasures, has an unspoilt coastline and grand, wild interior. The eastern (Ionian) coast is largely monotonous; except for a few towns such as Stilo and Rossano, the resort-dotted western (Tyrrhenian) littoral is more spectacular. The Calabrian interior comprises sun-baked plains and the rounded, wooded slopes of the Sila mountains, a large, sometimes rather laborious area to explore, but brimming with natural beauty and half-forgotten villages.

Basilicata Basilicata is Italy's poorest region. Its towns and villages are the country's least discovered, its intractable landscapes some of Europe's least spoilt. The Pollino mountains and hills of the Sauro valley offer magnificent drives, while Matera has the unmissable *sassi*, ancient cave-dwellings that riddle the ravines around the town. Melfi, the Normans' first southern power-base, is an attractive town and makes a good centre for exploring some of the region's more appealing abbeys and castles.

Apulia (Puglia) Apulia is by far the most rewarding part of the south. Rocky and sun-bleached, or smothered in vineyards and olive groves, it offers little fine scenery, except in the Gargano, a promontory of beaches, cliffs and forest that forms the spur of the Italian boot. But whitewashed, Greek-looking villages dot the coast, and the famous *trulli*, curious, beehive-like buildings of unknown antiquity, some still in use, scatter the countryside around Alberobello. Many towns are showcases for Apulian-Romanesque architecture, and in Lecce the Italian baroque finds its greatest expression.

▶▶　**Alberobello** (see page 223)　　*213D3*

▶▶　**Bari**　　　　　　　　　　　　　*213D3*

Bari's almost Arabic warren of medieval streets is in marked contrast to the mundane promenades of the modern city. At its heart lies the **Basilica di San Nicola**▶▶▶, a prototype for many of the region's great Apulian-Romanesque churches. Started in the 11th century, it was built to house the body of St Nicholas, the patron saint of Holy Russia, pawnbrokers, sailors and children (he is the St Nicholas of Santa Claus fame). Inside, the ciborium (altar canopy) and episcopal throne are two of the finest such works in Italy. Note also the silver altarpiece (1684) and the precious exhibits of the church Treasury. The body of St Nicholas (San Nicola) lies in the building's crypt.

The **Cattedrale di San Sabino**▶▶▶ close by is another exceptional if more austere Romanesque church. It contains an icon said to be the world's truest likeness of the Madonna. Also worth seeing are the **Castello**▶, rebuilt by Frederick II around 1240, and the **Museo Archeologico**▶▶ housing Apulia's most complete collection of antiquities.

Drive 17km west and Bitonto's quiet maze of medieval streets makes a welcome respite from Bari. Its fine 13th-century Apulian-Romanesque cathedral has an unusual *matroneum*, or women's gallery.

Safety
Crime can be a problem in urban southern Italy. The old quarters of Bari and Brindisi have a particularly bad reputation, but back streets should be avoided in most large towns after dark. Be especially careful of purse-snatching and car break-ins.

Barletta
Barletta is a shabby town famous for the *Colosso*, the largest Roman bronze statue in existence. Five metres high, it dates from the 4th century AD and probably depicts the Byzantine Emperor Valentinian (d. AD 375). Stolen by the Venetians from Constantinople in the 13th century, the statue was abandoned on the beach near Barletta when the boat bringing it to Venice foundered in a storm.

Left: decorated doorway of San Nicola, Bari
Below: Frederick II's enigmatic fortress, Castel del Monte

▶▶▶　**Castel del Monte**　　　　　*212D2*

This mighty fortress built around 1240 by Frederick II is one of the great medieval buildings of Europe. It is also one of the most mysterious, scholars having puzzled for centuries over its purpose and peculiar mathematical obsession. It is an octagonal building, built around an octagonal courtyard, flanked by eight towers which are also octagonal. Each of its floors contains eight rooms.

It may be that eight was a symbol of the crown, or that Frederick was imitating Jerusalem's octagonal Omar mosque. Another theory is that the castle's mathematical precision was astrological, as its proportions are supposed to relate to the movements of the planets. Others claim that it was a hunting lodge, or a refuge for pilgrims in search of the Holy Grail. In any event, it has few of the defensive features normally associated with medieval castles – only a magnificent position, its gloriously isolated bastions visible for miles around.

Part of the rocky coastline of the Gargano peninsula

▶▶▶ (II) Gargano 212E2

The 'spur'of the Italian boot is a hilly and largely wooded limestone peninsula edged with rocky cliffs, whitewashed villages and broad sandy beaches. While the interior remains unvisited, the coast – in summer at least – is crowded and commercialised. Come out of season, however, and the resorts are delightfully quiet.

Siponto▶ (Roman **Sipontum**) boasts a fine museum and the lovely 11th-century Romanesque church of **Santa Maria di Siponto**, but the Gargano starts in earnest at **Monte Sant'Angelo▶▶**. This windblown mountaintop eyrie was for almost 1,500 years one of Italy's most revered Christian shrines following several apparitions by the Archangel Michael in the 5th century. The most famous took place in a cave now contained in the **Santuario di San Michele▶▶** (note the beautiful bronze doors).

Moving around the coast, **Mattinata▶** is a small resort with a magnificent beach, linked by a scenic road to **Pugnochiuso▶**, set in a panoramic bay, and **Vieste▶▶**, the Gargano's busiest town. Nearby **Peschici▶▶**, however, makes a more attractive base, being quieter, prettier and well placed for access to beaches (and numerous small grottoes).

Stonework on the Santuario di San Michele, Monte Sant'Angelo

▶ Gerace 212A2

Rugged Gerace, perched on an impregnable crag, boasts Calabria's largest church, a Norman cathedral built in 1045 and enlarged by Frederick II in 1222. Its unadorned interior is supported by 20 ancient columns, many taken from the ruins of old Greek temples at nearby Locri. Be sure to see the Treasury with its exquisite Renaissance ivory crucifix. When you tire of exploring this unspoiled town, you might shop around for Gerace's distinctive local pottery.

▶▶▶ Lecce 213D4

Lecce is to the baroque what Florence is to the Renaissance. Counter-Reformationary zeal and mercantile money transformed much of the city in the 17th century. Churches, palaces – even houses and simple courtyards – were given a glorious baroque veneer of *putti*, gargoyles, garlands, stone curlicues and wreaths of exuberant decoration. There is so much to see, it is best to wander at random, but start with the 16th-century **Basilica di Santa Croce▶▶▶**, the apotheosis of Lecce's airy baroque style. Next door stands the **Palazzo del Governo▶**, designed by Zimbalo and Giuseppe Cino, architects responsible for many of the city's buildings. They also worked on **Piazza del Duomo's▶▶** cathedral and Palazzo del Seminario, as well as the Carmine, Gesù, Rosario and Santa Chiara churches. Non-baroque sights include Romanesque **SS Nicola e Cataldo▶**, the art and antiquities of the **Museo Provinciale▶▶**, and the ruins of the **Roman amphitheatre▶**, built at the time of Hadrian and capable of accommodating 20,000 spectators.

▶ Lucera 212E1

Lucera's windy hilltop site and tangle of inviting streets make it a wonderful place to explore. The **Duomo▶▶** is one of the region's more alluring medieval buildings, though the tremendous **Frederick II fortress▶▶** is more likely to command your attention. The second largest in southern Italy, its walls stretch over a kilometre.

Wine-tasting
Lecce's Enoteca Internazionale has an extensive range of Apulian, Italian and international wines served by the glass or bottle with light meals (Via Cesare Battisti 23).

Basilica di Santa Croce, Lecce

The Tavoliere
Lucera's lofty position and its immense fortress look down over the plains of the Tavoliere, or 'chessboard', named after the chequered pattern created by the region's wheatfields. The land has looked like this since Roman times, when it was parcelled up into squares for distribution to pensioned-off army officers.

■ **Apulia is perhaps best known for its remarkably vast number of Romanesque churches and cathedrals. Each in its way is a monument to the architectural styles bequeathed over the centuries by the region's many invaders. The influences of the Normans, Arabs, Lombards and Byzantines all coalesce to produce the magnificent hybrid which is known as Apulian-Romanesque.** ■

Why Apulia? Building a church was no easy matter. Political stability was needed for a start. Long-term projects required sustained peace and finance if they were to be completed. In Apulia, the strong government of Norman, Swabian and Angevin rulers allowed craftsmen long periods of creative endeavour. It also meant they could travel unmolested, absorbing new trends, and moving their workshops to where demand was highest. Apulia in this respect was a religious crucible, for it lay on several vital pilgrimage routes. Its ports were also points of embarkation for pilgrims bound for the Holy Land.

Lions and griffins guard the entrance to Ruvo di Puglia's fine Apulian-Romanesque cathedral

Rome and Byzantium No two Apulian churches are alike, and no set rules govern their architectural styles, but the variety, richness of decoration, and sculptural skill that make them one of the glories of Italian medieval art are bound by a few unifying strands. The earliest classical models reached Apulian church-builders via Byzantium. They contributed decorative motifs – crispcut and stylised – such as acanthus leaves, vine tendrils, animals and birds. Later, Roman portraiture and sarcophaghi also played their part.

The Lombards Lombard sculpture also had a great influence on Apulian churches: lions, snakes, centaurs, hunters, fishes and bizarre menageries frequently feature on church portals. Architecturally the Lombards contributed high central naves (with lower aisles), triform apsidal ends, and the arched corbel-table below the roof. They also provided the beautiful lateral galleries formed of open arcades.

Arabs and Normans Norman supremacy in the 11th century brought influences from France and Normandy, notably a grandeur of design and execution. Tuscan craftsmen were employed in northern Apulia, taking the 'striped' Pisan churches as their model. Oriental features filtered through from Arab Sicily, notably interlaced arches and pointed Saracenic arches. Finally, Frederick II reintroduced further classical Roman refinements.

►► Maratea 212C2

Pretty Maratea, on the Basilicata coast, is as pleasant as any of the resorts on the Calabrian seaboard to the south. It divides into several districts: Maratea Porto, with fishermen's cottages, bars and restaurants; hilltown Maratea Inferiore, home to most of the hotels and fun to explore; and Maratea Superiore, the upper town, from which you can climb to the evocative ruins of Maratea Vecchia (walk a little further and you come to the top of Monte San Biagio, with magnificent views over the Gulf of Policastro and Maratea's 22m statue of the Redeemer). The best beaches are 5km away at Maratea Marina, but the coast is studded with bays where you are able to swim in complete privacy.

► Martina Franca 213D3

Martina Franca's high-rise outskirts do not augur well, but the town centre is a marvellous showcase of baroque and rococo architecture. Its centrepiece is the church of **San Martino►►**, fronted by a soaring baroque façade. Walk down Via Cavour and you are also treated to numerous exuberantly decorated houses and *palazzi*. The 300-roomed **Palazzo Ducale►** should not be missed, nor the churches of the Carmine and San Domenico. Find time to wander the old **walls►** for a lovely panorama over the *trulli*-dotted patchwork of fields and vineyards of the Itria valley. The area's prime tourist attraction lies 28km north of the town, the **Grotte di Castellana**, a great cave system ending in the impressive Caverna Bianca.

Scenic drives
Calabria: the SS105 Belvedere Marittimo–Castrovillari; SS177 Rossano–Cosenza; SS179/SS109 San Giovanni in Fiore–Catanzaro; SS179 Stilo–Serra San Bruno; (*Aspromonte*) SS183/184 Reggio di Calabria–Gambarie–Melito. (*Basilicata*): SS7 Potenza–Matera; SS19 Lagonegro–Rivello–Mormanno–(Rotonda)–Castrovillari. (*Apulia*): SS89 Manfredonia–Monte Sant'Angelo–Vieste–Peschici–Rodi-Garganico; SS528 Monte Sant'Angelo–Vico del Gargano; SS172 Putignano–Alberobello–Martina Franca.

219

Martina Franca: the restrained elegance of the fountain (left) contrasts with the baroque flamboyance of the architectural detail (above)

► Massafra 213D3

Massafra bears striking similarities to Matera (see page 221). Divided in two by a deep ravine, the Gravina di San Marco, it is riddled with grottoes, troglodyte dwellings and early Greek Christian cave churches (which date from the 9th to 14th centuries). The best churches are San Marco, La Candelora and San Leonardo. Some of the town's buildings are rather badly signposted and difficult to reach, but a dramatic baroque staircase leads clearly to **Madonna della Scala►►**, built around an early cave church – with delicate 12th-century frescoes – and a primitive 8th-century crypt.

THE DEEP SOUTH

▶▶ **Matera** (see opposite page)   *212D2*

▶▶ **Melfi**   *212D2*

The Normans' occupation of Apulia began when 11 brothers came from Normandy offering their mercenary army in the service of local barons. In 1041 they captured Melfi and two years later elected William de Hauteville their leader. William's sons, Drogo and Humphrey were succeeded by Robert Guiscard, recognised as 'Duke of Apulia and Calabria' by Pope Nicholas II after campaigns against the Saracens (in 1059).

Dark and medieval Melfi still lies in the shadow of its Norman castle (1155), standing proud despite the earthquakes that have laid the town low over the centuries. Inside is a small museum with Greek, Roman and Byzantine finds, its prize exhibit a 1st-century Roman sarcophagus, the *Sarcofago di Rapolla*.

▶ **Metaponto**   *213C3*

Once home to Pythagoras, *Metapontion* in the 7th century BC was among the most flourishing colonies of Magna Graecia. Although its ruins today are the region's most extensive, they are spread over a large area and their effect is patchy – nor is modern Metaponto, despite its beaches, anything to write home about. The **Antiquarium**▶▶, however, is highly worthwhile, a well-presented museum of finds from the site. In its grounds is the **Tavole Paladine**▶▶, the 15-columned ruins of a 6th-century BC Doric temple. Most of the other remains lie scattered across the **Parco Archeologico**▶.

Turkish slaughter
In 1480 Otranto fell to the Turks after a 15-day siege. The town's archbishop was sawn in half for helping in the defence. Another 560 survivors were beheaded for failing to convert to Islam. The Turks' executioner is reputed to have converted to Christianity and refused to carry on with his work of slaughter.

The Tavole Paladine at Metaponto, a temple dedicated to the goddess Hera

▶ **Otranto**   *213C4*

Greek in origin, Italy's easternmost town nestles around a small harbour. It is an attractive fishing village, becoming increasingly popular despite its indifferent beach. Its cathedral, **Santa Maria Annunziata**▶▶, is remarkable for the fresco-covered crypt (1088) – supported by 42 tiny columns – and a beautiful mosaic (1165) that runs the length of the nave. In a mixture of themes, it portrays Biblical stories, illustrates the *Months of the Year* and *The Tree of Life*, and includes characters as diverse as King Arthur, Alexander the Great and the Queen of Sheba. Also see the town's mighty **Castello**▶ (an Aragonese fortress), and the 10th-century church of **San Pietro**▶.

■ **Bizarrely picturesque Matera is unique for its *sassi*, cave-dwellings dug from the living rock in the ravines around the town. Many have been inhabited since prehistoric times. A few have been turned into cave churches; others form an elaborate honeycomb of streets and alleys.** ■

Disease and designer dwellings Although Matera's *sassi* appear romantic today, earlier this century they represented the ugly face of Italy, racked by unimaginable poverty and riddled with diseases like malaria, dysentery and trachoma. Over the years their inhabitants have been rehoused in the modern apartments of the new town, only for the old caves to become the latest in designer homes for more affluent *materani*. About 700 people now live in the *sassi*.

The best way to get an overall picture of the labyrinth is on the Strada Panoramica, a scenic road specially built for sightseers. To see some of the nooks and crannies, and the rock churches, slip into the smaller back streets or employ one of the children who for a tip will take you to places you might not otherwise find.

Seeing the *sassi* The *sassi* divide into two main districts, the Sasso Caveoso (nearest the eastern end of the Strada Panoramica) and Sasso Barisano. Broadly speaking there are four types of cave: the oldest are the niches cut into the sides of the ravine, inhabited up to 7,000 years ago; the second type date from 2000 BC (and form the heart of the Sasso Caveoso); the third are 1,000 years old and lie along Via B Buozzi; the fourth are the dwellings around Via Fiorentini, most of which were excavated during the 17th century.

Rock churches Of special interest are the *chiese rupestri*, or cave churches, of which there are about 120 around the town. Most were carved by monks between the 8th and 13th centuries. Two of the best, San Pietro Caveoso and Santa Maria de Idris, lie close to one another. Both boast 14th-century Byzantine rock paintings. Santa Lucia alle Malve, a 10th-century church, is also worth a visit.

Past horrors
Matera's cave dwellings and their inhabitants were once emblematic of the poverty-stricken and disease-ridden lives of many peasants in Italy's deep South. Some 50 years ago, the sister of Carlo Levi (author of *Christ Stopped at Eboli*, a classic evocation of life in the south) compared the caves to scenes from Dante's *Inferno*. 'Never before have I seen such a spectacle of misery,' she wrote, going on to describe the 'wrinkled faces of the old men, emaciated by hunger, with hair crawling with lice and encrusted with scabs. Many of them had swollen bellies and yellowed faces, stricken with malaria.'

221

The grey labyrinth of sassi, extraordinary cave houses of Matera

► **Reggio di Calabria** 212A2

Calabria's grim capital is worth braving only for the **Museo Nazionale►►**, a splendid collection of material from archaeological sites all over Calabria and Basilicata. Its pride and joy, the *Bronzi di Riace*, were retrieved from the sea in a chance discovery in 1972. The two 5th-century BC sculptures depict a pair of Greek warriors, one at least believed to be the work of Phidias, regarded as the greatest sculptor of antiquity. Other prominent works include votive tablets from the Temple of Persephone at *Locri* and two paintings by Antonello da Messina, *Saint Jerome* and *Abraham and the Angels*.

One of the Greek Bronzi di Riace *in Reggio di Calabria's Museo Nazionale*

► **Riviera Calabrese (Calabrian Riviera)** 212B2

The Calabrian Riviera is a term of convenience for a fairly uniform succession of resorts, beaches and gently unassuming countryside on the region's Tyrrhenian coast. Development is often less marked than in Italy's northern resorts, but towns still have a wide choice of hotels, restaurants and nightlife. Most spots are crowded with Italian holiday-makers in summer, but sleepy and unspoilt out of season. Tropea (see page 225), is far and away the best destination, but other nice places include San Nicola Arcella; Diamante (an unusually chic resort); Amantea; and Pizzo (a reasonable alternative to Tropea).

► ► **Rossano** 213C3

This picturesque little hilltown was the most important Byzantine centre in the south during the 9th century. The greatest monument to its illustrious past is the *Codex Purpureus*, a beautifully illuminated 6th-century manuscript kept in the **Museo Diocesano►►►**. The 188-page volume contains the Gospels of St Matthew and St Mark, and was probably brought to Italy by monks fleeing Muslim persecution. While you are in Rossano, do not miss 10th-century **San Marco►►**, Calabria's finest Byzantine church, lent a strongly Middle Eastern flavour by its palm trees and tiny cupolas. Its terrace offers a fine view over Rossano's cave-riddled gorge. The town has several other frescoed Byzantine churches, most notably La Panaghia and Santa Maria del Pilerio.

► ► **Ruvo di Puglia** 212D2

Ruvo's **Museo Jatta►►** offers a collection of the 5th- to 3rd-century BC ceramics for which the town was famous. Among its 1,700-plus terracottas is the famous red-figured Greek vase known as the *Krater of Talos*. The **Duomo►►** is one of the region's more important pieces of Apulian-Romanesque architecture, its rather severe façade relieved by a richly decorated portal and exquisite rose window. (Notice the griffins flanking the main doorway and the little pagan figures around the sides of the building. It is thought they may have been copied from pieces of classical pottery.)

Aspromonte

The 'Bitter Mountain' is an incredibly wild region east of Reggio di Calabria. It is one of Italy's most isolated areas, and ways of life here have changed little in centuries. Aspromonte's mountain fastness is a traditional haunt of Calabria's kidnappers (though the area is perfectly safe). Excursions on its high roads offer astounding landscapes and ancient villages where Greek dialects are still spoken.

■ **Nobody knows the real age or origins of Apulia's *trulli*, the strange and conical dwellings that are found solely in a small region around Alberobello and nowhere else in Europe.** ■

Practical but puzzling *Trulli* are round, single-storey buildings made with uncemented stones. They are invariably whitewashed, and their tapered roofs are usually crowned with hieroglyphics – often a cross or some more arcane symbol (possibly of unknown magical significance). The oldest surviving example dates back to the 13th century, though most are no more than 300 years old. Their origins, however, are certainly more ancient.

At their most basic, the houses are practical – there is plenty of local limestone and they are simple to build; they remain cool in summer and are easily heated in winter. By these criteria, they should be found all over the Mediterranean. Why they occur only in Apulia is not known – though there is no shortage of theories.

Tax evasion? For a time it was thought they were built to outwit Ferdinand I of Aragon who, during his reign, forbade the Apulians to build permanent houses (in this way he could move labourers around as they were needed). The peasants responded by constructing houses which could be dismantled when the king's inspectors were spotted. This theory is now discredited, along with the notion that the houses were designed as a wily form of tax evasion. During Spanish rule a tax was levied on individual houses, only unfinished buildings being exempt, a clause, it is claimed, the *trulli*-owners exploited with their loose-stoned and easily removed roofs.

Greece or the Middle East A more persuasive idea links them with similar buildings at Mycenae, an idea which would connect the *trulli* with the Greek civilisation of 3000 BC. Apulian ports are the closest to Greece, and for centuries the region was part of Magna Graecia. On the same lines, and perhaps closer to the truth, is the theory that they were imported from the Middle East – a conjecture based on their similarity to the 'sugar loaf' houses of Syria and elsewhere. They were possibly introduced by Eastern monks – and used initially as tombs – or copied by soldiers returning from the Crusades.

One of Apulia's mysterious trulli

Train ride
A nice way to visit the best of Puglia's *trulli*, and see a slice of the region's prettiest countryside, is to take the little private railway operated by the *Ferrovie Sud-Est*. The line begins at Bari and ends at Taranto. En route it passes close to the Grotte di Castellana (see page 219), which lie just 2km from the Grotte di Castellana station. Then it proceeds to Putignano, beyond which you begin to see the first of the *trulli*. The largest concentration is found in and around Alberobello, a popular tourist destination, 20km beyond.You can leave the train here, and then reboard a later connection to take you on to Martina Franca (see page 219).

THE DEEP SOUTH

Excursion from the Sila
The scenic SS110 meanders lazily to Serra San Bruno (37km), with its Certosa di Santo Stefano, founded in 1090 by St Bruno, originator of the strict Carthusian order (the abbey is closed to women). A couple of kilometres away is the church of Santa Maria del Bosco, a church where you can see a cave where the saint is said to have prayed. The waters of the spring here are reputed to be effective for exorcisms.

The rolling forested landscape of the Sila

▶ **Sila** *212B2*

Calabria's mountainous interior divides into three jumbled massifs – the Sila Grande, Sila Piccola and Sila Greca – large areas of which are protected by the Parco Nazionale della Calabria. Almost the Apennines' last gasp, they have long been famous for their forests (from about the 6th century onwards, timber from the Sila provided the wooden roofs for many of Rome's churches). Today the scenery is wild and unspoilt, though the long rolling ridges and endless woods can become monotonous. Camigliatello and San Giovanni in Fiore (a less attractive town) are the main bases, Lakes Arvo, Cecita and Ampollino the most picturesque areas. Roads off the SS107 (SS177, SS179 and SS108bis) offer the best drives, and there is a superbly scenic little railway from Cosenza to San Giovanni in Fiore. The villages in the mountains are not terribly pretty – life is hard and poverty is rife – but they come alive during the numerous centuries-old festivals still held in many centres.

▶ **Stilo** *212A2*

Any fan of early church architecture should make a beeline for Stilo, home to **La Cattolica**▶▶, an important if rather ramshackle Byzantine church of indeterminate age (estimates range from 10th-century to 12th-century). Its brick and stone weathered to a lovely red-brown hue, the church looks out over a rocky valley, a major retreat for Basilian monks in southern Calabria (as Rossano was for their counterparts in the north of the region). Note the upturned ancient column in the nave, reputedly a symbol of Christianity's triumph over paganism. The town has several other churches of lesser antiquity.

▶ **Taranto** *213D3*

A large port and naval base, Taranto has one important tourist attraction, the **Museo Nazionale**▶▶▶. The museum's emphasis is on Magna Graecia, embracing a wide range of Greek statues, ceramics and the world's largest collection of Greek terracottas (50,000 pieces). Its centrepiece is the *Sala degli Ori*, a room devoted to goldware. Other highlights include a pair of *korai* (figurines of young girls); a series of Roman portraits; several actors' masks; busts of Apollo and Aphrodite; and a variety of bas-reliefs and mosaics from the town's tombs.

▶▶ Trani 212D2

Trani is an elegant and picturesque Apulian port, once a rival to Bari as the region's most important maritime power and still a cosmopolitan town. Today its fame rests on the **Duomo▶▶▶**, one of the area's finest examples of Apulian-Romanesque architecture. The cathedral's beauty is given added impact by the fact that it sits virtually on the sea's edge. Tremendous bronze doors, cast in 1180, usher you into a three-tiered church. Most of the interior is Norman, though part rests on the Ipogea di San Leucio, a 6th-century palaeo-Christian tomb. In the rest of town, try not to miss the church of Ognissanti, built as a hospice by the Knights Templar; the Palazzo Caccetta, a 15th-century Gothic palace (Gothic buildings are rare in Apulia); and the Castello, built for Frederick II in 1233 (but since rebuilt). Also walk around the medieval quarter, centred on Via Mario Pagano, and take time out in the Villa Comunale (Public Gardens) near the seafront.

▶▶ Troia 212E1

Quiet and windblown, Troia is a pretty village, distinguished by its splendid **cathedral▶▶▶**. Built in 1093, it has a sumptuous rose-window, as well as a pair of 12th-century bronze doors, all tinged with the classical, Saracen and Byzantine motifs that characterise Apulian-Romanesque architecture. Inside look at the curious carved 12th-century pulpit, the capitals and the paintings, manuscripts and furnishings of the **Museo Diocesano▶**.

▶▶ Tropea 212B2

A huddle of pastel-coloured houses perched above the sea, and surrounded by golden beaches, Tropea is by far the nicest resort on the Calabrian coast (the Riviera Calabrese). Although fashionable and popular, the town manages to retain its charm, and has hotels and *trattorie* in most price ranges. When not enjoying Tropea's beaches, seafood or picturesque streets, visit the church of Santa Maria dell'Isola, dramatically situated on a limestone crag near the sea. Also look into the Duomo, known for two strange works of art: an inlaid 16th-century Black Crucifix, and the Madonna of Rumania, reputedly painted by St Luke.

Trani's cathedral, a jewel of the Apulian-Romanesque style

Scylla and Charybdis
The legendary sea monsters of Homer's *Odyssey* were probably whirlpools created in the Straits of Messina by the meeting of the Ionian and Tyrrhenian seas. Ships to this day must navigate with care in these waters. Scylla corresponds to Calabria's modern-day village of Scilla; Charybdis is Cariddi on the Sicilian mainland.

The church of Santa Maria dell'Isola, Tropea

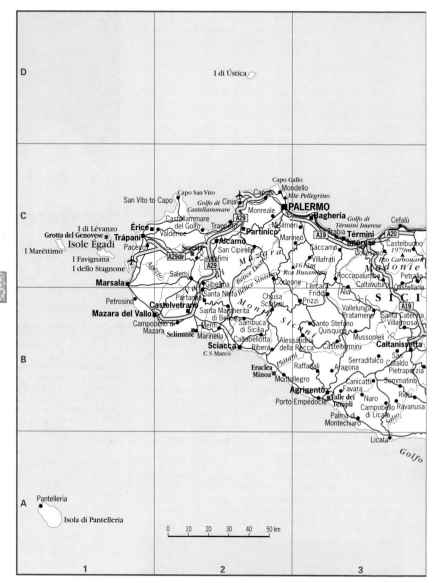

The island of Sicily

Colourful Sicilian
ceramics for the
tourist market

REGION HIGHLIGHTS ◄◄◄◄

AGRIGENTO *see page 230*
CEFALÙ *see page 232:*
THE DUOMO
MOUNT ETNA *see page 233*
MONREALE *see page 235*
PALERMO *see page 238:*
PALAZZO DEI NORMANNI,
CAPPELLA PALATINA
SEGESTA *see page 240*
PIAZZA ARMERINA
see page 241
SIRACUSA *see page 242:*
PARCO ARCHEOLOGICO
TAORMINA *see page 243:*
TEATRO GRECO, VIEWS

Sicily Cross the sea to Sicily and you do more than leave the Italian mainland. You cross to an island which stands on the edge of Europe, a place whose history and culture conspire to make it a world apart. Almost every Mediterranean power over the last 2,000 years has ruled its shores, not only leaving a mark on its art and architecture, but also moulding its cuisine and shaping its attitude to foreigners (a breed which for some Sicilians also includes other Italians). Although subjugation – together with poverty and the Mafia – have often crippled the island, they have rarely cowed its population. As a result you will find Sicilians some of the most singular and most hospitable of Italians.

SICILY

History Sicily is named after its early Siculo and Sicano tribes (1250 BC). Given the 500 years of Greek domination, (800–300 BC), it could as easily have kept its Greek name, *Trinacria* (after the island's triangular shape: Greek *treis* – three and *akra* – point). During this period cities like Syracuse and Agrigento were among the most powerful in Europe. Roman rule followed, superseded by the Vandals and then by the Byzantines. Two centuries of Arab rule from 827 produced another golden age, followed by a further upbeat period under the Normans (1061–1194). Henry IV, son of Frederick Barbarossa, imposed a period of imperial Swabian rule, soon followed by Angevin domination under Charles of Anjou (brother of the French king). The famous Sicilian Vespers (1282), after a brief period of independence, brought in the Spanish, who ruled Sicily in one guise or another until the 19th century.

228

The Greek temple of Segesta in its magnificent flower-strewn setting

Art and architecture Sicily is laden with monuments from each of its historical epochs, archaeological sites making up some of the island's most enticing attractions. The Greeks bequeathed the theatres of Syracuse and Taormina, and the temples of Agrigento, Selinunte and Segesta. The Romans created the mosaics of Piazza Armerina; Arabs, Byzantines and Normans left numerous fine buildings, and influenced the architecture of countless others. Swabians and Angevins built palaces and churches, many overlaid with the baroque stamp of the Spanish (most notably those in Noto and Ragusa). All the strands come together in Palermo, moribund and slightly knocked about in places, but still one of Italy's great artistic capitals. Few towns, however, are without treasures from one or more periods.

Landscapes The last 30 years have not been kind to the Sicilian coast. Time and again you come across ranks of derelict factories or half-built houses destroying what must once have been a coastal idyll. Cefalù and lovely Taormina are notable exceptions, and things are better on the islands – the unspoilt Egadi, for example, or the volcanic Lipari. In the interior they are better still, with landscapes as strange and spectacular as any in Italy. Modern housing has left its mark, but few could fail to be moved by Mount Etna, Europe's greatest volcano, or by the stark grandeur and lunar emptiness of the rolling interior plateaux. The mountains, too, are a revelation, especially the Madonie and Nebrodi, whose high, wooded ridges run along much of the northern coast.

Food Eating is one of Sicily's great pleasures, Greek, Arab, Norman and Spanish influences combining to form a unique cuisine. The quality and variety of fruit and vegetables in the markets is superb, and in restaurants the array of specialities is overwhelming. Seafood figures heavily, notably mussels (*cozze*), tuna (*tonno*), sardines (*sardi*) and swordfish (*pesce spada*). Fish sauces for pasta are good, especially *pasta con le sarde*. Chillis, capers, olives, peppers and aubergines are widely used (notably in *caponata*, a local 'sweet-and-sour' speciality). Sicilian desserts are legendary. Ice-cream was reputedly first made by the Arabs using snow from Etna. *Cassata* is an ice-cream cake, *granita* crushed ice flavoured with coffee or lemon. *Zabaglione*, a frothy whip of eggs and Marsala wine, and *cannoli*, a cream-filled cake, must both be sampled at least once.

When and how to go Spring is the best time to visit Sicily, when the weather is warm and the hills covered in wildflowers. July and August are uncomfortably hot and crowded, while September and October are pleasanter (and you can often swim as late as November). Be warned, though, that in the interior, and particularly in the mountains, the weather can be surprisingly cold and occasionally severe – snow is not unknown in April and May.

There are several ways of reaching Sicily from the mainland, including regular car ferries to Messina from Villa San Giovanni and Reggio di Calabria. Overnight car ferries operate daily from Naples to Palermo, and once a week to Catania and Syracuse.

Tourist information
Agrigento: Via Cesare Battisti 15 (tel: 0922/20 391).
Cefalù: Via Amendola 2 (tel: 0921/21 050).
Enna: Piazza Garibaldi 1 (tel: 0935/500 901).
Lipari: Corso Vittorio Emanuele 202 (tel: 090/988 0095).
Monreale: Piazza Duomo (tel: 091/640 2448).
Palermo: Piazza Castelnuovo 34–5 (tel: 091/605 8351 or 583 847).
Piazza Armerina: Via Cavour 15 (tel: 0935/680 201).
Siracusa: Via Maestranza 33 (tel: 0931/464 255).
Taormina: Piazza Santa Catarina (tel: 0942/23 243).

229

Mount Etna seen from Taormina

Scenic drives
(*Mount Etna*): Catania–Nicolosi–Rifugio Sapienza; Linguaglossa–Rifugio Citelli–Milo; SS120 Adrano–Bronte–Randazzo. (*Madonie mountains*): Cefalù–Collesano–Piano Battaglia–Petralia Soprana; SS286/SS120 Cefalù–Gibilmanna–Castelbuono–Gangi–Nicosia; SS117 Mistretta–Nicosia–Enna.

The Temple of Concord at Agrigento (ancient Acragas), one of the most complete Greek temples remaining

Operatic taste
There is a famous pasta speciality named after one of the operas of Catania-born composer Vincenzo Bellini. You should be able to sample *pasta alla Norma* (a tomato and aubergine sauce garnished with basil and cheese) in any of the *trattorias* on Via Etnea.

▶▶▶　**Agrigento** 226B3

Although modern Agrigento detracts from the setting, the **Valle dei Templi**▶▶▶ (Valley of the Temples) is one of Europe's greatest archaeological sites. Only ruins now remain of perhaps Magna Graecia's foremost city.

The eastern zone of the site contains the **Tempio di Ercole (Hercules)**▶▶, a temple built around the time of the colony's foundation in 582 BC. Near by are the ruins of a palaeo-Christian necropolis, and the tawny-stoned **Tempio della Concordia (Concord)**▶▶▶, the best-preserved Greek temple in the world after the Theseion in Athens. From here a path follows the old walls to the **Tempio di Giunone (Juno)**▶▶, a lonely and majestic ruin at the edge of the site.

In the western zone stands the **Tempio di Giove (Jupiter)**▶, planned as the Greek world's largest temple, but left unfinished after an attack by the Carthaginians in 405 BC. Here, too, is a *telamone*, a monumental column carved as a human figure, and the Tempio dei Dioscuri, a fake temple built in 1832 from miscellaneous fragments.

The **Museo Nazionale Archeologico**▶▶▶, a kilometre from the site, houses an overwhelming collection of artefacts removed from Agrigento and its environs. Outstanding are its *telamone*; a *krater*, or vase, depicting the *Battle of the Amazons*; the *Efebo*, a statue of a young man; a statuette known as the *Sitting Venus*; and several lion's head carvings removed from the temples.

Also pop into the adjacent church of **San Nicola**▶, both for its views of the temples, and for the Greek and Roman fragments incorporated in its walls.

▶　　　**Catania** 227B5

Sicily's second city is a modern and industrial place, whose chaotic and unpleasant streets may deter you from exploring its handful of ancient and medieval monuments (most of which have suffered over the years from earthquakes). The **Duomo**▶ and Sicily's largest church, San Nicolò, are worth a glance; so too the artistic and archaeological displays of the (often closed) **Museo Civico**▶.

Magna Graecia

■ ***Magna Graecia* (Greater Greece) was the network of scattered Greek colonies that sprang up over much of Sicily and southern Italy from about the 8th century BC. Greece had long traded with parts of Italy, most notably with the Etruscan cities of Tuscany, and it was inevitable that in time settlers should start to colonise areas near the Greek mainland. Over the centuries, the splendour of their cities came to rival and indeed sometimes exceed those of Greece itself.** ■

The colonies According to the historian Thucydides, the first settlers in Sicily established a foothold at Naxos (now Giardini-Naxos near Taormina) in 735 BC. They then quickly founded other colonies on Sicily's eastern coast at *Catana* (Catania), *Leontinoi* (Lentini) and *Zancle* (Messina). Within a year Greeks from Corinth had raised *Ortigia* (Syracuse), Magna Graecia's most powerful city, and five years later Megaran colonists, neighbours of the Corinthians in Greece, founded Megara Hyblaea, 25km to the north. Settlers from Crete and Rhodes created Gela in 689 BC, expanding westward a century later to settle *Acragas* (Agrigento). Pioneers from Rhodes founded Lipari, Sicily's last Greek colony, in 580 BC.

Sicilian riches Although the colonies retained links with Greece, they quickly became independent cities. Sicily's immense resources – especially its wheat-growing potential – brought them considerable wealth, a prosperity which can still be gauged from the splendour of the ruins in Syracuse and Agrigento. At the same time, however, the colonies were torn by internal jealousies and internecine warfare.

Greek jealousy As well as suffering civil war, the cities remained prey to two external adversaries. The first threat came from the mainland Greek states, who became jealous of Magna Graecia's increasing power. In 415 BC Athens sent an armada to attack Syracuse, suffering a defeat – after one of the greatest sea battles in ancient history – that left Syracuse and Magna Graecia at the peak of their powers.

Carthage The second threat came from Carthage, a North African power founded by the Phoenicians, who had cities of their own in western Sicily (Marsala and Palermo in particular). Battles raged between the two powers for centuries (and Carthage often sided with cities against their neighbours). In the 3rd century BC the two sides laid aside their differences and united to confront the growing power of Rome. The alliance was to no avail. The sack of Syracuse by Rome in 211 BC marked Magna Graecia's effective demise. For 700 years thereafter Sicily remained under Roman rule.

Magna Graecia today
Archaeological and historical remnants of the great Greek-influenced cities that once lay scattered across Sicily today make up some of the most enticing and rewarding sights on the island. The most obvious things to see are Magna Graecia's great surviving temples, particularly those at Segesta (see page 240), which is noted for its beautiful surroundings, and Agrigento (see page 230), celebrated as some of the best-preserved monuments from the ancient world. There are also the remains of no fewer than seven temples at Selinunte (see page 240), two of which are in an excellent state of preservation. You might also want to visit the Greek theatres at Taormina and Siracusa (Syracuse), and the museums of antiquities in these and other towns.

La Mattanza

Tuna are caught all over Sicily, but the most famous catch is Favignana's ritualised slaughter, *La Mattanza*. The age-old rite takes place around three times weekly in May and June. Under the head fisherman, or *rais* (an Arabic title), the fish are surrounded, netted, and then impaled and beaten to death. To many, in these days of ecological awareness, the ritual appears something of a bloodthirsty tourist attraction.

▶▶ **Cefalù**   226C3

Of all Sicily's coastal towns, bar Taormina, Cefalù is perhaps the most attractive. Nestled under a huge crag, it boasts good beaches and a tangle of tempting medieval streets. Its prime attraction is the beautiful **Duomo▶▶▶**, whose glorious mosaics (1148) are the earliest of any church in Sicily. Equally captivating is its balanced Norman-Romanesque façade, best seen from one of the outdoor cafés in the palm-fringed **Piazza del Duomo▶▶**. Close by lies the **Museo Mandralisca▶▶**, with a collection of Greek and Arab artefacts, and a famous painting by Sicily's most famous artist, Antonello da Messina, the *Portrait of an Unknown Man* (1472).

▶ **Egadi, Isole**   226C1

Ferries and hydrofoils run from Trapani to this archipelago just off Sicily's western coast. Favignana is the largest and most popular island, with many rocky coves but just one sandy beach, Cala Burrone. **Marettimo▶▶** is wilder and grander, an important sanctuary for wildlife, with gentle walks and hidden beaches. **Levanzo▶** is more primitive, rocky and sun-bleached, and known for the neolithic cave paintings of the Grotta del Genovese.

▶ **Enna**   227B4

If you explore Sicily's remote and beautiful interior, then consider making your base in Enna (the so-called 'navel of Sicily'). There is little to see, but the town has a welcoming provincial air and – from its incredible crag-top position – some of the finest views on the island. Two small museums, the Museo Alessi and Museo Varisano, have displays of Graeco-Roman finds and medieval church art. The **Castello▶** was built by Frederick II, on a site probably used as a defensive citadel for over 5,000 years.

▶▶ **Erice**   226C1

Erice is a tremendous mountain town, a sacred place and mighty fortress (*Eryx*) since time immemorial. Tour buses crowd in during the summer, drawn by the views from its limestone ramparts and the delightful medley of its tiny piazzas and cobbled streets, but the town has plenty of quiet corners in which to escape the throng.

Charming Cefalù is dominated by its superb Norman-Romanesque cathedral

►► **Etna**   *227B5*

Etna (3,323m) is one of the world's largest and most active volcanoes. Its smoking summit is a landmark over much of Sicily. The Arabs called it *Jebel*, the Mountain of Mountains. Ancient navigators thought it the highest point on earth. Pindar described it as the 'column which supports the sky'. The Greeks called it *aipho* (I burn), from which the present name derives. Reputedly, Arabs used

Etna smoulders under its blanket of snow

ice and snow from its summit to create the first *gelato* in the 8th century.

Eruptions For all its majesty, Etna is little more than 60,000 years old – a mere stripling in geological terms. There have been about 90 major eruptions since 475 BC (when the first was recorded) – the last was in 1991. The most catastrophic came in 1669, when a 25km fissure opened up in the mountain (Etna has a tendency to split at the seams, unlike most volcanoes, which erupt through the central cone). Around 350 minor craters have been created by these lateral eruptions). The rent unleashed a 2km-wide tongue of magma, engulfing Catania (40km away) and surrounding its castle with molten lava. The eruption continued for 122 days, throwing out ash that carried over 100km. In places the lava took eight years to cool. Chronicles describe peasants boiling water on the rocks long after the eruption.

Around the volcano Etna is an awe-inspiring sight, and a quarter of a million people a year now visit the crater (see panel). Its environs, however, offer as much to see as its highest slopes. For a good view of these varied surroundings you can either drive one of several scenic roads or take the Circumetnea railway that circles Etna's base, starting at Catania's Circumetnea station and finishing at Giarre-Riposto. Five trains daily ply the route. Most drivers approach from Catania, but roads from Linguaglossa►► and Adrano are equally spectacular – and less busy. All routes offer beautiful countryside, ranging from thick forests of oak and chestnut to the groves of orange, lemon, figs and olives that blanket Etna's fertile lower slopes.

Reaching the summit
Fully inclusive tours to Etna's summit run from Catania or Taormina. It is as easy (and cheaper), however, to make the trip by car or take the daily bus (8am) from Catania's FS railway station to the *Rifugio Sapienza* (1,881m). From here you can walk to the summit on a rough track provided for tourist minibuses. Allow three to four hours for the walk, wear boots or stout shoes, and take plenty of warm and waterproof clothing.

SERIE NS/A

REGIONE SICILIANA
ASSESSORATO DEI BENI CULTURALI, AM
E DELLA PUBBLICA ISTRUZIONE

BIGLIETTO D'INGRES
LIRE 2000

► **Gela** *227A4*

Gela is a town ravaged by textile factories and petrochemical plants. It is redeemed only by its **Museo Archeologico►**, known mainly for the collection of 5th-century BC pottery for which Greek Gela was famous. Four kilometres out of town is the more attractive area of **Capo Soprano►►**, where part of the fortifications that once surrounded the Greek city have been excavated.

►► **Lipari, Isola di** *227D4*

Lipari is the principal island of the Isole Eolie (Aeolian Islands), a seven-island volcanic archipelago off Sicily's northern coast. The group has become popular recently, visited mainly for its beaches and Stromboli's regular volcanic eruptions. The Aeolian islands were named after Aeolus, the Greek god of the winds and navigation (see panel).

Lipari is the busiest of the islands, easily reached by regular ferries from Milazzo, Messina, Naples and Reggio di Calabria. From its capital, Lipari, a picturesque port (with a good little museum), you can take boat trips around the coast or pick up bus connections to the rest of the island. You can also hire bikes and scooters (many roads offer lovely panoramas of Sicily and the archipelago). Good targets include Aquacalda, interesting for its pumice and obsidian quarries; San Calogero, which has mud baths and hot springs; and Canneto, 2km from Lipari's best beach, the Spiaggia Bianca. Much of the rugged interior also offers excellent walking.

To escape the crowds, visit the tiny yet dazzling island of Panarea, or the still unspoilt islets of Filicudi and Alicudi (each has a hotel and a few private rooms).

► **Messina** *227C5*

Most people see no more of the gateway to Sicily than is absolutely necessary. Despite an enchanting view from the ferry, Messina in the flesh is a battered and modern city (the result of earthquakes and 1943 bombing raids). If you have to linger there, try to be in Piazza del Duomo at noon for the performance of one of the world's largest astronomical clocks (the clock is housed in the campanile located to the side of the main cathedral building). It is also well worth paying a visit to the **Museo Regionale►**, which is graced with paintings by Caravaggio and Antonello da Messina.

►►► Monreale 226C2

Little outside the famous Norman cathedral of Monreale, 8km east of Palermo, suggests the splendour of what lies within – the most extensive and accomplished Christian mosaics in the world. Probably the work of Greek and Byzantine craftsmen, they were started around 1174 and completed in only 10 years. The apse portrays Christ, arms outstretched, flanked by St Peter and St Paul (the panels show the saints' martyrdoms – crucifixion and beheading respectively). The nave's gold-backed mosaics illustrate episodes from the Old and New Testaments.

Climb the tower for its views, then visit the cloister, an elegant arcade supported by 216 twin columns (no two of which are the same). To the cathedral's rear lies a garden, filled with banyan trees and other exotic vegetation. Little else in the town is worth exploring, though the views over Palermo and the Conca d'Oro, or 'Golden Shell' (the coastal area) are magnificent.

►► Noto 227A5

The earthquake which devasted much of eastern Sicily in 1693 had at least one silver lining – many of the cities it razed were beautifully rebuilt in the baroque style of the day. Noto's tawny-stoned churches and palaces are the most complete expression of this transformation. It is also one of the more heavily-promoted of the region's tourist attractions, so if you wish to stay – and the town makes a nice stop-over – then be prepared for high-season crowds.

During rebuilding, the town's residential and religio-political districts were deliberately separated. Most of the latter's buildings lie along Corso Vittorio Emanuele, the best on **Piazza del Municipio►►**, one of the most harmonious little squares in Sicily. Most of the *palazzi* have beautifully decorated façades, but perhaps the most famous is the **Palazzo Villadorata►►**, known for its billowing balconies (situated in Via Corrado Nicolaci, first right west of Piazza del Municipio).

Thomas à Becket
Among the ranks of saints below the mosaics of Christ and the Virgin, you should be able to pick out the figure of martyred archbishop of Canterbury, Thomas à Becket, canonised in 1173 shortly before Monreale cathedral's mosaics were started (he is marked *SCS Thomas Cantb*).

235

Baroque splendour in Noto, one of the gems of Sicily

RAPPORTI MAFIA · POLITICA:
INFLUENZA NELLE AMMINISTRAZIONI LOCALI
VENERDÌ 7 MAGGIO 1993 · Ore 18,30
CARMINE MANCUSO

■ **Many ambiguities surround the origins and identity of the Mafia. These days the old image of a criminal fraternity bound by family ties and codes of honour is a thing of the past. Mafia bosses are now slick-suited supremos (with politicians in their pockets), involved in every dubious trade from arms to heroin.** ■

Plus ça change…

One of the earliest allusions to the Mafia came in a report from the the British consul in 1866, who wrote: '*Maffie*-elected *juntas* share the earnings of the workmen, keep up intercourse with outcasts, and take malefactors under their wing and protection.'

236

The Mafia family

Mafia 'families' are groups united in crime – which do not always include blood relations. Each takes its name from its village of origin (Corleone, for example), or the city quarter it controls (in Palermo, the *Ciaculli, Porta Nova*, etc). Each has foot soldiers, lieutenants and a *capo*, or *padrino* (godfather). Families ally themselves in *cosche*, named after artichoke crowns (to symbolise the unity of many), but the network is often fractured by disputes within and between families.

The American Mafia

The hundreds of thousands of Sicilians who emigrated to the United States at the beginning of the century were a breeding ground for Mafia-style organisations (the so-called 'Black Hand'). During the period of Fascist rule many Italian *mafiosi* also fled to the US. Today, few doubt that there are links between Italian and American organised crime.

Mafia and mafia Everything about the Mafia is mysterious – even where its name comes from. The word may derive from the Arabic *mu'afàh* meaning 'protection' (though it also means 'skill', 'ability', 'beauty' and 'safety'). It appeared in Italian for the first time around 1860. Many commentators underline the idea of mafia as a mentality, 'a state of mind, a philosophy of life, a moral code, prevailing among all Sicilians' (Luigi Barzini, *The Italians*). This small 'm' mafia does not mean all Sicilians are criminals (nor that they condone criminality). It does, however, have a bearing on its upper case cousin – the criminal underworld known as the Mafia.

Origins How and why the Mafia (and mafia) developed are vexed questions. The answers lie in the gap that has always existed between southerners and authority – a breach historically filled by the Mafia. Two cultural phenomena go some way to explaining it: first, the value Sicilians attach to the ability to impose one's will on others; second, the historic distrust felt by southerners for the state, a feeling that stems from Sicily's catalogue of foreign rulers. Another reason is the island's isolation – its rugged interior proving a barrier to the imposition of authority. Yet another was the alienation of peasants from their feudal overlords, forced to work on Sicily's estates (*latifondi*) as serfs for absentee landlords in Naples or Palermo.

History Mafia activities go back hundreds of years, some say to the 12th century, when a secret sect was formed to oppose imperial rule. Under the Bourbons, ex-brigands were used to 'police' the interior, often taking kickbacks instead of arresting their erstwhile colleagues. Elsewhere, middlemen known as *gabellotti* acted as mediators between peasants and landowners. By intimidating one group and becoming agents for the other they quickly grew rich, becoming a distinct class, bound by mutual self-interest, established codes of honour and a semi-formal organisation.

Mussolini and the Mafia Little is known of the Mafia before World War II. It was under Fascism that Mussolini became the only political figure in Italy's history to damage the organisation. Through his legendary prefect, Cesare Mori, he set about the Mafia with a lethal – and illegal – efficiency. The Mafia was dealt a dose of its own medicine. It might well have proved fatal – but for the intervention of the Americans.

Allied deliverance When the Allies prepared to land in Sicily in 1943 they had only one organised source of intelligence and logistical support – the Mafia. In New York they talked to men like Lucky Luciano, who provided 'introductions' to the island's Mafia bosses (Luciano's 50-year prison sentence was repealed as a reward). This cleared the way for the Allies, and, in the aftermath of the invasion, also helped create the Allied Military Government. In organising political and military control of the island, the Allies entrusted responsibility for 62 of Sicily's 66 towns and cities to men with Mafia connections. Don Vito Genovese, on whom Mario Puzio based *The Godfather*, was one of these men.

The new Mafia Allied intervention left the Mafia well-placed to exploit Italy's post-war economic boom. With its criminal muscle and political connections it amassed huge fortunes (mainly from construction). Much of the money was 'laundered' through 'respectable' businesses, or used to finance the Mafia's expansion into arms and drug dealing (trades which brought immeasurable riches and changed the Mafia's character forever). Mafia tactics became increasingly ruthless as the stakes grew higher. Threats to its power were met by violent clan battles and the assassination of all who stood in its way. Despite recent 'maxi-trials' of hundreds of *mafiosi*, and the 'supergrass confessions' of men like Tommaso Buscetta, the Mafia's inextricable links with most aspects of Sicilian life make the prospect of its eradication extremely remote.

Words
Italians call the Mafia *la piovra*, or 'the octopus', because its tentacles infiltrate so many aspects of national life. The *mafiosi* themselves, however, are more circumspect. They would never address each other as such: Mafia men are *amici* (friends) or *uomini d'onore* (men of honour). They are members of *Cosa Nostra* (Our Thing) and protected by a code of silence – *omertà*.

Illustrious corpses
Since the 1970s the Mafia has murdered politicians, journalists and anyone else who threatened their position. These *cadaveri eccellenti* (illustrious corpses) reached a peak in 1982 with the assassination of General dalla Chiesa, gunned down as he prepared to investigate links between politicians and organised crime. In 1992 Italy was shocked by the killings of Giovane Falcone, one of the most effective and highly respected of Sicily's investigating magistrates, and of Judge Paolo Borsellino.

Sicily, 1950s: the coffin of another police officer killed in the daily fight against the Mafia

Glowing mosaics decorate the arches in Palermo's 12th-century Palatine Chapel

▶▶ Palermo   226C2

Past meets present head-on in Palermo. Norman, Arab and baroque monuments rise in Sicily's capital amid slums and back streets riddled with poverty and petty crime. Traffic and squalor assault the senses at every turn, ingredients in the city's strange mixture of criminal unease and decaying grandeur. Like Naples, this is not a place to all tastes, but in its tattered streets, its vibrant markets and magnificent art, it captures all the colour and contradictions that are so peculiarly Sicilian.

History Palermo started life as an 8th-century BC Phoenician trading post (though it takes its name from the Greek *Panormus* – 'all port'). Later it became a Carthaginian and then Roman stronghold. Its golden age came under the Arabs, when for 240 years (from 831) it became Europe's second most important city after Constantinople. It remained pre-eminent under the Normans (1072) and the Swabians (1194). Decline set in with the Angevins (1266) and – most markedly – with the Spaniards (who ruled for almost 600 years from 1282).

Cathedral and palace The Norman stamp is evident in the **Cattedrale▶▶**, at least in the exterior (1185), for the old interior was ruined by alterations in the 18th century. Its most interesting features are the royal tombs of Henry VI, Roger II and Frederick II (contained in two chapels of the south aisle). A reliquary (1631) close by contains the remains of St Rosalia, Palermo's patron saint. The treasury is crammed with precious objects, most notably a jewel-encrusted crown removed from the tomb of Constance of Aragon, wife of Frederick II.

Close to the cathedral stands the **Palazzo dei Normanni▶▶▶**, a monumental complex started by the Arabs and enlarged by the Normans (under whom it became one of Europe's leading courts). At its heart are the Sala di Re Ruggero (Hall of Roger II), decorated with mosaics of hunting scenes, and Palermo's undoubted artistic highlight, the **Cappella Palatina▶▶▶**. The latter,

The Sicilian Vespers
An island-wide uprising against Sicily's Angevin rulers was sparked in 1282 by a French insult to a woman in Palermo, traditionally said to have occurred after the bell for vespers (evening service) was rung in Palermo's church of Santo Spirito.

built by Roger II in 1132, is a largely Romanesque creation, though the interior rests on Roman columns and glitters with Byzantine-influenced mosaics. The wooden ceiling is Moorish, an intricate honeycomb of exquisite carving.

Churches Nearby San Giovanni degli Eremiti►► stands on the edge of the *Albergheria* district, a fascinating quarter teeming with baroque churches, busy markets and run-down back streets. The church (1132) retains its original Arabic-influenced domes, as well as a picturesque double cloister, filled with a wild profusion of palms, shrubs and lemon trees. It stands on the site of an old mosque (of which Palermo once had 200).

Three other important churches lie conveniently grouped around Piazza Pretoria►►. The finest, La Martorana►►, contains good 12th-century mosaics, while both San Giuseppe► and Santa Caterina► have wonderfully over-the-top baroque interiors.

Museum and gallery The Museo Archeologico►► is a small but excellent collection, prized for the carved friezes (or metopes) taken from the temples at Selinunte (see page 240). Other highlights include prehistoric cave paintings; lion's head fountains from temples at Himera; the *Ram of Syracuse*, a 3rd-century BC Greek bronze; and two Roman sculptures – *Hercules and the Stag* and *The Satyr Preparing to Drink*. The cream of Sicily's medieval treasures are contained in Palazzo Abatellis's Galleria Nazionale Siciliana►►►. Paintings are downstairs, sculptures upstairs, the masterpieces including Antonello da Messina's *Three Saints* and *Annunciation*, the Arab-styled *Malaga Vase*, and a delicate 15th-century *Bust of Eleanor of Aragon*.

Convento dei Cappuccini Italy has no stranger or more eerie sight than the thousands of mummies lining the catacombs of Palermo's Capuchin convent (in the west of the city at the corner of Via G Mosca and Via Pindemonte). The figures have parchment-yellow skin stretched across bones. All are wearing clothes – crumbling silks and dusty top hats; each is bizarre, comical or macabre by turns.

Monte Pellegrino
Monte Pellegrino overlooks Palermo, splitting off the city from the bay at Mondello. The scenic trip to the mountain is a popular Sunday excursion (bus No 12 runs here from the Teatro Politeama). Near the top is the Santuario di Santa Rosalia, a pilgrim church marking the spot where the bones of Palermo's patron saint were found in 1624. Paths and roads with fine views lead towards the summit.

Fishy decisions in Palermo's market

Markets
Palermo's Vucciria market sprawls over several streets south of Piazza San Domenico. Stalls sell everything from swordfish to coffee-percolators. The local delicacy, sold from stalls, is *guasteddi* (rolls filled with strips of calf's spleen, ricotta cheese and a hot sauce). The flea market is near the cathedral on Via Papireto (the antiques neighbourhood is in the same area).

Residents of the Catacombs

▶ Ragusa 227A4

Ragusa suffered in the same earthquake as Noto (see page 235) and was rebuilt along similar baroque lines. It is less visited than its neighbour, however, and you can wander around the atmospheric old town (*Ragusa Ibla*) in virtual solitude. The streets here are moribund and decrepit, without being depressing, the locked doors and shuttered windows creating the impression of an abandoned ghost town. While exploring, be sure to visit **San Giorgio**▶▶, among the more stately of Sicily's baroque churches.

The unfinished Greek temple of Segesta

▶▶▶ **Segesta** 226C2

Segesta's windswept **Greek temple**▶▶▶ rises in glorious isolation amid beautiful countryside, perhaps the grandest and most inspiring of all Sicily's great Hellenistic monuments. Started around 425 BC, it is all that remains of ancient *Segesta*, a colony with pre-Greek roots in the 12th century BC. The temple was never finished, though from its 36 columns and well-rounded appearance you would never know. Closer to, you see the columns remain unfluted and parts of the walls are missing, but this in no way detracts from the temple's harmonious proportions or the splendour of its natural setting.

Be sure to take the short road (2km) that wends through flower-strewn slopes to a small Greek theatre on a barren hilltop near by. The views are remarkable, especially at sunset, stretching to the sea across Monte Erice and the pastoral plains below.

▶▶▶ **Selinunte** 226B2

Founded in 628 BC and probably named after a wild parsley (*selinon* in Greek), Selinunte quickly became one of Magna Graecia's most prosperous colonies. It attracted many bitter rivals, notably Segesta, and suffered devastating attacks from the Carthaginians in 409 BC and 250 BC (blows from which it never fully recovered). The site today is among Sicily's finest, two of its original seven **temples**▶▶▶ as impressive as any on the island. Nobody knows to which gods Selinunte's temples were dedicated, so each is indicated only by a letter. They divide into two groups: the nearest to the entrance stand in a group (E, F, G) – Temple E was re-erected in the 1950s; the others lie together on the old acropolis to the west. Many of the site's treasures have been taken to Palermo's Museo Archeologico, but the ruins are still a lovely place to explore. The small fishing village and resort of Marinella just below the site makes a good base for the ruins.

■ **Even in the ruins of Herculaneum and Pompeii, even in Rome itself, there are no classical mosaics to compare in quality or extent with those of the Villa Casale near Piazza Armerina. Spread over 50 rooms, they are Sicily's finest Roman remains and one of the island's foremost attractions.** ■

A steep, cobbled lane leads from Piazza Armerina in central Sicily towards the Villa Casale, wending through open countryside before arriving at the little forested valley that shelters the ruins (5km). The villa probably served as a retreat and occasional hunting lodge, possibly for Emperor Maximianus Herculius, co-emperor with Diocletian between AD 286 and 305. It was used until as late as the 12th century, when a landslip covered it, preserving the mosaics until full-scale excavations began in the 1950s. The site has been skillfully laid out, new roofs serving both to protect the mosaics and to suggest how the villa might have looked in its heyday.

The mosaics All the components of a great Roman house are here, from the atrium, peristyle and baths to vast public halls and private apartments. Everything pales alongside the mosaics, however, 3,500sq m of exquisite works that unfold dramatically from room to room. Their style is reminiscent of Roman villas in North Africa, suggesting they are the work of Carthaginian craftsmen, a notion which helps to explain some of the more exotic scenes and animals they portray. Certainly the villa's cen-

Detail from a hunting scene: one of the extraordinary mosaics in the Villa Casale

trepiece seems set in Africa, the great *Hunting Scene* that stretches for over 60m along the edge of the courtyard's covered corridor. Its detailed and intertwined narrative depicts tigers, ostriches, elephants – even rhinos – being captured and caged for return to Rome's circuses and gladiatorial games.

Equally captivating are a circus scene and chariot race, or an enchanting children's hunt, where youngsters are chased by the hares and peacocks they are supposed to be catching. Another fine room vividly (and bloodily) depicts the labours of Hercules. Most people's favourite room, however, is the one that proves there is nothing new under the sun – with a mosaic showing 10 women athletes in Roman 'bikinis'.

SICILY

The baroque façade of Syracuse's cathedral

Syracuse: a fishing port for thousands of years

Fontana Aretusa
The Delphic oracles that first guided settlers to Syracuse spoke of the spring feeding Ortigia's Arethusa fountain. In Greek myth the nymph Arethusa rose here after swimming from Greece, transformed into a spring by Artemis to escape the clutches of the river god Alpheus. Admiral Nelson took on water from the spring *en route* for the Battle of the Nile. Today the spot is planted with papyrus and surrounded by pleasant cafés.

▶▶▶ **Siracusa (Syracuse)**　　　　227A5

Syracuse was founded by Greeks from Corinth in 733 BC. Within a hundred years it had become one of Europe's greatest cities. Today it divides into three areas: a dull modern town; Ortigia, the city's heart for 2,700 years; and the Parco Archeologico, a large area of Greek, Roman and early Christian remains.

The old town Ortigia▶▶, part medieval and part baroque, is an island, linked to the rest of the town by a bridge. It is graced with two pretty squares – **Piazza Duomo**▶▶ and Piazza Archimede (both popular meeting places with plenty of nice cafés). See the **Tempio di Apollo**▶, Sicily's oldest Doric temple (565 BC), and spend plenty of time wandering the port area and its old streets. Pay special attention to the **Duomo**▶▶, a fascinating patchwork of styles, its Norman walls embedded with columns from a 5th-century BC temple (much of the interior was also hacked from the temple). Further fragments hail from the 7th century, the date of the site's consecration as a Christian cathedral. The façade is 17th century.

The **Museo Nazionale**▶▶, part of the lovely Palazzo Bellomo, offers mainly medieval treasures, its highlights a ravishing *Annunciation* by Antonello da Messina and Caravaggio's *Burial of St Lucia*. There is also much sculpture, silverware, fabrics, furniture and religious vestments.

From the ancient world At the **Parco Archeologico**▶▶▶ the first thing you see after the souvenir stalls is the Ara di Ierone, the base of a colossal 3rd-century BC altar. In the past, it was the scene of sacrifices, orgies of blood-letting that saw up to 450 bulls slaughtered in one day. Close by is the 15,000-seat **Teatro Greco**▶▶, the most complete theatre in the Greek world (5th-century BC). Near it extends the Latomia del Paradiso, a lovely green area famous for the cave known as the Orecchio di Dionisio (Ear of Dionysius).

A kilometre from the park lies the **Museo Archeologico Nazionale**▶▶▶, a purpose-built museum whose wide-ranging collection covers finds from Syracuse, Agrigento and beyond. Its star turn is the *Venus Anadiomene* (Venus Rising from the Sea). Also outstanding are the *kouroi* (Greek statuettes) and a *Winged Victory*.

▶▶ **Taormina** *227C5*

Taormina is Sicily's most beautiful town, ringed around by mountains and perched above a turquoise sea. Etna rises majestically in the background. The climate is mild, the views matchless, and its vegetation a semi-tropical garden of palms, bougainvillea and orange trees.

What to see The town centre forms an intimate collection of tiny streets and flower-filled balconies. Wandering its twisting alleys or exploring its dark staircases is pleasure enough, with the chance of stumbling on quiet piazzas or of catching sudden views of the sea below.

Beyond the town's backstreet charm, there is really only one sight, the magnificently sited **Teatro Greco**▶▶▶. Built by the Greeks in the 3rd century BC, it was almost completely remodelled by the Romans. A small museum holds various archaeological fragments from the site.

What to do After seeing the theatre, many people confine themselves to a drink in one of the expensive but irresistible cafés on Piazza IX Aprile, Taormina's main square (or those on Corso Umberto I, its main street). You should also take time to stroll in the public gardens (on Via Croce) and to climb to the **Castello**▶▶ for more all-embracing views. Paths and roads (and buses) beyond the castle lead to Castelmola (5km), a tiny crag-top village with more nice bars and fine views.

Sadly, Taormina is too enticing to have to yourself. In high season – which runs from April to September – it becomes crowded and almost a caricature of itself. The streets are thronged, their smart shops outnumbered by souvenir stalls. Glitzy pizzerias compete at night with pounding discos. Ranks of glitterati attending film and theatre festivals preen and parade. Don't necessarily be deterred, but try to come off season if possible.

Taormina alternatives
If hotel prices and high-season crowds prevent you staying in Taormina, consider putting up in Spisone and Letojanni, less elegant but more affordable resorts near by. Better still, try Giardini-Naxos, the best place to stay near Taormina. It is a modern town, with a broad sandy beach and plenty of hotels at all prices. Regular buses run up to Taormina.

The Greek theatre above Taormina, with Etna beyond

SARDINIA

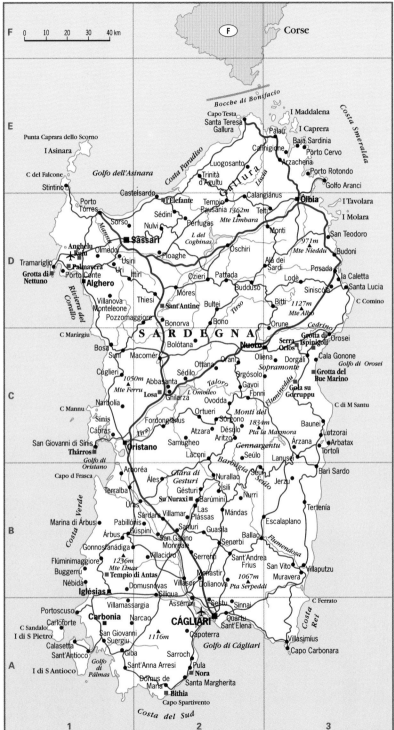

Sardinia (Sardegna) Italy's second-largest island differs from the Italian mainland in almost every respect, but for visitors its most vital difference is the lack of conventional sightseeing. You come here not for museums and monuments, but for some of Europe's finest beaches, or for the spectacle of the island's mountainous interior. The main cities, Cagliari and Sassari, are provincial spots, and – like most of the smaller towns – amount to little more than bases from which to venture further afield. If you do want to sightsee, you could happily potter around one of the island's classical or prehistoric sites (see page 249), or make a beeline for the coronet of Pisan-Romanesque churches near Sassari (see page 251).

Sea and sand Glorious beaches are what bring most people to Sardinia. The most famous beaches cluster around resorts on the Costa Smeralda, but there are plenty of smaller resorts, and a plethora of sandy coves and rocky inlets await those who make the effort to get off the beaten track. For the most part the sea is clean and beautifully clear, safe for swimming and ideal for any number of activities from sailing to snorkelling. Facilities at larger resorts allow you to indulge most seaside whims, though there are still plenty of unspoilt and scarcely developed spots.

The interior Sardinia's interior is varied and in many parts strikingly beautiful, ranging from gently rolling plains and endless scrub-covered hills to the upland hamlets and desolation of the Barbagia and Gennargentu mountains. Here, sheep and shepherds are often the only living creatures you encounter as you drive the lonely roads. Villages often preserve ancient customs and ceremonies, and you may still come across people in traditional costume. For the most part inland Sardinia is also unused to seeing many tourists, so expect facilities to be few and far between.

245

REGION HIGHLIGHTS ◄◄◄◄◄

CAGLIARI *see page 247:*
DUOMO

CALA GONONE *see page 248*

GENNARGENTU *see page 250*

SASSARI *see page 251:*
PISAN CHURCHES

GIARA DI GESTURI
see page 252:
SU NURAXI, LAS PLASSAS

ORISTANO *see page 254:*
SINIS PENINSULA

PORTO CONTE *see page 254:*
GROTTA DI NETTUNO

SARDINIA

Mosaic in Cagliari's cathedral

Tourist information
Alghero: Piazza Porta Terra 9 (tel: 079/979 054).
Cagliari: Via Mameli 97 (tel: 070/664 195).
Nuoro: Piazza Italia 19 (tel: 0784/32 307 or 30 083).
Oristano: Via Vittorio Emanuele 8 (tel: 0783/70 621).
Sassari: Viale Caprera 36 (tel: 079/299 544) and Viale Umberto 72 (tel: 079/233 534).

History Although prehistory bequeathed Sardinia's finest monuments – its great stone *nuraghi* – the Phoenicians, some of antiquity's greatest seafarers, are the first culture of which much is known. They arrived in the 8th century BC, followed by the Carthaginians and the Romans (238 BC). During the Middle Ages, Vandals, Byzantines and Arabs all left their mark. For a brief period, however, the island was ruled by the Giudicati, four independent duchies with close ties to Pisa and Genoa (hence the island's many Pisan-Romanesque churches). The Spanish gained control in 1479, remaining in charge until 1720, when the island passed by treaty to Piedmont's dukes of Savoy (the future kings of Italy). The island joined a united Italy in 1861.

Food Sardinian cuisine is the simple food of peasant and fisherman. On the coast you can sample just about every type of Mediterranean seafood, and in the interior cheeses such as *pecorini*, *casu marzu* and the yoghurt-like *gioddu* are common. First-course specialities include *malloreddus* (small dumplings); *culingiones* (ravioli); *favata* (pork and bean stew); *leppudrida* (meat and vegetable soup); and *sa fregula* (Sardinian couscous). For main courses you might be offered *aragosta* (crayfish); *burrida* (marinated fish), *porceddu* (suckling pig), or *buttarga* (tuna or mullet roe). *Sebadas* are cheese and honey pastries fried in oil; *suspirus* and *gueffus* are sweets bursting with almonds.

Facts and figures
Sardinia lies 180km from mainland Italy, and is 270km long by about 120km wide. It is Italy's third largest region, but has the country's lowest population density (1.6 million, a third of that of Sicily). The capital is Cagliari, and there are three provincial capitals – Nuoro, Oristano and Sassari.

Wine Several of Sardinia's unique grape varieties were introduced by the Phoenicians and Carthaginians. Despite their venerable provenance, they have not always been used to best effect, and the island's wines can be idiosyncratic – to say the least. The most famous vintage is the dry, sherry-like Vernaccia di Oristano (Contini is a good producer). The basic reds are Cannonau and Monica di Sardegna, slightly overshadowed by whites like Vermentino and Torbato di Alghero (the latter is produced by Sella & Mosca, one of Europe's largest estates). Malvasia di Bosa is a prized dessert wine. *Filu ferru* (steel thread) is the local grappa, so named because shepherds distilled it illegally and hid bottles underground – with a protruding piece of wire to enable them to locate the buried bottles later. Almost every cork in a bottle of Italian wine, incidentally, comes from the cork oak forests of northern Sardinia.

► **Alghero** 244D1

Alghero is one of Sardinia's busiest resorts, saved by its proud Catalan roots and down-to-earth fishing harbour from the tackiness that often blights tourist towns. There were so many Catalans here in the 14th century that the region became known as *Barcelonetta* (Little Barcelona). Many streets and monuments take Catalan names – *carrer* not *via*, for example; *plaça* not *piazza*; and *iglesia* for church, not *chiesa*).

Among the cobbled streets within the medieval walls, look for the town's seven large 15th-century towers, particularly the **Porta Torre**► and **Torre Sulis**►, and fine Aragonese-Gothic buildings like the **Casa Doria**►, **Palau Reial**► and **Palazzo d'Albis**►. The octagonal *campanile* is all that survives from the original 16th-century **Duomo**►. San Francesco is the most interesting church.

►► **Cagliari** 244A2

A large port, lots of industry and around 250,000 people should make Cagliari an unappetising prospect. In fact it is a pleasant place, blessed with a neat medieval centre, several modest monuments, and a hinterland of exquisite beaches and flamingo-filled lagoons. The old citadel above the harbour was founded by the Phoenicians, the forerunner of a port that over the centuries has remained one of the most important in the Mediterranean.

The **Citadella dei Musei-Museo Archeologico**►► is the island's premier museum, home to the cream of its prehistoric, pre-Roman and medieval treasures. Of these, the most important are the bronze figurines and other displays devoted to Sardinia's ancient Nuraghic culture (see page 249). The **Duomo**► near by is known for its crypt and two Pisan pulpits (1165). Elsewhere, see the **Torre San Pancrazio**►, which with the Torre dell'Elefante formed the cornerstone of the city's medieval defences, and **San Saturnino**►►, Sardinia's oldest church (5th-century). Also well worth seeing are the ruins of the Roman amphitheatre and the **Botanic Gardens**►►.

Below: marshland wildlife near Alghero
Bottom: Sunday market in Cagliari

247

SARDINIA

Boat trips

Two of the best coves south of Cala Gonone are Cala di Luna and Cala Sisine. Boats run to both, offering views of the deep gorges that cut through the coast's 900m-high mountains. Boats also visit the *Grotta del Bue Marino*, reputedly one of the last refuges of the Mediterranean monk seal, (*bue marino*) and a magical spot filled with stalactites and stalagmites.

L'Elefante

This little curiosity stands 4km out of Castelsardo on the SS134. It is an odd elephant-shaped rock which hangs over the road. Inside are several *domus de janas* tombs (see page 249), many etched with mysterious symbols and bull's head motifs. At Sedini (15km) another five-chambered *domus* has been turned into the Gothic church of San Andrea (1517).

The lovely bay at Cala Gonone

▶▶ **Cala Gonone**   244C3

Sardinia is so well known for its beaches that it is easy to forget the tremendous variety of its other coastal scenery. None is more spectacular than the east-coast mountainous cliffs surrounding the bay at Cala Gonone. Approach the area on the SS125 if possible (from Arbatax), a majestic road that climbs to over 1,000 metres as it wends through some of the island's wildest scenery. Its most breathtaking stretch offers views over the gorge of the Gola su Gorruppu▶▶▶.

Cala Gonone itself is approached from Dorgali, a town growing increasingly busy as more people discover the beauty of the coastline. Until a few years ago the bay and its tiny hamlet were accessible only from the sea. New hotels and villas which have sprouted since the building of a road have not yet spoiled the area's incomparable scenery. The best way to the area is to take a boat trip, either to marvel at the views, or to be dropped at one of the secluded coves up and down the coast (see panel).

▶▶ **Castelsardo**   244D2

Castelsardo, on the north coast, is a citadel town, founded in 1102 by the Genovese, whose formidable castle offers sweeping views over the sea and the town's maze of medieval streets. Similar views are to be had from the cliff-edge Duomo, worth popping into for its 15th-century icon, the *Madonna degli Angeli* by an unknown local painter. For beaches follow the scenic road to Porto Torres, fringed by a broad crescent of sand and turquoise seas.

Castelsardo is also known for its handicrafts, many of which are of dubious quality and authenticity. Bargains are to be had, though, if you rummage through the tat and stick to the weaving and palm-leaf baskets for which the town is most famous. Cork and coral goods, rugs, wrought iron and Sardinian masks (*mamathones*) are also available.

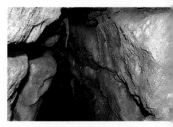

■ **Sardinia's prehistoric monuments provide some of the island's most memorable sights, from the great stone nuraghi that dot the countryside to the delicate bronze figurines of Cagliari's archaeological museum. That almost nothing is known of the culture which produced them only adds to the mysterious and intriguing appeal of the ancient remains.** ■

The earliest ruins The Sardinians could have come from almost anywhere: were they descended from Sardus, legendary son of Hercules, or from the Shardana tribes of ancient Libya? Or did they come from one of the countries around the Mediterranean? Nobody knows. Their earliest memorials are the *domus de janas* (elves' dwellings), tiny tombs cut into the rock which date from 2000–1800 BC. According to popular tradition they were the homes of elves, witches and fairies. Their other major monuments were the *tombe dei giganti* (giants' tombs), believed by locals to be the graves of their gigantic ancestors – in fact they were the temples and necropoli of the Nuraghic tribes that dominated prehistoric Sardinia from 1500 to 500 BC.

Nuraghi These same tribes also left the 7,000 or more *nuraghi* that scatter the island. These enigmatic structures are visible everywhere – on hills, at roadsides, or half-buried in scrub – either singly or in clusters. Most are conical in shape, with a round vaulted interior, linked by corridors and stairways to an upper terrace. Many are more than two or three storeys high. No two are the same. Some may have been dwellings, others fortified citadels.

The Sant'Antine nuraghe

Statuettes Sardinia has yielded around 500 Nuraghic statuettes, quirky bronze figurines between 15cm and 45cm tall, probably made around the 8th century BC from copper and tin ore imported from as far afield as Etruria and Cornwall. Many were votive offerings, made to decorate Nuraghic temples. They show immense vigour and invention, depicting not only people – anything from warriors to nursing mothers – but also objects such as houses, boats, gods, *nuraghi* and domestic animals.

These figures marked the apogee of Nuraghic culture. Around 1000 BC Sardinia began to fall prey to invading Phoenicians and Etruscans, far more skilled in the art of warfare than the local tribes (whose only weapons, according to the chroniclers, were stones and boulders rolled from hilltops).

Tombe dei Giganti
Sardinia's most significant concentration of *tombe* are at Anghelu Ruiu (10km north of Alghero on the road to Porto Torres). About 35 tombs riddle the hillside, eerie chambers connected by corridors and sloping passages. Some have lintels carved with symbolic shapes. Others are protected by large standing stones.

249

Finding *nuraghi*
Sardinia's best *nuraghi* are Su Nuraxi, outside Barumini; Losa, near Abbasanta; and Sant' Antine, between Macomer and Sassari. The most interesting of the smaller sites are Palmavera, west of Fertilia; Serra Orrios, near Dorgali; Bruncu de Madili, near Gesturi. You should have no trouble in discovering many more for yourself.

SARDINIA

Sardinian bread
Sardinia has over 300 types of bread. Be sure to try the best known, the old-fashioned *pane carasau*. Round, dry and wafer-thin, it was originally made by shepherds because it would keep for long periods. It is eaten crisp or softened by adding a few drops of water. Bread is shaped into flowers, animals – even lace – for weddings and christenings.

▶▶   **(La) Costa Smeralda**   *244E3*

The Emerald Coast started life as one resort – **Porto Cervo**▶▶ – an up-market holiday village built by the Aga Khan in the 1960s. Since then it has come to describe the string of smartish resorts that have sprung up along Sardinia's northeastern coast. Many of its villages are in the Porto Cervo mould – undeniably chic and tasteful, but also rather soulless and lacking in local colour. As oases of hedonistic retreat, however, they can hardly be bettered.

Other spots are still quite undeveloped, giving you Porto Cervo's beaches and facilities at a fraction of the cost. Close to **Santa Teresa Gallura**▶, for example, a relaxed and carefree resort on Sardinia's northern tip, lie three of the island's best beaches – Punta Falcone, La Marmorata and **Capo Testa**▶▶. Beyond them, more beach-fringed bays stretch as far as **Palau**▶, main port for the Maddalena archipelago (see page 253). Further east, villages like **Cannigione**▶ on the Golfo di Arzachena are also still relatively quiet. Nearby Baia Sardinia, Portisco and Porto Rotondo, however, are similar in style to Porto Cervo.

▶▶   **Gennargentu, Monti del**   *244C2*

The Gennargentu is Sardinia's mountainous heart, a region of ancient landscapes and ways of life that have scarcely changed in centuries. Its isolated and self-contained farming villages offer your best hope of seeing local costumes or stumbling on age-old festivals. It is also among Europe's last wilderness areas, recently having been designated a national park. Driving is the only practical way to explore, using either Mandas or Nuoro as your base (though infrequent trains from Cagliari run through the region to Sorgono and Arbatax). Most roads here offer lonely excursions, but try the Arbatax–Dorgali (SS125) ride in particular for its exhilarating views of the **Gola su Gorruppu**▶▶▶. To reach other breezy belvederes follow the Fonni to Aritzo road (and the spur to Bruncu Spina at 1,570m), or the scenic drives from Aritzo to Arcu Guddetorgiu (10km northeast of Aritzo) and Seui (45km southeast).

A quiet stretch of the Costa Smeralda

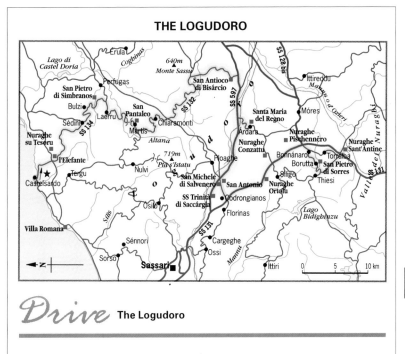

THE LOGUDORO

Drive The Logudoro

This route explores Sardinia's north-west corner – the Logudoro (Land of Gold) – famous for its remote 12th-century Pisan-Romanesque churches and several of the island's grandest prehistoric *nuraghi*.

You could start the tour in Sassari, but by starting at **Castelsardo**, (page 248), a magnificently sited old town, you have the chance of seeing not only San Pietro di Simbranos, one of the remotest of the Pisan churches, but also the famous Elefante rock and its prehistoric tombs. Tumbledown **San Antioco di Bisarcio** is the next church, followed by **Santa Maria del Regno**, a large, granite-fronted affair near Ardara (this now nondescript vil-lage was once capital of the Logudoro).

Moving southwest, you reach **San Antonio**, Pisan in style, but – as the red-and-white façade suggests – ren-ovated by the Aragonese. Next comes **San Michele di Salvenero**, then **Santissima Trinità di Saccargia►►**, part of a once-famous abbey (1116), now perhaps Sardinia's most notable church.

Pick up the main road (SS131) and turn off to Borutta, beyond which stands the beautifully situated church of **San Pietro di Sorres►**. Returning to the SS131 you come to the **Valle dei Nuraghi►►**, peppered with dozens of these enigmatic buildings, including the outstanding **Nuraghe Sant'Antine►►►**. It dates from the 14th century BC, and centres on an impressive 16m bastion. Be sure to visit the **Museo di Torralba**, the best of several *nuraghi* museums in the vicinity (2km north in Torralba).

The eye-catching church of Trinità di Saccargia

Giara di Gesturi: basalt and wildflowers

Buggerru
This seaside resort lies 40km north of Iglesias, surrounded by impressive beaches and dramatic countryside. To stay ahead of the crowd, explore the beautifully unspoilt Costa Verde north of Buggerru, reached on wild and picturesque roads from Guspini. Marina di Arbus is developed, but the cliffs and mountains to the south are still pristine.

Garibaldi and Caprera
Garibaldi first came to Caprera in 1855, seven years after his abortive attempt to form a Roman republic. In 1860 he set off from Maddalena with the thousand red-shirts (the famous *Mille*), his spectacular conquest of Sicily and Naples a prelude to the creation of a united Italy a year later. He then retired to lead the life of a simple farmer on Caprera. His house, garden and tomb are kept as a museum.

▶▶ **Giara di Gesturi** 244B2

Giare are strange basalt plateaux found all over Sardinia. None are odder or more alluring than the Giara di Gesturi. About 600m high and 12km across, its herb- and *maquis*-covered plains stretch to the horizon, broken by outcrops of pinky-black basalt and vast woods of cork oak (the forests contain an estimated 250,000 trees). After rain, trickling streams appear and areas of marsh form on the plateau rich in spring flowers and host to many migrating birds (the biggest such areas are Pauli Maiori and Pauli Minori). Roaming the heathland you may spot one of the plateau's famous wild horses – shy, tiny creatures similar to Shetland ponies and once common all over Sardinia. The area makes excellent walking country (for strolls long and short), and is easily accessed from surrounding villages. To get there, take the SS131 from Cagliari and after 40km branch east on the SS197 for Barumini: Gesturi village is 5km beyond.

You can combine a visit to the Giara di Gesturi with a trip to **Las Plassas**▶▶, a remarkable conical hill whose dramatic silhouette and ruined 12th-century castle are a landmark all around, and to **Su Nuraxi**▶▶▶, one of the island's finest *nuraghi*. *Su Nuraxi* means simply 'the *nuraghe*', a blunt title for the oldest, most splendid and most extensive *nuraghe* in Sardinia. It was probably deliberately buried by Sards or Carthaginians: only a severe storm in 1949 brought it to the notice of the modern world. If you see no other *nuraghi*, be sure to see this one, 1km west of Barumini.

▶ **Iglesias** 244B1

Gold, silver, iron, lead and zinc have been mined in the countryside around Iglesias for centuries. The town itself bears remarkably few signs of its industrial past. On the contrary, it is a pleasant and elegant spot, whose name derives from its numerous churches (Spanish *iglesia* – church). Its hub is Piazza Sella, a lively little square, backed by an old quarter of balconied houses and quiet cobbled streets. The secluded **Duomo**▶ is worth a quick glance, and there is also a museum devoted to the town's extensive mining heritage.

▶▶　La Maddalena　　244E3

This seven-isled archipelago has always had a naval presence. Nelson spent 15 months in its waters pursuing the French prior to the Battle of Trafalgar. Today, the island of Maddalena still has a huge NATO base, though assaults on the islands now come only from visitors flooding in from the Costa Smeralda. Most are here for the beaches, though the islands also have their scenic side – worn granite rocks, sparse *maquis* and wind-bent pines. Many people also come to pay homage to Garibaldi, Italy's nationalist hero, who lived for many years on the island of Caprera (see panel on page 252).

▶▶　Nora　　244A2

Sardinia's most compelling archaeological site occupies a narrow neck of land at Capo di Pula (32km west of Cagliari). Founded by the Phoenicians, the colony was later settled by the Carthaginians and then by the Romans. It was abandoned in the 3rd century AD, possibly in the wake of some natural disaster. Among the ruins you can see part of a burial ground, a Carthaginian temple to their chief goddess Astarte, a fine Roman theatre, fragments of four Roman baths, and a miscellany of houses, streets and well-preserved mosaic pavements. Part of the city is submerged, but still remains visible under the water close to the shoreline. Alongside the site stand the ruins of the 11th-century church of Sant'Efisio. Immediately below is a tempting sandy bay.

▶　Nuoro　　244C2

Nuoro has a grand mountain setting but as D H Lawrence observed when he visited the town earlier this century: 'There is nothing to see... which to tell the truth is always a relief. Sights are an irritating bore.' Little has changed, though these days the town boasts a folk museum, the **Museo della Vita e Tradizioni Popolari▶▶**, Sardinia's most complete collection of costumes, handicrafts and other mementoes of its rural past. Otherwise it is a rather shabby place, useful mainly as a springboard for excursions into the former bandit country to the south.

　Olbia　　244D3

Mainland ferries dock at Olbia, a modern but not unduly industrialised port. This makes it a lively but not particularly prepossessing place, and after seeing the 12th-century church of **San Simplicio▶▶** it probably makes sense to head for the string of resorts and beaches strung along the SS125. Lanes off the main road lead to small bays and sandy beaches. More developed facilities cluster around San Teodoro (25km) and Siniscola (55km), and around the coast's most picturesque little resorts, La Caletta and Santa Lucia (both about 7km east of Siniscola).

253

Costume display in Nuoro's Museo della Vita

SARDINIA

Tharros
Little remains of Tharros, founded by the Phoenicians in 800BC and later occupied by the Romans and Carthaginians. One of the most important classical sites in Sardinia nonetheless, it has the added attraction of a wild and beautiful setting, edged by clear seas and alluring beaches.

▶ **Oristano** 244C1

You often come to Sardinian towns only to leave them again for more interesting sights in the surrounding countryside. Oristano is no exception: it serves as a base for the **Sinis peninsula**▶▶, a patchwork of lagoons and desert-like dunes east of the town. As well as providing the background to ancient **Tharros**▶▶ (see panel), this is an area of solitary churches, ghost towns and virtually deserted white-sand beaches. As a sanctuary for flora and birds, notably flamingos, it is also a haven for botanists and naturalists. In Oristano itself, the bustling Piazza Roma and the tight historic core detain you only briefly. South of the town, however, leave time for the majestic 12th-century church of **Santa Giusta**▶▶.

Top: the marshland blooms near Oristano
Above: painting in the church of Santa Giusta, Oristano

▶▶ **Porto Conte** 244D1

Porto Conte is the main destination for many of Alghero's visitors. It is a sweeping bay of fine beaches and beautifully limpid seas that forms part of the *Riviera del Corallo* (named after the coral collected off the coast, much of which is made into jewellery that is sold in Alghero's shops). Two rocky promontories hold the bay in a protective embrace. The crook of the southern arm contains the **Nuraghi di Palmavera**▶▶, some 50 or so *nuraghi* gathered around a central domed 'palace'. Two good beaches occupy the promontory's southern shore, Lazzaretto and Le Bombarde.

The northern arm, Capo Caccia, rears up from the sea in a series of spectacular cliffs, easily seen by boat (from Alghero) or from the promontory's fine coastal road. It also harbours the **Grotta di Nettuno**▶▶▶, one of the Mediterranean's most fabulous sea caves. Single-file tours (on the hour) are conducted along a natural corridor past incredible displays of stalagmites and stalactites. The whole cavern is beautifully and dramatically lit. You can approach by boat from Alghero (15 minutes) or from Capo Caccia, where 654 dizzying steps – the *escala del cabriol* (goat's stairway) – drop to the cave's entrance at the foot of the cliffs. The stairway was only completed in 1954: before that the only access was via a precipitous and dangerous path.

► **Sant'Antioco, Isola di** 244A1

Access to Sant'Antioco, off southwest Sardinia, is via a causeway built by the Carthaginians. Halfway across look for the two rocks known as *Su Pàra* and *Sa Mongia* (the monk and the nun), two illicit lovers turned to stone by God as they fled the island. The town of Sant'Antioco on the other side has been inhabited since Phoenician times. Its main attractions date from later, principally the early Christian catacombs under the Romanesque church of Sant'Antioco. Dark, dank and chilling, these tombs still contain skeletons, some perhaps from an earlier Carthaginian tomb on the site. A more extensive Carthaginian burial site, or *tophet*, covers a hillside near by (signed from the village). The site has a small museum, numerous funerary urns and the remains of several ancient temples.

Many popular beaches dot the island, notably on the western coast, all linked by road to Calasetta and Sant'Antioco. Most are still pleasantly undeveloped.

► **San Pietro, Isola di** 244A1

Carloforte► on San Pietro can be reached by ferry from Portoscuro (22km southwest of Iglesias, page 252), or from Calasetta on its near neighbour, Sant'Antioco. Although partly spoilt by a large power station, individual parts of the island are attractive, notably **Capo Sandalo►►** and **La Caletta►►**, both accessible by road from Carloforte (13km). The island has endless stretches of rocky shoreline, perfect for swimming and snorkelling.

Sassari 244D1

Sardinia's second city has little to recommend it other than as a supplies stop to be visited from more agreeable spots on the coast. If you happen to pass through, spend a little time in the old quarter, whose claustrophobic maze of streets contrasts strikingly with the bland modern boulevards on the town's outskirts. See the **Duomo►** with its intricate baroque façade, and the **Museo Sanna►**, almost a carbon copy of Cagliari's archaeological museum. It offers similar displays of Nuraghic, Roman and Carthaginian artefacts, and examples of local costumes and handicrafts.

Beaches
A fine succession of beaches curves in a wide arc along the coast north of Sassari from Porto Torres to Castelsardo. All are linked by the SS200, a scenic seafront road.

255

Scenic drives
SS125 Arbatax–Dorgali–Nuoro; SS128/197 Nuoro–Fonni–Sorgono–Barumini; SS292 Oristano–Cuglieri–Bosa–Alghero; SS200/SS127 Sassari–Castelsardo–Costa Smeralda

Traces of former elegance in Sassari

■ **Much as Sardinia's coastline is nowadays synonymous with beaches and the pleasures of sand and sea, so the interior's vast tracts of lonely, sun-baked mountains have been associated since time immemorial with banditry, kidnapping and lethal, blood-soaked vendettas.** ■

Blood on the walls
Visitors to Orgosolo now search in vain for traces of its violent past, though locals have painted many houses with murals depicting some of the village's more blood-curdling historical episodes.

256

Banditry is by no means a new phenomenon; the capture of these French tourists made the headlines a hundred years ago

Capture de deux voyageurs français par des brigands en Sardaigne

The beginnings Banditry (the word comes from the Catalan *bandejat*, or *bandeado* in Spanish) has plagued Sardinia from Roman times. It has its roots in the traditional animosity and conflict of interests between the shepherds of the mountains – who required land for grazing – and the peasants of the lowlands who sought to tame the land for cultivation. At its simplest, lawlessness probably started with the looting of a few sheep, or the rustling of a few cattle, even today not seen as terribly heinous crimes among shepherds, who are more likely to be outraged at the theft of money, or the more practical items needed for everyday existence.

The blood feud If banditry's simple give and take were breached, or its basic rules broken – notably when blood was spilt – then blood feuds and vendettas (*bardana*) could develop which might escalate over decades to embrace not simply individuals but entire villages and districts. One notable *disamistade*, or enmity, for example, festered for years in Orgosolo, deep in the Barbagia mountains, banditry's traditional fortress, prompted by the disputed inheritance of the village's chief clansman. From 1903 over the course of 14 years virtually every member of the two families involved was wiped out. Between then and 1954 the village (population 4,000) had on average a killing every two months.

Robbery and kidnapping Simple highway robbery also became endemic, particularly after the war. One of the more infamous heists was the hold-up of 250 people in broad daylight in 1952 while the local police force celebrated its annual *festa*. Another came in 1973 when thieves made off with 230 sheep from the state agricultural penal colony. More recently, and more alarmingly, kidnapping has become the crime of choice, Sardinia's harsh interior providing the perfect cover for captors who know the terrain better than their pursuers. The numbers have soared. Between 1945 and 1965 there were 58 reported kidnappings on the island (and none on the Italian mainland); in just three years from 1979 to 1982 there were 22 abductions.

TRAVEL FACTS

Arriving
Passports only (no visas) are required for visitors from the UK and other EU (European Union) countries, the US, Canada, the Republic of Ireland, Australia and New Zealand.

Air Direct scheduled flights from the UK and Europe operate to Rome, Venice, Milan, Verona (BA flies direct), Turin, Bologna, Genoa, Florence, Pisa and Naples. Most long-haul flights fly to either Milan (Malpensa) or Rome (Leonardo da Vinci). Charter flights operate to the main cities plus Ancona, Alghero, Brindisi, Cagliari, Catania, Lamezia (Calabria), Olbia, Palermo, Pescara, Rimini and Verona.

Rail Trains run directly to Rome, Milan, Venice and Naples via Calais and Paris from London (Victoria) and other major European cities. Motorail services are available on some routes.

Road Entry to Italy by road is best made via the Mont Blanc tunnel (France); the Brenner Pass (Austria); and the St Bernard tunnel, Chiasso, or Simplon Pass (from Switzerland).

Camping
Most Italian campsites are on the coast or around lakes. Many open seasonally (typically June–September) and are extremely busy during July and August (so book ahead or arrive by 10am). Tourist offices have full details of current prices for sites, but if you are camping extensively invest in the widely available *Campeggi e Villaggi Turistici,* published by the Touring Club of Italy (TCI).

Car breakdowns see page 261

Car rentals see page 262

Children
All but budget hotels accept children and it is normal to take young children to restaurants in the evening. Nappies, accessories and baby foods are widely available. Children under four ride free on buses, trams and trains, and enjoy free admittance to museums and galleries. Children between four and 12 qualify for half-price reductions.

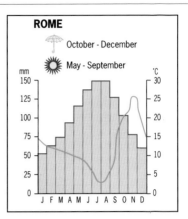

ROME

October - December

May - September

Climate
Despite its basically mild winters and warm summers, Italy has a surprisingly varied and extreme climate. In winter Venice can be colder than London, Turin chillier than Copenhagen. Manchester is milder than Milan and you can ski in several parts of the country during September. The best months for sightseeing are April, May, June, September and October, though rain and cold linger in northern and mountain areas throughout spring and autumn. July and August are the hottest months everywhere. Winters can be severe, particularly in the Alps and fog-bound plains of Lombardy and Emilia-Romagna.

Crime
The sheer number of visitors to Italy makes them an obvious target for the unscrupulous, especially in the larger cities and more depressed areas of the south. Of the horror stories told of unwitting tourists fleeced by Italy's criminal élite, however, few have much basis in fact. Common sense and a few precautions should keep you safe.

● Always carry cash in a belt or pouch – never in a pocket.

● Do not carry large amounts of cash: use credit cards or travellers' cheques.

● Wear your camera and never put it down on café tables – and beware of strap-cutting thieves.

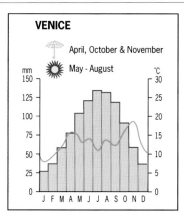

VENICE

April, October & November

May - August

mm 150 / 125 / 100 / 75 / 50 / 25 / 0

°C 30 / 25 / 20 / 15 / 10 / 5 / 0

J F M A M J J A S O N D

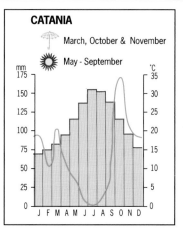

CATANIA

March, October & November

May - September

mm 175 / 150 / 125 / 100 / 75 / 50 / 25 / 0

°C 35 / 30 / 25 / 20 / 15 / 10 / 5 / 0

J F M A M J J A S O N D

259

- Do not flaunt valuables – better still, leave them at home.

- Leave all jewellery in the hotel safe (not rooms). Chains and earrings worn in the street are easily snatched by bold thieves.

- Women should hold bags across their front, never hung over one shoulder, where they can be easily rifled or grabbed.

- Be careful of pickpockets on crowded buses or where large groups of tourists congregate (particularly if you are confronted by gangs of determined-looking gypsy kids, who will jostle you and rifle through your pockets).

- After dark, women especially should not linger in non-commercial parts of town, in parks, or around railway stations.

- When driving always lock your car and never leave luggage, cameras or valuables inside.

Report any theft to your hotel and then to the police at the local *questura* (police station), many of which have a special department to deal with tourists' problems. They will issue documents (*denuncia*) to forward with any insurance claims. If you lose a passport report the loss to the police and then contact your consulate or embassy. To contact the police in an emergency call 113.

Customs Regulations

All items for personal or professional use may be brought into Italy free of charge, but take receipts for valuable articles to avoid paying duty on them. Travellers' allowances for Italy are the same as for other EU countries. To learn what you can take back *from* Italy to a non-EU country, contact that country's customs department.

Since 1 January 1993 throughout the EU there have been no restrictions on allowances for duty-paid goods (bought in local shops) that are for your own use (or as presents). Customs may ask questions if you exceed guide limits (800 cigarettes, 400 cigarillos, 200 cigars, 10 litres of spirits, 20 litres of fortified wine, 90 litres of wine, 110 litres of beer).

For duty-paid goods bought outside the EU and duty-free purchases, the following limits apply:

- **Tobacco:** 200 cigarettes or 100 cigarillos or 50 cigars or 250g tobacco

- **Alcohol** 1 litre of spirits (over 22 per cent proof) or 2 litres of fortified or sparkling wine, plus 2 litres of still wine

- **Perfume** 50g (60cc/ml) or 250cc/ml toilet water

- **Other goods** to the value of £36

Travellers with disabilities

Italy is not an easy country for people with physical disabilities, though facilities are improving – staff at airports, stations and museums are helpful (St Peter's and the Vatican museums are wheelchair accessible). Italian tourist offices in foreign countries (see page 270) provide a list of hotels equipped for people with disabilities, and addresses of helpful Italian associations in main cities. Some high-speed trains have wheelchair lifts (wheelchairs must be carried free by law): buses do not, though seats are reserved for passengers with disabilities.

Useful addresses

● **Australia:** Barrier-Free Travel, 36 Wheatley Street, North Bellingen NSW 2454 (tel: 066/551 773).

● **Canada:** Canadian Rehabilitation Council for the Disabled, 45 Sheppard Avenue E, Suite 801, Toronto, Ontario M2N 5W9 (tel: 416/250 7490).

● **Republic of Ireland:** National Rehabilitation Board, 24–5 Clyde Road, Ballsbridge, Dublin 4 (tel: 01/668 4181).

● **New Zealand:** Disabled Persons Assembly, PO Box 27–186, 63 Hinkey Street, Wellington (tel: 04/857828).

An alternative form of travel in Rome

● **UK:** RADAR, 12 City Forum, 250 City Road, London EC1V 8AF (tel: 0171/250 3222); Holiday Care Service, 2nd Floor, Imperial Buildings, Victoria Road, Horley, Surrey RH6 7P2 (tel: 01293/774 535).

● **US:** SATH (Society for the Advancement of Travel for the Handicapped), 347 Fifth Avenue, Suite 610, New York NY 10016 (tel: 212/447 7284).

The Project Phoenix Trust publishes a guide to Rome and Florence based on the personal experiences of disabled travellers; write to PPT, 56 Burnaby Road, Southend-on-Sea, Essex, UK (tel: 0702/466 412).

Domestic travel

Air Alitalia, its domestic affiliate ATI and several smaller national carriers offer frequent services between cities and islands. Prices are high and you will often find it cheaper and more convenient to travel by rail. Students and passengers between 12 and 25 qualify for 25 per cent discounts on certain Alitalia flights, and there are also 30 per cent reductions available on some night flights, as well as 50 per cent savings for family groups.

Boat The FS (see under **Rail**) and numerous private companies provide car ferries and hydrofoils to Sicily, Sardinia, Elba and the Tuscan archipelago, the Tremiti islands (Apulia), the Sicilian islands and the Bay of Naples islands. There are connections to Corsica, Malta, Tunisia, Egypt and Israel. Car ferry bookings for summer travel to Sardinia and Elba should be made several months in advance.

Bus Long haul coaches (*pullman*) run between most cities, but timetables, departure points and frequency can be hard to pin down. Ask about services at tourist offices or visit the local bus terminal (*autostazione*), often situated outside the town's railway station. Tickets must usually be bought beforehand from *tabacchi* (tobacconists) or the bus terminal. For city buses see page 268.

Rail Train is the best way of travelling around Italy without a car. The system is cheap and efficient. Bar a few private lines, the network is run by the Ferrovie dello Stato (FS). There are several train categories: *Rapido* and *Inter City*, which stop only at major stations and charge a 30 per cent supplement (*un supplemento*) which must be bought in addition to the normal ticket. *Espressi* and *diretti* stop at more stations, while *locali* stop at every station. There are two new categories: *Regionali* and *Inter-Regionali*; these are similar to *espressi* and *diretti*.

● **Tickets** (*biglietti*) are available as a single (*andata*) or return (*andata e ritorno*) in first (*prima*) or second class (*seconda classe*). Be sure to validate return tickets in yellow platform machines before travelling.

● **Fares** are calculated on a kilometric basis and are some of the cheapest in Europe. Return (3-day) tickets are discounted 15 per cent on distances up to 250km (50km on a day-return).

● **Validity** Tickets are valid for one day from the day of issue up to 250km, plus an extra day of validity for each additional 200km up to a maximum of 6 days. This validity takes effect from the moment you punch your ticket on platform machines. Tickets must be used within two months of purchase.

● **Reservations** Stations usually have separate ticket windows for reservations and sleepers (*cucetta*), the former worth considering for long journeys in summer when trains can be crowded.

● **Reductions** of 30 per cent are available for families with a *Carta Famiglia* (Family Card); for travellers between 12 and 26 with a *Carta Verde* (reductions are 20 per cent 26 June–14 August), and for men over 65 and women over 60 (with a *Carta d'Argento*).
  Cards are available from main stations and are valid for a year (except 26 June–14 August and 18–28

December for *Carta d'Argento*). Children between 4 and 12 travel half fare.

● **Passes** The FS issue three main passes: the *Chilometrico*, valid for 3,000km of travel over a maximum of 20 journeys; the *Italy Railcard*, a travel-at-will card available for 8-, 15-, 21- and 30-day periods (1st and 2nd class).

● **Timetables** If you use trains regularly be sure to buy the *Pozzorario*, a cheap biannual timetable. This is widely available in bookshops and station kiosks.

Driving
While many city centres are congested, the rest of Italy has a superb network of *autostrade* (motorways), *superstrade* (main roads) and *strade statali* (minor roads). Tolls are payable on motorways.

261

Accidents If you have an accident, place a warning triangle 50m behind the car and call the police (tel: 112 or 113). Do not admit liability or make statements which might later incriminate you. Ask any witness(es) to remain, make a statement to the police and exchange names, addresses, car details and insurance companies' names and addresses with other driver(s) involved.

Breakdowns Put on hazard warning lights and place a warning triangle behind the car. Call the Automobile Club d'Italia (ACI) 24-hour emergency number (tel: 116) and give your location, car registration and make. The car will be towed to an ACI affiliated garage. The service is free to any visiting motorist driving a foreign registered vehicle.

❏ For information on routes, road conditions, petrol stations and garages that repair foreign makes of cars, contact the Automobile Club d'Italia (ACI), Via Marsala 8, Rome (tel: 06/49 981). For road conditions call 1941/1942 ❏

CONVERSION CHARTS

FROM	TO	MULTIPLY BY
Inches	Centimetres	2.54
Centimetres	Inches	0.3937
Feet	Metres	0.3048
Metres	Feet	3.2810
Yards	Metres	0.9144
Metres	Yards	1.0940
Miles	Kilometres	1.6090
Kilometres	Miles	0.6214
Acres	Hectares	0.4047
Hectares	Acres	2.4710
Gallons	Litres	4.5460
Litres	Gallons	0.2200
Ounces	Grams	28.35
Grams	Ounces	0.0353
Pounds	Grams	453.6
Grams	Pounds	0.0022
Pounds	Kilograms	0.4536
Kilograms	Pounds	2.205
Tons	Tonnes	1.0160
Tonnes	Tons	0.9842

MEN'S SUITS

UK	36	38	40	42	44	46	48
Rest of Europe	46	48	50	52	54	56	58
US	36	38	40	42	44	46	48

DRESS SIZES

UK	8	10	12	14	16	18
France	36	38	40	42	44	46
Italy	38	40	42	44	46	48
Rest of Europe	34	36	38	40	42	44
US	6	8	10	12	14	16

MEN'S SHIRTS

UK	14	14.5	15	15.5	16	16.5	17
Rest of Europe	36	37	38	39/40	41	42	43
US	14	14.5	15	15.5	16	16.5	17

MEN'S SHOES

UK	7	7.5	8.5	9.5	10.5	11
Rest of Europe	41	42	43	44	45	46
US	8	8.5	9.5	10.5	11.5	12

WOMEN'S SHOES

UK	4.5	5	5.5	6	6.5	7
Rest of Europe	38	38	39	39	40	41
US	6	6.5	7	7.5	8	8.5

Documents Visitors bringing their own (foreign registered) car to Italy must be at least 18 years of age and carry the vehicle's registration documents (logbook) and a full, valid driving licence (*patente* in Italian).

Third-party insurance is compulsory; an international green card, though not compulsory, is recommended. A green UK, red Republic of Ireland or other foreign licence is acceptable if accompanied by a translation, available free from the ACI or the Italian State Tourist Office in the country of origin. The translation is not required for the new pink EU, UK or Republic of Ireland licence.

Parking Parking is often a nightmare in towns: parking spots (*parcheggi*) are invariably full and most historic centres are partially or fully closed to traffic. Try to leave your car in guarded parking areas, and never leave valuables or luggage in parked vehicles. Cars may be towed away if illegally parked: contact the local offices of the *Vigili Urbani* to effect recovery.

Petrol Petrol (*benzina*) in Italy is among the most expensive in Europe. Diesel (*gasolio*) is cheaper.

Petrol stations, except those on motorways (*Open* all day), tend to follow normal shop hours (*Closed* 1–4pm) and most close all day on Sunday (except on motorways). Self-service and 24-hour pumps which take L10,000 and L50,000 notes are increasingly common.

Renting a car Leading rental firms have offices in most cities and airports and, with local agencies, are listed in Yellow Pages under *Autonoleggio*. Fly-drive deals can be organised through travel agents. Drivers must be over 21 and hold a valid licence (an international driver's licence is sometimes required).

Rules of the road Italian traffic rules follow the Geneva Convention and Italy uses international road signs. Driving is on the right and you should give way at intersections to vehicles coming from your right. The speed limit in built-up areas is 50 kph: outside urban areas it is 110kph, unless otherwise marked (when it is usually 90kph). The limit on motorways is 130kph for vehicles over 1,100cc. Carrying warning triangles and wearing front seat belts are compulsory.

Electricity
The current is 220 volts AC, 50 cycles, with plugs of the two 'round' pin type: a travel plug is useful. In older hotels and houses you will find two-pin plugs of different specifications, but adapters are widely available.

Embassies and Consulates
All major countries are represented by an embassy in Rome. They include:
Australia: Via Alessandri 215 (tel: 06/852 271)
Canada: Via Zara 30 (tel: 06/440 3028)
Republic of Ireland: Largo Nazareno 3 (tel: 06/678 2541)
New Zealand: Via Zara 28 (tel: 06/440 2928)
UK: Via XX Settembre 80a (tel: 06/482 5441)
US: Via Vittorio Veneto 119a–121 (tel: 06/46 741)

Emergency Telephone Numbers

Police (*Carabinieri*) **112**
Emergency services (police, fire, ambulance) **113**
Fire (*Vigili di Fuoco*) **115**
Car breakdown **116**

Etiquette
● Do not wear shorts, short skirts or skimpy tops in churches.

● Do not intrude (or cause any sort of disturbance) while church services are in progress.

● Many churches forbid the use of flash with cameras, or ban photography altogether.

● There are still few non-smoking areas in restaurants and public places. Smoking is banned on buses and metros.

● Topless sunbathing is tolerated on out-of-the-way beaches.

● Bargaining is no longer appropriate in shops, though in markets (except food markets) and budget hotels you may be able to negotiate lower rates.

Health
Visitors from EU countries can claim treatment free from the Italian Health Service. Get Form E111 from any main post office before travelling. If you need treatment, exchange the form at a *Unita Sanitaria Locale* (USL) office in Italy – see Yellow Pages for locations. The Local Health Unit will provide you with a Certificate of Entitlement and a list of doctors and dentists who provide treatment free of charge. If a doctor refers you to a hospital, you will be given a further certificate for free treatment in certain hospitals. If you go directly to a hospital, give your E111 to the authorities there (if you have proof of EU citizenship, you will be treated even if you have no E111). Keep all paperwork for any retrospective claim for costs.

Though Italian hospitals may be a little rough and ready, and the queues long, the standards of care and treatment are high. Key health points to remember are:

● Vaccinations are unnecessary for entry into Italy unless you are travelling from a known infected area.

● Take out health insurance; keep all receipts for medicines and treatment from doctors, dentists and hospitals.

● For minor ailments visit a chemist (see **Pharmacies**, page 267).

● If you need a doctor (*un medico*), ask at your hotel or chemist, or consult the Yellow Pages under *Unita Sanitaria Locale* (USL).

● If you need first aid, visit the casualty department (*pronto soccorso*) of the nearest hospital (*ospedale*).

● If you need an ambulance (*ambulanza*) call the emergency services (tel: 113) or the Red Cross.

263

- Water is safe to drink unless marked *acqua non potabile*.

- To avoid heat exhaustion and sunstroke drink plenty of water, wear a hat and do not spend long in the sun.

- Levels of air pollution are high in most Italian cities.

- Snakebites are rarely fatal. If bitten, try to note the snake's appearance, and visit a doctor or pharmacy for the appropriate serum.

- Condoms (*profilatici*) are available over the counter from chemists and some supermarkets.

Language

Italians respond well to foreigners who make an effort to speak their language. In the more up-market hotels and restaurants, or in tourist cities, you should have few problems.

> ### Courtesies
>
> **Good morning:** buon giorno
>
> **Good afternoon/good evening:** buona sera
>
> **Good night:** buona notte
>
> **Hello/goodbye:** (informal) ciao
>
> **Goodbye:** arrivederci
>
> **Please:** per favore
>
> **Thank you:** (very much) grazie (mille)
>
> **You're welcome:** prego
>
> **How are you?:** (polite/informal) come sta/stai?
>
> **I'm fine:** bene
>
> **I'm sorry:** mi dispiace
>
> **Excuse me:** mi scusi
>
> **Excuse me:** (in a crowd) permesso

All Italian words are pronounced as written, with each vowel and consonant sounded. Major points to remember include:

- Use the polite, third person (*Lei*) to speak to strangers: use the second person (*tu*) to friends or children.

- The letter **c** is hard, as in the English 'cat' except when followed by **i** or **e**, when it becomes the soft *ch* of 'children'.

- The same applies to **g** when followed by **i** or **e** – soft in *giardino*, as in the English 'giant'; hard in *gatto*, as in 'gate'.

- Words ending in **o** are almost always masculine gender (plural: **i**); those ending in **a** are feminine (plural: **e**).

Lost Property

- Report losses to your hotel, then to the local police station (*questura*). Most larger bus terminals and railway stations have lost property offices.

- Report loss or theft of passports to the police and then contact your embassy or nearest consulate.

- If you lose your travellers' cheques or credit cards, notify the police, then follow the instructions given with the cards and cheques and inform the issuing company's nearest office.

Maps

Excellent 1:200 000 Touring Club Italiano (TCI) maps, ideal for driving and route-planning, are widely available in the UK and Italy. For walking maps, the main publishers are **Kompass, Tabacco, Multigraphic** and **Istituto Geografico Centrale** (IGC).

Tobacconists, street kiosks and bookshops sell maps, but adequate street maps of towns and cities are usually available from local tourist offices.

Media

Italy's main national newspapers (*giornali*) include the authoritative Milan-based *Corriere della Sera* (centre-right); the Turin-based *La Stampa*; and the Rome-based *La Repubblica* (centre-left). The biggest-selling papers are sports papers like the pink *Gazzetta dello Sport* and *Corriere dello Sport*. The leading news magazines (*riviste*) are *L'Espresso*, *Panorama*, *Europeo* and *Epoca*.

Foreign language newspapers and

magazines are available in major tourist areas at 2pm on the day of issue. The European editions of the *Financial Times*, *Guardian* and *International Herald Tribune* are widely available at news kiosks (*edicole*).

Italian radio and television are deregulated, and offer a vast range of national and local stations. Standards are low, with local networks geared mainly to advertising, pop music and old films. National stations are better, dividing equally between the three channels of the state RAI network and the stable of channels founded by Silvio Berlusconi (*Canale 5, Rete 4* and *Italia Uno*).

Money Matters

The unit of currency is the *lira* (plural *lire*), abbreviated to L, and is issued in denominations of: (notes) L1,000, L2,000, L5,000, L10,000, L50,000, L100,000; and (coins) L5, L10 (both rare), L50, L100, L200, L500. A L200 telephone token (*gettone*) can be used as a coin.

Italy is no longer plagued by a change shortage, but L50,000 and L100,000 notes can still cause problems. All the zeros can be confusing, so check change and all monetary transactions carefully.

Import and export

Visitors are advised to contact their banks for current information, but at present there are no restrictions on foreign currency brought into Italy. Up to L400,00 may be imported. To export more than L1,000,000 or the equivalent of more than L5,000,000 in foreign currency, you must sign form V2 at Customs on entry, and show it to Customs on leaving. Keep all receipts and stubs of transactions.

Travellers' cheques are free of upper limit restrictions, and all major cheques as well as Eurocheques are widely recognised. L300,000 may be charged to each Eurocheque, and most banks and exchange outlets allow you to cash up to three daily.

Credit cards (*carta di credito*) are slowly gaining acceptance in larger hotels, shops and restaurants, but an establishment may refuse a card, even though it displays a sticker for one of the principal cards. It is worth checking well before you have to pay the bill. Also be sure it is impossible for stubs to be tampered with once you have signed. Some cards (Visa, Amex) can be used for cash at certain banks and from automatic machines. Many petrol stations still will not accept cards.

Exchange Most banks will change foreign currency and travellers' cheques – look for the sign *cambio* – but queues are often long and the service laborious. Specialist exchange outlets may offer marginally worse rates, but they avoid frustration. Along with bureaux at airports and main railway stations they are also open beyond normal banking hours. In the last resort big hotels will change money, but at poor rates.

National Holidays
Shops, banks, offices and schools are closed on the following days:

1 January (New Year's Day)
6 January (Epiphany)
Easter Monday
Easter Sunday
25 April (Liberation Day)
1 May (Labour Day)
15 August (Assumption)
1 November (All Saints' Day)
8 December (Immaculate Conception)
Christmas Day
26 December (Santo Stefano)

Street café in Verona

When a public holiday falls on a Tuesday or Thursday it is customary to make a *ponte* (bridge) to the weekend and take the Monday or Friday off as well.

Opening Times
Archaeological sites Many sites are open all day from 9am to one hour before dusk, but it is always wise to check times with local tourist offices.

Banks are open weekdays 8.30am to 1.20pm, and some larger banks may open from 3 to 4pm.

Churches generally open around 7am and close towards noon, opening again between 4 and 7pm. Many churches remain closed except on Sundays and religious holidays: major cathedrals and basilicas like St Peter's are often open all day.

Museums and galleries run by the state usually open

Tuesday to Sunday from 9am to 1 or 2pm: almost all shut on Mondays. A few also open from 4 to 7pm, on selected days. Afternoon hours during winter are more restricted, especially in smaller galleries.

Parks and public gardens usually open from 9 to an hour before dusk.

Post offices usually open Monday to Friday 8 or 8.30 am to 2pm (to 12.30pm on Saturday). Main offices often stay open for some services until 8pm. Offices everywhere close at noon on the last working day of the month.

Restaurants and bars close once a week for a *riposo settimanale*.

Shops and offices are normally open from 8.30 or 9 until 1pm, reopening at 3.30 or 4 to 7.30 or 8pm. Most close on Sundays and on Monday mornings, and food shops may also close on Thursday afternoons. Garages are shut on Sundays; barbers and hairdressers on Sundays and Mondays. Supermarkets and department stores usually open 9.30am to 8pm.

Pharmacies

A chemist's shop (*farmacia*) is identified by a green cross. Pharmacies keep the same hours as shops, but also open late on a rotation basis. When closed (during lunch, holidays or at night), they display a list of chemists open near by.

Staff are well qualified to give advice on minor ailments, and can dispense medicines over the counter, including some only available on prescription in other countries. Brand names differ from country to country, so take finished medication to chemists to help with identification. Remember to bring any prescription or doctor's notes that might be required to obtain medicine.

Police

Dial 113 in an emergency, but in other situations go to the local police station (see **Crime** on page 258).

Police on the street divide into:

● The semi-military *carabinieri*, with smart black uniforms.

● The *polizia statale*, in blue uniforms, who perform most day-to-day policing.

● The *polizia urbana* and *vigili urbani*, who deal mainly with traffic control and parking offences.

Police registration In theory, you should register at a *questura* within three days of entering Italy. In practice no one does (hotels pass on their register instead).

Post Offices

For opening times see this page.

Stamps

(*francobolli*) can be bought from tobacconists (*tabacchi*) showing a blue 'T' sign, as well as the post office (*posta* or *ufficio postale*).

Mail to and from Italy can take three weeks. *Raccomandata* (registered) or *espresso* (express) are quicker. Letters can be sent *poste restante* to a town's main post office by addressing them *Fermo Posta*, followed by the name of the town. Take a passport when collecting mail: there is a small fee to pay. Filing can be haphazard, so check under your first and last names. **Telex**, fax and telegrams can be sent from larger post offices. **The Vatican** operates its own postal service, known for its greater efficiency than the Italian state system. There are post offices in the square in front of St Peter's in Rome.

Public Transport

Buses The urban bus (*autobus*) services of most towns and cities run along similar lines. Usually you must buy a ticket in advance from a machine, a news-stand, at *tabacchi* – or even from station bars – then validate it in a machine on the bus (roving inspectors and spot fines await anyone without a ticket). Tickets in some cities are valid for one journey, others for any number of journeys within a given time limit. Usually you enter by a bus's rear doors (marked *salita*) and leave by the centre doors (*uscita*). A bus stop is known as *una fermata*.

Metro Several cities have an underground system (*la metropolitana*), which provides the quickest way across the city. Tickets must be bought beforehand from shops, kiosks or metro stations.

Taxis Always check that your taxi is a registered cab and that the meter is running. Supplements to the meter fare are levied for additional passengers, for luggage, journeys after 8pm and on Sundays and public holidays. Many cities have set rates from the airport to the city centre. It can be difficult to hail taxis on the street, and most congregate at ranks. You can phone for cabs either through your hotel or by consulting Yellow Pages.

Senior Citizens

Men over 65 and women over 60 with identification gain free entry to state museums and art galleries. A 30 per cent discount on rail fares is on offer to the same age group with a *Carta d'Argento* (Silver Card), available form main-line stations – see page 261 for details.

Student and Youth Travel

Students and young travellers can enjoy reductions for rail and some air travel (see pages 260–1) as well as discounts to museums, galleries and archaeological sites on production of an ISIC card. There is free entrance to state museums for under-18s. Specialist youth travel agents Centro Turistico Studentesco e Giovanile (CTS) have over 90 offices throughout Italy.

Bicycles and scooters

Bicycle and scooter rental outlets are increasingly springing up in popular tourist areas. Most rent by the hour or day and require a credit card or passport as deposit.

Telephones

● Italy's state telephone company Telecom Italia provides public telephones in bars, on the street and in special SIP offices, all marked by a red or yellow sign showing a telephone dial and receiver.

● Most Italian phones accept L100, L200, and L500 coins as well as a L200 token, or *gettone*, which can be bought from most bars and tabacchi; the oldest phones, usually found in bars, may well only accept these tokens.

● Public phones are increasingly being modified to accept phone cards (*schede telefoniche*), on sale in L5,000, L10,000 and L15,000 denominations from *tabacchi*, or shops with a Telecom Italia sticker (remember to tear the corner off the card before using).

Telephone services
Operator **15**
International operator
  (Europe) **15**
International operator
  (Intercontinental) **170**
International Directory
  Enquiries **176**
Police **112/113**
Emergency services **113**
ACI car breakdowns **116**
Post office enquiries **160**
Time **161**
Road reports **1941/1942**
Snow reports **162**
Alarm call service **114**

International calls
To call abroad dial **00**, then the country code, followed by the town or city code, then the number (omitting the first zero in any town or city code).
To call Italy from the UK dial **010 39** plus the town code (minus the first zero) and number.
Country prefixes from Italy include:
Australia **00 61**
Canada **001**
New Zealand **00 64**
Republic of Ireland **00 353**
UK **00 44**
US **001**

● Peak period during weekdays is from 8am to 1pm, off-peak from 1pm to 8pm, and cheap at all other times. The cheap international rate is at weekends and 8pm to 8am during the week.

● Note that the Italian telephone system is currently undergoing another of its major overhauls and many numbers in this book will change as a result: free Telecom Italia announcements give new numbers.

● For international calls use phone cards or a *telefono a scatti*, where you speak first and pay later: these special cabins are found in some bars and hotels, post offices, some tourist offices and in most Telecom Italia offices.

● To make a collect or reverse charge call dial 15 (Europe) or 170 (Intercontinental) and ask to make *una chiamata con pagamento a destinazione*.

Time
Italy is 1 hour ahead of GMT in winter, 1 hour ahead of BST in summer, but as British clocks go back for winter a little later than in Italy, there is a short time in October when times are the same. New York and Montréal are 6 hours behind Italy. Sydney is 8 hours ahead of Italian time during the summer.

Tipping

● A 10 to 15 per cent service charge (*servizio*) is usually added to restaurant bills, but waiters expect a small tip in addition.

● Taxi drivers should be tipped 10 per cent.

● For quick service in bars you might wish to do as the locals do and slap down a L100 or L200 coin with your till receipt when ordering.

● Tip hotel staff (porters, doormen, room service) around L1,000–L2,000 depending on the standard of hotel.

● Cinema and theatre usherettes expect a small tip for showing you to your seats.

● Give something to custodians or sacristans if they have opened up churches or museums especially for your benefit, or outside normal opening hours.

tourist office known as an *Azienda Autonoma di Soggiorno e Turismo* (AAST). Most follow normal shop hours and offer maps, information and help with finding accommodation. (The *Ente Provinciale per il Turismo* (EPT) is usually more devoted to bureaucracy than information.) Villages may only have a small office known as a Pro Loco, with limited opening hours.

Italian State Tourist Offices abroad

Australia/NZ 61–69 Macquarie St, Sydney 2000, NSW (tel: 02/9247 8442) or 36 Grant Rd, Thorndon, Wellington (tel: 04/736 065).
Canada 1 Place Ville Marie, Montréal, Québec H3B 3M9 (tel: 514/866 7667)
Republic of Ireland 47 Merrion Street, Dublin 2 (tel: 01/766 397)
UK 1 Princes Street, London W1 8AY (tel: 0171/408 1254)
US 630 5th Avenue, Suite 1565, Rockefeller Center, New York NY 10111 (tel: 212/245 4822).

Valeting and Laundry

While Italy boasts very few coin-operated launderettes, virtually every town and village has an old-style cleaners (*una tintoria*), where your clothes are pressed and packaged. Most places also have dry-cleaning facilities (*lava a secco*).

Toilets

Public conveniences are rare in Italy, found mainly in railway stations and larger museums, and most of the time you have to use the grim facilities in bars and cafés. Ask for *il gabinetto* or *bagno* and do not confuse *signori* (Men) with *signore* (Women). Some larger places may have an attendant and small dish for gratuities – leave around L200.

Tourist Offices

The tourist system is currently being reorganised, but most towns, main railway stations and airports have a

Youth Hostels

Italy has about 50 youth hostels (*Alberghi per la Gioventù*) affiliated to Hostelling International (HI). Dormitory beds can be hard to come by without reservations in summer (many hostels close off season). In theory you should be a member of your national youth hostel association, but in practice many hostels allow you to join on the spot, or charge a higher fee to non-members.

HOTELS AND RESTAURANTS

ACCOMMODATION

budget (£): a double room for up to £40
moderate (££): a double room for between £40 and £75
expensive (£££): expect to pay more than £75 for a double room

ROME

The telephone code for Rome is 06.

Ambasciatori (£££) Via V Veneto 62 (tel: 47 493). Recently refurbished luxury hotel; impeccable service and facilities.
Carriage (££) Via delle Carrozze 36 (tel: 679 3312 or 699 0124). Renovated old world elegance near the Spanish Steps.
Columbus (££) Via della Conciliazione 33 (tel: 686 5435). Renaissance *palazzo* and gracious atmosphere; near St. Peter's and a favorite of visiting cardinals.
Della Lunetta (£) Piazza del Paradiso 68 (tel: 686 1080). Cheap, large but dowdy rooms; busy location near Campo dei Fiori.
Excelsior (£££) Via V Veneto 125 (tel: 4708). One of Rome's top hotels; polished and prestigious, but relaxed atmosphere.
Fiorella (£) Via del Babuino 196 (tel: 361 0597). Friendly, popular place with eight rooms near Piazza di Spagna. Pre-book.
Grand (£££) Via Vittorio Emanuele Orlando 3 (tel: 474 709). No longer a fine location, but still the haunt of VIPs and visiting royalty.
Hassler (£££) Piazza Trinità dei Monti 6 (tel: 678 2651). Grand position above Spanish Steps and one of Rome's top hotels.
Hotel d'Inghilterra (£££) Via Bocca di Leone 14 (tel: 672 161 or 69 981). Favourite of 19th-century writers and artists; at the heart of Rome's shopping district.
La Residenza (££) Via Emilia 22–4 (tel: 488 0789). Good value rooms in converted town house off Via V Veneto.
Locarno (££) Via della Penna 22 (tel: 361 0841). Atmospheric old favorite in side street near Piazza del Popolo.
Lord Byron (£££) Via G de Notaris 5 (tel: 361 3041). Parkland setting in Parioli; exclusive and perhaps most splendid of Rome's luxury hotels.
Margutta (££) Via Laurina 34 (tel: 679 8440). Pretty, with average rooms in quiet location near Piazza del Popolo.
Perugia (£) Via del Colosseo 7 (tel: 679 7200). On quiet side street near Colosseum.
Pomezia (£) Via dei Chiavari 12 (tel: 686 1371). Bargain rooms near Piazza Navona.
Portoghesi (££) Via dei Portoghesi 1 (tel: 686 4231). Once a bargain, now no longer cheap, but still popular; near Piazza Navona; fine roof terrace and views.
Raphael (£££) Largo di Febo 2 (tel: 682 831 or 683 8881). Beautiful, stylish hotel opposite the parliament.
Sistina (££) Via Sistina 136 (tel: 4890 0316). Quiet and reliable hotel near Piazza di Spagna; lovely terrace.

Smeraldo (£) Via dei Chiodaroli 11 (tel: 687 5929). Refitted, comfortable and popular hotel 2 minutes from Campo dei Fiori.
Sole (£) Via del Biscione 76 (tel: 6880 6873 or 687 9446). Well-known backpackers' favourite; busy rooms off Campo dei Fiori.

THE NORTHWEST

Aosta
Europe (£££) Piazza Narbonne 8 (tel: 0165/236 363). Central 5-story hotel renovated in 1991.
Rayon du Soleil (££) Saraillon 16 (tel: 0165/262 247). Traditional hotel in the hills.

Asti
Alermo (£££) Via E Filiberto 13 (tel: 0141/595 661). Best hotel in town.
Cavour (£) Piazza Marconi 18 (tel: 0141/530 222). A good, modern and cheap hotel.
Rainero (££) Via Cavour 85 (tel: 0141/353 866). Oldish family-run hotel near centre.

Cinque Terre
Porto Roca (£££) Via Corone 1 (tel: 0187/817 502). Quietly situated on a hill near the town. Sea views.

Genova (Genoa)
Agnello d'Oro (£) Via delle Monachette 6 (tel: 010/246 2084). Centrally placed near the station; simple but air-conditioned.
Bristol Palace (£££) Via XX Settembre 35 (tel: 010/592 541). Top-class hotel in the fashionable part of the city.
Major (£) Vico Spada 4 (tel: 010/293 449). A bargain; central, modern and clean.
Pagoda Residence (£££) Via Capolungo 15, Nervi (tel: 010/326 161). Idiosyncratic small hotel 6 miles out.

Riviera di Levante
Cenobio dei Dogi (£££) Via Cuneo 34, Camogli (tel: 0185/770 041). Modernised former summer villa of Genoa's doges.
Eden (£–££) Vico Dritto 18, Portofino (tel: 0185/269 091). Nice 2-star in 1920s Ligurian house, close to village square.
Piccolo Hotel (££) Portofino (tel: 0185/69 015). Small and modern, overlooking the harbour; attracts younger set.
Royal Sporting (££) Via dell' Olivo 345, Portovenere (tel: 0187/900 326). Modern beach hotel; excellent sports facilities.
Splendido (£££) Salita Baratta 12, Portofino (tel:0185/269 551). About as luxurious and expensive as an Italian hotel gets.

Riviera di Ponente
Grand Hotel Capo Ampelio (£££) Via Virgilio 5, Bordighera (tel: 0184/264 333). Quietly located hilltop villa.
Grand Hotel del Mare ((£££) Via Portico della Punta 34, Bordighera (tel: 0184/262 201). Top-quality hotel on a hill above the beach; great views and good facilities.
Paradiso (££) Via Roccasterone 12, San Remo (tel: 0184/571 211). Quiet modern hotel set in its own garden.

Royal (£££) Corso Imperatrice 80, San Remo (tel: 0184/53 91). Luxury hotel near the casino where the top people stay.

Torino (Turin)
Astoria (£) Via XX Settembre 4 (tel: 011/562 0653). A good cheap hotel.
Jolly Ligure (££) Piazza Carlo Felice 85 (tel: 011/55 641). Large, centrally situated hotel in a restored and modernised old building.
Principi di Piemonte (£££) Via P. Gobetti 15 (tel: 011/562 9693). Elegant hotel patronised by the rich and famous.
Victoria (££) Via Nino Costa 4 (tel: 011/561 1909). Central, pleasant and modern, decorated in idiosyncratic style.

LOMBARDY AND EMILIA-ROMAGNA
Bergamo
Agnello d'Oro (£) Via Gombito 22 (tel: 035/249 883). One of the few cheap places in the old town.
Excelsior San Marco (£££) Piazza della Repubblica 6 (tel: 035/366 111). Top hotel with a renowned quality restaurant.

Bologna
Apollo (£) Via Drapperie 5 (tel: 051/237 904). Clean, spacious and central.
Corona d'Oro (£££) Via Oberdan 12 (tel: 051/236 456). Old hotel, once a printing house.
Orologio (££) Via IV Novembre 10 (tel: 051/231 243). Quiet, central hotel. Reserve.
Roma (££) Via Massimo d'Azeglio 9 (tel: 051/226 322). Traditional hotel.

Como, Lago di
Barchetta Excelsior (£££) Piazza Cavour 1, Como (tel: 031/3221). Hotel with lakefront setting (not all rooms have a view).
Du Lac (££) Piazza Mazzini 32, Bellagio (tel: 031/950 320). Lakeside hotel in village centre; great views from roof terrace.
Tre Re (££) Via Boldoni 20, Como (tel: 031/265 374). Modernised 16th-century palace with popular terrace restaurant.
Villa d'Este (£££) Via Regina 40, Cernobbio (tel: 031/511 471). The most famous and expensive hotel in the Lakes region.

Ferrara
Ripagrande (£££) Via Ripagrande 21 (tel: 0532/765 250). Restored medieval *palazzo* in the centre of the old town.
San Paolo (£–££) Via Baluardi 9 (tel: 0532/762 040). Quiet budget hotel.

Garda, Lago di
Catullo (££) Piazza Flaminia 7, Sirmione (tel: 030/990 5811). Recently refurbished, with fine views. In the old town.
Sirmione (££) Piazza Castello 19, Sirmione (tel: 030/916 331). Lakeside hotel in a charming garden setting.
Villa del Sogno (£££) Corso Zanardelli 107, Gardone Riviera (tel: 0365/290 181). Situated above the lake: very relaxing.

Lago Maggiore
Des Iles Borromées (£££) Lungolago Umberto I 167, Stresa (tel: 0323/30 431). Famous, palatial and highly expensive hotel, in business since 1863.
Milan au Lac (££) Piazza Marconi, Stresa (tel: 0323/31 190). Large, traditional hotel. Watch the boats at the nearby dock.
Primavera (££) Via Cavour 39 (tel: 0323/31 286 or 31 191). Clean, simple 3-star rooms in quiet pedestrianised centre of town.

Mantova (Mantua)
Bianchi Stazione (£) Piazza Don E Leoni 24 (tel: 0376/321 504). Good budget spot near the station. Can be noisy.
San Lorenzo (£££) Piazza Concordia 14 (tel: 0376/220 500). Character hotel in old *palazzo* in the historic centre.

Milano (Milan)
Antica Locanda Solferino (££) Via Castelfidardo 2 (tel: 02/657 0129). Popular inn in Brera district. Booking essential.
Diana Majestic (£££) Viale Piave 42 (tel: 021/2951 3404). Charming, smart art-deco hotel run by Cigna group.
Manzoni (££) Via Santo Spirito 20 (tel: 02/7600 5700). Excellent central location, and popular – reserve ahead.
Rovello (£) Via Rovello 18a (tel: 02/8646 4654). Basic décor in this small budget *pensione*, a favorite with the young.

273

Parma
Button (££) Via Saline 7 (tel: 0521/208 039). Excellent central 3-star in quiet side-street.
Lazzaro (£) Via XX Marzo 14 (tel: 0521/208 944). Small, central 1-star above a good restaurant. Arrive early.
Torino (££) Via Mazza 7 (tel: 0521/281 046). Agreeable and friendly, central yet quiet.

Ravenna
Bisanzio (£££) Via Salara 30 (tel: 0544/217 111). Smooth, comfortable central hotel.
Ravenna (£) Via Maroncelli 12 (tel: 0544/212 204). Modern hotel, handy for the station. Gets full in season.

VENICE
The telephone code for Venice is 041.
Accademia (££) Fondamenta Bollani, Dorsoduro 1058 (tel: 521 0188). One of the city's most popular hotels (book up to a year ahead). Ample rooms, though not always quiet; homey; reasonable rates.
Agli Alboretti (££) Rio Terrà Sant'Agnese, Dorsoduro 882/4 (tel: 523 0058). Simple, attractive family-run hotel; modern rooms but cosy atmosphere; central location.
American (££) Fondamenta Bragadin, Rio di San Vio, Dorsoduro 628 (tel: 041/520 4733). Good 3-star just a few minutes from the Accademia in pretty location.
Ca' Foscari (£) Calle della Frescada, Dorsoduro 3888 (tel: 522 5817). Quiet, attractive and easygoing.

HOTELS AND RESTAURANTS

Caneva (£) Ramo della Fava, Castello 5515 (tel: 522 8118). Close to the Rialto but still quiet; most rooms overlook a canal.

Casa Petrarca (£) Calle delle Colonne, San Marco 4386 (tel: 520 0430). Friendly, only seven rooms. Near San Marco.

Casa Verardo (£) Ruga Giuffa, Castello 4765 (tel: 528 6127). Probably the best choice in this part of the city.

Cipriani (£££) Giudecca 10 (tel: 520 7744). Famous and luxurious, but away from the heart of the city.

Danieli (£££) Riva degli Schiavoni, Castello 4196 (tel: 522 6480). Famous since 1822; still celebrity-packed despite a fading reputation; rooms vary; avoid the annexe.

Flora (££) Calle Bergamaschi, off Calle Larga XXII Marzo, San Marco 2283a (tel: 520 5844). Delightful relaxing hotel (though some rooms are dark or cramped); garden.

Gritti Palace (£££) Campo Santa Maria del Giglio, San Marco 2467 (tel: 794 611). Superb location and setting; elegant service and supreme old-world luxury.

La Fenice et des Artistes (££) Campiello della Fenice 1936, San Marco (tel: 523 2333). Slightly arty; rooms vary – those in the old wing are more appealing.

La Residenza (£) Campo Bandiera e Moro 3608 (tel: 528 5315). Small, low-key hotel with a feeling of old Venice.

Londra Palace (£££) Riva degli Schiavoni 4171 (tel: 520 0533). Distinguished atmosphere; watery views.

Metropole (£££) Riva degli Schiavoni 4149 (tel: 520 5044). Small, exclusive hotel which offers both canal and garden rooms.

Monaco and Grand Canal (£££) Calle Vallaresso, San Marco 1325 (tel: 520 0211). Intimate luxury hotel on the Grand Canal; some rooms rather small; excellent service.

Pausania (££) Fondamenta Gherardini, Dorsoduro 2824 (tel: 522 2083). Quiet, 3-star near Campo Santa Margherita.

Sant'Anna (£) Corte del Bianco, Castello 269 (tel: 520 4203). Away from the centre and crowds; good for families.

Santo Stefano (££) Campo Santo Stefano, San Marco 2957 (tel: 520 0166). Tiny, immaculate hotel; modest sized rooms.

THE NORTHEAST
Asolo
Villa Cipriani (£££) Via Canova 298 (tel: 0423/952 166). One of the most beautiful and alluring of all the CIGA chain's hotels.

Bolzano-Bozen
Fiechter (£–££) Via Grappoli 15 (tel: 0471/978 768). Good 2-star hotel close to the centre; convenient for the station.

Grifone-Greif (£££) Piazza Walther (tel: 0471/977 056). Venerable hotel located on the central square; noted restaurant.

Luna-Mondschein (££) Via Piave 15 (tel: 0471/975 642). Established and run by the same family for two centuries, this hotel is central, tranquil and friendly.

Padova (Padua)
Bellevue (£) Via L Belludi 11 (tel: 049/862 493). Nice rooms around a courtyard.

Europa (££) Largo Europa 9 (tel: 049/661 200). Central hotel but unexciting.

Trento
Accademia (£££) Vicolo Collico 4/6 (tel: 0461/233 600). Central and amiable hotel in medieval building. Noted restaurant.

Treviso
Campeol (£) Piazza Ancillotto 8 (tel: 0422/56 601). A reliable mid-range hotel in centre.

Continental (£££) Via Roma 16 (tel: 0422/411 216). Convenient for the old town; comfortable rooms.

Le Beccherie (£) Piazza Ancillotto 11 (tel: 0422/540 871). Budget first choice.

Trieste
Duchi d'Aosta (£££) Piazza dell'Unità d'Italia 2 (tel: 040/7351). Central, beautifully appointed hotel with elegant restaurant.

Hotel al Teatro (££) Via Capo di Piazza G. Bartoli 1 (tel: 040/ 366 220). Old-style neoclassical hotel near the opera.

Verona
Colomba d'Oro (£££) Via Cattaneo 10 (tel: 045/595 300). Quiet and comfortable hotel close to the Arena.

Giulietta e Romeo (££) Vicolo Tre Marchetti 3 (tel: 045/800 3554). Unpretentious hotel; good value and well placed for sightseeing.

Il Torcolo (££) Vicolo Listone 3 (tel: 045/800 7512). Close to the Arena and like all Verona's hotels must be pre-booked during the opera season.

Victoria (£££) Via Adua 8 (tel: 045/590 566). Small, plush and quiet.

Vicenza
Giardini (££) Via Giuriolo 10 (tel: 0444/326 458). Renovated 3-star close to the Teatro Olimpico and town centre.

FLORENCE
The telephone code for Florence is 055.

Annalena (££) Via Romana 34 (tel: 222 402). Famous 14th-century hotel near Pitti and Boboli gardens.

Ausinia e Rimini (£) (tel: 496 547) & **Kursal** (tel: 496 324) Via Nazionale 22. Refitted hotels near the station.

Beacci Tornabuoni (£££) Via dei Tornabuoni 3 (tel: 212 645 or 268 377). Famously quaint and archetypal old-world *pensione* (half board required).

Excelsior (£££) Piazza Ognissanti 3 (tel: 264 201). Top rate luxury class hotel; part of the CIGA chain. Its renowned *Il Cestello* restaurant has magnificent views of the city from its summer roof terrace.

Grand Hotel Villa Cora (£££) Viale Machiavelli 18 (tel: 229 8451). Venerable and opulent rooms, pool, large garden.

Hermitage (££) Vicolo Marzio 1 (tel: 287 216). Popular with UK and US visitors. Good 3-star hotel overlooking the River Arno.
Kraft (££) Via Solferino 2 (tel: 284 273). Quiet, comfortable and spacious; small pool and panoramic roof terrace.
La Mia Casa (£) Piazza Santa Maria Novella 23 (tel: 213 061). Best of several hotels on this square.
Loggiato dei Serviti (££) Piazza della Santissima Annunziata 3 (tel: 289 592). 19th-century elegance and 20th-century comfort in a quiet pleasant square.
Maxim (£) Via de'Medici 4/Via dei Calzaiouli (tel: 217 474). Welcoming, very central budget choice; some quiet courtyard rooms.
Monna Lisa (£££) Borgo Pinti 27 (tel: 247 9751). Cosy, rather small rooms, but aristocratic fittings and public areas; in a Renaissance *palazzo* near to the Duomo.
Regency Umbria (£££) Piazza d'Azeglio 3 (tel: 245 247). Quiet and charm at top prices. Noted restaurant.
Rigatti (££) Lungarno Diaz 2 (tel: 213 022). Airy rooms with plush antique fittings in 19th century *palazzo*; booking essential.
Sorelle Bandini (£) Piazza Santo Spirito 9 (tel: 215 308). Fine choice in Oltrrarno; views, lofty rooms and lovely fittings.
Splendor (£) Via S Gallo 30 (tel: 483 427). Quiet and congenial hotel near San Marco.
Villa San Michele (£££) Via Doccia 4, Fiesole (tel: 59 451). Small, romantic and exclusive hotel in hills outside the city.

TUSCANY
Arezzo
Continentale (££) Piazza Guido Monaco 7 (tel: 0575/320 251). Well equipped and cheerfully furnished; near station and sights.

Lucca
Piccolo Puccini (££) Via di Poggio 9 (tel: 0583/ 55 421). Small, very pleasant 3-star hotel close to the centre and Puccini's house.
Universo (££) Piazza del Giglio, off Piazza Napoleone (tel: 0583/493 678). Traditional; highest ranking spot in the town centre.
Villa La Principessa (£££) Massa Pisana, 2 miles from Lucca on Via Nuova (tel: 0583/ 379 737). Lots of old-world charm in this lovely country house set in its own park.

Pisa
Cavalieri (£££) Piazza della Stazione 2 (tel: 050/43 290). All mod cons, and handy for the station and airport.
Royal Victoria (££) Lungarno Pacinotti 12 (tel: 050/940 111). Comfortable *palazzo* 10 minutes from the cathedral square.

San Gimignano
La Cisterna (££) Piazza della Cisterna (tel: 0577/940 328). Venerable old inn in the centre of town, with respected restaurant.
Pescille (££) (tel: 0577/940 186). Tasteful hotel 2 miles from San Gimignano; pool, garden and views of the village.

Siena
Certosa di Maggiano (£££) Via Certosa 82 (tel: 0577/288 180). Exclusive hotel in former monastery 2km outside town.
Palazzo Ravizza (££) Via Pian dei Mantellini 34 (tel: 0577/280 462). Traditional hotel in 17th-century *palazzo* – completely restored.
Santa Caterina (£) Via Piccolomini 7 (tel: 0577/221 105). Town house converted into a small modern hotel; garden.

Volterra
San Lino (££) Via San Lino 26, near Porta San Francesco (tel: 0588/85 250). Central choice with pool; formerly a convent.
Villa Nencini (££) Borgo Santo Stefano 55 (tel: 0588/ 86 386). Just out of town centre.

UMBRIA & THE MARCHES
Assisi
Hotel Umbra (££) Via degli Archi 6 (tel: 075/812 240). A 400-year-old building in a traffic-free location; rooms have terraces.
La Rocca (£) Via di Porta Perlici 27 (tel: 075/812 284). In a quiet part of town.
Subasio (£££) Via Frate Elia 2 (tel: 075/812 206). Lots of old world elegance close to the Basilica; rooms with views.

275

Gubbio
Ai Cappuccini (£££) Via Tifernate (tel: 075/922 9234). Modern luxury in converted 14th-century monastery.
Bosone (££) Via XX Settembre 22 (tel: 075/922 0688). In a frescoed palace in the heart of Gubbio.
Dei Consoli (££) Via dei Consoli 59 (tel: 075/927 3335). Excellent location in central medieval street.
Hotel Gattapone (£) Via Ansidei 6 (tel: 075/ 927 2489). Small family-run hotel in the town centre; comfortable and informal.

Norcia
Grotta Azzurra (££) Via Alfieri 12 (tel: 0743/ 816 513). Perfect, amiable central hotel with a great restaurant.

Orvieto
La Badia (£££) La Badia, 3 miles south of Orvieto (tel: 0763/90 359). Monastery converted into famous country hotel.
Maitani (££) Via Maitani 5 (tel: 0763/42 011). Baroque palace in town centre with comfortable, if not over-modern, rooms.
Virgilio (££) Piazza del Duomo 5 (tel: 0763/ 41 882). Small unassuming hotel by the cathedral; nice rooms.

Perugia
Locanda della Posta (£££) Corso Vannucci 97 (tel: 075/572 8925). Lovely small hotel in the old quarter with views over the town.
Palace Hotel Bellavista (££) Piazza d'Italia 12 (tel: 075/572 0741). Grand hotel in a 19th-century *palazzo*.
Umbria (£) Via Boncambi 37 (tel: 075/572 1203). A reasonable 2-star hotel.

HOTELS AND RESTAURANTS

Spoleto
Aurora (£) Via dell'Apollinare 4 (tel: 0743/220 315). Small, central and quiet place in the upper town.
Dei Duchi (£££) Viale Matteotti 2 (tel: 0743/44 541). Fine town-centre hotel with garden, close to Roman amphitheater.
Gattapone (£££) Via del Ponte 6 (tel: 0743/223 447). Tiny hotel with tempting views and lovely rooms.

Todi
Bramante (£££) Via Orvietana 48 (tel: 075/894 8381). Converted medieval convent near S M della Consolazione.
Fonte Cesia (£££) Via Lorenzo Leoni 3 (tel: 075/894 3737). Brand new and very nice 4-star right in the heart of town.

Urbino
Bonconte (£££) Via delle Mura 28 (tel: 0722 2363). Avoid the small top-floor rooms.
Hotel San Giovanni (££) Via Barocci 13 (tel: 0722/2827). Unpretentious but comfortable hotel in a converted medieval building.

LAZIO & ABRUZZO
L'Aquila
Duomo (£) Via Dragonetti 10 (tel: 0862/410 893). A 2-star hotel with 27 rooms in a quiet and very central position.
Sole (£) Largo Silvestre dell'Aquila 4 (tel: 0862/24 041). Airy, sunny rooms in a quiet street near Piazza del Duomo.

Parco Nazionale d'Abruzzo
Cristiana (££) Pescasseroli (tel: 0863/910 795). Popular and welcoming wooden chalet-type mountain hotel.

Subiaco
Belvedere (££) Via dei Monasteri 33 (tel: 0774/85 531). On the road between the town and the monasteries; has a welcoming restaurant.

Sulmona
Europa Park (££) (tel: 0864/251 260). 105-room hotel in rural setting out of town.
Italia (£) Piazza Tommaso 3, off Plazza XX Settembre (tel: 0864/52 308). Popular, central and cheap; Puccini was one of the first guests.

Tarquinia
Tarconte (££) Via Tuscia 23 (tel: 0766/856 585). Modern and perfunctory, but outstanding views from some rooms.

CAMPANIA
Amalfi
Amalfi (££) Via dei Pastai 3 (tel: 089/872 440). A good mid-range choice with spotless rooms; reservations essential.
Hotel Luna Convento (£££) Via P. Comite 19 (tel: 089/871 002 or 871 050). A lovely, converted 13th-century abbey; it is advisable to avoid street-side rooms.

Lidomare (££) Via Piccolomini 9 (tel: 089/871 332). Smart, small and clean.
Miramalfi (££) Via Quasimodo 3 (tel: 089/871 588). Quietly located modern hotel 1km out of town, overlooking the sea.
Santa Caterina (£££) Strada Amalfitana 9 (tel: 089/871 012). One of the area's best hotels; swimming pool and lovely grounds.
Sole (£) Largo della Zecca (tel: 089/871 147). Cheap place near the cathedral.

Capri
Quattro Stagioni (£) Via Marina Piccola 1, Capri Town (tel: 081/837 0041). Cosy rooms with views.
Quisisana (£££) Via Camerelle 2, Capri Town (tel: 081/837 0788). Island's top hotel; very expensive.
Scalinatella (£££) Via Tragara 8, Capri Town (tel: 081/837 0633). Intimate modern hotel with views, pool and luxury features.
Villa Brunella (££) Via Tragara 24, Capri Town (tel: 081/837 0122). Tasteful; with terraces, views, pool and noted restaurant.
Villa Eva (£) Via La Fabbrica 8, Anacapri (tel: 081/837 2040). Secluded bliss.
Villa Krupp (££) Via Matteotti 12, near Giardini di Augusto (tel: 081/837 0362). Quiet and small; Lenin and Gorky stayed here.

Ischia
Delle Rose (£) Via Casa Mennella 9 (tel: 081/994 682). In cheaper village of Casamicciola.
La Villarosa (££) Via Giacinto Gigante 5 (tel: 081/991 316). Tasteful hotel in lovely garden setting. Private swimming pool.
Regina Isabella (£££) Piazza Restituita, Lacco Ameno (tel: 081/994 322). The island's top luxury hotel.
San Montano (££) Via Monte Vicco (tel: 081/994 033). Modern hotel with fine view.

Napoli (Naples)
Ausonia (£) Via Caracciolo 11 (tel: 081/682 278 or 664 536). One of Naples' better budget hotels: seafront position in Mergellina.
Cavour (££) Piazza Garibaldi 32 (tel: 081/283 122). This is one of the better hotels in this otherwise dingy area near the station.
Excelsior (£££) Via Partenope 48 (tel: 081/764 0111). The city's top hotel.
Rex (££) Via Palepoli 12 (tel: 081/764 9389). In a convenient and relatively quiet location near the Santa Lucia waterfront.

Positano
California (£) Via Colombo 141 (tel: 089/875 382). Good budget choice.
Casa Albertina (£££) Via Tavolozza 3 (tel: 089/875 143). Friendly, family-owned, small hotel; view from terrace and roof garden.
Palazzo Murat (££) Via dei Mulini 23 (tel: 089/875 177). Town centre location with garden setting and elegant old-world charm.
San Pietro (£££) Amalfi Coast Road (tel: 089/875 455). The best in the area; over-the-top luxury and exclusivity.

Sirenuse (£££) Via Cristoforo Colombo 30 (tel: 089/875 066). Luxury hotel in centre; views, pool and large, tasteful rooms.

Ravello
Belvedere Caruso (££) Via San Giovanni del Toro 52 (tel: 089/857 111). Charming old-fashioned villa hotel; lovely garden and restaurant; first choice in the range.
Palumbo (£££) Palazzo Gonfalone (tel: 089/857 244). Just eight attractive rooms here; very elegant and very expensive.
Villa Amore (£) Via Santa Chiara 5 (tel: 089/857 135). Garden looking over cliffs and sea.
Villa Maria (£) Via Santa Chiara 2 (tel: 089/857 255). Small and quiet *pensione* with pretty garden and friendly ambience.

Sorrento
Bellevue Syrene (££) Piazza della Vittoria 5 (tel: 081/878 1024 or 878 1604). Old-style comfort in this villa-hotel; garden.
Cocumella (£££) Via Cocumella 7 (tel: 081/878 2933). This ex-monastery is now a fine welcoming hotel.
Eden (££) Via Correale 25 (tel: 081/878 1909). Central but reasonably quiet; pleasant rooms (some at budget price).
Excelsior Vittoria (£££) Piazza Tasso 34 (tel: 081/807 1044 or 878 1900). Renowned hotel; faded grandeur but comfortable.

THE DEEP SOUTH
Alberobello
Astoria (£) Viale Bari 11 (tel: 080/721 190). Functional hotel near the station.
Dei Trulli (£££) Via Cadore 28 (tel: 080/932 3555). Trulli-style rooms in a wooded setting.

Bari
Boston (££) Via Piccinni 155 (tel: 080/521 6633). Medium-sized modern hotel near the Old Town; some rooms have balconies.
Sheraton Nicolaus (£££) Via Rosalba 27 (tel: 080/504 2626). Large chain hotel with the usual facilities for business clientele.

Gargano
Al Castello (£) Via Castello 29, Peschici (tel: 0884/964 038). Hotel with noted restaurant.
Pizzomunno (£££) Lungomare Enrico Mattei, Vieste (tel: 0884/708 741). Upmarket complex; numerous facilities.
Rotary (£) Via per Pulsano, Monte Sant'Angelo (tel: 0884/62·146). Simple and modern hotel with views; just out of town.
Valle Clavia (££) Valle Clavia, Peschici (tel: 0884/964 012). Stolid modern hotel near beach in pinewoods.

Lecce
President (£££) Via Salandra 6 (tel: 0832/311 881). Sleek, modern spot in the new business part of town.
Risorgimento (££) Via Augusto Imperatore 19 (tel: 0832/242 125). Large *palazzo* in the baroque old town; old-fashioned charm.

Matera
Roma (£) Via Roma 62 (tel: 0835/333 912). Clean and central – but it fills up quickly.

Trani
Lucy (££) Piazza Plebiscito 11 (tel: 0883/41 022). Small friendly place; airy rooms with balconies; near the seafront.
Royal (££) Via De Robertis 29 (tel: 0883/588 777). A 4-star hotel in the centre.

SICILY
Agrigento
Bella Napoli (£) Piazza Lana 6, off Via Bac Bac (tel: 0922/20 435). Roof terrace overlooking the valley.
Jolly dei Templi (££) Parco Angeli, Villagio Mose (tel: 0922/606 144). Reliable hotel, 8km southeast of the town.
Villa Athena (£££) Via dei Templi 33 (tel: 0922/596 288). Only hotel near the temples, so busy as a result; book ahead.

Cefalù
Cangelosi (£) Via Umberto I 26 (tel: 0921/421 591). Cheap, central choice.
Kalura (£££) Contrada Caldura (tel: 0921/421 354 or 422 501). Beautifully set hotel with private beach and terraces.
Villa Belvedere (££) Via Mulini (tel: 0921/421 593). Hotel with antique appeal and quiet palm-tree garden.

Enna
Grande Albergo Sicilia (£) Piazza N Colajanni 5, off via Roma (tel: 0935/500 850). Friendly, reliable and central.

Erice
Elimo (££) Via V. Emanuele 75 (tel: 0923/869 377). Comfortable hotel in medieval town house.

Noto
Stella (£) Via F Maiore 44, corner of Via Napoli (tel: 0931/835 695). Noto's only hotel.

Palermo
Grande Albergo e delle Palme (£££) Via Roma 398 (tel: 091/583 933). Famous and faded, but still the best hotel in central Palermo; rooms vary greatly in quality.
Orientale (£) Via Maqueda 26 (tel: 091/616 5727). Located in 17th-century *palazzo*.
Pensione Sud (£) Via Maqueda 8 (tel: 091/617 5700). Handy for the station.
Sole (££) Corso Vittorio Emanuele 291 (tel: 091/581 811). Best of the mid-range central hotels, though some rooms noisy.
Villa Igiea (£££) Via Belmonte 43, Acquasanta (tel: 091/543 744). Art-nouveau building; the city's most luxurious hotel.

Piazza Armerina
Hotel Park Paradiso (££) (tel: 0935/680 841). Located 1km north of the town beyond the church of Sant'Andrea.

HOTELS AND RESTAURANTS

Siracusa (Syracuse)
Gran Bretagna (£) Via Savoia 21 (tel: 0931/68 765). Easily the best Ortigia choice and often full as a result. A cheap and reliable restaurant lurks downstairs.
Jolly Hotel (£££) Corso Gelone 45 (tel: 0931/461 111). Reliable big-chain hotel near the station and archeological zone.
Motel Agip (£££) Viale Teracati 30 (tel: 0931/463 232). Usual motel facilities and decent restaurant. Convenient for the archeological zone.

Taormina
Palazzo Vecchio (££) Salita Ciampoli 9 (tel: 0942/23 033). Elegant and central.
San Domenico Palace (£££) Piazza San Domenico 5 (tel: 0942/23 701). First choice for atmosphere and luxury; expensive.
Svizzera (£) Via Pirandello 26 (tel: 0942/23 790). Excellent and popular choice; lovely building; clean rooms and sea views.
Villa Fiorita (££) Via Pirandello 39 (tel: 0942/24 122). Swimming pool and small garden; rooms with fine views of the coast.
Villa San Michele (££) Via Damiano Rosso 11/bis (tel: 0942/24 327). Very central hotel: recently renovated 3-star rooms.

SARDINIA
Alghero
San Francesco (£) Via Machin 2 (tel: 079/980 330). At the centre of the old town; quiet and clean rooms; book ahead.
Tarragona (££) Via Gallura (tel: 079/952 270). A pleasant establishment situated near the port.
Villa Las Tronas (£££) Lungomare Valencia 1 (tel: 079/981 818). Top hotel; characterful villa just east of the town centre.

Cagliari
Firenze (£) Corso Vittorio Emanuele 50 (tel: 070/653 678). Only has 5 rooms, but they are very popular, so book well in advance.
La Perla (£) Via Sardegna 18 (tel: 070/669 446). One of many budget options on this street.
Regina Margherita (£££) Viale Regina Margherita 44 (tel: 070/670 342). The city's top hotel.

Costa Smeralda
Balocco (£££) Liscia di Vacca, Porto Cervo (tel: 0789/91 555). A touch cheaper than most hotels in Porto Cervo.
Pitrizza (£££) Porto Cervo (tel: 0789/91 500; closed October-May). Very exclusive hotel.

Nuoro
Su Gologone (££) Su Gologone, Oliena (tel: 0784/287 512). About 8km from Oliena; smart hotel and well-known restaurant.

Oristano
Cama (£) Via V Veneto 119 (tel: 0783/74 374). Close to the station and the old town; parking and air-conditioning.

Mistral (££) Via Martiri di Belfiore (tel: 0783/212 505). Edge of town hotel with new annexe in the town centre.

RESTAURANTS

Note Always try to book a table at expensive (£££) restaurants (and preferably in moderate (££) ones as well). Few restaurants have a dress code, but a jacket (and sometimes a tie) is in order at most expensive places.

ROME
The telephone code for Rome is 06.

Al Leoncino (£) Via del Leoncino 28. Superb pizzeria one block off Via del Corso; wood oven and interior unchanged for 30 years.
Baffetto (£) Via Governo Vecchio 114. Legendary pizzeria near Piazza Navona; queues common; amiable atmosphere.
Birreria Tempera (£) Via San Marcello 19. Great old beer hall behind Piazza Venezia; perfect for lunch and snacks.
Checchino dal 1887 (£££) Via di Monte Testaccio 30 (tel: 574 6318). Long renowned as the place to sample classic Roman dishes – tripe, brains and other oft-ignored offal; among Rome's best wine lists.
Da Giggetto (££) Via Portico d'Ottavia 21a. Famous Jewish-Roman cuisine in old-fashioned setting.
Da Nerone (££) Via delle Terme di Tito 96 (tel: 474 5207). Best eating near the Colosseum; excellent buffet *antipasti* and homemade Tuscan wine.
El Toulà (£££) Via della Lupa 29b (tel: 687 3498). High prices, swanky, and often rated Rome's best; plenty of famous faces.
Grappola d'Oro (££) Piazza della Cancelleria 80. Little-known place near Campo dei Fiori; perhaps the archetypal old Roman *trattoria*.
Ivo (£) Via di San Francesco a Ripa 157. Quintessential Roman pizzeria; fast turnover; arrive early to avoid the queues.
La Fraschetta (£) Via di San Francesco a Ripa 134. A few doors from Ivo's and quieter but almost as good; excellent desserts.
L'Eau Vive (£££) Via Monterone 85 (tel: 654 1095 or 6880 1095). An institution, mainly because food is served by nuns; good place to go cardinal-spotting; cheaper lunch menu.
Mario (££) Via della Vite 55 (tel: 678 3818). Good value Tuscan food; 30-year old institution; invariably busy, so book.
Papà Giovanni (£££) Via dei Sediari 4 (tel: 061/686 5308). Light, innovative cooking, currently rated one of Rome's best.
Paris (££) Piazza San Callisto 7a (tel: 061 581 5378). Ever-reliable and stylish restaurant.

THE NORTHWEST
Aosta
La Brasserie du Commerce (£) Via de Tillier 10 (tel: 0165/ 35 613). Centrally located, small and friendly.

Taverna da Nando (£) Via De Tillier 41
(tel: 0165/44 455). A good local trattoria.
Vecchia Aosta (££) Via Porta Pretoriane 4
(tel: 0165/361 186). Elegant and atmospheric
place with local cuisine and good wines.

Asti
L'Angolo del Beato (££) Via Guttuari 12
(tel: 0141/531 668). A reliable, upper price-
bracket restaurant in the historic centre.
Gener Neuv (£££) Lungo Tanaro 4 (tel: 0141/
557 270). Among Italy's top restaurants;
very good but very expensive.

Genova (Genoa)
Enoteca Sola (££) Corso Barabino 120r (tel:
010/594 513). A small, old-fashioned restaurant with light Ligurian cooking.
Gran Gotto (£££) Via Fiume 11r, near Piazza
della Vittoria (tel: 010/564 344). Small and
smart. One of the city's classic spots.
Sa Pesta (£) Via Giustiniani 16r, near Piazza
Matteotti. For lunch only.

Riviera di Levante
Manuelina (££) Via Roma 300, Recco (tel:
0185/731 019). One of the Riviera's more
celebrated spots.
Savoia (£) Piazza IV Novembre 3, Rapallo
(tel: 0185/247 021). Handy pizza place.
Terrazza Bellini (££) Via XX Settembre 62 (tel:
0185/770 737). Not scenic, but good food.

Riviera di Ponente
Bagatto (££) Via Matteotti 145, San Remo
(tel: 0184/531 925). In the town centre;
serves national and regional dishes.
Degli Amici (£) Via Lunga 2, Bordighera.
Reasonably-priced seafood in the old town.
La Reserve Tastevin (£££) Via Arziglia 20,
Capo Sant'Ampelio, Bordighera (tel:
0184/261 322). Excellent views and seafood.

Torino (Turin)
Brek (£) Piazza Carlo Felice 18. Sleek self-
service.
Da Giuseppe (££) Via San Massimo 34
(tel: 011/812 2090). Piedmontese specialties
served; popular with locals.
Vecchia Lanterna (£££) Corso Re Umberto
21 (tel: 011/537 047). One of Italy's top
five restaurants; very expensive.

LOMBARDY AND EMILIA-ROMAGNA
Bergamo
Da Vittorio (£££) Via Giovanni XXIII 21 (tel:
035/ 218 060). A top restaurant. Reasonably
priced lunch menu. Excellent pastries.
Taverna del Colleoni (£££) Piazza Vecchia
(tel: 035/ 232 596). Smart place in the heart
of the old town.

Bologna
Antica Brunetti (££) Via Caduti di Cefalonia
5 (tel: 051/234 441). Busy restaurant-pizzeria
near Piazza Maggiore.
Bertino (£) Via delle Lame 55 (tel: 051/522
230). Cheap, popular *trattoria*.

Da Cesari (££) Via de Carbonesi 8 (tel:
051/237 710). Interesting dishes at a
reasonable price.
Tre Frecce (£££) Strada Maggiore 19 (tel:
051/231 200). Mouthwatering cooking in a
medieval *palazzo* setting.

Como, Lago di
La Pergola (££) Pescallo (tel: 031/950 263).
Enjoy freshly caught fish beside the lake,
1km from Bellagio.
La Scuderia (£) Piazza Matteotti 4, Como.
Lively pizzeria.
Sant'Anna (£££) Via F Turati 3, Como (tel:
031/505 266). Family-run, rather smart,
business-oriented spot.

Ferrara
Da Noemi (£) Via Ragno 31a, off Corso
Porta Reno. Simple, family-run place in
business over 30 years.
La Provvidenza (£££) Corso Ercole d'Este 92
(tel: 0532/21 937). Worthy and well known,
so booking advisable.

Garda, Lago di
Vecchia Luguna (££) Piazzale Vecchia
Luguna 1 (tel: 030/919 012). One of the
region's leading restaurants.

Lago Maggiore
Piemontese (££) Via Mazzini 25 (tel: 0323/30
235). Superb food, only narrowly pipped to
the post by the more expensive **L'Emiliano**.
L'Emiliano (£££) Corso Italia 50 (tel: 0323/31
396). An elegant, high-quality restaurant.

Mantova (Mantua)
Dei Martini (££) Piazza dell' Arco 1 (tel:
0376/7202 0224). A lovely restaurant with
many local specialties.
L'Aquila Nigra (££) Vicolo Bonacolsi 4, near
Palazzo Ducale (tel: 0376/327 180). Lovely
frescoed dining room; Mantuan specialties;
reservations required.

Milano (Milan)
Boeucc (£££) Piazza Belgioioso 2 (tel:
02/7207 0224). Venerable Milanese dining
spot near La Scala, with luxurious decor
and varied menu.
Grande Italia (£) Via Palermo 5. Lively
central spot for pasta and pizzas.
La Giara (£) Viale Monza 10. Pugliese cooking at rustic wooden benches.
La Libera (££) Via Palermo 21 (tel: 02/805
3603). Trendy spot in Brera district, with
draught beer, and jazz, to accompany the
delicious food.

Parma
Corrieri (£) Via Conservatorio 1. Popular
with locals.
Enoteca Fontana di Parma (£) Via Farini 22a.
Excellent selection of wines and light meals.
La Greppia (£££) Via Garibaldi 39a (tel:
0521/233 686). Parma's best and smartest
restaurant.

HOTELS AND RESTAURANTS

Ravenna
La Gardela (£) Via Ponte Marino 3. Fine, homely *trattoria* two minutes from Piazza del Popolo.
Tre Spade (£££) Via Faentinci 136 (tel: 0544/500 522). Converted mill near the Duomo serving immaculate and inventive food.

VENICE
The telephone code for Venice is 041.

Agli Alboretti (££) Rio Terrà Sant' Agnese, Dorsoduro 882 (tel: 523 0058). Slightly up-market place near the Accademia.
Ai Cugnai (£) Calle Nuova Sant'Agnese 857 (tel: 528 9238). A tavern, handy for the Accademia, serving Venetian specialties.
Ai Promessi Sposi (£) Calle dell'Oca, Castello 4367. Seafood dishes and lively bar.
Al Mascaron (£) Calle Lunga S M Formosa 5225 (tel: 522 5995). Informal and often busy with Venetians.
Antico Martini (£££) Campo San Fantin 1983 (tel: 522 4121). A Venetian institution; but prices are far from old-fashioned.
Antica Mola (£–££) Fondamenta degli Ormesini 2800, Cannaregio. Excellent, family-run trattoria near Ghetto. Increasingly well-known.
Da Fiore (££) Calle dello Scaleter, San Polo 2202 (tel: 721 308). Local favourite now discovered by tourists, so book ahead.
Da Franz (£££) Fondamenta Sant'Isepo, Castello 754 (tel: 045/522 7505). Regularly rated among Venice's best restaurants. Excellent fish.
Da Silvio (£) Calle San Pantalon, San Polo 429. Best of the options locally; garden dining in summer.
Fiaschetteria Toscana (£££) Campo San Giovanni Crisostomo, Cannaregio 5719 (tel: 528 5281). Friendly atmosphere, setting and food make this a popular choice with locals.
Madonna (££) Calle della Madonna, San Polo 594 (tel: 523 3824). Large and busy fish restaurant.
Montin (££) Fondamenta di Borgo, Dorsoduro 1147 (tel: 522 7151). Favoured by Pound, Hemingway, *et al*; erratic cooking, slightly overpriced, but still popular.
San Bartolomeo (£) Calle della Bissa, San Marco 5424a. Good selection of self-service snacks.

THE NORTHEAST
Bolzano-Bozen
Amadè (££–£££) Via Cavour – Vicolo Cà de'Bezzi (tel: 047/971 278). Elegant and serious restaurant with food that merits the high prices.
Rössel Via dei Bottai 6. Popular, central and authentic *bierkeller* with up to 100 Tyrolean dishes.

Padova (Padua)
Antico Brolo (££) Corso Milano 22 (tel: 0491 664 555). Housed in 15th-century *palazzo*. The food lives up to the surroundings.

Dotto Via Squarcione 23 (tel: 049/875 1490). Reliable old-world place in the city centre.

Trento
Alla Mora (££) Via Roggia Grande 8 (tel: 0461/984 675). Delightful restaurant with courtyard, good, varied menu.
Chiesa (££) Via San Marco 64 (tel: 0461/238 766). Medieval setting and medieval recipes.

Treviso
Beccherie (££) Piazza Ancillotto 10 (tel: 0422/540 871). Rustic inn in the old town.

Trieste
Antica Suban (££) Via Emilio Comici 2 (tel: 040/54 368). On the edge of town; many good local dishes.

Verona
Dodici Apostoli (£££) Corticella San Marco 3 (tel: 045/596 999). One of Verona's top restaurants; medieval setting.
Il Desco (£££) Via dietro San Sebastiano 7 (tel: 045/593 358). Vies with Dodici Apostoli for the role of the city's best restaurant.
La Greppia (££) Vicolo Samaritana 3 (tel: 045/800 4577). Good local dishes are offered here, in old-fashioned surroundings.

Vicenza
Da Remo (££) Via Ca'Impenta 14 (tel: 0444/911 007). Venetian dishes are served in a charming villa 2km from Vicenza.
Scudo di Francia (££) Contrà Piancoli 4 (tel: 0444/323 322). Simply decorated central place with local specialties.

FLORENCE
The telephone code for Florence is 055.

Alle Murate (£) Via Ghibellina 52r (tel: 240 618). Increasingly popular, but still reasonably priced. Light, innovative cuisine.
Al Lume di Candela (£££) Via delle Terme 23r (tel: 294 566). *The* place for a romantic meal; small and elegant and housed in a medieval tower.
Angiolino (££) Via Santo Spirito 36r (tel: 239 8976). Busy with locals and tourists, with wood-burning stove and charcoal grill, but cooking occasionally erratic.
Belle Donne (£–££) Via delle Belle Donne 1br (tel: 238 2609). Tiny place with shared tables and eye-catching décor. Good for light lunches.
Da Mario (£) Via Rosina 2r, Piazza del Mercato. Low prices, friendly atmosphere, shared tables with students and market traders; traditional no-frills food.
Enoteca Pinchiorri (£££) Via Ghibellina 87 (tel: 242 777). Often called Italy's best restaurant, though perhaps over-formal; 80,000 bottles of best French and Italian wine. Reservations required.
Il Cibrèo (££) Via de' Macci 118r (tel: 234 1100). Sometimes over-adventurous

Tuscan specialties and Italian standards with a hint of *nouvelle cuisine*; great desserts and good wine list.

Il Contadino (£) Via Palazzuolo 69r. Basic meals and backpackers' favorite.

La Capannina di Sante (£££) Piazza Ravenna (tel: 688 345). Casual and simple place; this is the city's best fish restaurant.

Latini (£) Via Palchetti 6r (tel: 210 916). Bustling and always busy (lines likely after 8p.m.); shared tables and deliberate quasi-rustic atmosphere.

Le Fonticine (££) Via Nazionale 79r (tel: 282 106). Highly-rated restaurant combining Tuscan and Emilia-Romagnan dishes.

TUSCANY
Arezzo
Buca di San Francesco (££) Piazza San Francesco I. Tourist filled, but offers reliable food.

La Lancia d'Oro (££) Piazza Grande 18, Logge Vasari (tel: 0575/21 033). Arezzo's best restaurant, located on the town's impressive main square.

Cortona
La Loggetta (££) Piazza Peschiera 3. Lovely medieval dining room, fine food and well-chosen wines.

Lucca
Buca di Sant'Antonio (££) Via della Cervia 3 (tel: 0583/55 881). This former inn is now considered Lucca's finest restaurant. Some unusual dishes are on offer.

Da Giulio (£) Via delle Conce 47, near Palazzo Mansi (tel: 0583/55 948). Packed and popular so book or arrive early.

Solferino (£££) San Macario in Piano, 6km from Lucca on Viareggio road (tel: 0583/ 59 118). Place of Tuscan-wide renown run by same family for four generations.

Montalcino
Grappola Blu (££) Via Scale di Moglio 1 (tel: 0577/847 150). Small but with innovative cooking, and nice medieval dining area.

Pisa
Da Bruno (££) Via Luigi Bianchi 12 (tel: 050/560 818). Traditional Tuscan cooking, near the old town.

Sergio (£££) Lungarno Pacinotti 1 (tel: 050/580 580). Smart riverside restaurant in an ancient palace. The owner cooks both well and imaginatively.

Stelio (£) Piazza Dante 11. Popular pizza and pasta joint, especially so with students.

San Gimignano
Bel Soggiorno (££) Via San Giovanni 91 (0577/940 375). You can enjoy local dishes and splendid views here on the top floor of a 19th-century inn.

Le Terrazze (££) Hotel La Cisterna, Piazza della Cisterna 23 (tel: 0577/940 328). You dine overlooking the town and surrounding country in this well-known restaurant. Tuscan dishes dominate the menu.

Siena
Al Marsili (££) Via del Castoro 3 (tel: 0577/47 154). Siena's best; reservations essential.

La Torre (££) Via Salicotto 7. Friendly, tiny *trattoria* just off the Campo, so arrive early to be sure of a table.

Le Logge (££) Via del Porrione 33 (tel: 0577/ 48 013). Pretty and popular spot offering Tuscan specialties; reserve a table.

Volterra
Etruria (££) Piazza dei Priori 6 (tel: 0588/87 377). There is no need to book at this place in the heart of town, but the local dishes are good.

UMBRIA AND THE MARCHES
Assisi
Fortezza (££) Vicolo della Fortezza (tel: 075/ 812 418). Good, unpretentious food and setting.

Il Medio Evo (£££) Via dell'Arco dei Priori (tel: 075/813 068). Beautiful medieval dining rooms are the setting for some of Umbria's best food.

Palotta (£) Via San Rufino 4 (tel: 075/812 649 or 812 307). It is best to arrive early to be sure of a table (12:30 for lunch) in this popular restaurant.

281

Gubbio
Fornace di Maestro Giorgio (££) Via Maestro Giorgio 2 (tel: 075/927 5740). Located in a medieval workshop; table d'hôte menus and Umbrian dishes.

Taverna del Lupo (££) Via Ansidei 21a (tel: 075/927 4368). Large and very stylish medieval dining hall.

Montefalco
Il Coccorone (£) Via Fabbri-Largo Tempestivi. One of Umbria's finest restaurants.

Norcia
Grotta Azzurra (££) Via Alfieri 12. A temple to Umbrian cuisine, with truffle dishes and medieval dining rooms.

Orvieto
Grotta (£) Via Signorelli 15. Friendly, simple and good value *trattoria*.

Maurizio (££) Via del Duomo 78 (tel: 0763/41 114). Self-consciously modern décor, and often touristy, but good food in central location.

Perugia
Café del Cambio (£) Corso Vannucci 29. Good for quick, cheap lunches.

Falchetto (££) Via Bartolo 20. Sound choice just behind the Duomo; two small dining rooms and good food.

Osteria del Bartolo (£££) Via Bartolo 30 (tel: 075/61 461). Elegant setting and occasionally exotic food.

HOTELS AND RESTAURANTS

Spello
La Cantina (£) Via Cavour 2. Excellent local specialties in pleasant medieval setting.

Spoleto
Pentagramma (££) Via Tommaso Martini 4, off Piazza Libertà (tel: 0743/37 233). Specialises in rustic Umbrian dishes.
Sabatini (££) Corso Mazzini 54. Clever interior and fine, innovative cooking.

Todi
Umbria (££) Via S Bonaventura 13, off Piazza del Popolo (tel: 075/894 737). Superb outside terrace.

Urbino
Vecchia Urbino (££) Via dei Vasari 3 (tel: 0722/4447). The best place for a treat in Urbino.

LAZIO & ABRUZZO
L'Aquila
Ernesto (£–££) Piazza Palazzo 22 (tel: 0862/21 094). Varied local cooking with the occasional novelty.
Tre Marie (££) Via Tre Marie 3 (tel: 0862/413 191). The spot to come to sample classic Abruzzese food and wines; 17th-century setting and cosy atmosphere. Reserve.

282

Bolsena
Da Picchietto (££) Via Porta Fiorentina 15, Bolsena (tel: 0761/799 158). Homemade pasta and lake specialities like grilled eels.

Palestrina
Coccia (££) Albergo Coccia, Piazzale Liberazione (tel: 06/953 8172). Busy hotel dining-room with views over town gardens.

Sulmona
Cesedio (£) Piazza Solimo 25. Family-run place near Corso Ovidio and local favourite.
Italia (£) Piazza XX Settembre. Inventive additions to traditional Abruzzese fare. A good first choice.

Tarquinia
Corneto (£) Via Garibaldi 12-Via Cavallotti. Not much to look at, but they do serve generous portions of pizza and pasta.

Tivoli
Cinque Statue (££) Via Quintilio Varo 1-Largo S Angelo (tel: 0774/20 366). At the entrance to the Villa Gregoriana; veranda for al fresco eating.
Del Falcone (£) Via Trevio 34 (tel: 0774/22 358). Central and well-patronised rustic-look restaurant; try to book ahead.

Viterbo
Porta Romana (£) Via della Bontà. Local favourite.
Richiastro (££) Via della Marrocca 16 (tel: 0761/236 909). Pretty garden restaurant on cobbled street.

CAMPANIA
Amalfi
Da Bararacca (££) Piazza Ferrari. The town's oldest restaurant; fish specialities.
Il Tari (£) Via P Capuano 9. Small and modest; good for snacks and sandwiches.
La Caravella (££) Via M Camera 12 (tel: 089/871 029). Unpromising entrance hides intimate interior; choice of mainly fish dishes.

Capri
Da Gemma (££) Via Madre Serafina 6 (tel: 081/837 0461). One of Capri's longest-established restaurants.
Il Solitario (££) Via G. Orlandi 54, Anacapri (tel: 081/837 1382). Intimate spot with garden. Advance booking is essential.
La Capannina (£££) Via delle Botteghe 14, Capri Town (tel: 081/837 0732). Widely considered the island's top restaurant.
La Pigna (£££) Via Roma 30, Capri Town (tel: 081/837 0280). Veranda and al fresco dining; in one of Capri's favourite restaurants.

Ischia
Giardini Eden (££) Ischia Ponte, Via Nuova Cartaromana (tel: 081/993 909). The island's top restaurant.

Napoli (Naples)
Avellinese da Peppino (£) Via Silvio Spaventa 31–5. Great favourite with tourists and locals near Piazza Garibaldi; welcoming and excellent food.
Bellini (£) Via Santa Maria di Constantinopli 80, corner of Via San Pietro (tel: 081/459 774). Popular with Neapolitans; somewhat slow service but great pizzas and other dishes.
Bersagliera (££) Borgo Marinaro 10 (tel: 081/764 6016). On the waterfront and touristy as a result, but still fun for a first night – and the food is good.
Ciro a Santa Brigada (££) Via Santa Brigada 71, off Via Toledo (tel: 081/552 4072). Pizza and fish specialities; favoured by artists, journalists and the like.
La Sacrista (£££) Via Orazio 116 (tel: 081/664 186). One of southern Italy's finest restaurants.

Positano
Buca di Bacco (££) Via Rampa Teglia 8 (tel: 089/875 699). Above the town's most fashionable café; terrace dining overlooking the beach. Reservations required in the evening.
O'Capurale (££) Via Marina (tel: 089/875 374). Book ahead for outdoor tables in the cheapest and best of the many restaurants on and near Positano's waterfront.

Ravello
Cumpa Cosimo (£) Via Roma 44 (tel: 089/857 156). Friendly and pleasant good-sized restaurant, popular with tourists. The food is good.
Villa Maria (£) Via di Santa Chiara. Romantic place with garden overlooking the sea.

Sorrento
Parrucchiano (££) Corso Italia 71 (tel: 081/878 1321). One of the town's most popular restaurants; beautiful setting and tempting local dishes; reservations advised.
Sant'Antonino (£) Via Santa Maria delle Grazie 6. Popular with locals and visitors alike; low prices and flower-filled patio.

THE DEEP SOUTH
Alberobello
Il Poeta Contadino (££) Via Indipendenza 21 (tel: 080/721 917). Best restaurant in the area; almost worth a special trip.
Trullo d'Oro (££) Via F Cavallotti 29 (tel: 080/721 820). Rustic and atmospheric restaurant arranged in five *trulli*.

Bari
La Pignata (££) Corso Vittorio Emanuele 173 (tel: 080/523 2481). The best of Bari's many fine restaurants.
Taverna Verde (£) Largo Adua 18/19, end of Corso Cavour (tel: 080/554 0870). On the waterfront; popular with locals; book early.

Lecce
Barbablu' (£) Via Umberto I 7 (tel: 0832/241 183). Local favourite.

Matera
Il Terrazzino (£) Piazza Vittorio Veneto-Vico S Giuseppe 7 (tel: 0835/332 503). In an old *sasso* dug into the rock; outdoor terrace; excellent pizzas and local dishes.
Lucana (£) Via Lucana 48, off Via Roma (tel: 0835/336 117). Best restaurant in town.

Trani
La Antica Cattedrale (££) Piazza Archivio 2 (tel: 0883/586 568). Lovely old dining-room; tables outside; reserve on weekends.

SICILY
Agrigento
Caprice (££) Via Panoramica dei Templi 51 (tel: 0922/26 469). Popular place near the temples.
Leon d'Oro (£) Via Emporium, near Lungomare di San Leone (tel: 0922/414 400). Fine old trattoria; under the same management for 30 years.
Vigneto (£) Via Cavaleri Magazzeni 11 (tel: 0922/414 319). Reserve or arrive early to secure a table on the terrace.

Cefalù
Arkade Grill (£) Via Vanni 9. Excellent Tunisian cooking plus a few Italian dishes.
La Brace (£) Via XXV Novembre 10 (tel: 0921/23 570). Wonderfully eclectic cooking: sicilian meets the Far East.

Erice
Monte San Giuliano (£) Via San Rocco 7 (tel: 0923/869 595). Arab cuisine influences some of the dishes served in this popular friendly place. Reserve a table.

Noto
Trieste (£) Via Napoli 17. Busy and excellent-value restaurant on the edge of the Giardino Pubblico.

Palermo
Antica Focacceria San Francesco (£) Via Paternostro 58 (tel: 091/320 264). Marvellous turn-of-the-century institution with authentic Sicilian specialities.
Charleston (£££) Piazza Ungheria 30 (tel; 091/321 366) or, 16 June to 25 September, Viale Regina Elena, Mondello (tel: 091/450 171). The best in the city. Moves 8km out of town during high season.
La Scudiera (££) Via del Fonte 9 (tel: 091/520 323). Relaxed atmosphere and outstanding Palermitan specialities.
Shanghai (£) Vicolo de Mezzani 34, overlooking Piazza Caracciolo. Not Chinese, despite the name, but wonderfully atmospheric place in the midst of the Vucciria market.

Siracusa (Syracuse)
Archimede (££) Via Gemmellaro 8 (tel: 0931/69 701). Small, tasteful and popular Ortigia spot with good game and seafood.
Do Scugghiu (£) Via Scina 11, off Piazza Archimede. Local institution with huge choice of pasta dishes.
Minosse (££) Via Mirabella 6 (tel: 0931/66 366). Relaxing and elegant: the town's top restaurant.

Taormina
La Griglia (££) Corso Umberto 54 (tel: 0942/23 980). Probably the best of the many restaurants on Corso Umberto.
Pace (£) Piazza San Pancrazio 3. Bustling pizza and pasta place with outdoor tables.

SARDINIA
Alghero
Da Pietro (£) Via A Machin 20 (tel: 079/979 645). Busy vaulted restaurant in the old town; excellent seafood.
La Lepanto (££) Via Carlo Alberto 135 (tel: 079/979 116). One of the island's leading seafood spots.

Cagliari
Antica Osteria (££) Via Cavour 60 (tel: 070/665 870). Rivals Dal Corsaro as Cagliari's best restaurant, but prices are lower.
Da Serafino (£) Via Sardegna 109. Good value and popular with locals.
Dal Corsaro (£££) Viale Regina Margherita 28 (tel: 070/664 318). One of Sardinia's best-known restaurants – so booking essential.

Oristano
Il Faro (£££) Via Bellini 25 (tel: 0783/70 002). Recognised as one of the area's top seafood restaurants.
Da Gino (£) Via Tirso 13 (tel: 0783/71 428). Excellent good-value trattoria close to central Piazza Roma.

Index

A

Abruzzo *see* Lazio and Abruzzo
Abruzzo, Parco Nazionale d' 183, 194–5, 276
  accommodation 272–8
Agrigento 230
  accommodation 277
  eating out 283
  Museo Nazionale Archeologico 230
  Valle dei Templi 230
air travel 258, 260
Alassio 64, 72
Alatri 184
Alba 65
Albano Laziale 185
Albenga 72
Albergo-Rifugio Campo Imperatore 188
Alberobello 223, 277, 283
Alghero 247, 278, 283
Amalfi 199, 276
Amantea 222
Anagni 184
Ancona 166–7
Angelico, Fra 142
Angera 87
Anghelu Ruiu 249
Anticoli Corrado 191
Aeolian Islands 234
Aosta 64, 65, 76, 272, 279
Aosta, Valle d' 64, 76
Apulia 214, 218
Aquileia 118
Arezzo 150, 152, 275, 281
Argentera, Parco Naturale dell' 70
Armenzano 172
art and architecture
  baroque 36–7
  Byzantine 31
  classical 30
  18th, 19th and 20th centuries 38
  Gothic 32
  pre-Renaissance 33
  Renaissance 34–5
  Romanesque 32, 218
Ascoli Piceno 167
Asolo 116, 118, 274
Aspromonte 222
Assisi 165, 168, 179
  accommodation 275
  Basilica di San Francesco 168
  Duomo 168
  eating out 281
  Museo-Tesoro della Basilica 168
  Oratorio dei Pellegrini 168
  Piazza del Comune 168
  San Damiano 168
  San Pietro 168
Asti 65, 272, 279
Avigliana 77
Avise 76
Ayas, Val d' 64, 77

B

Badia, Val 123
Bagnaia 193
Bagni di Lucca 154

Bagno Vignoni 155
Baldo, Monte 85, 86
bandits 256
Bard 76
Barga 154
Bari 215, 277, 283
Barletta 215
Barrea 194
Basilicata 214
Bassano del Grappa 118
Baveno 87
Bella, Isola 87
Bellagio 83
Bellini family 98–9
Belluno 118
Benevento 199
Bergamo 82, 279
Bevagna 170, 172
bicycle and scooter rental 268
Bisentina 184
Bitonto 215
Blanc, Mont 76
Bologna 81, 82
  accommodation 273
  Archiginnasio 82
  eating out 279
  Pinacoteca Nazionale 82
  San Domenico 82
  San Giacomo Maggiore 82
  San Petronio 82
Bolsena 184, 282
Bolsena, Lago di 184
Bolzano (Bozen) 119, 274, 280
Bomarzo 193
Bordighera 72
Borromee, Isole 87
Bregagno, Monte 86
Brescia 82
Brolio 153
Brusson 77
Buggerru 252
Buonconvento 155
bus and coach services 260, 268
Byron, Lord 69, 106

C

Cagliari 247, 278
Cala Gonone 248
Calabria 214
Camigliatello 224
Camogli 69
Campania 196–211
  accommodation 276–7
  cuisine 198
  eating out 282–3
  essential sights 197
  tourist information 199
Campi Flegrei 199
camping 258
Campo Imperatore 188
Canaletto 99
Cannero Riviera 87
Cannigione 250
Capo Testa 250
Capodimonte 184
Capraia 154
Caprarola 184–5
  Palazzo Farnese 184–5
Caprese Michelangelo 152
Capri 197–8, 204
  accommodation 276
  Anacapri 204

  eating out 282
  La Grotta Azzurra 204
Carezza, Lago di 121
Cariddi 225
Casamari, Abbazia di 188
Cascata del Varone 85
Cascia 178
Casentino 152
Caserta 204
Caserta Vecchia 204
Caso 178
Castagneto Carducci 157
Castel Gandolfo 185
Castel del Monte 215, 277
Castel Rigone 177
Castelli Romani 182, 185
Castello Rancolo 119
Castelluccio 178
Castelsardo 248, 251
Castiglione del Lago 177
Castiglione Olana 83
Castiglione della Pescaia 157
Catania 230
Catholic Church 12
Cefalù 232, 277–8, 283
Cernobbio 83
Certosa di Pavia 91
Certosa di Pisa 156
Certosa di Santo Stefano 224
Cerveteri 182, 186–7
Cervo 87
Champoluc 77
Chianti 153
Chiarone 183
chiese rupestri 221
children 258
Cilento 198, 210
cinema 18
Cinque Terre 64, 66, 71, 272
Circeo, Parco Nazionale del 185
Civetta, Monte 122
Cividale del Friuli 120
Civita 184
Civitella Alfedena 194
climate 258
Cogne 68
Cogne, Val di 64, 68
Collalbo 119
Collepino 172
Columbus, Christopher 67
Como 81, 83
Como, Lago di (Lake Como) 80, 83, 86, 273, 279
Conero, Monte 166–7
confetti 193
conversion chart 262
Cornaro, Caterina 118
Corniglia 66
Cortina d'Ampezzo 123
Cortona 150, 153, 281
Costa Smeralda 250, 278
Cremona 81, 84
crete 151, 155
crime 215, 258–9
Customs regulations 259

D

d'Annunzio, Gabriele 85
Deep South 212–25
  accommodation 277

  eating out 283
  essential sights 213
  social problems 16
  tourist information 212
  wines 214
Diamante 222
Diano Marina 72
disabilities, travellers with 260
Dobbiacomare 123
Dolomiti (Dolomites) 116, 120–3
Dolomiti Bellunesi 118
Dolomiti di Brenta 120, 123
Dolomiti di Sesto 123
domestic travel 260–1
Donizetti, Gaetano 82
Dorgali 248
driving
  accidents and breakdowns 261
  car rental 262
  documents 262
  parking 262
  petrol 262
  regulations 262–3
  to Italy 258

E

Ega, Val d' 121
Egadi, Isole 232
Elba, Isola di 154
  Capoliveri 154
  Marciana 154
  Marina di Campo 154
  Poggio 154
  Portoferraio 154
electricity 263
embassies and consulates 263
emergency telephone numbers 263
Emilia-Romagna *see* Lombardy and Emilia-Romagna
Enna 232, 278
Eremo delle Carceri 172
Erice 232, 278, 283
etiquette 263
Etna 233
Etruscan tombs 163
Etruscan towns 186–7

F

Faenza 84
  Museo Internazionale delle Ceramiche 84
family, importance of 11
Fenis 76
Ferrara 84, 273, 279–80
Ferrari factory 91
ferry services 260
Finale Ligure 72
Florence (Firenze) 132–47
  accommodation 146, 274–5
  art galleries 140
  Bargello, Museo Nazionale del 140
  Battistero (Baptistery) 137
  Campanile 137
  Casa Buonarroti (Michelangelo Museum) 141

churches 134, 137–9
David 140
Duomo 137
eating out 147, 280–1
essential sights 133
festivals 134
Galleria dell'Accademia 140
Galleria degli Uffizi 140
Giardino di Boboli 144
Giardino dei Semplici 141
history 134–5
Loggia della Signoria 142
markets 138, 141
Mercato Centrale 138
Museo dell'Antica Casa Fiorentina 141
Museo Archeologico 141
Museo dell'Opera del Duomo 141
Museo di San Marco (Fra Angelico Museum) 142
Museo Stibbert 142
Museo di Storia della Scienza 142
Museo di Zoologia 143
museums and palaces 141–3
Oltrarno 144
Orsanmichele 138
Palazzo Medici-Riccardi 142
Palazzo Pitti 143
Palazzo Vecchio 143
Piazza del Duomo 144
Piazza della Signoria 134, 144
Ponte Vecchio 143
public transport 145
Santissima Annunziata 138
Santa Croce 138
San Lorenzo 139
Santa Maria del Carmine 139
Santa Maria Novella 139
San Miniato al Monte 139
shopping 145
tourist information 134
Foligno 170
Fonte Cerreto 188
food and drink
cuisine *see* regions
eating out *see* locations
meals 13
olive oil 177
truffles 174
wines 13
see also regions
Foresti Casentinesi 152
Forni, Valle dei 86
Forte dei Marmi 154
Frascati 182, 185
Frederick II 214
Fregene 183
Friuli-Venezia Giulia 117
Funivia del Monte Bianco 76

G

Gaeta 183
Gaiole in Chianti 153

Garda, Lago di (Lake Garda) 84–5, 86, 273, 280
Gardena, Val 123
Gardone Riviera 85
Garfagnana 154
Gargano 214, 216, 277
Garibaldi, Giuseppe 252
Gavelli 178
Gela 234
Gennargentu, Monti del 250
Genoa (Genova) 64, 67
accommodation 272
eating out 279
Galleria Nazionale di Palazzo Spinola 67
Museo Chiossone 67
Palazzo Bianco 67
Palazzo Rosso 67
Piazza San Matteo 67
San Lorenzo 67
Via Garibaldi 67
Gerace 216
Ghiberti, Lorenzo 137
Ghiffa 87
Giara di Gesturi 252
Giardino Alpino 68
Giorgione 99
Giotto 33
Gola su Gorruppu 248, 250
Golfo dei Poeti 69
Grado 118
Gradoli 184
Gran Paradiso, Parco Nazionale del 68, 70
Gran San Bernardo, Valle del 77
Gran Sasso d'Italia 183, 188
Grand Tour 136
Grappa, Monte 119
Gressoney, Val di 64, 77
Gressoney-La-Trinité 77
Gressoney-St-Jean 77
Greve in Chianti 153
Grotta del Bue Marino 248
Grotta Gigante 126
Grotta di Nettuno 254
Grotta di Smeraldo 209
Grottaferata 185
Grotte di Castellana 219
Grotte di Catullo 85
Gualdo Cattaneo 172
Gualdo Tadino 179
Gubbio 165, 170
accommodation 275
eating out 281
Loggia dei Tiratori 170
Palazzo dei Consoli 170
San Francesco 170

H

Hanbury Gardens 73
health 263–4
Herculaneum 205
history of Italy 20–9

I

Iglesias 252
Il Vittoriale degli Italiani 85
Ischia 198, 204
accommodation 276
eating out 282
Fontana 204

Monte Epomeo 204
Sant'Angelo 204
Iseo, Lago di 85
Isernia 183
Isola, Monte 85
Issogne 76
Italian character 10
Italian Lakes 80–1

L

La Caletta 253
La Grande Strada delle Dolomiti 121
La Maddalena 253
La Morra 70
La Palud 76
La Verna 152
Ladispoli 183
Lago Maggiore (Lake Maggiore) 80, 87, 273, 280
Laiguelia 72
language 17,264
L'Aquila 183, 184
accommodation 276
eating out 282
Museo Nazionale d'Abruzzo 184
San Bernardino 184
Santa Maria di Collemaggio 184
Las Plassas 252
Lazio and Abruzzo 180–95
accommodation 276
eating out 282
essential sights 181
tourist information 183
wines 184, 185
Le Langhe 70
Lecce 214, 217
accommodation 277
amphitheatre 217
Basilica di Santa Croce 217
eating out 283
Museo Provinciale 217
Palazzo del Governo 217
SS Nicola e Cataldo 217
L'Elefante 248
Lerici 69
Levanto 66
Liguria 64
Linguaglossa 233
Lipari, Isola di 234
Lippi, Fra Filippo 142
Logudoro 251
Lombardy and Emilia-Romagna 78–93
accommodation 273
cuisine 81, 82, 88
eating out 279–80
essential sights 79
tourist information 80
wines 88
lost property 264
Lucca 150, 156
accommodation 275
Duomo di San Martino 156
eating out 281
Museo Nazionale Guinigi 156
Piazza del Anfiteatro 156

Pinacoteca Nazionale 156
San Frediano 156
San Michele in Foro 156
Lucera 217
Frederick II fortress 217

M

Madonna di Campiglio 120, 123
Madre, Isola 87
Mafia 16, 236–7
Maggiore, Isola 177
Maggiore, Lago (Lake Maggiore) 80, 87, 273, 280
Magna Graecia 214, 231
Malcesine 81, 85
Manarola 66
Mantua (Mantova) 81, 87
accommodation 273
eating out 279
Palazzo Ducale 87
Palazzo Te 87
Piazza delle Erbe 87
Sant'Andrea 87
maps 264
Maratea 219
Maratea Marina 219
Marches, The *see* Umbria and The Marches
Maremma 150–1, 157
Maremma, Parco Naturale della 151, 157
Marina di Alberese 157
Marinella 240
Martina Franca 219
Maser 118
Massa Marittima 157
Massafra 219
Matera 221, 277, 283
Mattinata 216
media 264–5
medical treatment 263–4
Medici family 134–5
Melfi 214, 220
Menaggio 83
Merano (Meran) 124
Messina 234
Metaponto 220
Michelangelo 35, 48, 55, 138, 140
Milan (Milano) 80, 88–90
Accademia Brera 89
accommodation 273
Castello Sforzesco 88–9
Duomo 88
eating out 88, 279
La Scala 88
Museo d'Arte Antica 89
Museo Poldi Pezzoli 88
Palazzo dell'Ambrosiana 89
Pinacoteca 89
Sant'Ambrogio 89
Santa Maria delle Grazie 89
shopping 89
The Last Supper 88, 90
Miramare 126
Modena 91
Molise 183
money
credit cards 265
currency 265

INDEX

exchange facilities 265
travellers' cheques 265
Monreale 235
Montalcino 150, 157, 281
Monte Cucco, Parco
  Naturale del 179
Monte di Portofino,
  Parco Naturale del 69,
  70–1
Monte Oliveto Maggiore,
  Abbazia di 150, 155, 157
Montecassino 188
Montefalco 165, 169,
  170, 172, 281–2
Montefiascone 184
Monteleone di Spoleto
  178
Montepulciano 150, 158
Monterchi 152
Monteriggioni 161
Monterosso 66
Monteverdi, Claudio 127
Monti Sibillini, Parco
  Nazionale dei 179
Montseuc 68
mosaics
  Piazza Armerina 241
  Ravenna 93
Mostri, Parco dei 193
Mussolini, Benito 28, 83

Naples (Napoli) 197,
  206–7
accommodation 276
Duomo 206
eating out 282
Museo Archeologico
  Nazionale 206, 207
Palazzo Reale di
  Capodimonte 206
Santa Anna dei
  Lombardi 206
San Lorenzo Maggiore
  206
Teatro San Carlo 206
Napoleon 26, 154
Noli 72
Nora 253
Norcia 171, 276, 282
Northeast Italy 114–31
  accommodation 274
  cuisine 116–17
  eating out 280
  essential sights 116
  tourist information 115
Northwest Italy 62–77
  accommodation 272–3
  cuisine 65, 66, 67
  eating out 278–9
  essential sights 63
  tourist information 64
  wines 65, 66
Noto 235, 278, 283
Nuoro 253, 278
  Museo della Vita e
    Tradizioni Popolari
    253
Nuraghe Sant'Antine 251
nuraghi 249
Nuraghi di Palmavera 254
Nuraghi, Valle dei 251

Olbia 253
opening times 266–7

opera 127
Opi 194
Orcia 186
Orecchiella 154
Oristano 254, 278, 283
Orsiera-Rocciavré 77
Orta, Lago di 80, 91
Orta-San Giulio 91
Ortisei Canazei 123
Orvieto 165, 171
  accommodation 275
  Duomo 171
  eating out 281
  Pozzo di San Patrizio
    171
  San Giovenale 171
Ostia 190
Ostia Antica 182, 190
Otranto 220

Padua (Padova) 116, 124
  accommodation 274
  Basilica di Sant'Antonio
    124
  Cappella degli
    Scrovegni 124
  eating out 280
Paestum 208
Palau 250
Palermo 238–9
  accommodation 277
  Cappella Palatina 238–9
  Cattedrale 238
  Convento dei
    Cappuccini 239
  eating out 283
  Galleria Nazionale
    Siciliana 239
  La Martorana 239
  markets 239
  Museo Archeologico
    239
  Palazzo dei Normanni
    238
  Piazza Pretoria 239
  Santa Caterina 239
  San Giovanni degli
    Eremiti 239
  San Giuseppe 239
Palestrina 182, 190, 191,
  282
Palinuro 210
Palladio, Andrea 103,
  131
Parma 81, 91
  accommodation 273
  Baptistery 91
  Duomo 91
  eating out 279
  Palazzo della Pilotta 91
  San Giovanni
    Evangelista 91
Passignano 177
Pavia 91
Pellegrino, Monte 239
Perugia 165, 175
  accommodation 275
  Collegio del Cambio
    173
  eating out 281
  Fontana Maggiore 173
  Galleria Nazionale
    dell'Umbria 173
  Museo Archeologico
    Nazionale dell'Umbria
    173

Oratorio di San
  Bernardino 173
  Sala del Collegio della
    Mercanzia 173
  San Domenico 173
  San Pietro 173
Pesaro 173
Pescasseroli 194
Pescatori, Isola 87
Peschici 216
pharmacies 267
Piacenza 92
Piano Grande 165, 175
Piazza Armerina 241, 278
Piemonte (Piedmont) 64
Pienza 150, 158
Piero della Francesca 34,
  152
Pineto 183
Pisa 150, 158
  accommodation 275
  Baptistery 158
  Camposanto 158
  Duomo 158
  eating out 281
  Leaning Tower 158
  Museo dell' Opera del
    Duomo 158
  Museo delle Sinopie
    158
Pisano, Nicola 33
Pistoia 159
Pitigliano 150, 157, 163
Pizzo 222
police 267
politics 14–15
Pompeii 201–3
Pont-St-Martin 76
Ponza, Isola di 182, 192
Poppi 152
Porto Cervo 250
Porto Conte 254
Porto Ercole 157
Porto Santo Stefano 157
Portofino 69, 70–1
Portovenere 69
Positano 208, 277,
  282–3
postal services 267
Praiano 208
Procida, Isola di 198, 209
public transport 268
Puccini, Giacomo 127,
  156
Pugnochiuso 216
Punta Ala 157
Punta di San Vigilio 85

Radda in Chianti 153
Ragusa 240
rail travel 258, 261
Rapallo 69
Ravello 209
  accommodation 277
  eating out 282
  Villa Cimbrone 209
  Villa Rufolo 209
Ravenna 92–3
  accommodation 273
  Basilica di San Vitale
    93
  eating out 280
  Mausoleo di Galla
    Placidia 93
  mosaics 93
  Museo Nazionale 93

Oratorio di Sant'Andrea
  93
Sant'Apollinare in
  Classe 93
Sant'Apollinare Nuovo
  93
'Red Train' 81
Reggio di Calabria 222
Rimini 92
Riomaggiore 66
Riva del Garda 85
Riva di Solto 85
Riviera Calabrese 222
Riviera di Levante 68–9,
  272, 279
Riviera di Ponente 72,
  272–3, 279
Rocca di Papa 185
Rocca Scaligera 85
Roccalbegna 157
Rome 39–61
  accommodation 57,
    272
  Ara Pacis Augustae 44
  Arch of Constantine 44
  Bocca della Verità 52
  Capitoline Museums
    46–7
  Castel Sant'Angelo 46
  Catacombs 44
  churches 51–3
  city areas 43
  Colosseum 50
  eating out 58, 278
  essential sights 39
  Farnese Gardens 44
  Fontana di Trevi 54
  Galleria Borghese 46
  Galleria Nazionale
    d'Arte Antica-Palazzo
    Barberini 46
  Gesù 51
  guided tours 57
  history 21–3
  imperial forums 44
  itinerary 43
  Jewish Ghetto 45
  map 40–1
  monuments 44–5
  Museo di Palazzo
    Venezia 47
  Museo Nazionale
    Etrusco 47
  Museo Nazionale
    Romano 47
  museums and galleries
    46–7
  nightlife 60
  Palatino 44
  Palazzo-Galleria Doria
    Pamphili 47
  Pantheon 44–5
  Piazza Barberini 54
  Piazza Campo dei Fiori
    54
  Piazza Colonna 54
  Piazza Mattei 54
  Piazza Navona 54
  Piazza Sant'Ignazio 54
  Piazza di Spagna 54
  Piazza Venezia 54
  piazzas and fountains
    54
  public transport 61
  Roman Forum 44
  Sant'Andrea al
    Quirinale 51
  San Carlino 51

Santa Cecilia in Trastevere 51
San Clemente 51
San Giovanni in Laterano 51
San Luigi dei Francesi 52
Santa Maria in Aracoeli 52
Santa Maria in Cosmedin 52
Santa Maria Maggiore 52
Santa Maria sopra Minerva 53
Santa Maria del Popolo 53
Santa Maria in Trastevere 53
San Pietro (St Peter's) 55
San Pietro in Vincoli 53
shopping 59
Sistine Chapel 48–9
Spanish Steps 54
Teatro di Marcello 45
Terme di Caracalla 45
Trajan's Column 44
Vatican City 12, 48–9
Vatican Museums 48–9
Via Appia Antica 45
Villa Giulia 47
Rossano 222
Rossini, Gioacchino 127, 173
Ruvo di Puglia 222

S

Sabaudia 183
Sacra di San Michele 77
St Benedict 169, 193
St Bernard Pass 77
St Bruno 224
St Clare 169
St Francis 168, 169
St-Pierre 76
St-Vincent 76
saints 169
Salbertrand 77
Salerno 209
Salò 85
Sambucheto 178
San Clemente a Casauria 192
San Felice Circeo 183
San Galgano 150
San Gimignano 150, 159
  accommodation 275
  Collegiata 159
  eating out 281
  Sant'Agostino 159
San Giovanni in Fiore 224
San Giulio, Isola 91
San Leo 175
San Marco 210
San Marino 175
San Nicola Arcella 222
San Pellegrino in Alpe 154
San Pietro, Isola di 255
  Capo Sandalo 255
  La Caletta 255
San Pietro in Valle 178
San Quirico d'Orcia 155
San Remo 64, 72
San Teodoro 253

San Terenzo 69
Sansepolcro 152
Sansovino, Jacopo 98
Sant' Anatolia di Narco 178
Sant'Antimo 150, 155, 157
Sant'Antioco, Isola di 255
Santa Lucia 253
Santa Maria Capua Vetere 210
  amphitheatre 210
  Mithraeum 210
  Museo Campano 210
Santa Maria di Castellabate 210
Santa Marinella 183
Santa Severa 183
Santa Teresa Gallura 250
Sant'Angelo, Monte 216
Sant'Eutizio 169
Santissima Trinità di Saccargia 251
Sardinia 244–56
  accommodation 278
  cuisine 246, 250
  eating out 283
  essential sights 245
  tourist information 246
  wines 246
Sarnico 85
Sarre 76
Sassari 255
sassi (cave-dwellings) 221
Sassovivo, Abbazia di 170
Savona 72
Scilla 225
Sedini 248
Segesta 240
Selinunte 240
Senales, Val di 124
senior citizens 268
Sesto 123
Sestri Levante 69
Shelley, Percy Bysshe 69, 208
Sicily 226–43
  accommodation 277–8
  cuisine 229, 230
  eating out 283
  essential sights 227
  tourist information 229
Siena 150, 160–2
  accommodation 275
  Campo 161
  Duomo 161
  eating out 281
  Museo dell'Opera del Duomo 161
  Ospedale di Santa Maria della Scala 161
  Palazzo Pubblico 161
  Palio 162
  Pinacoteca Nazionale 161
  Torre del Mangia 161
Sila 224
Sinis peninsula 254
Siniscola 253
Siponto 216
Siracusa (Syracuse) 242
  accommodation 278
  eating out 283
  Museo Archeologico Nazionale 242

Museo Nazionale 242
  Ortigia 242
  Parco Archeologico 242
  Piazza Duomo 242
  Teatro Greco 242
  Tempio di Apollo 242
Sirmione 84–5
skiing 270
Sorano 150, 163
Sorrento 198, 210, 277, 283
Sovana 150, 157, 163
Spello 165, 172, 175, 282
Sperlonga 183, 192
Spoleto 165, 176
  accommodation 276
  arts festival 176
  Duomo 176
  eating out 282
  Ponte delle Torri 176
  Sant'Eufemia 176
  San Gregorio 176
  San Pietro 176
  San Salvatore 176
Stelvio, Parco Nazionale dello 86
Stilo 224
Strada Chiantigiana 153
Stradivari, Antonio 84
Straits of Messina 225
Stresa 81, 87
Stromboli 234
student and youth travel 268
Su Nuraxi 252
Subasio, Monte 172
Subiaco 182, 193, 276
Sulmona 183, 191, 193, 276, 282
Susa 77
Susa, Valle di 77
Sutri 187

T

Taormina 243
  accommodation 278
  Castello 243
  eating out 283
  Teatro Greco 243
Taranto 224
  Museo Nazionale 224
Tarquinia 182, 187, 276, 282
Tavernola 85
Tavoliere 217
taxis 268
telephones 268–9
Termoli 183
Terra di Lavoro 210
Terracina 192
Testa Grigia 77
Tharros 254
time 269
Tintoretto 99, 108
tipping 270
Titian 99
Tivoli 182, 189
  eating out 282
  Villa Adriana 182, 189
  Villa d'Este 182, 189
  Villa Gregoriana 189
Todi 165, 176
  accommodation 276
  Duomo 176
  eating out 282
  Piazza del Popolo 176
  San Fortunato 176

Santa Maria della Consolazione 176
toilets 270
Tomba Ildebranda 163
tourist offices 270
Trani 225, 277, 283
Trasimeno, Lago (Lake Trasimeno) 165, 177
travel arrangements 258
Tre Cime di Lavaredo 123
Tremezzo 83
Trentino-Alto Adige 116–17
Trento (Trent) 125, 274, 280
Trevi 172, 177
Treviso 125, 274, 280
Trieste 117, 126, 274, 280
Troia 225
Tropea 222, 225
trulli 223
Turin (Torino) 64, 74–5
  accommodation 273
  Armeria Reale 74
  Basilica di Superga 74
  eating out 279
  Galleria Sabauda 74
  Mole Antonelliana 74
  Museo Egizio 74
  Museo Nazionale del Risorgimento 74
  Palazzo Madama 74
  Palazzo Reale 74
  Turin Shroud 75
Tuscany 148–63
  accommodation 275
  cuisine 151
  eating out 281
  essential sights 149
  tourist information 150
  wines 151, 153, 159

U

Uccellina, Monti dell' 151
Udine 126
Umbria and the Marches 164–79
  accommodation 275–6
  cuisine 166
  eating out 281–2
  essential sights 165
  tourist information 167
  wines 166
Urbino 166, 177
  accommodation 276
  eating out 282
  Galleria Nazionale delle Marche 177
  Palazzo Ducale 177

V

valeting and laundry 270
Valnontey 68
Valpelline 77
Varenna 83
Vasto 183
Veneto 116
Venice (Venezia) 94–113
  Accademia 106
  accommodation 112, 273–4
  Arsenale 109
  artistic heritage 98–9
  Basilica di San Marco 100

INDEX

Burano 104
Ca' d'Oro e Galleria Franchetti 106
Ca' Pesaro 107
Ca' Rezzonico e Museo del Settecento Veneziano 107
Campanile di San Marco 101
Campo San Zaccaria 103
Campo Santa Margherita 108
Canal Grande 106, 110
churches 101–3
Colleoni Monument 109
Collezione Guggenheim 107
eating out 113, 280
essential sights 95
floods and pollution 105
frari 102
Ghetto 110
gondolas 111
history 96–7
Il Redentore 103
lagoon 104
landmarks 109
Lido 104
Madonna dell'Orto 101
Murano 104
Museo Civico Correr 107
Museo Storico Navale 107
Museo Vetrario 104
museums and galleries 106–8
Palazzo Ducale (Doge's Palace) 107

Palazzo Mocenigo 108
Palazzo Querini-Stampalia 108
Piazza San Marco 110
Ponte dei Sospiri (Bridge of Sighs) 107
Ponte di Rialto 109
Rialto 109
San Giorgio Maggiore 101
San Giovanni in Bragora 101
Santi Giovanni e Paolo (San Zanipolo) 101
Santa Maria Assunta (Gesuiti) 102
Santa Maria Formosa 102
Santa Maria Gloriosa dei Frari 102
Santa Maria dei Miracoli 102
Santa Maria della Salute 102
San Pantalon 102
San Salvatore 102
San Sebastiano 103
San Stae 103
Santo Stefano 103
San Zaccaria 103
Scuola dei Merletti 104
Scuola di San Giorgio degli Schiavoni 108
Scuola Grande di San Rocco 108
shopping 111
Torcello 104
Torre dell'Orologio 109
tourist information 97
water buses 111

Venosta, Val 124
Ventotene 192
Verdi, Giuseppe 127
Vernazza 66
Verona 116, 128–9
accommodation 274
Arche Scaligere 129
Arena 128
Capulets and Montagues 128
Casa di Giulietta (Juliet's House) 128
Castelvecchio 129
Duomo 129
eating out 280
osterie (wine shops) 129
Piazza delle Erbe 128
Piazza dei Signori 128–9
Sant'Anastasia 129
San Giorgio in Braida 129
San Zeno Maggiore 129
Teatro Romano 129
Torre dei Lamberti 129
Via Mazzini 128
Veronese, Paolo 99
Verres 76
Vesuvius 200
Vezzolano, Abbazia di 65
Viareggio 163
Vicenza 116, 130
accommodation 274
Basilica 130
Corso Andrea Palladio 130
eating out 280
Loggia del Capitanio 130

Santa Corona 130
Teatro Olimpico 130
Vico, Lago di 193
Vieste 216
Villa Barbaro 118
Villa Casale 241
Villa Cordellina-Lombardi 130
Villa Junker 91
Villa Lante 193
Villa Monastero 83
Villa Taranto 87
Villa Valmarana 130
Villetta Barrea 194
Visso 178
Viterbo 193, 282
Vivarini family 35, 98
Volterra 150, 163
accommodation 275
eating out 281
Museo Etrusco Guarnacci 163
Parco Archeologico 163
Piazza dei Priori 163
Pinacoteca Comunale 163

W

Wagner, Richard 106, 209
wine routes 125, 153

Y

youth hostels 270

Z

Zebrù, Valle dello 86

288

Picture credits

The Automobile Association would like to thank the following for their assistance in the preparation of this book:
J ALLAN CASH PHOTO LIBRARY 72 San Remo harbour, 77a St Bernard Tunnel, 119a Traditional houses, Bolzano, 119b Bassano del Grappa market, 124 Equestrian statue Padua, 126 Trieste. ASSOCIATED PRESS/TOPHAM 237a Funeral at Palermo. MARTIN BLACK/IMPACT PHOTOS 70 Walkers. BRIDGEMAN ART LIBRARY front cover c, 26b Napoleon crossing Alps by David, Jacques Louis (1748–1825) Schloss Charlottenburg, Berlin, 27b General Garibaldi by Barucco, F (fl 1864–6) Guildhall Art Gallery, Corporation of London, 30b Golden Etruscan bowl, 7th century BC by courtesy of the Board of Trustees of the V & A, 38a Marble sculpture of the Three Graces by Canova, Antonio (1757–1822), Belvoir Castle, Leics, 38b A Seated Man Leaning on a Table by Modigliani, Amedeo (1884–1920), Jesi Collection, Milan, 98b The Tempest by Giorgione, Giorgio (1476/8–1510) Galleria dell'Accademia, Venice, 99a The Miracle of the Cross on San Lorenzo Bridge by Bellini, Gentile (c 1429–1507) Galleria dell'Accademia, Venice, 136b Venice: San Giorgio from the Dogana, Sunrise by Turner, Joseph Mallord William (1775–1851) British Museum, London, 187 Etruscan vase showing boxers fighting c 500BC, British Museum, London, 207 Spring – maiden gathering flowers – wall painting from Stabiae (1st century AD) Archaeological Museum, Naples. JAMES DAVIS 234 Messina. STEVE DAY 120, 121, 122b Dolomites. CHRIS DONAGHUE 131 San Giorgio Maggiore E T ARCHIVE 75b Turin Shroud. MARY EVANS PICTURE LIBRARY 21a Punic Wars, 22b Assassination of Caesar, 24b Pope Gregory VII, 256b Bandits. RONALD GRANT ARCHIVE 18a Città Aperta, 18b Ossessione. HULTON DEUTSCH COLLECTION LTD 28a, 28b Mussolini, 29b Student riot. T JEPSON 68 Parco Nazionale del Gran Paradiso. NATURE PHOTOGRAPHERS LTD 195a Grey wolf (E A Janes), 195b European brown bear (P R Sterry). PICTURES COLOUR LIBRARY front cover a. REX FEATURES LTD 14b Coins, 15 Italian election. ROYAL GEOGRAPHICAL SOCIETY 25b Map. SPECTRUM COLOUR LIBRARY 67 Genoa Campanile, 74 Turin, 75a Replica of Turin Shroud, 75c Turin San Giovanni Cathedral, 122–3a Skiers Vigo di Fassa, 123 Skiers Dolomites, 127a Verona Aida, 162a,b Siena Palio, 200a,b Vesuvius, 204 Capri, 256a Sheep. TONY STONE IMAGES front cover b. THE GARDEN PICTURE LIBRARY 73a,b,c, Hanbury Gardens. THE MANSELL COLLECTION LTD 20b Phoenician merchant ships, 21b Julius Caesar, 23a Barbarians, 23b Charlemagne, 24a Henry IV, 99b Titian. TOPHAM PICTURE SOURCE 237b Coffin of policeman. ZEFA PICTURE LIBRARY (UK) LTD Spine.
All remaining pictures are held in the Association's own library (AA PHOTO LIBRARY) with contributions from: ADRIAN BAKER 77b. PETE BENNETT 26a. JERRY EDMANSON 34a,b, 137, 141, 142, 144a, 145, 152. JIM HOLMES 257b. DARIO MITIDIERI 12b, 19, 22c, 27a, 31b, 35, 36b, 37a,b, 39, 45a,b, 47, 48a, 52, 53, 58, 60, 61. ERIC MEACHER 13b. RICHARD NEWTON 98a, 101, 103, 104a, 106, 108. KEN PATERSON 11a,b. 16a, 30a,c, 33a,b, 135, 139, 140, 143a,b, 144b, 146, 147, 149, 150, 151, 153, 154, 156, 157, 158, 159, 160, 161a,b, 163, 164–5, 168, 169a,b, 170, 171, 173, 174a,b, 175a, 176a,b, 177, 179b, 186a. CLIVE SAWYER 2, 3, 4, 5a,b, 6–7a, 7b, 9a,b, 10b, 14a, 16b,c, 17a,b, 19, 20a, 31a, 32c, 36a, 39b, 42, 46, 48b, 49b, 50a, 54, 56, 63, 65, 70, 71, 76a,b, 79, 80–a, 82, 83, 85, 87a,b, 88, 89, 90a,b, 95, 96, 97, 100a,b, 104b, 105a,b, 107, 109, 110a,b, 111a,b, 112, 113, 115, 117, 125, 127b, 128, 129, 130, 132, 134, 165, 166, 167, 175b, 180, 181, 184, 185, 188, 189a,b, 190, 192, 193, 194a,b, 196–7, 19, 201a,b, 202, 203, 209b, 210, 211, 215a,b, 216a,b, 217, 219a,b, 222, 223a,b, 224, 225b, 226, 227, 228, 229, 230, 231, 232, 233, 235a,b, 236, 238, 239a,b, 240, 242a,b, 243, 245a,b,, 246, 247a,b, 248, 249a,b, 250, 251, 252, 253, 254a,b, 255, 260, 266, 270, 271. BARRIE SMITH front cover d, 25a, 29a, 33c, 132, 138, 268. ANTONY SOUTER 2, 8, 13a, 21c, 32a,b, 55b, 66, 69, 84, 91, 92, 93a,b, 131a, 172, 178, 179a, 182a,b, 183, 186b, 187b, 191, 197b, 198, 205a,b, 207a,b, 208, 209a, 213, 218a,b, 220, 221a,b, 225a, 271. PETER WILSON 10a, 12a, 22a, 37c, 43, 49a, 50b, 51, 55a, 57, 59.

Contributors

Revision verifier: Tim Jepson
Original copy editor: Audrey Horne   Revision copy editor: Nia Williams